BENJAMIN RUSH

BENJAMIN RUSH

BENJAMIN RUSH

Revolutionary Gadfly

BY

DAVID FREEMAN HAWKE

THE BOBBS-MERRILL COMPANY, INC.

Indianapolis & New York

A MULTITUDE OF CAUSES

BENJAMIN RUSH

Preface

THIS VOLUME covers forty-three years of Benjamin Rush's moderately long, inordinately full life, which ended in 1813, shortly after he had reached sixty-eight. The working title for the book was "Benjamin Rush: Physician in the Revolution"—a rather flat identification that obscured a lively personality. It also perpetuated a cliché. Most people, if they know anything about Rush, think of him principally as a physician. He is considered one of the most influential doctors in American history, and those acquainted with his writings on the mentally ill regard him as "the father of American psychiatry." Down to the Civil War, half, if not more, of all college-trained physicians in the United States propagated views and prescribed cures absorbed from Rush's lectures at the College of Philadelphia. His widely read volumes on medicine indoctrinated those who missed him in the classroom.

The medical side of Rush's career is not, however, emphasized in this book, for his fame as a physician rests mainly on work done during the last twenty-five years of his life. Prior to 1790, his commitment to medicine was more practical than passionate: it provided the income to care for his family. Medicine occupied Rush's mind and time only incidentally during the American Revolution. His "mission," as he called it, lay elsewhere. He might have objected to the label "revolutionary gadfly," but to one who, through Rush's extensive literary remains, has lived with him for several years, this phrase seems marvelously exact and descriptive; James Thomas Flexner can be thanked for suggesting it. One would like to think that in a candid moment Rush himself would admit that it serves more than adequately to summarize his role during the years the new nation took shape.

Thanks must first be given to the Richard Prentice Ettinger Foundation which awarded the grant that launched this biography. Pace College continued here, as it has for the past decade, to give unobtrusive but consistent support.

A number of libraries have extended, as a friend puts it, "not only assistance but hospitality." First, chronologically, comes the library of Dartmouth College, which gave to a visitor the privileges of a faculty member. In New York City thanks are due the New York Academy of Medicine, the New-York Historical Society, Pace College, and especially the New York Public Library, which honored me with the privileges of the Frederick Lewis Allen Room. In Philadelphia much was asked and more received from librarians at the College of Physicians, the Presbyterian Historical Society, the University of Pennsylvania, the American Philosophical Society, the Library Company of Philadelphia, and the Historical Society of Pennsylvania.

I forbear to name individuals in these institutions for fear of overlooking someone who was helpful. But one person must be mentioned—William Hoth, a tireless critic, a magnificent worrier over details, and, above all, a superb editor. This is a better book for the care he gave to it.

All quotations from the writings of Rush and his contemporaries have been standardized along the lines laid down by Lyman H. Butterfield in his edition of the *Letters of Benjamin Rush*—that is, spelling, punctuation, and capitalization have been adjusted, in almost all instances, to modern usage—with this principal exception: proper names, place names particularly, have also been altered to fit modern orthography.

TO

John E. Flaherty

AND

Edward S. Brown

Contents

Starting
Out

1

Youth

1746–1760

1

DR. BENJAMIN RUSH'S wife believed no one in history resembled her eminent husband so much as Martin Luther. Both, she held, were ardent in their pursuits, fearless of the consequences when they attacked old prejudices, and often hasty in the way they spoke of their enemies. Dr. Rush, who seldom differed with his wife in their long and affectionate marriage, admitted he shared Luther's defects in temper and conduct, but, he added, there was "a character in the Old Testament which more nearly accords with mine," and then went on to use the words of the prophet Jeremiah to pass judgment on himself: "Woe is me, my mother, that thou hast borne me, a man of *strife* and a man of contention to the whole earth. I have neither lent on usury, nor have men lent to me on usury, yet every one of them doth curse me."[1]

Benjamin Rush managed during the last half of the eighteenth century and the early years of the nineteenth to become a man of contention if not to the whole world then at least to a good part of it, but it was Philadelphia that served as the principal battleground for nearly all his sixty-eight years. Naturally, the city came in for a full share of the firm, moralistic, and usually censorious judgments he dispensed almost as regularly as he exhaled. He might in an off moment admit that "from habit, from necessity, and from local circumstances, all the States view our city as the capital of the new world," but more often he deplored its defects—the low state of its

5

literature, the godless, obtuse quality of its inhabitants, the miserable summers, the filth, the noise. "Alas," Rush wrote when sixteen, "I am sorry to say this is a seat of corruption, and happy are they who escape its evils and come off conquerors." He never amended that youthful judgment. "Cities contain the combustible matter of vice," he said in 1783, and in 1800 he told Thomas Jefferson they resembled "abscesses on the human body." And yet, like a contemporary who found the harsh music of rattling carriages "preferable to croaking frogs and screeching owls," he rarely endured the country for long.[2]

Rush only twice visited the countryside where he was born, though it lay but a short distance beyond what was then the north boundary of Philadelphia. The first visit was brief; it occurred during the Revolution, "a time when war and news and politics occupied my mind so entirely as to exclude all moral and domestic reflections." The second came in 1812, the year before he died. This time, more in the mood for reflection, he stopped by the country cemetery where his father's kinsmen were buried. He imagined as he stood over the graves of his ancestors, all of whom had been farmers, that they must have wondered about the intrusion of this gentleman dressed in city clothes. Rush had a ready explanation: he came "to claim affinity with you and do homage to your Christian and rural virtues." As the foremost physician in the United States, a signer of the Declaration of Independence, a friend of two Presidents, John Adams and Thomas Jefferson, he had moved in a lofty sphere through life, but "I have acquired and received nothing from the world which I prize so highly as the religious principles I inherited from you, and I possess nothing that I value so much as the innocence and purity of your characters."[3]

Little has survived to verify either the innocence or the purity of Rush's ancestors. Those on his father's side seem to have sprung from yeoman stock in England. John Rush, patriarch of the family's American branch, commanded a troop of horse in the Puritan army during England's Civil War. Cromwell, according to family legend, judged him among his best officers. Benjamin Rush believed that from the virtues and exploits of the "Old Trooper," as he liked to call his great-great-grandfather, came "a large portion of my republican temper and principles." In later life he went to some trouble to retrieve the old gentleman's watch from a collateral descendant. The sword John Rush fought with, dyed "with the blood of the minions of arbitrary power," hung in Rush's bedroom, and to its sight he believed he owed "much of the spirit which animated me in 1774."[4]

After the Civil War John Rush married and settled down to farming and rearing a family. About 1660 he became a Quaker, and he held to that persuasion throughout the Restoration, a harsh time for those who refused to conform to the Church of England. When William Penn opened his "holy experiment" for settlement, the Old Trooper, then sixty-three, sold off his holdings in Oxfordshire and in 1683 crossed the ocean to Pennsylvania with the Rush clan—his wife, a daughter, and six sons who brought with them their families. Shortly before departing, a relative urged him to leave behind at least one of his grandchildren. "No, no, I won't," he said. "I won't leave even a *hoof* of my family behind me." Long afterward it pleased Rush to recall that his great-great-grandfather had "left his native country in a fit of indignation at its then intolerant government."[5]

The Rushes settled in Byberry Township, then twelve miles up the Delaware River from Philadelphia. The Old Trooper had been drawn there by a daughter and son-in-law who had come over with William Penn and staked a claim to some five hundred acres in the township. The Indians had unwittingly made the district attractive to settlers by setting fire to the grass and timber each year during hunting season, thus clearing the land and eliminating the major hardship most immigrants to colonial America faced. The several families of Rushes prospered in a modest way from the start. They remained much as they had been in England—country people concerned with their farms, their families, and the local community. The nearby city interested them primarily as a place to market their crops.

John Rush's eldest son William, the great-grandfather of Benjamin, died five years after the family reached Pennsylvania. He left three children, of whom James, Benjamin Rush's grandfather, was the eldest. James Rush was an industrious farmer, an "uncommonly ingenious" gunsmith, and a devout man who had no trouble attending to both worlds. When he died in 1727 at the age of forty-eight, he bequeathed "a considerable property for that time," all of it free of debt. John, Benjamin Rush's father, inherited the family farm and the father's trade as a gunsmith.

John Rush, so far as his son could learn, "was a man of meek and peaceable spirit." He was also "agreeable and engaging in person and manners" and "exemplary in his life." He married Susanna Hall Harvey, who brought with her a daughter from a previous, unpleasant marriage that had been "terminated in three or four years by the extravagance and intemperance of her young husband." She also brought a lineage that traced itself in America almost as far back as the Rushes—to 1685, when the Halls migrated from England. Benjamin Rush regarded his mother, who had been taught "the common branches of female education" at a Philadelphia boarding school, as well educated for the times. But one of his own sons thought otherwise. "She was a woman of good sense, high temper, and energy in her affairs," he said, "but having perhaps that coarseness which those qualities are apt to be attended with in low life and consequently uneducated life."[6]

Susanna Rush gave her husband seven children. Benjamin, the fourth, was born in the family farmhouse in Byberry on Christmas Eve, 1745.* (His birthday became 4 January 1746 when the Gregorian calendar was introduced into the colonies in 1752.) Rush, one of four of Susanna's children to live to maturity, made his "first *unwelcome* noise in the world," as he put it, in a bedroom on the second floor of the stone farmhouse. It was a treacherous year for infants. A disease that contemporary physicians called angina maligna, but that sounds like diphtheria, ravaged the Pennsylvania countryside "with mortal rage," according to one chronicler. "It swept off all before it, baffling every attempt to stop its progress," he added. "Villages were almost depopulated, and numerous parents were left to bewail the loss of their tender offspring."[8]

The house in which Rush was born sat on ninety acres of rich farmland. Before it flowed a "small but deep creek abounding with panfish." Two years after Rush's birth his father, apparently little taken with the virtues of the rural life his son would extol, moved the family to Philadelphia, where he gave full time to gunsmithing. But ties with the farm must have remained, for Rush recalled living there, at least off and on, until he was six, and when he returned the year before his own death he searched for the cedar tree his father had planted in front of the house (it had been cut down and its wood used for the veranda that had since been added), and looked

---

*This is the date always given for Rush's birth. His sons accepted it and so, apparently, did he. "I have seen a letter from him written in his own well-known hand to Dr. Finley in which he says December 24th 1745," David Ramsay wrote when preparing his eulogy of Rush.[7] For whatever it is worth, it can be noted that among the Rush papers at the Historical Society of Pennsylvania there is a notebook labeled "Letters and Thoughts" and on page 70 in "his own well-known hand" Rush has, curiously, listed his birthday a year earlier as 24 December 1744.

sadly at what was left of the apple orchard that had once flourished under John Rush's care.[9]

The city that John Rush carried his family to was then the second largest in America, numbering some thirteen thousand inhabitants. Though the youngest of the continent's large towns, it would soon outstrip Boston in size; during the ensuing decade, while the Massachusetts capital lost population, Philadelphia would nearly double its inhabitants as immigrants from Europe, enticed by William Penn's policy of welcoming men of all religious faiths, poured in. The gridiron layout Penn had devised for Philadelphia's streets had created on paper a city of giant squares. The plan had been that these would be split into generous lots surrounded with sufficient light and lawn to prevent the development of squalid tenements. The early settlers, however, subdivided the lots, cut through the large squares with dingy alleyways, and instead of expanding westward toward the Schuylkill River, as Penn envisioned, most of the city stayed jammed against the Delaware River on which it fronted. Here, within earshot of the wharves, "the voice of industry perpetually resounds," a citizen remarked, "and every wharf within my view is surrounded with groves of masts and heaped with commodities of every kind, from almost every quarter of the globe."[10]

During Rush's youth, Philadelphia still sufficiently resembled Penn's dream of "a green country town" that when a man advertised for his lost red-and-white cow, he considered it enough to note that she "had two small hind teats and a star in her forehead."[11] Hogs ran wild. A constant stench arose from Dock Creek, a stream that twisted through the heart of the city and was flanked by stables and tanyards that used it for an open sewer. Filth accumulated in the streets until heavy rains washed it away. Flies blackened uncovered food, and bedbugs, mosquitoes, and roaches tormented residents through the sweltering summers.

Summers were dreaded by all. "The heat in this city is excessive, the sun's rays being reflected with such power from the brick houses and from the street pavement, which is brick," one man reported. "The people commonly use awnings of painted cloth or duck over their shop doors and windows and, at sunset, throw buckets full of water upon the pavement which gives a sensible cool. They are stocked with plenty of excellent water in this city, there being a pump at almost every fifty paces distance. There are a great number of balconies to their houses where sometimes the men sit in a cool habit and smoke."[12]

An attentive mother like Susanna Rush must have had a troublesome time keeping the sordid side of city life from her children. Brawls were common, and one witnessed by a stranger between "an unwieldly, pot-gutted" master and his "muscular, rawboned" servant, who favored such epithets as "little bastard" and "shitten elf," terms the observer found "ill applied to such a pursy load of flesh," must have resembled many young Rush saw as he moved about the streets. Rush grew up taking for granted much that outsiders found curious. The city awoke early, with shops opening at five in the morning, earlier on market days when farm wagons rumbled in long before dawn. There were few "public gay diversions," and travelers often complained about the lack of dancing and music. Most social life took place in the home or in the tavern.[13]

The taverns offered strangers a "mixed company of different nations and religions" like nothing else to be found in all America. "There were Scots, English, Dutch, Germans, and Irish," one visitor reported; "there were Roman Catholics, Churchmen, Presbyterians, Anabaptists, and one Jew. The whole company consisted of twenty-five planted round an oblong table in a great hall well stoked with flies. The company divided into com-mittees in conversation; the prevailing topic was politics and conjectures of a French war. A knot of Quakers there talked only about selling of flour and the price it bore. They touched a little upon religion, and high words arose among some of the sectaries, but their blood was not hot enough to quarrel, or, to speak in the canting phrase, their zeal wanted fervency."[14]

2

Benjamin Rush was baptized in the Church of England and as a child attended services at Philadelphia's Christ Church. Religion would occupy a large part of life for Rush, and it always gratified him that the Old Trooper had come to the wilderness of Pennsylvania "in order to enjoy the privileges of worshiping God according to the dictates of his own conscience." The dictates of that conscience, however, were unsteady. Down through the years the Rush clan virtually boxed the compass of Protestantism. Old John Rush reared a devout family but one unsure of the form its devotion should take. The family split from the orthodox Quakers in 1691 and joined a separatist movement headed by George Keith; eight years later it migrated to the Baptists. Rush's grandfather, James, eventually became a Presbyterian, but his father lived and died a member of the Church of England, spending his free time reading religious books; Rush would later read Bishop William Beveridge's *Private Thoughts on Religion* "only because my mother informed me that he valued it next to the Bible." During his lifetime, Rush capped the religious wanderings of his ancestors by following an even more erratic course.[15]

John Rush died in July of 1751 at the age of thirty-nine. He went peacefully, saying over and over, "Lord! Lord! Lord!" and his wife saw him buried as he wished in the cemetery behind Christ Church. "He was an angel to me in life," Susanna Rush said toward the end of her own, and though she had taken herself and the children out of the Anglican Church and into the Presbyterian promptly after her husband died, she advised when asked where she wished to be buried: "Let me lie by him in death."

Susanna Rush was thirty-four when her husband left her with seven children—a daughter by the first marriage, who was then about sixteen, plus James, twelve years old; Rachel, ten; Rebecca, seven; Benjamin, five and a half; Jacob, four; and John, an infant. The widow sold her husband's gunsmith shop and tools and his "likely Negro woman," though she kept at least one of the slaves as a family servant. The income from these sales, together with that from two houses which John Rush had owned in the city and which were now rented, was not sufficient, however, to rear a family of seven. Under the sign of the Blazing Star, Mrs. Rush opened a shop above Second Street, opposite the immense colonnaded market shed that stretched the length of two city squares down the center of High Street. Here she sold groceries and liquor—it was "somewhat like a country store," according to one of her grandsons—and, later, in another shop across the street which Rebecca would in due time manage, she added chinaware. "Her industry and uncommon talents and address in doing business commanded success," her son recalled, "so that she was enabled not only to educate her children agreeably to her wishes, but to save money."[16]

For all Mrs. Rush's acumen, misfortune continued to overshadow her life. Her youngest son, John, died soon after her husband, and the eldest, James, who had been "much afflicted with a nervous disease" that had apparently been cured after a tour of duty before the mast, died of yellow fever in 1760 in his twenty-first year. Silence pervades the family records regarding James's "nervous disease," but in the eighteenth century the phrase generally meant a mental breakdown. She took for a third husband one Richard Morris, a distiller, who, according to Rush, was "rough, unkind, and often abusive in his treatment of her," a judgment of questionable worth, coming as it did from a stepson no doubt resentful of any intruder on his mother's affections. Nonetheless, remarriage failed to bring her happiness; the union lasted sixteen years, ending with Morris's death.

Through all this Susanna Rush Morris survived for seventy-eight years, dying on 2 July 1795 in her bedroom in Benjamin's home, where, on his insistence, she had come to live out her last years. How he felt about her while growing up is unknown, for none of their letters to each other survive; in later years he revealed only deep affection for her. "Her company was at all times delightful," he said, and "as a mother she had no superior in kindness, generosity, and attention to the morals and religious principles of her children." She was determined never to be a burden to her children; even before the Revolution she purchased a small farmhouse outside the city, and after the war she sold her business and retired to it. She was, to use her son's word, an "uncommon" woman.[17]

<h2 style="text-align:center">3</h2>

In later life Rush admitted "it was always one of my numerous weaknesses to hold great men in too much veneration."[18] The first of the fatherless boy's heroes was Samuel Finley, a Presbyterian minister married to his mother's sister. In 1754, when Rush was eight, he and his seven-year-old brother Jacob were sent to Reverend Finley's boarding school, Nottingham Academy, located some fifty miles south of Philadelphia near the Pennsylvania-Maryland border.

Finley had come from Ulster to Pennsylvania in 1734, when he was nineteen. Sometime later he became a student of William Tennent, a Presbyterian divine who had settled north of Philadelphia in Bucks County and there opened a school which those who opposed his religious views patronizingly called the "Log College." When Finley came under Tennent's influence, the Presbyterian Church in America was splitting apart. The "Old Side"—or "Old Lights" as the faction was later called—was almost more Calvinistic than Calvin; it demanded doctrinal purity, a strict adherence to the Westminster Confession of Faith laid down in Cromwell's time, as the essential test for the ministry. The "New Side"—or "New Lights"—

led by Tennent, held that too many pulpits had become filled with men doc-
trinally pure but of little faith, that the church was ruled by "Pharisee
Teachers" who preached from cold hearts. This quarrel concerning the
clergy overlaid a deeper cause for division. The Old Side clergy fought to
keep the church as its members had known it in Ulster and Scotland. They
wanted to import all ministers from "home"; they wanted the church run
by a central body, the synod, as it was in Scotland. The New Side sought to
fashion the church to the American experience. Here, where mixed bloods
made up congregations, the words of a Scottish-trained clergy would sound
empty; here, where the provincial government was weak and the county
strong, the local presbytery rather than the synod should determine a congregation's affairs.

Tennent, then, knowingly or not, sought to make the Presbyterian
Church an American church, and Finley was among the chosen to assist in
the conversion. He received a license to preach in 1740, the year the English
evangelist George Whitefield, spurred on by Tennent, initiated the Great
Awakening, America's first continental religious revival. It was, however,
more than a religious revival. Contained within the sermons of the Awakeners was a set of social and political values that were to have an enduring
effect on a generation of Americans, among them Benjamin Rush—who was
shepherded into adulthood by two of the greatest Awakeners, Samuel Finley and Samuel Davies.

Despite Calvinism's pessimistic view of man's nature, the Awakening
propagated an optimistic view of life. Central to the revival was the concept
of rebirth or regeneration, defined by Davies as "that great change of temper, that extirpation of the corrupt principles of nature, and that implan-
tation of holy and supernatural principles of action."[19] God offered
regeneration to all who opened their hearts to Him, regardless of their race
or rank in society; and regeneration alone, not wealth or political power or
other supposed signs of God's favor, put man on the road to happiness.
This spiritual happiness gained by the reborn man carried with it public
duties: he must work with God to bring heaven down to earth. All Awakeners preached constantly of the millennium's swift approach, for never
before in man's history had its arrival seemed more certain than now in
America.

Tied to and justifying the optimistic view that God's Kingdom would
soon arrive was a set of ideas that made the revival anathema to a considerable segment of America. The Awakeners offended those who loved

England and patterned their lives on English ways, for they held that God obviously had abandoned that hopelessly corrupt and degenerate nation. They railed against cities, where people became prey to "immoderate desires, fears, and cares about earthly things." They condemned commerce—it played upon man's acquisitive instincts—and praised the simple virtues of rural life. They attacked the rich, holding that men "grow in wickedness in proportion to the increase of their wealth." They talked about the equality of men, saying that "considered as men, they share in the same common nature, and are so far equal," and this view led some, like Davies, to condemn Negro slavery as contrary to God's law. In a day when established churches prevailed in most colonies, they spoke up for religious liberty; God, they said, cared not a whit about the forms of worship so long as men worshiped from the heart. These beliefs the Awakeners broadcast through the land as God's truth. Those who opposed them, said Finley, committed an "unpardonable sin against the Holy Ghost." They were "sinners to the same degree of guilt as were those who opposed Jesus Christ himself."[20]

After being ordained in 1742 by a New Side presbytery, Finley set out to awaken Connecticut, only to be quickly evicted for preaching to a congregation unrecognized by the civil authority. Two years of wandering from pulpit to pulpit followed, then in June of 1744 he accepted a call to Nottingham, where he was to live out all but the last few years of his life.

Finley came to Nottingham ready to teach as well as preach. His friend Gilbert Tennent, the son of his mentor, had once said that if the church was to be stocked with a faithful ministry, new schools "under the care of skillful and experienced Christians" must be established.[21] To that end Finley opened Nottingham Academy. It soon became a preparatory school for the College of New Jersey, which the New Side Presbyterians founded in 1746 to assure a stream of American-trained ministers into their church. Finley hoped, of course, that his students would be drawn into the ministry. But for those who failed to receive the call from God there were other useful fields to enter. Medicine was one. When the Rush boys arrived at the academy in 1754 two of its brightest graduates—and two names Rush would never forget—John Morgan and William Shippen, Jr., were studying medicine in Philadelphia and would soon go abroad to continue their training.

In Benjamin Rush's day the school had an enrollment of about fifteen students. Among them were William Williams of Virginia, John Archer of Maryland, and Thomas Ruston of Pennsylvania, all of whom became physicians; Gerardus Clarkson, some eight or nine years older than Rush and another future physician of whom Rush said many years later: "I loved him like a brother"; and Ebenezer Hazard, who for a time would become Rush's closest friend. All were from Presbyterian homes and usually from nearby points, though occasionally a boy appeared from as far away as South Carolina. Finley and his wife, even with eight children of their own, served as proxy parents to all the boys. They reproved and praised and watched over them as if they were their own, for in the eighteenth century anyone living beneath one's roof automatically became a member of the family. Mrs. Finley, who fed and reprimanded her platoon of youngsters the year round, was coolly and perhaps uncharitably remembered by her nephew for "the irritability of her temper," but judged "in every other respect a good housewife"; Finley impressed Rush and his classmates far more favorably. "I never met with one of them who did not admire, esteem, and love him," Rush said. "Some of them," he added, implicitly including himself, "expressed their respect for his memory in terms bordering upon idolatry."[22]

Finley, though fiery in the pulpit, was a gentle man with a round, ruddy face set on a stocky frame. He ruled his family with a "strict but never severe or arbitrary" hand, preferring to terrify his students into obedience with words rather than blows. When punishment was called for, he tore a switch from a convenient bush or tree, then talked of folly and wickedness until the offender stood trembling and weeping. At that point he ordered a palm outstretched, gave it three light taps with the switch, and said: "There, go about your business. I mean shame and not pain [to] be your punishment in the present instance." Once, beside himself, he boxed Rush's ears for having pegged a stone at a withered apple hanging on an otherwise bare tree. There was "no excuse for your offense," he said when Rush complained of the punishment. "By throwing at that decayed apple you injure the tree. You have, moreover, broken a law, which though apparently trifling, will lead you to break laws of more importance." Finley held that laws as rigid as those Newton had found for the heavens regulated human conduct, and he meant to see that his charges learned early in life to obey them. Years later when Rush sought to impress on his own son that there must be no "disobedience to my authority," he admitted to his wife it was *he* who got the "severe blow from Dr. Finley," but when retelling the story to his children in his autobiography the culprit became simply "a boy" at the school.[23]

Finley missed no chance to mold the boys. At dinner he often told stories with central characters like Bill Slovenly, with whom "he connected all the usual follies and improprieties of boys," and Johnny Courtly, "who was an example of all that was proper and amiable in the conduct of a young man." He made the dinner-table tales palatable by interspersing them "with anecdotes that excited a burst of laughter." The boys got the idea when they were told to work in the fields that exercise was pleasant and useful, that it "begat health and helped to implant more deeply in our minds the native passion for rural life." Rush carried through life a finger scar as a memento of his effort to learn to reap at Finley's school.

Each day began and ended with prayers. All, as might be expected, attended church faithfully, and during the Sunday evening instruction period they were required to tell what they could remember of the sermon. Somehow, though Finley was an awkward speaker and stammered, his message got through. Rush later credited "my not having at any time of my life ever entertained a doubt of the divine origin of the Bible" to Finley's plain way of stating "the most striking and intelligible evidence of the truth of the Christian religion."[24]

As a Calvinist, Finley taught his students to "struggle against the corruptions and temptations of a wicked world," to avoid indolence, and, above all, to lead purposeful lives. He sought principally to promote a boy's usefulness to society. For this reason, students learned arithmetic, geometry, and geography—as well as Latin and Greek because no professional man, be he doctor, lawyer, or minister, could work without it. He taught the students to read, write, and speak English "with great care and success" for the same reason. He touched only lightly on science, or natural philosophy as it was then called, because, according to Rush, "he was unfortunately tied down to the principles and forms that were common in the schools of that day."[25]

In the spring of 1759, when Rush was thirteen and a half, Finley judged him sufficiently prepared to enter the College of New Jersey as a junior. He was a last-minute addition to the group of three Finley sent to the college that year. As late as April 26 he did not yet "know his parents' intention," but approval for Rush to go on to the college must have been received soon after from Susanna Morris—"your mammy," as Finley called her. The College of Philadelphia would have been a more convenient school, for Rush could have saved his mother money by living at home, but

such a choice was unthinkable. Anglicans and Old Side Presbyterians controlled the Philadelphia school, and though the Great Awakening had occurred more than a quarter of a century ago, the ill feelings it had raised
still flourished. Rush departed with an affection for Finley and Nottingham
Academy that never dimmed. Later he would regard as wasted the time
spent learning Latin and Greek during his four years there; the only other
flaw he could recall about Finley's pedagogy was the encouragement of such
idle pursuits as hunting, which Rush believed depressed "the relish for
study" and tended to risk "health and morals." He would blush, too, to
recollect the time wasted "playing cat and five and steal-clothes." Finley,
however, always remained on a pedestal, and five—indeed, fifty-five—years
after Rush left the school he saw himself "nobly striving to imitate *his*
example."[26]

4

When the College of New Jersey in 1756 moved south from its early
home in Newark to Prince Town—or Princeton, as it would soon be called—
Gov. Jonathan Belcher, sensing perhaps the awkwardness of the intended
name, Belcher Hall, asked that the building that housed the school be
called Nassau Hall, "as it will express the honor we retain . . . to the im-
mortal memory of the glorious King William III, who was a branch of the
illustrious house of Nassau."[27] Nassau Hall and the college were one and
the same for Rush and his contemporaries. They headed their letters "from
Nassau Hall," and the displeasure some boys from other colonies felt in
being associated with a college of New Jersey contributed to the name's
being changed eventually to Princeton.

The building where Rush for the next year and a half lived and studied and, being "sometimes a mischievous boy,"[28] idled away more hours
than he liked to recall, was a sturdy though not particularly impressive example of Georgian architecture—a large central block of stonework topped by
a bell tower and flanked by two extensive wings. When Rush mounted the
stone steps and passed through the main entrance in the spring of 1759, he
found himself in a dark hallway bounded by classrooms, the corridor ending at the door to the prayer room. He found the library on the second

floor and the kitchen and dining room in the basement. The wings of the
building held student and faculty living quarters, most of which consisted
of small suites partitioned into a bedroom and two studies.

Rush arrived at Nassau Hall comforted by the sight of familiar faces.
Three friends from Nottingham Academy—Joseph Alexander, Archer, and
Ruston—entered the college with him, and a fourth, Hazard, would turn up
a few months later. Some fifty students lived in the college in Rush's day
and the faculty numbered four. Adjustment to college life offered slight
difficulty, for the routine differed little from the one Rush had known at
Finley's school. The bell in the cupola rang at five every morning, after
which a servant went pounding from door to door until all were awake.
Prayers came at half-past five, followed by an hour for study, then breakfast. Classes lasted from nine to one o'clock. After dinner the boys were at
liberty until three; they studied until five, when evening prayers began, and
ate supper at seven. They went to bed at nine; to go before was considered
"reproachful." Everyone rose at the usual hour on Sunday, went to church
at eleven and listened to another sermon at three in the afternoon in Nassau
Hall. This regimen lasted through the year, broken only by a six-week vacation after both the first semester (November to May) and the second (June
to October). Tuition was £4 a year, and the charge for room and board
amounted to about £20. Total expenses, when clothing, travel, books, and
incidentals were added in, probably came to something more than £30 a
year, about half what it took to keep a family of seven in Philadelphia at
the subsistence level, about one-third what it cost a single gentleman to live
comfortably in the city. In short, keeping Rush in college must have taxed
his mother's financial means.[29]

Most of the boys thrived on dormitory life, but in some way never
specified it scarred Rush. "Vices of the same species attract each other with
the most force," he said years later when forming plans for his own college.
"Hence the bad consequences of crowding young men (whose propensities
are generally the same) under one roof, in our modern plans of education."
When his eldest son went to Princeton, Rush saw him housed in the village
with a private family, "for I consider a *college life* and *college society* to
boys of his age as alike fatal to morals and manners." Since Rush, even in
the relatively mellow years of his forties, regarded card playing on Sunday
as sufficiently sinful to pull his son out of college ("He can never recover
his character so as to appear to advantage either with his masters or among

his fellow students"), perhaps the sins of his own college years ranked small by modern standards. Then again, perhaps not.[30]

The curriculum for upperclassmen when Rush arrived consisted of advanced courses in mathematics, logic, Latin and Greek, and other subjects he had been exposed to at Finley's school. He had hardly settled in, however, when a change came; in July 1759 the college acquired a new president, Samuel Davies, the second of Rush's youthful heroes. (When Davies died eighteen months later, Rush told a classmate, "You and I have lost a father, a friend."[31]) Davies had been reared on a farm in Delaware and was, according to Rush, a "self-made man" who had "surmounted the disadvantages of scanty circumstances and a confined education by the strength and activity of a great and original genius."[32] He, like Finley, had been caught up in the Great Awakening. After a tour as an itinerant clergyman that established his reputation as one of the greatest preachers of the day, he accepted a call to Hanover County in Virginia, and there, where each year he rode a five-hundred-mile circuit through the backcountry, he became known as the "father of the Presbyterian Church in Virginia." His evangelical sermons managed to be at once both dignified and moving, and the years in the more rural regions did not deprive him of "the most elegant and commanding manners." He acquired in the South a warm feeling for the "neglected Negroes" and hid from no one that "these poor unhappy Africans are objects of my compassion." "Your Negroes may be ignorant and stupid as to divine things, not for want of capacity, but for want of instruction; not through their perverseness, but through your negligence," he told Virginia slave owners in 1758. "From the many trials I have made, I have reason to conclude, that making allowance for their low and barbarous education, their imperfect acquaintance with our language, their having no opportunity for intellectual improvements, and the like, they are generally as capable of instruction as the white people."[33]

Also while in Virginia, Davies had warmly supported the French and Indian War, which had begun in the wilderness of western Pennsylvania in the year Rush arrived at Nottingham and came to a climax with Wolfe's victory at Quebec during the year he left for college. Braddock's defeat in 1755 had led Davies to preach on the close ties between religion and patriotism. In that sermon he castigated the elite of America, whose main concern with public affairs had been to oppress and harass "harmless dissenters" and thereby estrange them from their governments; he also praised a then unknown man named George Washington, who had been with Braddock, wondering aloud whether Providence had preserved "that heroic youth . . . in so signal a manner" because he was destined for "some important service of his country."[34]

When Davies arrived at the college with his wife and five children, he was thirty-six years old, a gaunt, handsome man who suffered from an advanced case of tuberculosis. Nevertheless, he drove himself hard, rising at dawn "to remedy fancied defects in scholarship," and rarely retiring before midnight. Within a few months he was reshaping the college as much as Tennent had reshaped the church. Under Davies' guidance, it ceased to be a school designed solely to produce ministers. He asked that something be done about the marked lack of books on "mathematics and Newtonian philosophy" among the library's 1,200 volumes; he stiffened entrance requirements, insisting that none could be admitted without some knowledge of "vulgar arithmetic."[35] The religious side of the school was played down to such an extent that a 1760 print of Nassau Hall was adorned not with the Bible, as might be expected, but with a microscope, a sextant, a pair of dividers, and other paraphernalia of the utilitarian and scientific worlds.

Davies managed, without overturning the old curriculum, to slip into it several new subjects—a course in metaphysics, for instance, and another in English literature—and, said Rush, he "gave to the old branches of education a new and popular complexion." As a man who cared for words—in addition to sermons, Davies composed hymns and patriotic poems—he emphasized English composition. (Davies praised poetry as a "glorious enterprise" that in the right hands could point up a moral more effectively than a sermon. Two of his favorite poems were Edward Young's *Night Thoughts* and James Thomson's *The Seasons,* both of which remained lifelong favorites of Rush's.) As an orator, he made it a requirement that members of the senior class must deliver monthly orations. The classics were not, to be sure, neglected; he urged the boys to keep a commonplace book, or "Liber Selectorum" as he called it, in which to record passages from the classics that struck them forcibly. "By recording these passages," Rush later said, "I was led afterwards to record facts and opinions. To this I owe perhaps in part the frequent use I have made of pen and ink."[36]

Not all that Davies did pleased Rush. The continued stress on Latin and Greek left a lasting distaste for those languages. Metaphysics, Davies' specialty, bored him. Thirty years later he still recollected with disgust the hours he had listened to Davies talk "of possible existences, the infinity of space, the ubiquity of spirit, and many other such subtleties of the learning of the thirteenth and fourteenth centuries." And yet to the end he kept among his papers a meticulously worked out "Synoptical Compend of Metaphysicks," a synopsis in Latin of the course that Davies had drawn up for the class.[37]

Rush attracted Davies' attention promptly. The boy had a quick, sure memory, and in a day when rote learning was the scholastic pattern, this impressed the president "so far that he gave me credit for much more capacity than I possessed." Davies as a teacher inspired Rush with a love for knowledge that lasted through life, but otherwise, so he said, he "derived little from his instruction." His views of politics and society especially disheartened Rush—or so he would recollect. Davies believed "that no government could be safe or durable where there was no kingly and aristocratic power, and that the British constitution included in it the perfections of every species of government without any of their imperfections."[38]

Aside from Davies' affection for the classics and metaphysics and his notions of "kingly and aristocratical power," Rush rejected little else. During the next fifteen years, it would be difficult to distinguish where his thoughts began and Davies' ended when he wrote about slavery, religion, education, or patriotism. When in 1775 Congress debated the choice for commander in chief of the Continental army, Rush spoke his mind by pulling out Davies' remarks made twenty years earlier on Washington and having them reprinted in a Philadelphia newspaper.

If words can shape men's minds, Davies perhaps had his most enduring effect with the last sermon Rush heard from him. Graduation for Rush and the ten others in his class came in the fall of 1760. Davies delivered the baccalaureate sermon on Sunday, September 21, choosing for his theme religion and public spirit. "It deserves to be printed in letters of gold in every young candidate's heart," Rush said when he learned it was to be published, and the copy he bought remained in his library to the end.[39]

Davies opened with a sentiment especially suitable to Rush. "Great and good characters are often formed by *imitation*," he said. "And if we would shine in any sphere, we must propose to ourselves some illustrious examples." He urged the graduates to be like David, to cherish a public spirit, for devoid of this "your lives will be of little use to the community, and all the valuable ends of a liberal education will be lost upon you. . . . Bravely live and die, serving your *generation*—your *own* generation. This *David did!*" By all means "be ambitious to survive yourselves," he went on, "but *your own* generation is the special and appropriate sphere of your usefulness."

Davies cautioned the students that, young as they were, they had but a brief time to work, for "the day of life is short." They must "seize therefore, the present flying moments," and above all "let religion be the source of your benevolence and public spirit, as it was with David." As a Calvinist he warned them: "Be not ambitious of self-government, but resign yourselves to the will of God." As one of the Great Awakeners, he reminded them that without a regenerated spirit, without a new heart, "you can never arrive at the finished character of good and great men." Without a spiritual rebirth "it would be better for you to be Hottentots, or even the most abject and miserable creatures among the meanest and most noxious of the brutal tribes, than to be the sons of NASSAU HALL."

A string of homilies carried the sermon to its conclusion. Continue to study, otherwise "you will live your age *backward,* and be less wise at sixty than at twenty." When you come to your profession, "follow Nature and consult the public good." After a final warning against the world's snares— among others, bad company, idleness, and trifling—he dismissed the students with obvious sadness, as if sensing these boys would be the last he would send from his care "into the wide world to shift for [themselves]."[40]

Commencement came three days after Davies' final sermon. The morning exercises opened with an oration in Latin by Jonathan Bayard Smith, a special friend of Rush's. A syllogistic debate, also in Latin, followed. "When this was concluded," went a Philadelphia newspaper account by someone eager to praise a fourteen-year-old hometown boy, "MR. BENJAMIN RUSH arose, and in a very sprightly and entertaining manner delivered an ingenious English harangue in praise of oratory." The harangue was succeeded by "a forensic dispute in English," then "a Latin dispute in a Socratic way," and finally "a well-composed valedictory oration in English." The singing of an ode on science written by Davies concluded the morning exercises. The afternoon audience had to endure only one dispute in Latin, which was, of course, "learnedly defended and ingeniously opposed." That done, President Davies "descended from the rostrum, and with the usual formalities conferred the degree of Bachelor of Arts and Master of Arts." Soon afterward came the singing of an ode on peace, also written by Davies. The ceremonies then ended, "to the universal pleasure and satisfaction of a numerous auditory."[41]

2

Apprenticeship

1760–1766

1

PEOPLE OF THE DAY described Benjamin Rush as "a comely young man." He stood five feet nine inches high, then considered "above middle size," had a slender frame that would thicken only slightly through life, alert, "highly animated" blue eyes, and an expressive face seldom seen in repose. He had a prominent forehead and an aquiline nose, but it was his head—"the diameter of his head from back to front was uncommonly large," said a contemporary—that impressed most observers. It was thought, to use the language of the age, that "the general traits of his physiognomy bespoke strength and activity of intellect."

Women generally regarded Rush as good-looking, and he appears never to have been at a loss for young ladies to squire about town. He was a companionable beau, rarely dull, an easy person to while away an afternoon with in idle chatter. When with him, a girl never needed to work at stitching over gaps in a conversation, for Rush, above all else, loved to talk. Those who liked him commented on "his great powers of conversation"; those who held him in less regard always remembered his ability to talk "incessantly."[1]

In conversation he found it easy to be himself—lively, colloquial, relaxed. But when he wrote in these days, before he found the style that suited him, another person came forth—stiff, turgid, even pompous, to judge by a letter of his in 1761 from Philadelphia to a college classmate living in the country far "from the world of iniquity." In that letter he spoke of President Davies, who, having served his generation, had "fallen asleep" early in February; then in rotund, oratorical sentences that suggested his way of writing still sagged under the weight of Davies' sermons, he continued: "Our poor parent Nassau-Hall again left desolate and melancholy. Oh, it is a wound too fatal—the stroke is almost too severe. When the silver locks of old age and unusefulness are taken away, then indeed it's vain to grieve. But when the charms of beauty, vigor, health, and youth, and all the united splendors of utility are snatched away, the blow is heavy and portends something important."

Rush went on to relate his wavering views about a career. During the last months in college, he had given much thought to the future. For a boy with no displayed leaning toward business and without family connections to advance him in that field, the choice of a career in the eighteenth century was limited to the church, the law, or medicine. Rush believed that "every pursuit of life must dwindle into nought when Divinity appears," but he dismissed the ministry for himself because of "my incapacity," a vague explanation he never cared to clarify. Medicine seemed out of the question, for "I had an uncommon aversion from seeing such sights as are connected with its practice." His reputation as an orator in college suggested that law, "the babblative art," would suit best. Davies agreed and assured him he would "make a better figure at the bar than in the walks of a hospital." That "fixed my determination," and word went out to his mother to search for a lawyer to take him on as a student.[2]

Before settling down to a legal career, Rush visited a classmate in Maryland, and on the trip back to Philadelphia he stopped off in Nottingham. One afternoon when talking with Finley on the front porch, he revealed the decision to enter law. The news distressed Finley. He disliked "such temptations and dangers as are in the law way," he said. His antipathy toward lawyers reflected a feeling embedded in the American past. The Virginia Assembly had banned all lawyers from the colony in 1658, and more than a half century passed before they were allowed to reappear. The Fundamental Constitutions of Carolina called "it a base and vile thing to plead for money or reward." A New Englander of the day viewed the "law to be very much like a lottery—great charge, little benefit." These attitudes waned in the eighteenth century as American life took on some of the complexities of civilization, and the need for competent lawyers became obligatory. Abler men began to enter a profession that had once been dominated by riff-raff. Men like Thomas Jefferson in Virginia and John Adams in Massachusetts were giving it a dignity and integrity it had once lacked. But in Finley's eyes, the profession still rated low. He urged Rush to give thought to medicine, a much more useful field of endeavor. "But before you determine on anything," he said, "set apart a day for fasting and prayer, and ask God to direct you in your choice of a profession."

Rush avoided the day of fasting and prayer, for Finley's plea had sufficed to unsettle his mind. He reversed his former decision and on Davies' next visit to Philadelphia obtained from him "a letter of recommendation to Dr. John Redman to become his pupil." No inner compulsion but rather Finley's desire appeared to have determined his course. That, and Davies' advice to "consult the public good." "To spend and be spent for the good of mankind is what I chiefly aim at," he told a classmate who wondered about the choice. "This earthly frame, a minute fabric, a center of wonders, is forever subject to diseases and death," he added sententiously.[3]

Physicians could do much to make the world a better place to live in. They could also expect to make a good living in Philadelphia, where disease, endemic and epidemic, flourished steadily the year round. The inhabitants unwittingly did their best to assure the physicians prosperous practices. A family's water well often shared the backyard with the privy and perhaps a cow, a horse or two, and a brood of chickens. Garbage piled in the streets, flies and mosquitoes transmitted diseases, and Dock Creek drained through the city like a running sore.

Rush's decision delighted Finley. "I hope the Governor of the world will direct your course of life, to his glory and your good," he wrote, adding: "On him be your dependence! Eye his hand, marking all his dispensations towards you! So doing you will better understand his loving kindness." To Rush, these lofty sentiments never disguised the warm, human qualities of Finley, a man of earthly ties who ended the letter saying: "Give my best and most affectionate regards to your mammy—to Mr. Morris—to your sisters. Tell your mammy I received hers by Cousin Becky. . . ." And it must have relieved his anxiety over the future of Nassau Hall when, a few months later, Samuel Finley was chosen by the board of trustees to replace Davies as president of the College of New Jersey. Nevertheless, for years afterward Rush, like so many others who follow the profession urged on them by their fathers, wondered if medicine had been the right choice.

At least once he deserted it and began to study law, and only toward the end of his life did he see "the hand of heaven" in the decision he—or Finley—had made in 1760.[4]

2

In February 1761, the month Davies died, Rush, just fifteen, went to live as an apprentice with Dr. Redman, a devout Presbyterian who at the age of thirty-nine had built one of the largest, most lucrative practices in Philadelphia. The short, swarthy Redman had lively black eyes, a quick temper that died away as swiftly as it blew up, and something Rush forever lacked—a sense of humor. A friend seeking free medical advice once stopped the doctor on the street to ask about a chest pain; Redman tilted back his wig—the better to hear, for he was slightly deaf—then after ruminating a moment said, "Consult your physician," and walked on. Rush was his apprentice for five and a half years, finding him, so he said near the end of his tenure, "not only the indulgent master but the sincere friend and tender father."[5]

Redman, like Finley, had matured during the Great Awakening. He, too, had been educated at William Tennent's Log College, but for reasons never revealed he had shunned the ministry to become a medical apprentice in the early 1740's. A loan from William Allen, chief justice of Pennsylvania and friend of aspiring young men—he had contributed to the painter Benjamin West's trip to England and would later underwrite John Morgan's studies abroad—helped to finance Redman's studies at Edinburgh and Leyden. He received his M.D. from the University of Leyden, topped off his academic training with a winter of practical experience in a London hospital, and in 1749 returned to Philadelphia, from which he departed only on brief trips during the remaining sixty years of his life.[6]

Redman once told Rush that knowledge and discipline helped to make a man more useful, but faith in God alone could "make us happy in ourselves, a real blessing in our generation." To him, a physician's role resembled a minister's, for he must "be every hour engaged in doing good to rich and poor, relieving the distresses of poor suffering fellow mortals, and perhaps receiving daily blessings of those who are ready to perish." He held that "no life can be happy or pleasing to God but what is useful to man."[7] Daily he drummed in sentiments heard since Rush had come under Finley's wing. Moreover, like Finley, he, too, watched over the boy as if he were his father, partly out of affection, partly because apprentices were considered members of their masters' families. In the years Rush lived under Redman's roof, he absented himself from the doctor's business only eleven days and in all that time "never spent more than three evenings out of his house."[8]

Rush learned the rudiments of the profession first in Redman's apothecary shop. American physicians then made and sold their own prescriptions, and their apprentices ran the shop while the doctor called on patients. The job took more time than intelligence, for the materia medica then extended little beyond such drugs as calomel, opium, ipecac, mercury, magnesia, laudanum, castor oil, rattlesnake root, Jesuits' bark (cinchona, a crude version of quinine), and a few others. Prescriptions were compounded on such simple and haphazard instructions as: enough opium "to lie on a penknife's point" or "a pretty draught" of mercury or pulverized root "the size of a walnut."

Citizens availed themselves of this pharmacopeia only after exhausting their own medicinal repertoire. A foot trod upon by a galloping horse was soaked in cold spring water, then covered with "a cataplasm of cow dung"; only if the home remedy failed was the physician called. A doctor's lance might relieve a bad sty on the eyelid, but first the efficacy of a rotten apple applied to the swelling had to be tried. A man who rammed a nail into his arm had the wound dressed with rabbit fat. Sore corns were rubbed with "spirits of wine." The foul-smelling, highly poisonous Jamestown weed was smoked in a pipe to relieve asthma; sun-dried pokeberries served "as a plaster of great virtue for the cancer"; goldenrod cured dysentery; magnolia berries steeped in brandy relieved consumption.

The physician, restrained by his "scientific" training, brought a less imaginative approach to the problem of illness. His medicine bag held no stethoscope, no clinical thermometer, no watch to count the pulse; the lance was his favored instrument and he used it principally to open a vein for bleeding "morbific matters" from the patient's body. "Bleeding is proper at the beginning of all inflammatory fevers, as pleurisies, peripneumonies, etc.," according to a contemporary medical handbook. "It is likewise proper in all topical inflammations, as those of the intestines, womb, bladder, stomach, kidneys, . . . rheumatisms, the apoplexy, epilepsy, and the bloody flux.

After falls, blows, bruises, or any violent hurt received either externally or internally, bleeding is necessary." For topical or local infections, leeches or the cup were generally used. Leeches in Rush's day were coming into disfavor, for "it is impossible to know what quantity of blood is taken away by leeches; besides, the bleeding is often very difficult to stop, and the wounds are not easily healed." Cupping, done with a bell-shaped glass with a syringe fastened to the bottom, was preferred. Heat applied to the outside of the glass created a vacuum that raised the skin and made it easier to insert the syringe and withdraw a calculated amount of blood.[9]

Eventually, Rush was able to escape the apothecary shop and accompany Redman on calls and on rounds through the wards of the Pennsylvania Hospital, where his master served as consulting physician. Most visitors found the hospital an elegant building, but one sight-seeing physician said that the "strong smell of sores and nastiness rendered it insupportable even to me who have been pretty much used to such places." The hospital, as everyone knew, served as a port of last resort—for the poor, the aged, the insane, or any ill person who had become an unbearable burden to his family. Those who could afford it were treated at home. On cases that required constant attention, Rush often performed "many little offices of a nurse to them." In time he learned to bleed patients, dress their wounds, and even share in surgical operations; physicians then doubled as surgeons, whose work was largely limited to amputations, cutting out ulcerous sores, and pulling teeth. He also kept the account books up to date.

None of Redman's patients died of "heart attacks" or "tuberculosis," and few even of "cancer"; the eighteenth century had its own nomenclature of diseases. People died of fits, convulsions, and apoplexy; of dropsy, pleurisy, and "scorbutic and scrophulous ulcers"; of "decay" and "flux." Occasionally a disease might be sorted out of this vague lexicon and given a specific name—such as smallpox, whooping cough, scarlet fever, or syphilis —but for the most part physicians accepted the layman's designations. A man whose chest ached more than likely had "pleurisy" or "a pleuritical disorder." Blood in the sputum usually indicated "pulmonary consumption." The "throat distemper" or "putrid sore throat" might be diphtheria, scarlet fever, or any number of streptococcus infections. The "bloody flux" could possibly be typhoid or cholera but usually referred to dysentery.

Most people in the latter half of the eighteenth century spent their lives nagged by some physical disorder of varying severity that physicians commonly associated with a single symptom—fever. "Intermittent fevers" came and went at regular intervals; "remittent fevers" rose and subsided irregularly; "continued fevers" remained steady but could develop, if they rose, into "putrid fevers." Typhoid usually went under the name of "nervous fever," typhus under "hospital fever" or "jail fever." The "bilious remitting fever" more often than not referred to yellow fever. The "slow chronic fever" plagued the community in autumn. Any fever accompanied by chills became an "ague"; "tertian ague," which meant the chills came every third day, generally connoted malaria.

Invariably, each year an epidemic of one or more of these fevers overwhelmed Philadelphia. The winter Rush began his apprenticeship, the "epidemic cold" or influenza struck. The "malignant sore throat" (diphtheria?) carried off a number of children in the winter of 1763. The following year scarlet fever swept through the city. The greatest onslaught came during the second year of Rush's apprenticeship, in 1762, when two epidemics struck back to back. Smallpox hit first. Cotton Mather had battled for inoculation forty years earlier in Boston, and by mid-century most physicians accepted the idea that an induced local infection protected patients against the full effects of the disease. The trouble with inoculation was that it required up to six weeks of professional care, and only the well-to-do could afford that. Redman had worked to popularize a simplified inoculation procedure, but colleagues rejected the reform. As a result, the epidemic of 1762 proved "very mortal," especially among the poor.[10]

In August, as the smallpox epidemic abated, yellow fever appeared. Physicians believed, mistakenly, that it was contagious; schools were closed and many left the city for the apparently immune countryside. The disease's confinement to tenements around Dock Creek, to squares near the wharves that lined the Delaware River, and to the south part of town adjacent to a stretch of marshland, made it clear in the light of contemporary theory that it came from a contaminated miasma or effluvia rising off the marshes and river water. Redman saw no more than twenty patients a day, for his practice lay outside the infected areas, among the city's prosperous. Whenever he and Rush visited a yellow-fever victim, each chewed a wad of tobacco in order to prevent swallowing the saliva that could carry the disease into his body. In every sickroom they ordered a bowl of vinegar with a steaming hot iron to disinfect the air. Even with these precautions, Redman later admitted, "a sense of danger frequently affected me."[11]

The epidemic lasted until the first frost. When Rush came to report the experience, he still sounded grandiloquent: "Numbers die daily— a solemn call this to *prepare for Death!* You may perhaps reply, 'Fine times for the physicians.' Such a retort as this might only be adapted to those inhuman *monsters* who estimate their happiness by the miseries and infelicities of their fellow creatures; as for my part, I can assure you it awakens my compassion and calls forth every generous passion to sympathize with the afflicted."[12]

3

Rush's confessed tendency to fritter away time vanished during the apprenticeship years. "The confinement and restraint which now imposed upon me gave me no alternative but business and study," he recalled, "both of which became in a short time agreeable to me." Redman believed practical experience should be balanced by a knowledge of medical theory, and Rush soon found himself reading "at late and early hours" two of his master's favorite authors—Thomas Sydenham, the seventeenth-century "English Hippocrates," and the Dutch physician and Leyden professor, Hermann Boerhaave.[13]

Sydenham survives today for his work as a clinician. His accurate eye made him the first to diagnose measles as a distinct disease, the first to distinguish between gout and rheumatism, the first to give a careful description of Saint Vitus's Dance, the first to establish the psychic character of hysteria. Doctors of Redman's generation found much more in his writings that they regarded as gold but that has since proved to be dross. Sydenham held that disease resulted from the accumulation of "morbific matter" in the body and only when it had been drained off by bleeding, purging, or sweating would health return. Once the body had been cleansed, he called for a mild therapy—rest, light foods, fresh air—to encourage nature's healing powers. Sydenham attributed the spread of disease to an effluvia in the air that insinuated itself into the body, mixed with the blood, and tainted the whole human frame. He emphasized the influence of climatic and atmospheric change on the cause and spread of disease and held that every season and each year had its peculiar "epidemic constitution" in which a particular disease with particular characteristics would prevail. All Sydenham's thought

Rush absorbed—so much so that he deserved for this reason alone the title for which he always yearned—"the American Sydenham."

Philadelphia physicians honored Sydenham, but they idolized Boerhaave, who, though he had died in 1738, still dominated European, and thus American, medical thought. Redman had arrived at the University of Leyden, where Boerhaave had taught for forty-two years, when tales of his genius could still be heard from those who had known him, and where a coterie of disciples perpetuated his doctrines. Naturally, Rush found himself studying Boerhaave's lectures on physiology and pathology "with the closest attention." An apprentice could obtain much specific and useful information from these volumes, but Redman's chief purpose in giving them to Rush was to expose him to Boerhaave's system of medicine.

In an era when physicians were as eager to distinguish themselves from quacks and "empirics" as natural philosophers were from alchemists, Boerhaave had erected a "system" for medicine as neat and as seemingly exact as the one Newton had recently created for the universe. He did this by adapting to medicine the mechanical principles of Newtonian science. "The human body is undoubtedly an hydraulic machine through whose numerous orders of wonderfully variant vessels, or pipes, there is a constant motion of different fluids," was the way a later colleague of Rush's explained Boerhaave's system, adding: "The increase or declension of this motion from a due standard may be accounted the cause of disease. Perhaps the whole art of physic is little more than regulating, i.e. increasing or retarding this motion in due time and order."[14] Physicians, for instance, had long been puzzled by the cause of inflammation. Boerhaave's system drew on physics for the answer: it resulted from an obstruction in the small arteries; the increased speed of the blood stream as it attempted to slip past the blocked spot created sufficient heat to inflame the surrounding area.

Sydenham and Boerhaave complemented each other. One offered physicians a satisfying system that explained the cause of *all* disease, the other reminded them that the world was filled with a disturbing number of diseases, each, once it had been identified, requiring a specific treatment. Any doctor who considered himself a Boerhaavian also revealed himself a follower of Sydenham when he wrote: blend in a "natural sagacity and diligent observation" and these will "in the end prove the surest resort for the afflicted patient."

The chief mark Boerhaavians had against Sydenham was that doctors could find in his theories what they wished. He had admonished physicians to "consult nature" in dealing out their cures, but his own treatments hardly followed this advice. "Blood-letting and anodynes are the principle tools of our practitioners," one physician complained of the American followers of Sydenham, adding that his colleagues also "follow Sydenham too much in giving paregorics, after cathartics, which is playing fast and loose," and in their "frequent use of vitriolics and opiates." The Boerhaavians, in Rush's day, wielded greater influence and it was incumbent upon all Sydenham enthusiasts to avoid one pitfall: never, however deep their respect for Sydenham, reject Boerhaave. To do so risked being dismissed, as one American physician was by a colleague, as one "of the clinical class of physicians" who "cries up empiricism."[15]

4

In November 1762, shortly after the yellow-fever epidemic ended, Dr. William Shippen, Jr., announced a series of lectures on anatomy, the first given in America. Shippen, after graduating from Finley's academy and the College of New Jersey (Class of 1754), had studied surgery in London, then gone on to Edinburgh, where he received his medical degree in 1761. The lecture series initiated a grand scheme he and John Morgan had concocted while studying together in London—to start a medical school in Philadelphia. The opening talk, held in the State House, was advertised "for the entertainment of any gentleman who may have curiosity to understand the anatomy of the human frame," but the other nine were designed for those "now engaged in the study of physic" and lacked the means to go "abroad for improvement to the anatomical schools in Europe." The lectures were held in a laboratory built onto the back of the elder Shippen's house. Rush at the time seems to have had little notion of studying abroad; he enrolled as one of ten students and attended the full series. He found Shippen "eloquent, luminous, and pleasing," but otherwise had nothing to say about the course. He never mentioned, for example, that less than a month after the course began a Negro cut his throat with a piece of glass and that "after the coroner's inquest had pronounced him guilty of self-murder, his body was immediately ordered, by authority, to Dr. Shippen's anatomical theater."[16]

For that matter, he commented little on the medical side of life during the apprenticeship years. The primary source for his thoughts in this period survives in letters to his then close friend Ebenezer Hazard. These letters, filled with stilted phrases and sentimental ramblings about the past, seem those of a tottering old man. " 'Twas in my tender years, when each noble passion was taking birth, you took deep root in my bosom," he wrote of the friendship that began at Finley's school. Religious matters preoccupied him. He rejoiced to hear from Hazard, then working in New York as a bookseller, that "the work of God" progresses nicely there, and that at least a few souls "are crying out what they shall do to be saved." Alas, matters proceeded less well in Philadelphia, where "vice and profanity openly prevail," where the "Sabbaths are boldly profaned," and the youth "are wholly devoted to pleasure and sensuality." "O my dear Ebenezer, let not the deadly contagion reach us," he concluded. "May the Son of God arise and shine upon our souls. May we be made to feel our vileness and undone situation, and earnestly cry aloud to Jesus till he opens our eyes to behold his all-sufficiency and fitness to be our Redeemer."[17]

These effusions may have been prompted by the fear of death. In the winter of 1764 a "pulmonary complaint" came upon Rush, severe enough that occasionally he spat up blood during coughing spells. The complaint hung on for more than twenty years, he recalled near the end of his life, until he was almost forty. Possibly Rush suffered from a mild case of chronic pulmonary tuberculosis, or consumption as people then also called it. Except when smallpox raged in epidemic proportions, consumption year in and year out led the list of diseases that caused death in Philadelphia. Between 1761 and 1763, for example, it claimed 273 people in the Christ Church parish alone. It was particularly virulent among "the fashionable women of Philadelphia," because, said a contemporary, "they dance too much and then drink cold or iced water, or eat cold unripe fruit when they are hot; they drink boiling tea; they dress too lightly in winter and pay no attention to the changes of temperature so frequent in Philadelphia." It was also thought that "eating too much meat" and "drinking too many spirits" made people susceptible to it, and the treatment Rush adopted for his case reflected these presuppositions. "During that long period I lived chiefly upon vegetables, tea, coffee, and a small quantity of animal food," he said. "When most free of my disorder, I drank malt liquors and wine and took bark with advantage."[18]

The feeling that his end might be near was probably intensified by the death that winter of Gilbert Tennent, Rush's pastor at the Second Presbyterian Church, Samuel Finley's close friend, and one of the most fervent leaders of the Great Awakening. The event led to Rush's first known published essay, a eulogy to Tennent under the by-line of "a young gentleman of Philadelphia," and published at the tail end of Finley's own sermon, *The Successful Minister of Christ Distinguished in Glory*. The essay had all the markings of a production by an eighteen-year-old who had lost an idol. It opened with a rhetorical flourish: shall the hero "who bleeds with transport for his country," shall the legislator "who with a generous wisdom plans the good of mankind," shall the patriot who strives "to promote the honor of his king"—shall these alone be "enrolled in the records of fame?" Obviously not. Come, then, Rush continued, "and attend a few minutes, while we endeavor to portray the character and present to the public view a few golden threads from the sacred mantle of the late Reverend Mr. GILBERT TENNENT."

In the twelve pages that followed, Rush managed to use virtually every cliché and platitude currently available. Tennent's "tender soul" was pierced with grief when "ruthless, bloodthirsty Indians," carrying the "murdering hatchet," the "poisoned arrow," snatched infants "from their weeping, affrighted mothers' arms." In old age, his "soul, like the setting sun, broke through the clouds of infirmity," his wisdom "bloomed upon his silver locks, and while the cold hand of time snowed upon his head, his heart glowed with redoubled love for the church."

Yet through this lush forest of prose, Rush evoked something of Tennent's powerful presence in the pulpit. "The old Puritan spirit that had for a series of years been asleep, seemed to revive and blaze forth in him with a genuine luster." He thundered when offended by a breach of God's commandments and "he made it his constant practice to sound the alarm of God's curse abiding on the whole human race." But, added Rush, "as he knew how to wound, so he knew how to pour the oil of consolation on the bleeding conscience." He was, as it seemed fitting for Rush to say, a father to his people, who "counseled, warned, and reproved them with all the tenderness and solicitude of a father's heart." He rose above prejudice. "His soul extended toward the human race, and he ever estimated his happiness in proportion to his usefulness in the world." All men, rich and poor, black and white, "had equally free access to his person."

5

Rush found little time for literary pursuits in 1765. Early in the year Redman fell ill, with the result that, according to Rush, "the whole weight of his business is now on my young shoulders." He found time amidst his labors to philosophize on the brevity of life; the more he thought about it, "the more am I animated to exert myself in the arduous work Providence has assigned me." He must review his life, pry into his heart, to make certain he did not court the admiring throng but worked only to promote the glory of God in the world.[19] His solemnity increased with the arrival of George Whitefield, who in mid-May returned to the city where fifteen years earlier he had sparked a local revival into the Great Awakening. When Whitefield spoke to the congregation of the Second Presbyterian Church, "his soul catched fire at the thoughts, and earth seemed scarce able to contain him," said Rush. " 'Twas a heaven upon earth I believe to many souls, for I think I never see more attention and solemnity in a place of worship in my life before."[20]

While Whitefield was stirring the devout, John Morgan was agitating the physicians. Morgan, whose schooling at Nottingham Academy and the College of New Jersey was followed by five years of study in Europe, returned home to become "the general subject of conversation" in the spring of 1765. The public was convinced he had the "eccentricities of genius" by the silk umbrella he carried about town to ward off the summer sun, an affectation then judged "a scouted effeminacy" but that he pulled off without loss of reputation.[21] If academic honors can make the man, then Morgan at the age of thirty had come back the most prominent physician in the colonies. Europeans had elected or approved him for election to the Royal Society, the Royal Academy of Surgery of Paris, the Royal College of Physicians of London, and the Royal College of Physicians of Edinburgh. James Boswell had judged the man rather than the physician and found him humorless, a "fat bonhomme," and John Hunter, England's greatest anatomist, suspected Morgan had sought to promote his own reputation by palming off as his the work of Hunter and his assistant. But Dr. John Fothergill, friend and protector of American medical students in London, liked Morgan and believed he would serve as an "able assistant" to Shippen in the reformation of Philadelphia's medical profession.[22]

Morgan was not cut out to be anyone's assistant, let alone Shippen's, and he made it clear soon after his return that any medical reformation would be directed by him. He had two plans for improving the status as well as the quality of American physicians. The first, which he discussed with friends before airing it in public, concerned the scope of a physician's work. Morgan held that a physician must cut all ties with the apothecary shop and with "the low drudgery of surgery" and concentrate on the practice of medicine. A general must know his army, but that does not mean "he should act as a pioneer and dig in a trench," he said. "No more, then, is a physician obliged from his office to handle a knife with a surgeon, to cull herbs with the botanist, to distill simples with the chemist, or compound drugs with the apothecary." Without specialization, the field of medicine cannot advance in America as it has in Europe. "Whilst we labor amidst such a variety of pursuits, all improvement must be kept at a stand. Whereas, let each cultivate his respective branch apart, the physician, surgeon, apothecary, etc., the knowledge of medicine will be then daily improved and it may be practiced with greater accuracy and skill as well as at less expense."[23]

The year of the Stamp Act was no time to call for the Anglicization of American medicine, but in any year Morgan's program would have met with a sour reception. Redman warned his former apprentice he risked being "almost buried and, as it were, rusting for want of employment" if he put the plan into operation. Worse, his income "would be so small as ill to repay you for your extraordinary expense of time and money in qualifying yourself." Rush, echoing his master, reported that for Morgan to practice what he preached would, "notwithstanding his reputation, prevent his getting much business." Morgan persisted in his views to the extent of publishing them, but stopped at that point. His apprentice, John Archer, a friend of Rush's from Nottingham days, found himself "daily at Dr. Morgan's shop" compounding medicines like any other apprentice.[24]

A formal announcement of Morgan's second plan for improving American medicine was issued May 9 when the trustees of the College of Philadelphia revealed his election as professor of the theory and practice of medicine and said he would deliver an address at the college commencement three weeks hence "in order to show the expediency of instituting medical schools in this seminary." The announcement concluded: "Dr. Morgan's plan has been warmly recommended to the trustees by persons of eminence in England, and his known abilities and great industry give the utmost reason to hope it will be successful and tend much to the public utility."[25]

By calling it "Dr. Morgan's plan" the trustees credited him with a vision that Morgan originally shared with Shippen. Shippen later told them he had only "waited to be joined by Dr. Morgan, to whom I first communicated my plan in England, and who promised to unite with me in every scheme we might think necessary for the execution of so important a point." In his commencement address Morgan mentioned that Shippen had "proposed some hints of a plan" for medical lectures, "but I do not learn that he recommended at all a collegiate undertaking of this kind." The knife in, he twisted it. "Should the trustees of the college think proper to found a professorship in anatomy, Dr. Shippen having been concerned already in teaching that branch of medical science is a circumstance favorable to our wishes."[26]

From the sidelines, Rush watched these opening moves in the feud between Morgan and Shippen that would eventually bring both men to the ground. Within the small medical circle of Philadelphia, however, no one could long maintain neutrality.

6

Sometime during the last years of the apprenticeship, Rush determined to continue his medical education abroad. No doubt Redman, Shippen, and Morgan joined to encourage the venture, and his mother—and possibly his stepfather—agreed to underwrite the heavy expense of sending a young man across the ocean for three years of study in Edinburgh and London.[27] Originally, Rush planned to depart in the summer of 1765, but he postponed the trip for a year, by which time he hoped "by hard study and longer attendance on the practice of physic to fit myself better to make a figure in Europe and be of more use to society when I return." Perhaps Shippen and Morgan urged him to stay until he had taken their courses, which began at the college in the fall of 1765. Perhaps Redman convinced him to brush up his Latin and Greek, neither of which he excelled in, before entering the academic world. Perhaps love detained him, for by this time Rush had become smitten with a girl named Mary (Polly) Fisher. "She is the only woman whom I ever loved," he said a year later, "and, I may add,

ever shall. If ever I do marry, other motives of a sordid nature must influence me. *Love* never will." Parental objections blocked serious thought of
marriage. His mother and stepfather gave him the "unwelcome orders not
to think of a wife for eight or ten years to come," he said, "as it would
effectually shut the door against my providing for my sisters and their sons."
Both Rachel and Rebecca had recently been widowed and together had
three sons to rear. Also he had his younger brother, Jacob, to think about.
Jacob had just graduated from the College of New Jersey and apprenticed
himself to a Philadelphia lawyer, and in time he, like Benjamin, might want
to round off his education by studying in London.[28]

Rush planned his future with care during the last year of the apprenticeship. He saw that a new doctor in Philadelphia, already well-stocked
with European-trained physicians—fourteen of the seventeen respected doctors had been schooled abroad—would have to scramble for business, and for
that reason he set about "to learn the Dutch language inasmuch as so great
a part of our city consists of that nation." Rush would repeat the resolve several times in his lifetime, but to the end fluency in German eluded him. He
also pulled out college textbooks and boned up on Greek and Latin. Greek,
"in which I find myself lamentably deficient," gave trouble, but in a short
while he was, so he said, taking "great pleasure in reading Latin authors and
have of late read more physic in Latin than ever."[29]

Ebenezer Hazard responded to this news by suggesting a correspondence in Latin. Rush agreed reluctantly, pointing out that years had passed
"since I learned the Latin language." The ordeal lasted through two or
three letters when an incontestable excuse to end it came along. "Public
commotions and calamities are increasing too fast to admit of a communication of sentiments in Latin," Rush wrote with ill-suppressed joy. He
referred to agitation over the Stamp Act. "Let us therefore dispense with
its usefulness for some time, till the restoration of peace and tranquillity to
our distressed country gives us more time to pursue that useful branch of
improvement." All men of the day, from John Adams in Massachusetts to
Thomas Jefferson in Virginia, referred to their colony as "my country."
To all thirteen "countries," peace and tranquillity took time to return. By
then, "my country" had a new significance. One aspect of the revolution
that occurred in men's minds during the 1770's was an outward broadening
of their loyalties from the provincial level to the continental, and no one
better exemplifies this change than Benjamin Rush.[30]

7

The Stamp Act aroused Rush's interest for the first time in political affairs. Since the Peace of Paris of 1763, which had ended the Seven Years' War—or the French and Indian War, as the colonists called it—England had been searching for ways to make the empire in America a self-sustaining operation. The Revenue Act of 1764 had tightened up and enlarged the customs service in the colonies, and warships were assigned to the coast to pick up smugglers. Such products as hides, potash, iron, and lumber that Americans had once been allowed to export directly to Europe now had to be funneled through England in order to give merchants there a cut of the profits before they were reexported to the Continent. While the colonists were still adjusting to these new restrictions, Parliament, in line with making the colonies self-supporting, passed the Stamp Act. The act imposed a tax on virtually every paper-made product that circulated in the colonies. Duties varied from a halfpenny on newspapers to two pounds on diplomas; they were levied on all colonial bills of lading, licenses, wills, bonds, deeds, indentures, contracts, leases, newspaper advertisements, almanacs, playing cards, dice—the list seemed endless.

The law provoked a bitter reaction in all thirteen colonies. In Pennsylvania it became a political issue in which the Presbyterians—long at loggerheads with the ruling majority of Quakers and Anglicans—saw their chance to appear more American than Americans whose roots in the colony were at least a half century deeper than theirs, for a majority of the Presbyterians had arrived only within the last generation. "The first open identification of the Presbyterians, *as a Church,* with the cause of colonial liberties," one historian has said, "came during the Stamp Act controversy."[31]

Rush's reaction to the controversy was predictable and his sympathies immediately obvious. "Philadelphia is cursed with a set of men who seem resolved to counteract all our efforts against the Stamp Act, and are daily endeavoring to suppress the spirit of liberty among us," he said, speaking as a Presbyterian as well as an American. "You know I mean the Quakers. They have openly spoke in favor of the act and declare it high treason to speak against the English Parliament." Benjamin Franklin, who as Pennsylvania's agent in England had done little to block passage of the Stamp Act—indeed, appeared to have favored it—came in for Rush's severest blows. "O, *Franklin, Franklin,* thou curse to Pennsylvania and America, may the most accumulated vengeance burst speedily on thy guilty head!" John Hughes, an amiable gentleman who had accepted the appointment as stamp distributor that his friend Franklin had wangled for him, became for Rush "a man so devoid of public spirit as to be willing to enslave his country if others will." Since Hughes refused to resign his commission, Rush wished the people, the *"mobility"* as he put it, would "extort a full and ample resignation from him, the present precarious state of our charter at home by no means admitting of our exerting ourselves in the seditious way. . . ." For Rush, in politics as in religion, there were only saints and villains.[32]

At the height of the uproar over the Stamp Act in the autumn of 1765, Shippen and Morgan began their courses, now for the first time offered under the aegis of the College of Philadelphia. Rush sidestepped entanglement in the feud between the two men—to take sides might endanger his career—by signing up for Morgan's course on materia medica and chemistry and repeating Shippen's on anatomy. Somehow without antagonizing Shippen, he established close ties with Morgan. He joined a short-lived medical society organized by Morgan and opposed by the two Shippens and most of the established physicians of the city, virtually none of whom Morgan invited to become members.[33] He listened as Morgan planned out his schedule at the University of Edinburgh—Alexander Monro, secundus, for anatomy; James Russell for natural philosophy; William Cullen, whom Morgan called "the Boerhaave of his age," for the institutes of medicine; and, above all, Joseph Black for his "ingenious lectures on chemistry." Morgan emphasized Black's course, for he promised that the professorship of chemistry would be waiting when Rush returned from Europe.

Politics and medicine absorbed Rush's time through 1765 and 1766, but they did little to dim a still constant anxiety over the state of his soul. Early in 1766 he admitted being one of those fools, those madmen, who "banish God from their thoughts, and plunge themselves into a gulf of sin, and thus ripen their souls for the torments of hell perhaps before they arrive at the age of twenty." Rush had just arrived at that age. The summit of guilt, he said, had been at Nassau Hall, but since his apprenticeship with Redman "my temper became more and more uniform, and I began to delight in reading religious books, in hearing good sermons, and in convenings with pious people." Nonetheless, he remained convinced sin dominated his soul. "This drove me sometimes to my knees, and made me importunate with God for a change of heart." He continued in his "former state of security in sin" until December, when God's gracious spirit seemed to shine down upon him. A sermon by Samuel Blair, a college classmate who now preached in Philadelphia, and much private meditation revealed "my exceeding aggravated guilt and insecurity," Rush confessed in a letter to Hazard. "Jesus Christ spoke to my soul as he did to the woman of *Samaria* when he told her that he with whom she lived was not her husband," he went on, adding vaguely: "One particular *sin* lay heavy upon my conscience, which brought to my *view all the things that ever I did.*" Obviously, Rush felt compelled to reveal to Hazard that he had slept with a married woman. But confession did not clear his conscience. The "particular *sin*" continued to haunt him through life, and more than thirty years later he repeated in his autobiography the oblique confession made to Hazard, possibly in the hope that by admitting it to his children he would at last expunge its evil effect from his soul. While convinced in 1766 of "being the chief sinner," Rush found his "heart more and more excited to an ardent, vehement desire after a *new nature* and an interest in Christ Jesus." His conversion, if it can be called that, left his "mind more tender to sin of every kind."[34]

About the time spiritual peace was descending upon Rush, rumors floated through the city that Parliament would soon repeal the Stamp Act. "The liberty of the press was yesterday revived in a plain, decent coffin and carried in triumph through our streets with drums beating, colors flying, and other suitable demonstrations of joy," he wrote Hazard at the end of March. "I wish our rejoicing may not be turned into sorrow. Blow, ye winds, and conspire, ye water, and swiftly roll into our waiting, trembling ports the welcome barge that shall confirm the joyful tidings!"[35]

Those tidings came a few days later and helped to put him in a beneficent mood toward the mother country he was about to visit. But he had little chance to rejoice over the repeal or think much about political matters his last hectic weeks in Philadelphia. "Dr. Redman is now out of town," he wrote early in July, less than a month before departure, "and I am so busied from morning to evening in visiting his patients that I have little time to devote to friendship." While Rush carried on the heavy practice, he had the added worry of Redman's young daughter Nancy, who had come down with a case of cholera infantum. The child survived the treatment of puking and purging, and Rush had pronounced her "happily recovered" when he learned that Samuel Finley at the age of fifty-one was nearing death. With Redman's absence, Rush became Finley's physician, or so he assumed. Shippen, however, dropped in from time to time, and it was he who first told the minister "he could live but a few days longer." Rush "sat up with him every night," and aware of a momentous event, he recorded Finley's dying remarks. During one vigil Finley asked how his pulse beat and rejoiced to hear "it was fluttering or irregular." During another he urged Rush to avoid a life of indolence. "I was ashamed to take rest here," he said. "Eternity will be long enough to rest." In repeating the remark years later, Rush added: "I hope I shall be able in my last moments to derive comfort from the same reflection."[36]

Rush sat by when Finley bade farewell to his daughter and son-in-law, urging them constantly to live seeking God's favor. "He will support you when all earthly friends are removed," he said. "He has long been my Friend and Guardian and has preserved me from a thousand dangers and temptations. Seek, seek, then, my dear children, an interest in His favor, and among other motives to engage you in this work, remember 'twas the last dying advice of your father." Rush slipped from the room with tears on his face.

At about one in the morning, July 17, Finley died—"without a sigh or a groan or any kind of motion sufficient to alarm his wife and those friends who were about his bed." Rush leaned over to perform "the distressing office of closing his eyes." Finley had ended his days "tortured with the most excruciating pains," yet not once did he fail to treat those around him "with that same sweetness and ease that were so peculiar and natural to him," Rush observed. "In fine, he was a most striking example of that *faith* which kindles love in the heart, and produces the sweet fruits of meekness, gentleness, patience, and every Christian grace and virtue."[37]

3

Edinburgh

1766–1768

1

ON THE LAST DAY of August 1766, a "mournful Sunday," Benjamin Rush set sail for Liverpool "with a view of proceeding from thence to Edinburgh in order to prosecute my studies in medicine." The master of the *Friendship* was Capt. Thomas Pearce, whose piety pleased Rush. His companions were Jonathan Potts, a fellow Pennsylvanian who also planned to study medicine at Edinburgh, and James Cummins, a young Scotsman returning home after losing his fortune and health in the West Indies. Several unnamed "bosom friends" came down to the wharf to bid farewell, and Rush was properly sad. "The sun that day to me had lost all its luster, and I fancied all nature around me corresponded with the gloomy situation of my mind." Uneasiness filled him as the ship glided down the bay into rough water. He felt well, "but oh! I dread tomorrow!" he said as the ship passed Cape Henlopen and pushed into the Atlantic.[1]

The dread proved valid; the *Friendship* had no sooner entered the Atlantic when Rush experienced "a most violent vomiting and seasickness" that stayed with him for ten straight days "without one moment's respite." He was recovering lost strength and appetite when "a most violent gale of wind" arose and continued to blow for the next three days. Rush dosed himself with laudanum and waited out the storm in his berth, all the while condemning "that thirst for knowledge which induced me to leave my native country." While he waited "with trembling anxiety for the fatal

wave that should engulf us forever in the sea," he pondered the scant comfort riches and power could give at a time like this, a thought that spurred
further philosophical contemplations: " 'Twas religion alone that could
support the soul, and bear her up amidst the awful prospects of approaching
death." At one point, Potts and Rush heard the captain call out: "Clear the
boats!" They leaped from their berths and rushed topside to public prayers.
Rush found the rolling motion of the ship made it impossible even to sit up,
and after prayers he returned to his berth, "resolved to meet death"; there
Rush said he "lay for some time pouring forth my soul in the most ardent
prayers" until the captain came down to "bid me not to be alarmed."

Rush, it can be said, derived little pleasure from the crossing. A month
of foul weather followed the initial storm, and not until October 18 were
his eyes "once more blessed with a sight of land." The next day, however,
the ship nearly smashed to splinters on rocks along the Irish coast, an event
that would have been doubly calamitous for Rush, for the land was "inhabited entirely by Roman Catholics who are as savage as their remote
situation and religion can make them." Two days later they were nearly
wrecked off the presumably more hospitable coast of Wales.

The *Friendship* docked at Liverpool on October 21, after seven weeks
and two days at sea. The joy felt when Rush touched "once more upon *terra
firma*" was tainted by the news that he and Potts could not carry away their
trunks until they had been inspected at the customs house. Later, after the
trunks had been thoroughly searched, the inspectors demanded half a crown.
"Pray, how do you think the freeborn sons of America bore this unac-
customed treatment?" Rush asked rhetorically.

The day after arriving, he sent a note off to London to Benjamin
Franklin, whom he had never met, asking him to "write to such as your
friends in Edinburgh in behalf of my good friend Mr. Potts and myself as
you think will be most useful to us in the prosecution of our studies." That
done, the two men spent a week sight-seeing. In his journal and letters
home, Rush spoke of the kind treatment received from families in the city
to whom he had letters of introduction; he admired the public infirmary and
the charity school that accommodated nearly two hundred children from
poor families; he condemned a Presbyterian splinter group that leaned
toward deism and openly denied the divinity of Christ. He condemned, too,
the city's heavy involvement in the African slave trade: it is an "inhuman
practice that men should grow rich by the calamities of their fellow crea-

tures!" The size of the city seemed to astound him; a waterfront that could handle three hundred ships made Philadelphia resemble a backwater village.

One afternoon during a tour of Liverpool, Cummins broke away, saying he must return to their rooms for he felt indisposed. That night he awoke "with a noise like a person in convulsions." Rush called for candles and opened a vein in his arm, hoping a good bleeding would check the fits and restore his reason. A respected local physician was called in, but by the next night Cummins was dead—"a most afflicting event, for he became very dear to us by our fellowship in dangers," Rush said. "We showed our respect for him by burying him at our own expense in a graveyard belonging to an Episcopal Church in the town." Two days later, on October 31, Rush and Potts set off for Edinburgh.

2

Age as well as size distinguished Liverpool from Philadelphia, but Rush and Potts had also found much in the city to remind them of home. On the trip to Edinburgh they moved into a world that more clearly set the old apart from the new. They came upon poverty that exceeded anything known in the American countryside. "We would as we rode along," he said, "see many houses where the husband, wife, children, hogs, horses, and cows all lived together in one room in an undistinguished manner. I had often heard that some of the poor families in Scotland lived in this manner but never believed it before." A swollen stream that blocked the road forced them to put up one night at "a poor little dirty cottage," where the farmer and his wife generously shared their supper—a bowl of milk—and then turned over the single bed to the visitors, who "lay all night in fur coats to avoid catching the itch, but all our precautions did not avail, for poor Mr. Potts the next day enjoyed much of the royal pleasure of scratching himself."

In the evening of November 3 Rush and Potts saw the great, gray Castle Rock rise from the dark and knew they had arrived at Edinburgh. Virtually the entire city clustered beneath the shadow of the castle atop the rock, stretching a mile down the sloping spine of stone to the now empty palace of former Scottish kings. The next day they walked the cobblestones of High Street, the main thoroughfare. Narrow stone buildings, taller than any Rush had ever seen, flanked the street, and a glimpse down the tunnel-like alleys cutting away to the right and left revealed further clusters of these soaring houses.

The shroud of sooty smoke that hung in the air most of the year had led Scotsmen to call their city "Auld Reekie." Rush suspected another reason for the nickname. The height of their houses and the number of families within them "subjects the inhabitants to many inconveniences," he observed, "for as they have no yards or cellars, they have of course no necessary houses, and all their filth of every kind is thrown out of their windows." Those unfortunate enough to be abroad after ten o'clock at night ran the risk of receiving "the flowers of Edinburgh"—a gift once received *"naturalized"* the visitor, Rush remarked with emphasis. "As yet I have happily escaped being made a freeman of the city in this way, but my unfortunate friend Potts has gained the honor before me."[2]

"Silence pervaded the streets of that great city after ten o'clock at night," Rush years later told his children with unconscious humor, for he meant the remark to illustrate the high moral tone of Edinburgh life. The churches, he noted, were always filled on Sundays. He never "saw a pack of cards in either a public or private house." Genteel people preferred dancing to insipid conversation, they rarely swore, and never got drunk; among the common people drunkenness was a rarity, fraud scarcely known, and integrity omnipresent. Rush always conveniently forgot anything that marred his conception of the city and its citizens, as, for example, the night his future father-in-law was attacked by a robber and only "after a severe contest, in which he successfully and skillfully defended himself with a small sword," escaped with his life; nothing unseemly about Edinburgh ever appeared in Rush's journal or the letters home. Even the games of the Scots provided moral uplift. A man who played golf, for instance, "would live ten years the longer for using this exercise once or twice a week." Rush, hoping to popularize the sport in America, later explained it to friends: "A large common in which there are several little holes is chosen for the purpose. It is played with little leather balls stuffed with feathers and sticks made somewhat in the form of a bandy-wicket. He who puts a ball into a given number of holes, with the fewest strokes, gets the game."[3]

The Scots could do no wrong, but one of their characteristics did puzzle Rush. He found that though they "live together in their human hives," they remained "entire strangers to one another." In the building where he and Potts rented rooms from two spinsters, he never got to know the names of the families that lived above and below his floor. The anonymity of the city's life seemed cold, even frightening, to Rush, who had known nothing like it in Philadelphia.[4]

Once he and Potts had found rooms, they went around to the university. The first sight must have jolted them, for the buildings resembled "more a pile of old stables than a Temple of Science." They called on the professors whose lectures they wanted to attend, paid their fees, and secured the customary admission tickets to the courses. The tall, slender Cullen, who stood with a stoop, left an especially vivid first impression. Years later Rush remembered his long face, pendulous lower lip and large nose, but particularly his "air of mildness and thought." The two young men said they brought letters from Philadelphia. "I hope from my good friend Dr. Morgan," Cullen replied, and after reading the letters took Rush and Potts by the hand, welcomed them to the university, then went on to explain that his lectures and private practice kept him so busy that he lacked the time to be as hospitable to students as he would like. "But however close my attention may be to these necessary avocations," he said, "young gentlemen recommended to me from Dr. Morgan may always depend upon my immediate patronage and friendship."[5]

The letter from Morgan satisfied the entrance requirements so far as Cullen and the other professors were concerned, but the young men were not formally matriculated until they had visited the provost and listened to him read in Latin the students' obligations to the university—to obey its rules, respect its professors, desist from participating in any riots or tumults, and apply themselves to their studies. Once they had signed the matriculation book they were accredited students of the University of Edinburgh, home of what was then considered the most prestigious medical school in the western world.

3

"I find it a painful piece of labor to attend these lectures as I should do," Rush wrote Morgan at the end of his second week in Edinburgh, "and I am now more fully convinced than ever how much sleep you must have sacrificed in transcribing those volumes of learning you carried with you to

America."[6] He found many of the students had come equipped to take shorthand in order to preserve every nugget dropped by the professors. Those like Rush who knew no shorthand customarily gathered after a lecture to concoct a literal report of what they had heard.

The value of an Edinburgh education, students assumed, came from listening to professors who worked on the frontiers of their specialties and in their lectures set forth doctrines that each day overturned some ancient medical practice or theory. "The present era will be famous for a revolution in physic," Rush told a college classmate a few months after arrival. "The old [Boerhaavian] doctrines of the blood, nerves, etc., are now exploded, and much more rational ones substituted in their room," he added with assurance. "DR. MONRO in his public lectures refutes Dr. Shippen's theory of the child's nutrition in the womb and Dr. Morgan's notions of the secretion of pus. These if you remember were the subjects of their inaugural dissertations. The theory of physic is like our dress always changing, and we are always best pleased with that which is most fashionable."[7]

Enthusiasm for Monro's course in anatomy, a subject that never especially interested Rush, was fashionable. Every season some two hundred students turned up to watch him perform from the podium in the "elegant" anatomical theater. He spoke without notes in rounded, polished sentences that were occasionally brightened by flashes of dry humor. Rush missed the humor and judged Monro "a most complete, accomplished scholar," a man of "great politeness and humanity."[8]

Neither Dr. John Gregory, who taught the practice of physic, nor Dr. John Hope, professor of botany, came off so well. Hope was dismissed as "a man of little genius but great application." Gregory had the good taste to reflect in his lectures "upon infidelity" and sought "to convince young minds that true honor could only consist in a regard to religion." He was a gentleman of "genius and learning," much "beloved as a man," but his lectures, delivered in a low voice without flourishes, contained nothing "new or interesting." The students in disgust petitioned Cullen to give his own version of the course, which he did. "Had it not been for these invaluable lectures of Dr. Cullen's," Rush said later, "I should have returned but little wiser in the practical parts of medicine than I came here."[9]

Rush gave his fullest attention to Dr. Black, because of the subject, and to Dr. Cullen, because of the man. Black, who was easily the greatest scientist on the faculty, had studied chemistry under Cullen at Glasgow.

His doctoral dissertation, one of the most significant ever published in chemistry, announced the discovery of carbon dioxide, or "fixed air" as it was then called. Up to that point, chemists had believed air was the only gas, but when Black "showed that fixed air was consistently distinguishable from normal air," he opened the way for the discovery of other gasses, notably oxygen. Rush's first year at Edinburgh was also Black's, who assumed a course Cullen had made one of the most popular in the medical school. Black's execrable platform presence—so bad that one student felt the need to "blush for his delivery"—led Rush, where he gave paragraphs and even pages to other professors in his journal, to state simply that Black was one "passionately fond" of his specialty and a man who "will not fail in a short time of rendering his name famous all over the world."[10]

If Black as a lecturer disappointed, Rush let no one at home know it. He called chemistry "my favorite study," as, indeed, it ought to be if he were to teach it. "I know of no science in the world which affords more rational entertainment than this," he said. "It is not only a science of importance in itself, but serves as a key to a thousand other sources of knowledge." In truth, however, Black, a pure scientist, showed little interest in the utilitarian aspects that principally interested Rush, and it took Rush more than a quarter of a century to appreciate him fully. He still told students years after returning to Philadelphia that "among all the chemists who adorn the present day Dr. Cullen of Edinburgh deserves to be mentioned with the most respect."[11]

Rush venerated no man more than Cullen. No one could possibly "do justice to this great man's character either as a scholar, a physician, or a man." Familiar with all science, he also knew history, politics, and belles lettres and could ramble fluently in at least six languages. He served, said Rush, as "the father of all his pupils," yet could lay aside distance without loss of dignity and mix with students "upon terms of the most endearing equality." He excelled in the classroom, his lectures so smooth "it was hard to tell which most to admire, their ingenuity or their order." Though later generations would credit Cullen with few permanent contributions to medicine, his students, most of whom felt about him as Rush did, believed he had enriched all its branches "with the most invaluable discoveries" and that "his fame and merit will be better known and more acknowledged a hundred years hence than it is at present."[12]

That fame would rest on two rocks—his nosology and his system of medicine. Nosology, according to an eighteenth-century definition, "consists in a systematic distribution of disease into classes, orders, genera, and species, on the plan of natural history." Cullen hoped that he, in his classifications of diseases by symptoms, would do for medicine what Linnaeus had done for botany. When finished, he had found a niche for 1,720 diseases, but the beautiful pattern crumbled before he died, with Rush one of the subverters. "An undue reliance upon nosology, and allowing it to substitute names for realities, seems to have produced the mischief which has thrown it into discredit," a physician of the day wrote by way of an obituary.[13]

Cullen's system of medicine sought to supplant Boerhaave's. Boerhaave located the source of all disease in the fluids of the body; Cullen held that it lay in the solids. He maintained that life emanated from the "energy of the brain," which passed from there through the nervous system to the solid organs and muscles. Disease resulted from a malfunction of the brain that caused, in turn, either tension or laxness throughout the body; treatment of any disease, then, depended on whether nervous energy needed to be built up or diminished. Appropriate drugs and diet were available for restoring energy, and bleeding and purging were recommended for reducing it. For more than half his professional career, Rush preached the medical gospel according to Cullen, only eventually to discard the master's theory for one of his own devising. But even then Cullen exerted an influence, for it was his emphasis on the brain and on the functions and disorders of the nervous system—it was he who coined the word "neurosis"—that alerted Rush to an aspect of medicine then given little attention: mental illness.[14]

4

Everything went well for Rush during the first term. A student's day normally began about seven. He studied in his room through the morning, spent the afternoon in classes and touring the infirmary wards, with an hour out for dinner between two and three o'clock. After a light supper at six, he settled down for the evening to copy over notes and do some general reading, retiring about midnight. The routine varied only on Sunday and lasted from November to May. Rush ended the year with praise from professors and an invitation to join the medical society, which students had founded thirty years earlier and was "now so reputable that most of the professors in the college are members of it." The society gathered every Saturday morning during the term in a room in the Royal Infirmary. "Each member is obliged to write a long dissertation in his turn upon a disease, or upon some of the animal functions, or any other subject the president of the society may propose to him, and is obliged to defend it publicly against all attacks from any person in the society."[15]

During the summer of 1767 Rush studied Spanish and Italian on his own and French with a tutor, no doubt with an eye to making the most of a Continental tour if he could manage one before returning home. Also, he still had to contend with the old burden of Latin, even though he now believed he read it "with a rapidity and pleasure I never had known before." Edinburgh had modernized to the point where lectures were delivered in English, but all dissertations had to be written in Latin. Rush blamed his past troubles with Latin on being forced to read the classics at an age when "they are so little relished, or so imperfectly understood, by young men."[16]

A busy social life began the first day in the city, when he "waited upon several gentlemen to whom I was recommended," and continued full from then on, though doubtless largely confined to Sundays during the term; from May until the following November the relaxed pace of his academic schedule allowed him to circulate about the city more freely. Franklin had written his friend Sir Alexander Dick, president of the Royal Society of Physicians, that Rush and Potts were "young gentlemen of ingenuity and application and excellent morals," and before the first month ended Rush found himself dining at Sir Alexander's table with David Hume. He judged the philosopher a "rather ungenteel and clumsy" person who spoke little but always amiably and to the point and did not flaunt his deism. He met William Robertson, principal of the college and widely known for a recently completed history of England, and this "haughty prelate" he condemned as a man of "arbitrary spirit," a persecutor of the pious who numbered among his close friends that deist Hume. He became friendly with two prominent bankers in the city, William Hogg, a venerable gentleman of seventy-two who died two months after Rush's arrival, and his son Thomas Hogg, with whose family he became particularly close. The younger Hogg introduced him to the Earl of Leven, owner of an estate some twelve miles from Edinburgh that Rush visited several times during the summer. "It was here I first saw true domestic happiness in its highest perfection." He admired Lord Leven as "the patron and friend of everything that's good" and Lady Leven as "(I had almost said) an angel incarnate." He liked the sons, Alexander and David, and he fell in love with the daughter, Jane, sixteen years old, which for Rush, then twenty-one, marked the age where "youth, beauty, and virtue appear to the greatest advantage."

Never before had Rush met anyone like Lady Jane. The girls of Philadelphia paled beside her. Her radiance blotted out all thought of Polly Fisher, whom Rush had promised to love forever. Her beauty left him speechless, or almost speechless. And when such beauty was blended "with all the additional strength which education, virtue, spotless innocence and sweetness of temper give, then its power becomes irresistible," he confided to his journal. More than that, "when these amiable endowments meet in a person of high rank and fortune they strike us with something divine." She had "a complete knowledge of music," and she sang Scottish airs with a lisp that left him limp with delight. She spoke French. "What politeness! What an address, what an insinuating manner does she possess! *The law of kindness is written in her heart.* Words like honey drop from her tongue. In a word, *Heaven is in her eye, grace in her look."* Rush said nothing about Lady Jane in his letters to friends back home, but clearly the young woman obsessed him and would for some time.[17]

Rush's social success owed something to his charm—he was good company, an intelligent as well as companionable presence at the dinner table— something to his letters of introduction from the obliging Franklin and from Philadelphians who had friends in the city, and something to the fact he was an American, a species of man Scotsmen had seen few of. There was, of course, more to it than that. Rush worked at building up his social connections. He was a gregarious young man and as curious about the Scots as they were about Americans. But he also relished the heady sensation of circulating, as he never had in Philadelphia, among the cream—and the wealthy —of society. Rush did not catalog Lady Jane's "high rank and fortune" among her lesser virtues. He also became friends with Robert Scott Moncrief, "a gentleman of considerable fortune"; Archibald Wallace, brother of a Philadelphia merchant, "the friend and promoter of every useful institution"; John Waikon, "a man of fortune"; William Galloway, a scholarly merchant and master of seven languages.

Naturally, he found time, too, for the clergy, dining with Whitefield when he visited the city, and visiting frequently with the blind, somewhat solemn poet-scholar-preacher Thomas Blacklock and with John Erskine, a minister so absentminded he once tipped his hat to his wife in the street as if she were a stranger. Erskine, a friend through correspondence with a number of American ministers, worried about the establishment of a military government in the colonies, and in 1769 published a pamphlet entitled *Shall I Go to War with American Brethren?* wherein he argued that if war did materialize, the Americans, using Indian tactics, might defeat the British.[18]

Rush liked Erskine personally and for his political views, but his sensible sermons failed to excite him. He preferred the "nervous" style of Robert Walker, whose church he regularly attended and whose sermons contained "all the beauties of composition and graces of elocution." The grace rather than the spiritual power of a sermon seemed the new touchstone. Since his traumatic religious experience in 1766, when Christ had spoken to his soul about having slept with a married woman, Rush had made a habit of secret daily prayer; yet now, only months later, that devotion had become "often a mere form, and carelessly and irreverently performed." He had avoided contact in Edinburgh with the "common sense" philosophy popularized by Francis Hut:heson, for it verged too close to deism for comfort. He despised the liberal wing of Presbyterianism led by Robertson, for it countenanced card playing and theatergoing and sought to erect a theology based as much on reason as on faith. He moved in an orthodox circle, the Scottish counterpart of the New Side environment he had been reared in. And yet in Scotland, of all places, where Calvinism prevailed and Presbyterianism seeped into every crevice of life, Rush's sense of sin waned, and for the first time he seemed at peace with himself and the world. Perhaps the attitude of his all but flawless hero Cullen—"with regard to revealed religion he professes himself a skeptic"—helped to relax him. Whatever the reason, Rush in later years preferred to blame his lost "spiritual sensibility" on travel, "for traveling is unfavorable to the growth and even to the existence of religion in the soul."[19]

5

In February 1767 Jonathan Potts left for home. Potts's fiancée called him back because she had become "greatly indisposed" by his absence. He testified affection for his roommate by promising to name his first son

Benjamin, though Rush supposed after Franklin rather than himself. Potts's departure created a void that Rush filled by circulating more widely among fellow students. Rush knew and was known by all his colleagues. Talk—and Rush loved to talk, finding it "a constant source of excitement to my mind" —usually centered on matters medical. With the American students, however, it also involved matters financial, for most of them worried about the expense of an Edinburgh education. Costs ran between £100 and £120 a year, a considerable sum for Rush's mother and stepfather to provide, if it was they who were underwriting his venture. One of Rush's friends, Walter Jones of Virginia, had come to Edinburgh expecting to live on £90 a year; he ended spending £118 a year, and though this was £30 to £40 less than friends had spent to keep up "a tolerable genteel character," his three-year stay nearly bankrupted his brother, who was footing the bill. "Boarding is now become so excessive high in Edinburgh," Rush wrote home in 1768, "that few students will be able to come here hereafter from America."[20]

Among the British students Rush knew best was a lad named John Bostock, whose aunt he had met in Liverpool and whose political views were to exert a lasting influence. The friendship blossomed when Bostock learned that Rush, like himself, had an ancestor who had served in Cromwell's army. "He now opened his mind fully to me, and declared himself to be an advocate for the republican principles for which our ancestors had fought." Bostock rhapsodized over the character and writings of Algernon Sidney, especially his treatise on government, and he criticized the validity of the monarchical system of rule, flatly contradicting Samuel Davies' view that kings were "nearly as essential to political order as the sun is to the order of our solar system." Rush now reviewed his political—as he had perhaps his religious—beliefs. "I renounced the prejudices of my education upon [monarchy]," he recollected years later, "and from that time to the present all my reading, observations and reflections have tended more and more to show the absurdity of hereditary power, and to prove that no form of government can be rational but that which is derived from the suffrages of the people who are the subjects to it."[21] This recollection, however, rather neatly overlooked the fact that at the time Rush was presumably denouncing "the absurdity of hereditary power," he had declared "his zealous attachment to his Majesty, King George the Third, and our present happy Constitution in Church and State," and had, thereupon, been admitted a member of the Revolution Club of Edinburgh.[22]

Without much question, however, Bostock's political views made a great impression. To recognize the validity of a government based on the "suffrages of the people . . . became a ferment in my mind. I now suspected error in everything I had been taught, or believed, and as far as I was able began to try the foundations of my opinions upon many other subjects." Later, back in Philadelphia, Rush did "try the foundations of my opinions upon many other subjects," but nothing indicates these experiments got under way at Edinburgh. His friendships among students, especially the fifteen or so from America, were close but based largely on a common involvement in medicine. Seldom in letters that flowed out after his classmates had returned to their homes in England, Virginia, Maryland, South Carolina, and the West Indies is there discussion of subjects outside medicine and personal affairs.

In February 1767 Rush's routine was broken by a visit from Richard Stockton of Princeton. Stockton, a lawyer and member of the board of trustees of the College of New Jersey, had come to Scotland mainly to inform Rev. John Witherspoon, who lived in the village of Paisley, about five miles beyond Glasgow, that the college had chosen him to succeed Finley as president. A short while after Stockton fulfilled his mission, Rush learned that Witherspoon had refused the honor. He had "a strong bias to America," but his wife feared the long sea voyage and refused to budge from Scotland. Rush viewed the refusal as disastrous for the college. To him, Witherspoon "revived in one" the genius of Davies and the knowledge of Finley. One who knew Witherspoon later said "he had more of the quality called *presence*" than any other man of his time except George Washington. His sermons were "loaded with good sense," delivered without notes and in a melodious voice "with all the elegance and beauty that language can give them." Witherspoon had been selected by the college trustees as a man who would not be dominated by the Old Side of the Presbyterian Church that sought to control the school, and on this point, too, Rush was reassuring. "He is the 'homo factus ad unguem' ['a man to his very fingertips'], and is admirably calculated for overthrowing all the strategems of *those* who have hitherto combined to ruin our college."[23]

Rush took it upon himself to persuade Witherspoon to accept the call. "All America waits, I am sure with trembling impatience, for your answer," he wrote with his usual proneness for hyperbole, "and should you refuse the call they would look upon the dispensations of Providence towards that college as more gloomy and mysterious than ever they have been." Think not only of the college but of yourself, he continued. "Here your talents have been in some measure buried, but at Princeton they will be called into action, and the evening of your life will be much more effulgent than your brightest meridian days have been. . . ."[24]

Witherspoon answered this effusion a month later by saying that his refusal was irrevocable. "I was thunderstruck," Rush replied. "What shall I say?" he asked—rhetorically, for he had plenty to say. He drew a dreadful picture of the consequences of Witherspoon's rejection, the worst aspect being that Dr. Francis Alison, an Old Side clergyman, might get the post. Did Witherspoon wish to hand over the college to the devil's disciple? "How awful would such a step be to the interests of religion in that extensive and growing country! He is a man of the most virulent, bitter temper, and has from the beginning of his life showed himself an enemy to vital religion." Rush, in the role of the loyal "old grad," now moved into a passionate peroration. "Suffer me to conjure you by everything you look upon as sacred not to refuse the call, if you have any regard to religion, to your family, and to your own private happiness. Let not the college with her last breath proclaim you as the cause of her dissolution. Let not the enemies of the college triumph over her dejected, heartbroken friends. Every tear they shed and every pang of grief they feel will be felt by you. O! *Nassau Hall, Nassau Hall!* in vain rescued and cherished by every lover of religion, since thou art now to fall into the hands of some _____. But I cannot express it —my heart bleeds within me—O Nassau Hall, Nassau Hall!"[25]

In mid-August Rush visited the Witherspoons at Paisley in order "to cooperate with the doctor in endeavoring to remove his wife's objections to going to America." Witherspoon held out little hope of success, doubting his wife would even "enter into conversation" with Rush. But she did. The technique to charm her out of the corner seems to have been to ignore her and in conversations with Witherspoon to lament "often in the presence of his wife his not accepting of the charge of the Jersey college." Soon, apparently, Mrs. Witherspoon joined the talk and aired her fears of the ocean voyage and of settling in a strange new land. Somehow Rush, who had only recently spent seven terrifying weeks at sea, "obviated such of the objections as she had formerly made to crossing the ocean." Before the visit ended, Mrs. Witherspoon had agreed that her husband should go to America and that she would accompany him. Witherspoon was both pleased and disconcerted at the change worked upon his wife. Rush was, as he had observed before, "a most agreeable young man," but his addiction to "strong and superlative expressions" gave Witherspoon no little "uneasiness."[26]

6

Despite warnings from friends to take life easier, Rush had ended the first term with his "health somewhat impaired by too much confinement and close study." A brief vacation to Glasgow and a relatively languid summer sufficed to revive him for the term that began in the fall of 1767. "I have a thousand things to communicate to you in physic," he wrote Morgan soon after classes resumed. He was attending Cullen's lectures a second time, a common practice with students to make sure they missed nothing the great man had to offer, and his enthusiasm waxed rather than waned. "His lectures upon the nervous system and upon pathology are worth their weight in gold. I am in hopes I shall be able to transplant most of his doctrines to Philadelphia." A second time round with Dr. Black's course in chemistry led to a friendship with that "very amiable and learned gentleman" and to "many distinguishing marks of favor." He said nothing about the course in materia medica, taught by John Hope, that man "of little genius." John Gregory's lectures on the practice of physic abounded with "excellent practical observations" but in no way equaled those of Cullen's, "whose merit is beyond all praise."[27]

Midway in the second term Rush prepared to work on his dissertation, the major requirement remaining for the M.D. after completing the necessary courses. He chose to do research on digestion, a subject that had intrigued physicians for the past century. Cullen reflected eighteenth-century ignorance when he explained digestion by "the presence and necessity of an acid generated in the stomach." (The nineteenth century showed that the stomach only initiated "the first of a series of profound changes taking place along nearly the whole length of the alimentary canal.") A currently popular theory held that fermentation lay at the root of the digestive process.[28] Rush's search for an answer led to a mild ordeal; his technical approach to the problem was awkward and unimaginative and his findings inaccurate, but a flair for the dramatic obscured these shortcomings. He made four experiments, three upon himself and one upon a friend, that

involved vomiting a full meal and testing the remains for acid. Rush later
vividly summarized the experiments:

> Having dined on beef, peas, and bread, I puked up, about three
> hours afterwards, the contents of my stomach, by means of a
> grain of tartar emetic, and found them not only acid to the taste,
> but likewise that they afforded a red color, upon being mixed
> with the syrup of violets—an invariable mark this, of acidity,
> among chemists! The same phenomena took place, after having
> eat[en] veal, poultry, and several other kinds of flesh. The bread
> I made use of in one of the experiments was not fermented, and
> before dining, each time, I took a few grains of a fixed alkali, in
> order to destroy the least particle of an acid, which the preceding
> meal might have left in my stomach. I repeat, therefore, what I
> formerly advanced, that digestion is carried on *chiefly* by fer-
> mentation, and that the stomach stands in need of no other exer-
> cise, during this process, than its own gentle peristaltic motions,
> which serve both to mix the aliment, and to discharge it from the
> stomach.[29]

By January 1768 he had written up the experiments in English and was
"busily employed" in translating the work into Latin.

As Rush worked through Black's chemistry course a second time, he
came to consider himself "now master of the science" and convinced he
"could teach it with confidence and ease." Morgan told him the chemistry
professorship at the college remained open until he returned but that Redman spoke less certainly; though not on the faculty, Redman's stature among
Philadelphia physicians, together with his close ties with Rush, made his
approval of the appointment obligatory. Rush responded to this news with
a long, furious letter excoriating Redman. His help in securing the professorship "was the first favor I ever implored from him, and I am resolved
it shall be the last." Rush may have been exhausted from studies and extra-
curricular activities. "I expect," he told Morgan at the time, "to stand forth
in a few nights to defend my papers in the medical society. One of them is
on the *bilious fever,* the other on the *venereal disease.*" Or his outburst may
have been prompted by an eagerness to reject his medical "father." It is also
possible that Rush was unnerved by the thought that Adam Kuhn, who had
recently received his M.D. from Edinburgh and returned to Philadelphia

to become professor of botany, might usurp the coveted chemistry post. Regardless of why he lashed out, he soon regretted it. Hardly had the letter to Morgan been posted when one arrived from Redman filled with fondness for a favorite among his "professional children." In a later letter Redman explained that the trustees should not promise a professorship "so long before the qualifications of a person could be certainly determined." Be assured, he said, your friends can block all applications till your return, "nor has the person you might suspect (or any other) applied, well knowing from proper hints what he might expect if he had." Redman ended on a note of affection; for him the incident was closed, though not for Rush. The father-son relationship of old had died, and when friendship resumed between the two, it would be on Rush's terms as equals.[30]

During the spring of 1768 Rush again found time to encourage—and advise—Witherspoon. The irony of a twenty-two-year-old admonishing a gentleman of forty-five escaped him. "Prudence should be mixed with zeal to constitute it such," he cautioned. "We may often miss the prize we aim at by running too swift as well as too slow." In May he traveled back to Paisley to convey to its presbytery the official notice of Witherspoon's call to the College of New Jersey, and a few days later the couple sailed for Philadelphia. Ahead of them sped a letter from Rush to friends at home urging a warm welcome, especially for Mrs. Witherspoon, who "has atoned for her former reluctance by her present cheerfulness in complying with the call to America." Witherspoon reported soon after reaching Princeton in mid-August that their reception "even exceeded your own hyperbolical promises."[31]

Rush publicly defended his thesis and took the final examinations in June, a month after the Witherspoons' departure. The ordeal of qualifying for a degree followed a pattern that a friend of Rush's described this way:

> On the first day I had not the most distant hint what was to be the subject of my trial. I went in, I confess, trembling, and Dr. Cullen began my examination by asking me some general definitions, as "Quid est medicina?" and so on. He then went to the structure of the stomach and alimentary canal, thence made a digression to their diseases with their diagnosis and method of cure. Then young Dr. Munro [Monro] followed upon similar topics. This ended my first examination, which lasted near an

hour. My next consisted in writing commentaries upon two apho-
risms of Hippocrates and defending them against old Dr. Munro
and Dr. Cullen, which took up one hour also. My last private one
was writing commentaries upon two cases in practice . . . which
I defended against Dr. Munro and Dr. Cullen. This examination
took up an hour and a half; and lastly I was called upon publicly in the hall to defend my thesis. During all these trials my
exercises were not only written in Latin, but I was obliged to
defend them in the same language; not even in the first where I
was ignorant of my subject being allowed to speak a word of
English.[32]

Having survived the defense of the thesis, the candidates left the hall to
don black gowns. "When we returned," said Rush, "an oath was administered to us in which we swore that we would never wantonly try experiments with any of our patients, nor yet divulge any thing that had been
told us as a secret," then "a cap was put on our heads and we were declared
publicly Doctors of Physic."[33]

Soon afterward, Rush's dissertation was published as a thirty-page
pamphlet entitled *De Coctione Ciborum in Ventriculo,* which in less imposing English became "On the Digestion of Food in the Stomach." Months earlier Rush had asked Morgan's permission "to prefix your name to it together
with Dr. Franklin's, Dr. Black's, Dr. Shippen's and Redman's." Ultimately
the pamphlet was dedicated to Franklin, and below his name came Black,
Redman, Shippen, Morgan, in that order, followed by Rush's college friend
Jonathan Bayard Smith and his brother Jacob Rush. The absence of Cullen's
name must have been by request. Rush had pondered the arrangement of
names. The one arrived at satisfied both himself and protocol, or so it
seemed then.[34]

7

As late as May 1768 Rush had planned to head for London after receiving his degree and continue his studies there, but between May and
June he was prevailed on to stay in Edinburgh through the summer. He
attended Cullen's lectures on the practice of physic, which unfolded "each

day some new secret to us in the animal economy," but otherwise he spent the summer months visiting with friends. Early July found him taking his ease at the country seat of Lord Leven and remarking "how insipid are all lectures and studies when set in composition with the *pleasures of friendship* and a rural life!" The allure of a country vacation was enhanced, obviously, by the presence of Lady Jane Leslie.[35]

Rush's student friends considered him something of a ladies' man, a judgment borne out by an awkward situation that came to a head during his last summer in Edinburgh. Earlier he had received information that his friend Thomas Bradford had fallen in love with Mary Fisher. Rush responded to the news generously, telling Bradford he could not "think of a wife for eight or ten years to come," or at least not until he could provide for his widowed sisters and their young sons. While circumstances forced him to relinquish the blessed Miss Fisher, she should "know how often I have walked up and down my room for whole nights together since I came to Scotland, thinking upon nothing but her." Could that dear girl but "see my *heart,* my honest heart," she would know "I will never cease as long as I live to esteem her the loveliest and best woman in the world." Rush ended blessing a marriage he assumed already consummated. In June, however, he learned Bradford and Miss Fisher apparently still considered his love a bar to the union; this time he spoke bluntly and less effusively. "I have detached my affections so much from her," he wrote Bradford, "that if I found her single when I returned, I should not think of courting her." Rush encouraged a prompt wedding and then ended with this ingenious sentence: "I had rather hear of it than see it, lest the old flame which I think is now extinguished, should revive again, and revive to no purpose; for whether you married her or no, she would be equally lost to me."[36] (Bradford and Miss Fisher were married on November 23.)

As quickly as possible in the correspondence with Bradford he closed off the embarrassing discussion about Miss Fisher and shifted none too subtly to other matters. "Yes, we will be revenged of the mother country," he wrote. "For my part, I am resolved to devote my head, my heart, and my pen entirely to the service of America, and promise myself much assistance from you in everything of this kind that I shall attempt through life." He now cherished "his native country above all places in the world," and, as he had told Morgan, he saw Philadelphia soon becoming "the *Edinburgh of America.*" To achieve that goal entailed more than a great medical school.

"Why don't you set a circulating library on foot?" he asked Bradford, who eventually did. "I think you had better alter the form of your newspaper," he added, referring to the *Pennsylvania Journal* which Bradford, with his father William, published; Rush advised essays on agriculture and manufacturing. His plans were endless. Why don't we establish "a *literary and physical society* in Philadelphia, in imitation of the Edinburgh society of the same name?" he suggested to Morgan.[37]

Dreams of projects to enhance Philadelphia faded with news that Redman and Morgan, but especially Morgan, disliked their positions in the dissertation's dedicatory list. Rush answered an angry letter from Morgan by dismissing the issue as "a matter of no consequence," by claiming that if he had considered it otherwise "your name should have been first," and by asserting somewhat petulantly that Redman followed Black because, "sir, there are *teaching* and *ruling* masters" and Redman had taught him nothing. Rush had "pounded his mortar" and "posted his books six long years" and received no favors except "such as he was bound to do by the common rules of decency and good manners." (The dispute boiled on for months and clouded Rush's homecoming. Morgan came to think his protégé sided with Shippen, and nearly a year later sent a confused twelve-page letter of complaints: Rush *had* given thought to the order of names, he wrote, for Morgan knew from "a gentleman at Edinburgh" that Rush had been warned to place his name above Shippen's, as "I was the eldest medical professor; but you maintained a contrary opinion. . . .") Morgan in another context suggested that while Rush continued his studies in London he would do well to take another course in chemistry. Rush waved aside the admonition, too. He could think of no greater "dishonor to my ingenious master" than attending another. Moreover, after listening to Black for two years he now knew all there was to know about chemistry.[38]

Morgan, too, could be arrogant, vindictive, and self-pitying, as his letter showed, but it must have surprised him to find Rush displaying these qualities. Yet Rush knew himself, knew that his outburst exposed a side of him that, unattractive as it was, he must live with. You have less reason to reproach yourself, he told Ebenezer Hazard at about the same time he wrote Morgan; then followed a revealing sentence: "Your temper was ever less impetuous, and your whole behavior more of a piece than mine."[39]

Shortly after Cullen's lectures ended in mid-September, Rush set out for London. He left with a full heart and a deep attachment for Scotland.

"The happiest part of my life is now over," he said at the time. "My halcyon days have been spent in Edinburgh." That feeling never ebbed. "The two years I spent in Edinburgh," he wrote long afterward, "I consider as the most important in their influence upon my character and conduct of any period of my life." Years later when his son James was in Edinburgh he wrote: "However wistfully you may cast your eyes across the Atlantic and long for a seat at your father's fireside, be assured you will often lick your fingers in reviewing the days and hours you are now spending in the highly cultivated society of Edinburgh. Perhaps there is at present no spot upon the earth where religion, science, and literature combine more to produce moral and intellectual pleasures than in the metropolis of Scotland. What a contrast between an evening at Mrs. Hamilton's or Mrs. Fletcher's, or a seat at the tea table of the venerable Mrs. Hogg, or a chair next to Miss A. Hogg—and the convivial dinners and insipid tea parties of Philadelphia!"[40]

4

London and Paris

1768–1769

1

JUDGE RICHARD PETERS of Philadelphia, who knew Benjamin Rush better and longer than almost anyone, once said of him: "I admire his abilities, lament his foibles, and with them all sincerely love him, therefore I cannot but wish him gratified."[1] Peters in a sentence caught perfectly the complex reaction Rush evoked from contemporaries. Philadelphians, except those with whom he fought—no small number—felt much as the judge did. So, too, did those he came to know in Edinburgh, a remarkable number of whom remained friends for life, with only the years of the Revolution interrupting their stream of letters across the ocean. London would react to the garrulous, the charming, the mercurial Rush as Philadelphia and Edinburgh had.

His letters from Edinburgh had not held much on the course of political affairs, though relations with England had worsened steadily through 1767. Parliament that year, prodded by Charles Townshend, had inflicted a new set of custom duties on such items as paint, glass, tea, silk, and lead. The most cogent attack on the duties came from Philadelphia in the form of twelve *Letters from a Farmer in Pennsylvania to the Inhabitants of the British Colonies,* written by John Dickinson, a respected, politically moderate attorney who had studied in London. Dickinson argued "that we [Americans] cannot be happy, without being free; that we cannot be free without being secure in our property; that we cannot be secure in our property, if, without our consent, others may, as by right, take it away; that taxes imposed on us by Parliament, do thus take it away." He said nothing new, but he said it more effectively than anyone else. The Farmer quickly became a man for whom "no mark of honor and respect" was "thought equal to his merit." Though nonimportation and nonexportation agreements were fashioned in all the colonies after the Farmer's letters appeared, Britain had still not repealed the Townshend duties when Rush arrived in London. Indeed, after learning of a mob's attack on custom officers in Boston, talk of appeasing the colonies died in Parliament and in September 1768, the month Rush set out for London, troops stationed at Halifax were ordered to occupy Boston.

Rush headed for London filled with much confidence and slight enthusiasm. He expected to learn little "from the random prescriptions of the London physicians," but since "my reputation may be influenced by it, I shall follow them faithfully for some months." He found rooms first in the busy Strand, but since they were too far from the hospitals he soon moved to the Haymarket district, settling in with his cousin Thomas Coombe, then in London to be ordained in the Anglican Church. They lived in the home of Hannah Jeffries, a widow who became a proxy mother to Rush, privy to his love for Miss Leslie and other personal matters.[2]

Rush remained in London from the end of September 1768 to mid-February of the following year. The damp, foggy London weather bothered his lungs, and only after he had returned to Philadelphia did he lose, as a friend was glad to hear, "that complaint which you labored under when you and I were at London last." But the weather had to be endured, for Rush had timed his stay to fit in the "autumn course" of anatomical lectures given by Dr. William Hunter. There were two Hunters, William and John, brothers as well as Scotsmen and both distinguished—the shy, awkward John as a surgeon and the greatest anatomist of the century, William as an extraordinary lecturer and an obstetrician who had made the profession of man-midwife for the first time a respectable pursuit for physicians, especially after the queen chose him as her physician. As a lecturer William attracted not only medical students but also such notables as Edmund Burke and Edward Gibbon, holding them spellbound during his two-hour talks. Gibbon became so intrigued by the mysteries of the human anatomy that he refused to leave London until Hunter's series of talks had ended. Rush found Hunter "entertaining as well as instructing," a mild judgment perhaps conditioned by the twice-taken anatomy course of Shippen, an ex-student of both Hunters.[3]

The early weeks of the course centered on William Hunter's lectures; dissection began only when "the weather [became] cold enough to admit bringing dead bodies into the theater." The apparent ease with which bodies were produced for dissection—John Hunter had established excellent contacts with grave robbers—must have amazed Rush. He could remember the day shortly before leaving Philadelphia when Shippen had been hounded by a mob convinced he had dissected a body other than a hanged felon; at Edinburgh he had been warned that a student ran the risk of expulsion from both the medical school and the city "if it was known he had a body in his possession." Students' dissections at the time Rush attended the Hunter school were directed by William's partner, William Hewson, John having become a surgeon at Saint George's Hospital.[4]

Years earlier John Morgan had attended Hunter's school and had struck up a friendship with Hewson. Rush did the same. And because of this, Rush, no doubt chatting away as he dissected a body, happened to be at Hewson's side when the surgeon completed a delicate operation that "proved the existence of lymphatic vessels in fishes." The function of the vessels in humans had long been disputed. The Hunters and Hewson argued that they helped absorb fluids from the body and food from the intestine; Albrecht von Haller, a distinguished Swiss pathologist, rejected this view, insisting that mammals alone carried lymphatic vessels. Hewson had earlier, with extraordinary skill, uncovered them in a turtle, and now to find them in fish (and later in birds) both refuted Haller and cleared the way for verifying the Hunter-Hewson view of their function.[5]

A letter of introduction to another of Morgan's British friends, Dr. Richard Huck, decided the choice of mentor for Rush's practical training while in London. With Huck he walked the wards of Middlesex Hospital, and when Huck moved to Saint Thomas, the city's oldest hospital, Rush followed along. The distinctions that British medicine insisted upon between surgeons and physicians—surgeons, who but twenty-five years earlier had broken away from the barbers' guild, were known as "mister" and only physicians with their university-granted M.D.'s could be addressed as "doctor"—carried over to the hospital routine. Huck's "walking student" fee of approximately twenty guineas allowed Rush to tour the hospital wards daily and to watch Huck prescribe for his patients, but to enter the operating room he had to pay an additional fee to one of the staff surgeons. The surgeon's fee was high—generally about fifty pounds—and either for that reason or because the course with Hunter and Hewson offered all he wanted to know about surgery, Rush was satisfied to see the hospital routine solely through a physician's eyes.[6]

Some doctors, like the poet-physician Mark Akenside whom Rush saw at Saint Thomas, were "distant and formal" with their students. Others, like Huck, accepted them as friends and equals. Huck lived "very elegantly" as a bachelor, but the formal style of his life contrasted with his easy, genial personality. Though one of London's foremost physicians, "he was so modest that he seldom spoke even at his own table without blushing." He liked Americans and knew America, having served there and in the West Indies as an army physician during the Seven Years' War. Rush was "charmed with his character" and soon found he could "visit him at all hours and derive considerable improvement." To Rush, the man had but a single flaw—"he was a high-toned Royalist." American opposition against the crown angered Huck as little else did. Whatever the crown did was right; if it bribed members of Parliament to get a majority, then "it was necessary to bribe the rascals in order to make them honest."[7]

Rush soon found himself invited to join a weekly gathering of physicians at Huck's house, and often he was asked to dine "with him in large and highly polished companies." Through Huck he came to meet Sir John Pringle, former surgeon-general of the British army, the royal family's favorite physician, and soon to be president of the Royal Society. Though in his sixties, Pringle carried on a full professional and social life. The first time he met Rush he pumped question after question at him in genial curiosity. Rush must have handled himself well, for Pringle invited him to join a medical society that met every Wednesday night at his house. "The plan of it is not unlike the medical society you established in Philadelphia," Rush told Morgan, adding somewhat boastfully: "It consists of only eight or ten members, who are all Sir John's particular friends."[8]

Within a month Rush had revised his judgment of London physicians and what he could learn from them. "Few of them indeed practice medicine upon philosophical principles, but, notwithstanding this, they have enriched the science with a number of very useful facts." One of these facts concerned a new, simplified technique for inoculating against smallpox, the "Suttonian system," as it was called. At an Inoculating Hospital for the poor, Rush saw some one hundred patients who had been inoculated by Dr. Daniel Sutton's method, and all were "doing very well." He told Morgan that "the manner of making the incision is different" and that "the cool regimen is the grand secret." His account by mail, however, was so vague that the Suttonian system could not be introduced in Philadelphia until Rush returned to demonstrate it. By "cool regimen" Rush meant the "cooling treatment" Sydenham had introduced in the previous century and for which he had been ridiculed by contemporary physicians. Normally smallpox patients were put to bed and swathed in blankets and dosed with medicines to induce sweating, the aim being to hasten the disease's departure from the body. Sydenham preferred to let nature take its course. He allowed the patient to move freely about the house until approximately the fourth day of the fever when the pustules erupted; he then put the patient to bed, fed him fluids, and covered him only with light bedcovers. Sutton's refinement on Sydenham's treatment called for, as a modern physician has described it, "the clear serum from an early lesion in the blister stage, before it was contaminated with pus." This reduced the chance of secondary infection. Formerly, the infected matter was placed in a long incision. Sutton required only a light puncture, no larger, said Rush, "than is sufficient to draw one drop of blood."[9]

Vagueness characterized much of what Rush had to say about the professional side of his life in London. He commented little in letters home about Hunter's lectures, about the queasy experience of cutting apart stolen bodies in Hewson's dissection room, about the stench and filth of the packed wards of Saint Thomas. In London, it was people and politics that fascinated him most.

2

Through letters of introduction from home, Rush entered the circle of Dr. John Fothergill, a warm friend of Americans in London, especially medical students. Fothergill, a Quaker, had befriended Shippen and Morgan and encouraged their then shared vision of a medical school for Philadelphia. He also liked his new visitor from Philadelphia, though he thought him "too ardent a politician" and occasionally felt the need to "moderate the sanguine temperament." Soon Rush, who never missed the chance for good talk, found himself breakfasting once a week at Fother-gill's table. The conversation, always elevated and animated, usually cen-tered on politics, British and American, medicine, some philanthropic project that had currently engaged Fothergill's interest, or pacifism, a sub-ject close to the doctor's heart. "He often spoke with horror of war," Rush recalled, "and lamented the prevailing custom of the English and French nations considering each other as 'natural enemies.' "[10]

At the breakfast table Rush met John Coakley Lettsom, another young physician who had been reared in the West Indies and now lived with Fothergill while getting established in London. A warm friendship de-veloped between them, the closest Rush made in London. The two resem-bled each other strikingly in character, temperament, and energy, so much so that when Fothergill privately censured one for his volubility and en-thusiasm he soon afterward found himself applying similar words to the other. Friends judged both men "unstable as water." Both liked and at-tracted pretty women, and the remark made of Lettsom that he was a young man who "can trifle agreeably with females" could have been made of Rush. Both were ambitious for themselves, yet idealists eager to make the world a better place to live. Lettsom, the senior by three years, made an enduring impression on Rush. A condensed version of Lettsom's doctoral thesis on the ill effects of tea drinking appeared in an essay by Rush written shortly after he returned to America. After the Revolution Rush took the lead in Philadelphia in setting up a medical dispensary for the poor, a medical society for physicians, and a humane society; all three were pat-terned on similar organizations originally established in London by Lettsom, who had urged Rush to duplicate them in America. Lettsom's experiences on a West Indian plantation, where he saw firsthand the brutal effects of slavery, may also have led Rush toward the abolitionist views he was to express a few years later.

The friendship between the two continued by mail until Rush's death, when Lettsom published one of the few affectionate eulogies his old friend received from a contemporary on either side of the ocean. In that tribute he recalled a visit the pair had made to a "disputing society." One of the ora-tors had ended a speech that inveighed against America's rebellious spirit by insinuating "that if the Americans possessed even cannon, they had not a ball to fire." Rush shot to his feet and, as Lettsom remembered it, said "that if the Americans possessed no cannonballs, they could supply the

deficiency by digging up the skulls of those ancestors who had courted ex-
patriation from the old hemisphere under the vivid hope of enjoying more
ample freedom in the new one."[11]

3

After the social success produced by Franklin's letters of introduction
to Edinburgh acquaintances, Rush counted on "being introduced by him to
some of his friends" in London. He had heard before arriving that Franklin
had sailed for Pennsylvania, but the rumor proved false. Rush called on the
old gentleman—he was almost exactly forty years older than Rush—soon
after arriving in the city and, as did most visiting Americans, he received
a warm welcome. "It was my peculiar happiness to be domesticated in his
family," Rush said, meaning only that the door was always open to him,
not that he lived there. During the London stay Franklin treated Rush as a
son. He carried him to literary gatherings and once to court, where he
"pointed out to me many of the most distinguished public characters of
the nation," Rush recalled. "I never visited him without learning something." Nineteen years later he would be able in a small way to repay these
kindnesses by seeing to it that Franklin, after being passed over, was added
to the Pennsylvania delegation to the Constitutional Convention.[12]

The people Franklin introduced him to helped strengthen Rush's
prejudices against the British government. Probably through Franklin Rush
met Richard Price, nonconformist minister, and Edward and Charles Dilly,
nonconformists in religion and booksellers and publishers by profession—
all three warm friends of America by inclination. Rush went to the Pennsylvania Coffee House to get news and letters from home, but for local literary
gossip he visited the Dillys' bookstore. There he met "many gentlemen of
literary character" who before he left London had passed him on to one
well-known author after another. The talk at Dillys' was always stimulating
but occasionally too one-sided for Edward Dilly, noted for the elasticity of
his tongue; he was, said a friend, "one of the greatest talkers I ever met with;
tongue, hands, and head all moving at a time with so much rapidity that I
wonder how his lungs can sustain it." Edward chattered constantly and seldom strayed far from his favorite subject—politics; Charles, inured to the
verbal cascade, seldom bothered to speak.[13]

Possibly through Franklin but perhaps on his own, since they shared mutual friends back in Philadelphia, Rush met Benjamin West, another London-based American. West, though at the height of his fame as a painter of historic scenes, put on no airs with Rush. He painted his portrait and gossiped away about "the king and the royal family, also of many of the nobility of England," relived the years he had studied in Italy, and reminisced longingly about the countryside around Philadelphia and the people of "simple manners" among whom he had been reared. Through West, Rush met Sir Joshua Reynolds, who invited him to dine with Dr. Samuel Johnson, Oliver Goldsmith, and several other distinguished literary characters.[14]

Rush regarded the day spent with Johnson and Goldsmith "one of the most memorable I passed while abroad." The company had gathered by the time Johnson arrived. He entered the room as Sir Joshua was consoling Goldsmith about a drubbing recently taken from reviewers. "Don't mind them," Johnson said. "Where is the advantage of a man having a great deal of money but that the loss of a little will not hurt him? And where is the advantage of a man having a great deal of reputation but that the loss of a little will not hurt him? You can bear it."

Johnson dominated the talk the rest of the day. "He instructed upon all subjects," Rush recalled. "One of them was drunkenness, upon which he discovered much of that original energy of thought and expression which were so peculiar to him." At one point conversation turned to a scientific question—was the *anemone maritima* of the vegetable or animal kingdom? "It is animal," said Johnson, "for its ashes have been analyzed, and they yield a volatile alkali, and this we know is the criterion of animal matter as distinguished from vegetable, which yields a fixed alkali." Rush had no way of knowing whether or not Johnson was correct (he was, to the degree that the ash between the two differs), but he was astonished to hear a man whose work had "been confined to moral and philological subjects decide so confidently upon a controversy in natural history."

The talk turned to James Boswell: "He appears, doctor, from some passages in his book, to be one of your acquaintances," Goldsmith said, no doubt with false innocence.

"Yes," said Johnson, "I know him."

"And pray, what do you think of him?" Goldsmith asked.

"He is well enough—well enough."

"I have heard he is much given to asking questions in company."

"Yes, he is," Johnson said, "and his questions are not of the most interesting nature. They are such as this—'Pray, doctor, why is an apple round, and why is a pear not so?' "

Sir Joshua placed Rush between Johnson and Goldsmith at the table. During the meal Goldsmith asked several questions about the manners and customs of American Indians. One of them provoked the eavesdropping Johnson. He turned to Goldsmith, whom Rush regarded as a gentle, unoffending man, and said: "There is not an Indian in North America who would have asked such a foolish question." Goldsmith shot back: "I am sure there is not a savage in America that would have made so rude a speech to a gentleman."

After dinner Heaton Wilkes, brother of the (to Johnson) infamous John Wilkes, came by. Johnson and he were soon disputing the recent firing upon a mob in Saint George Fields by government troops. Wilkes condemned the action and held the mob could have been dispersed by peaceful means. "That may be," Johnson said. "Some men have a knack in quelling riots, which others have not, just as you, sir, have a knack in defending them, which I have not."

Rush found Johnson bigoted in political and ecclesiastical matters, and occasionally "offensive in his manners," but his "massy understanding in the scale of Christianity" overbalanced these failings. "I left his company under an impression that I had passed a day which deserved always to be remembered with pleasure."[15]

The dinner at Sir Joshua's led later to Rush's presence at Oliver Goldsmith's table. The company talked of *The Vicar of Wakefield* and Goldsmith revealed that the vicar's wife "was intended for his mother." The book was a favorite of Rush's; in his letters to Lady Jane Leslie he used the names of Edwin and Angelina, taken from a tearful poem of parted but eventually reunited lovers that Goldsmith had inserted in the story, as pseudonyms for himself and his love. Goldsmith read in an animated manner and an Irish accent from an unpublished poem that two years later came forth as *The Deserted Village*. Rush found him entertaining but wanting in the "usual marks of great and original genius."[16]

Rush avoided talk of politics with men like Johnson and Goldsmith, although the subject never strayed far from his mind. Curiously, however, the republican sentiments supposedly acquired in Scotland abated during a visit to Parliament; on entering the House of Lords he expressed the feeling of walking "on sacred ground," and the sight of the royal throne so stirred him that he begged the guide to sit on it. The guide refused, "but upon my importuning him a good deal I prevailed upon him to allow me the liberty." To sit where kings had sat awed Rush. "This is the golden period of the worldly man's wishes," he said to himself, taking the words of his favorite poet, Edward Young. "His passions conceive, his hopes aspire after nothing beyond *this Throne.*"[17]

The House of Commons provoked less reverent thoughts. This "cursed haunt of venality, bribery, and corruption!" had robbed the king of his supremacy over the colonies. Here "the infernal scheme for enslaving America was first broached." The guide pointed out the spot where William Pitt had argued for repeal of the Stamp Act, and Rush, "fancying myself surrounded with a crowded House," stood there repeating what he remembered from the speech: "Americans are the sons, not the bastards, of Englishmen. I rejoice that America has resisted."[18]

Rush was of the opinion that British government had for the past century been slipping steadily downhill, for he had been indoctrinated since youth to believe its high point had been reached under Oliver Cromwell. During the Great Awakening, preachers like Finley and Davies had spoken often and admiringly of Cromwell. Davies had chosen David in his final sermon to exemplify a man "after God's own heart"; he might equally well have talked of Cromwell as one who combined religion and public service and "became an extensive blessing to the church and his country." At the head of a militant church, Cromwell had commanded a grand rebellion that cleansed England of evil and let Calvinism prevail. Rush had been reared in a tradition still thriving in America that held, as one clergyman put it, that "England was never more happy before, nor much more since, than after the head of the first Stuart was severed from his body, and while it was under the protectorship of Oliver Cromwell." And Rush had a direct tie to that army of Christian soldiers through his great-great-grandfather. He determined to meet a descendant of John Rush's commander in chief before leaving England. From a friend he wangled a letter that introduced him to Oliver Cromwell's great-grandson William, a shy, retiring man then nearly seventy. William Cromwell received Rush courteously, pulled out several of the great man's letters and also his watch. When Rush admired the seals that dangled from the watch—one of the family coat of arms, another of the commonwealth—Cromwell gave him wax impressions of them as a gift. "I still possess them both," Rush was to tell his children. What he did not tell them was that only ten years after visiting the grandson, when he had come to hate not only monarchy but all authoritarian government, he disowned his hero. "Are you sure we have no Caesars nor Cromwells in this country?" he asked in 1779.[19]

Rush also met in London two living "defenders of the faith," though they bore little resemblance to Cromwell except in their passion for a cause— theirs being American liberty. The first was the historian Catharine Macaulay, who invited him to her weekly "evening coterie," where Rush met "some of the first literary and political characters in the British nation." Mrs. Macaulay was a devout Anglican but a nonconformist in all else. She rouged her cheeks, which elicited no comment from Rush but had prompted Dr. Johnson to remark that it was better she should "redden her own cheeks" than "blacken other people's characters"; Johnson was referring obliquely to her multivolume history of England, then being hailed as one of the great works of the age, in which she used the Stuarts to besmirch the current ministry.[20]

Rush found Mrs. Macaulay "sensible and eloquent but visionary in some of her ideas of government." Her schemes bothered him to the extent that one day in January 1769 he sat at a table in the Pennsylvania Coffee House and wrote a rebuttal to views she had outlined in a public letter to Pasquale di Paoli, the Corsican patriot. Rush contended that military officers should be excluded from a legislature. He believed taxes should be levied by a popularly elected assembly rather than an appointed senate, as Mrs. Macaulay preferred, because members of the assembly would "represent the greatest part of the people" and "all parts of the commonwealth," and also because "they (from their greater numbers) are naturally supposed to have more property in the state, and therefore have a better right to give it away for the purposes of government." Rush ended on an obsequious and artificial note: "Perhaps I am wrong in both these observations. If I am, I expect to be rectified by you, madam, who are so well skilled in the science of government. I am but a young scholar in the school of politics, although I have made great progress in the love of liberty; for *this,* let me assure you madam, was among the first passions that warmed my breast."[21] Mrs. Macaulay printed the letter, with asterisks in place of Rush's name, in the second edition that came out that year of her *Loose Remarks on Certain*

Positions to Be Found in Mr. Hobbes' Philosophical Rudiments of Government and Society, which contained her letter to Paoli.

Arthur Lee, a brother-in-law of William Shippen, Jr., and a Virginian who had received his medical degree at Edinburgh but now studied law in London, carried Rush to dine with England's most vociferous supporter of the American cause, John Wilkes, then a comfortable resident of King's Bench Prison. Rush expected to meet "a monster of immorality"; he found instead a "perfectly well bred" gentleman, chaste in language, amusing in conversation, and in every way as opinionated as Dr. Johnson. Wilkes detested the Scots, who unfailingly voted for all anti-American bills introduced in Parliament. He believed that John Dickinson's *Letters from a Farmer* were "superior to anything of the kind that was ever published in any age or country." "He is an enthusiast for AMERICAN liberty," Rush reported home, "and says if you can but preserve an equality among one another, you will always be free in spite of everything." Rush could fault the man on only one point: the "commonplace literature" that made up his library gave "an indifferent opinion of his taste and judgment."[22]

Sometime before Rush left Philadelphia, the Bradfords had suggested to him that he keep an eye out for material that could be used in their newspaper. Several of Rush's letters from Edinburgh were obviously written with a thought to publication, but thus far only three or four small excerpts had been used. The account of the visit to Wilkes's prison apartment, however, was printed in full, 30 March 1769. A week later the *Journal* published an even longer account by Rush. This opened with a grim review of anti-American feeling in London. Only the friends of Wilkes supported the American cause, and many of them were so disheartened with their "arbitrary" government that they talked of emigration. Mrs. Macaulay, for instance, spoke "of ending her days on the banks of the Ohio." The House of Lords had recently thanked the king for his prompt dispatch of troops from Halifax to suppress "the riotous disposition of the people of Boston." It had also called for a "strict inquiry" into the origins of the illegal convention of Massachusetts politicians held after the governor had dissolved the assembly, and demanded that once the instigators had been found they should "be sent over here to be tried for their *lives.*"[23]

Rush ended his "news dispatch" with a plea to "save our sinking country" by promoting American manufactures. America could raise nearly all it now took from abroad—grapes for wine, sheep for wool, mulberry trees for silkworms. "Banish forever from our tables" bohea and green tea, now imported, for a bowl of homegrown "sage and baum tea is worth an ocean of both of them." American craftsmen complain of low incomes because "we consume too little of their manufactures to keep them employed the whole year round," but once "American manufactures become general, this complaint will have no foundation, and hundreds of artificers of every kind would be invited to come over from England and settle among us."[24]

Whatever else the months in England had done, they clearly had not strengthened Rush's affection for the British government and its domination of the American colonies. If, as he believed, Scotland made him a republican, then London did much to make him a rebel, though at the time he was no more aware of this than his wise friend Benjamin Franklin.

4

Probably because Edinburgh had cost more than expected, Rush came to London determined to make the next stop Philadelphia, but somewhere along the line he decided to visit Paris before leaving for home. Franklin, who perhaps urged the trip, equipped him with letters of introduction "to several of his philosophical friends." Though Rush insisted he had money enough, Franklin also gave him "a credit upon a banker in Paris for two or three hundred guineas."[25]

Rush set out for Paris in mid-February and visited there slightly more than a month. It took but a few days for him to decide that visually Paris had much to offer "a man of taste," though many of the statues, he wrote in the journal he kept of the trip, "want that chastity which we would wish to find in all civilized, but more especially in all Christian, countries." It especially distressed him to see the *Rape of Orithyia* in a public place. The French stage bored him, except for the comedies which he liked because they were "designed to expose living vices." His comment that he had "never read a French comedy in my life that had even a double entendre in it" reveals more about his command of French than his perception.[26]

French women proved "very beautiful," though Rush noticed that it took considerable "painting" to achieve the effect. They repaired their faces in public, and it fascinated him "to see them take out a little box of paint, which they always carry in their pockets, together with a small looking glass, and a fine pencil, and daub their cheeks over in their coaches, when they are going to an assembly or any public entertainment." Red paint on the cheeks, he said, "is only imitating nature, and notwithstanding all that has been said against it, adds much to its beauty." Years later, when writing up the Paris trip for his children, he omitted this warm defense of "painting."

Rush, fancying himself the tolerant sophisticate, the "man of taste," also observed that French women had been censured for allowing men to pay calls to their bed chambers in the morning and for using "certain expressions in conversation" that might be considered indelicate. But why, he wondered, is it permissible to see a lady in ordinary dress, but wrong to visit her while she lies under a pile of bed coverings? "Much more of the body is exposed in the former case (even by our most delicate English ladies) than in the latter." Indeed, he added, "I have heard some Scotch ladies (who are remarkable for their delicacy in most things) make use of expressions in public companies which I should blush to have repeated."

From his wide experience, Rush judged French women "the most entertaining companions in the world." He found them unusually well read, and he now decided that education could "add much to the native charms of a woman, and render her in every respect a more agreeable companion to a man of sense." Rush had been reared to think learning made women vain, but his Parisian experience brought him round to the view that "were their education more attended to, and a little knowledge in the fine arts more common among them, it would in a short time destroy that preeminence in a few which is the chief cause of their vanity."

Rush, perhaps understandably, had less to say and less to praise about Parisian gentlemen. Franklin's letters allowed him to meet the distinguished surgeon Jean-Joseph Sue; Bernard de Jussieu and Augustin Roux, two highly esteemed physicians; and such chemists as Antoine Baumé and Pierre Joseph Macquer. None of these gentlemen nor French medicine generally impressed Rush. "Physic is not cultivated here by men of rank and fortune, nor is the profession looked upon so liberal in this country, as it is in England or America. I visited most of their hospitals and convened with several of the principal physicians in Paris and was sorry to find them at least fifty years behind the physicians in England and Scotland in medical knowledge."

Jacques Barbeu-Dubourg, physician, botanist, and friend of Franklin, alone among the gentlemen of Paris won much space in Rush's journal. The two met while Dubourg was in the midst of translating Dickinson's *Letters from a Farmer*. He asked Rush at once if he knew the author of the letters. "I told him I had that honor," Rush answered. "He then broke out into a great many fine encomiums upon them, and said that in his opinion the Roman Cicero was less eloquent than the Pennsylvania Farmer." That touched Rush. "I took him into my arms, nay, more. I took him into my heart."

Dubourg carried Rush to the Marquis de Mirabeau. They arrived at the door of a large room filled with "the first literary characters in Paris." Dubourg silenced the group and announced: "Voila! Un ami de M. Franklin." Mirabeau hurried to the doorway, grasped Rush by the hand, and said: "C'est assez."

The philosophes Rush met at Mirabeau's gathering and elsewhere in Paris had their effect, temporarily at least. "There is no life so agreeable as that of the savage," he said at one point in his journal. "It is free and independent, and in this consists the highest happiness of man." His remarks on agriculture could have been written by Diderot, with whom he spent an afternoon: "Agriculture is the only solid basis of the riches of any country. It is owing to this that the American colonies have in so short a space of time arisen to such a pitch of grandeur and riches. Where this is neglected, here can be neither riches nor grandeur." Without perceiving the contradiction between his words here and in the *Pennsylvania Journal* on manufacturing, he added: "In a word, where there are riches, there will be power, and where there is power, there will be freedom and independence."

For once he had nothing derogatory to say against deism, though he did mention that most men of learning were deists and he condemned the established Catholic Church as warmly as any philosophe. "Were the clergy less powerful the human mind might become unfettered there," he said. He called the monastical life one of "indolent and cowardly piety," then went on: "Heavens! thought I, such a religion must be unworthy of God and unfit for man which dissolves his ties with society, and obliges him to pass thro' the world a stranger to the tenderest names of husband, father, friend. Religion does not forbid us the enjoyments of any of the good things in life. It only teaches us to enjoy them in moderation, and in subordination to better things."

Rush spent a day at Versailles, arriving as a herald passed through a gallery calling, "Le roi venien." Louis XV brushed by on his way to mass.

"He is between fifty-nine and sixty years of age, but looks so well that no one would take him to be above forty-five," Rush said. The "remarkably coarse featured" gentleman he saw later in the day turned out to be the dauphin, who in five years would become Louis XVI. He "stoops in his shoulders, has a brown skin, and is very awkward in every respect." During the royal dinner, which visitors were allowed to observe, Rush saw the dauphin pull from his mouth a piece of meat he had been chewing, study it for a few moments, then throw it beneath the table. The king's daughters wore "a prodigious quantity of paint upon their cheeks" but not enough to conceal their ages "or to supply the want of beauty which nature had denied them." All this pointed to a moral: "Let such as maintain the divine right of kings come and behold this monarch, setting . . . with a common prostitute, picked up a few years ago from the streets of Paris."

Despite censure of the king and of French religious habits, Rush concluded generously that the French had learned "the art of living" as no one else. "They cultivate the social principle by a thousand arts, to which Englishmen are strangers." The genial and generous tone of Rush's Paris journal resembles little else found in his earlier writings. He could be as opinionated, prudish, and wrongheaded as ever, but much of the mawkish sentiment of the youthful letters has now faded. The rotund sentences have been replaced by a crisper, more natural style, and the religious emphasis that cloaked previous writings has been overlaid with a less rigid, though still far from sophisticated, view. Possibly he wrote the journal as a gift to Franklin. If so, this may have shaped his report. Rush later in life credited this shift in his literary style to having read when twenty-two—he went to Paris when twenty-three—Robert Lowth's *Short Introduction to English Grammar,* David Hume's *History of England,* and the works of Jonathan Swift. "By means of these authors I learned to put words together," he said.[27]

Rush left Paris on March 21, spending a leisurely four days on the road to Calais and a miserable twenty-three hours crossing the channel. He also had a brief trial once in England. En route to London his carriage suddenly pulled up short as the driver spied a woman in labor lying off the side of the road. Rush jumped out, announced he was a physician, and asked if he could help. Ten minutes later he, with assistance from another passenger, had delivered the woman "of a fine boy," which he subsequently heard was named after him.

In London he called at once on Franklin to report that he had spent

more money than planned in Paris and "had been obliged to avail [himself]
of [Franklin's] kind offer, by drawing upon his banker for thirty guineas."
Franklin was delighted Rush had enjoyed himself and told him to pay back
the debt to his wife in Philadelphia whenever it was convenient. "I take
great pleasure in recording this delicate act of paternal friendship in Dr.
Franklin," Rush wrote years later. "It attached me to him during the remainder of his life, and it has, since his death, disposed me to respect and
love all the branches of his family."[28]

5

Rush lingered in London for two months, passing the time paying last
visits to friends. He delivered a letter from Diderot to Hume, apparently
then in the city unless Rush made an unmentioned quick trip to Edinburgh
to see Miss Leslie; during the visit with Hume, Rush noticed a picture of
Rousseau, which Hume said was a good likeness of his "peevish countenance." From Timothy Bevan, a Quaker merchant of pharmaceutical
supplies who did much business with Philadelphia physicians, he ordered
on credit £100 worth of merchandise. Dr. Fothergill wrote out a recommendation of his professional abilities and then passed him on to Thomas
Penn, proprietor of Pennsylvania, who in turn recommended him to the
notice of the trustees of the College of Philadelphia and added that Rush
was bringing with him a "chemical apparatus" selected by Fothergill but a
gift from Penn to the college.

The warm send-off from London friends would have been dimmed if
Rush had known of a note Fothergill had sent to a Philadelphia acquaintance. Fothergill was still uneasy about Rush's character and feared that life
thus far had perhaps treated him too well. He hoped he would not be
"spoiled by too early an introduction to public favors," he said. "Not that
I want to have difficulties thrown in his way, but let him acquire reputation
by his own conduct, rather than by the too hasty suffrage of his friends."[29]

Rush boarded the *Edward*, commanded by a Captain Salmon, a tactful
Scotsman, on May 26. From the stern of the ship he gave a pensive, last
look at the white cliffs of Dover, then settled in for the ordeal he knew
lay ahead. Again the voyage lasted seven weeks. However, this time the
sea behaved and Rush had to endure only a day of seasickness. The pas-

sengers on the whole were an agreeable lot, and Rush particularly enjoyed the company of Abigail Streate Coxe, her son Daniel, and an army lieutenant who had seen action in the Seven Years' War. He told Mrs. Coxe all about his love for Lady Jane Leslie, he listened for hours to Lt. Richard Dysart's war stories, but he soon began to fidget. His own books had been sent ahead on another ship, and so he was forced to borrow reading material. Daniel Coxe loaned him the first three volumes—the fourth would not be out for another year—of Blackstone's *Commentaries,* which he read "with uncommon attention and pleasure," and the captain handed him an Italian novel that "helped to render a few hours of several days less tedious." It took only a week or so to work his way through most of the literature on board. Dysart rescued him from restlessness by offering to teach him German, and after a few weeks of intensive study Rush was able, so he said, to read in a borrowed German Bible "with but little aid from a translation or a dictionary."[30] Whether he did or not, this second attempt to learn German succeeded no better than the first, and Rush went through life confounded by the complexities of that language.

The *Edward* reached New York on July 14. Ebenezer Hazard, still in the publishing and bookselling business, met him at the pier. For the first meal ashore, Rush ordered a cup of tea and a slice of bread and butter, which after two years abroad and seven weeks at sea "had a relish to me which I never before perceived in food of any kind." He spent the following day walking about the city. "Three things struck me in the appearance of the people I saw in the streets of New York. . . . They had less color . . . they walked less erect . . . and they moved with a less quick step" than Londoners. The second evening ashore he "felt an uncommon depression," which he accepted as "the usual effect of a high tide of joy upon the system." All the tales "of melancholy and even suicide following similar emotions of the mind," which before he had doubted, he now believed.[31]

Years later Rush confessed to a friend that the day he stepped ashore from the ship that brought him home he resolved that no woman, regardless of her personal charms, her fortune, or her family connections, would "tempt him to perpetrate matrimony till he had extended his studies so far that a family would be no impediment to his farther progress." It was a promise kept, for as the friend later remarked, Benjamin Rush had "resolved to be a great man."[32]

5

Fledgling Physician

1769–1773

1

A FEW DAYS after the return from Europe, Rush's name came up in "one of the first circles" of Philadelphia society. Someone in the gathering, either with wit or innocence, asked whether Dr. Rush was a doctor of divinity or physic. The supposed insult rankled for years, and Rush repeated it to his children to underscore the hardship he had endured to get established. Perhaps he was no more prickly than most ambitious young men who seek to climb from the class into which they were born, but he found it difficult to forget that he was the son of a gunsmith, that his mother ran a grocery store, that he was a Presbyterian in a city whose elite were Quakers and Anglicans.

Fothergill's fear of an early success brought on by the "too hasty suffrage" of friends would have seemed, if Rush had known of it, a monstrous joke. To his knowledge, no friends hovered around to promote his career; indeed, the city seemed leagued against him. He lacked "the patronage of a great man"; his "family connections were few and without power or influence"; by those "who called themselves great in the city," he was "neglected or unknown." The Anglicans ignored him, the Quakers gave their business to those "who belonged to their society or who favored their own views in politics," and his own Presbyterians were "too small and too much divided to afford me much support."[1]

All this was true. But Rush later emphasized these handicaps from a desire to make his success seem self-made. He overlooked, for instance, the helping hand colleagues extended in those early melancholy weeks that all neophyte physicians are forced to endure. On August 3, two days after he had seen his first patient and three after he had opened for business, a Dr. Bayard called him in to consult on a case. On August 18, Drs. Thomas Bond, Thomas Cadwalader, Shippen, and Bayard asked his advice in the puzzling illness of Capt. John McPherson. (The McPherson family from then on became his regular patients.) Shortly afterward Shippen requested his "attendance in consultation," for which he received £1 7s. The consultations diminished gradually as Rush gained patients of his own. From a low of seven patients the first month, the number mounted steadily—nine in September, fifteen in October, eighteen in November, twenty in December. By April 1770 he averaged about thirty-five patients each month; his monthly billings were between £35 and £40, and the cash income never dropped below £15.[2] This, coupled with fees from apprentices—each of whom brought in approximately £100—and from students who signed up for the chemistry course he began teaching at the college, resulted in a fairly decent income almost from the start.

Rush's prosperity owed something to the times. He later estimated that when he began to practice, the annual death rate in Philadelphia was at least one in every twenty-five citizens (in contrast with one in fifty in 1809).[3] It would have been difficult for a Philadelphia physician not to have fared well. The month Rush saw his first patient scarlet fever raged among the children, and in December an epidemic of "hives" or croup struck, concentrated again among the children. The next winter, 1770–1771, influenza took scores of lives. The city succumbed to a continental epidemic of measles in 1772, and in the following year smallpox hit with uncommon severity, leaving behind more than three hundred dead. "As the chief of them were the children of poor people," the press reported, "a number of gentlemen . . . formed a Society for Inoculating the Poor, free of expense to them." Rush was among the physicians who volunteered their services.[4]

For a young man beginning his professional career, Rush lived well during these years. A partial list of goods stolen from him in March 1770—"six new-fashioned silver tablespoons, marked with a wolf's head crest, a common sized chased cream pot, a pair of tea tongs, together with a half dozen teaspoons"—hardly suggests the shabby quarters usually associated with a young bachelor. He and his brother Jacob, an apprentice lawyer, shared a house—since the age of eight Rush had avoided one way or another living with his mother and stepfather—kept for them by their sister Rebecca Stamper. Rebecca, who, as it was vaguely put, "had been unfortunate in her marriage," looked after Rush until he married; long afterward she thanked him for "the seven years that we lived together and the very great tenderness, more like that of a father than a brother," that he had displayed toward her. When Jacob left in the fall of 1770 to study in London, Rush, with Rebecca, moved near the waterfront to a house with a balcony off the second-floor study that gave a view of the wharves, the traffic on the Delaware, and the Jersey coast beyond. Here he brought his bride in 1776 and lived until his first child was born in 1780.[5]

Soon after returning home Rush acquired a slave for a servant and took on two apprentices—one "idle but worthy," the other "idle, acute"— and at first they lived in, as he had with Redman. In 1771, after these two had left, he acquired seven more apprentices. These paying novices were an indication of Rush's need for money—Redman, for instance, never took on more than two—for by now he was financing Jacob's studies abroad. Seven youngsters kept the house in a turmoil; sanity required a break with tradition, and Rush arranged for them to bed down dormitory-style in a neighboring loft, out of earshot but close enough to keep an eye on their antics.

Though still in his twenties, he watched over the apprentices as if he were their father. He could be firm ("Learn from this to subdue your temper"), generous ("I forgave you long before you saw or acknowledged your folly"), and he never hesitated to draw a moral ("Happy is the man who can review the period between the sixteenth and twentieth years of his life without marking it with more fault than even an enemy"). Many of them became friends for life, and Rush never failed when they wrote for advice on a difficult case to send back full and precise instructions ("Dress the bone with lint dipt in a tincture of myrrh and aloes." "Let her live on liquid aliment. Let her drink plentifully"). The boys ran the apothecary shop and the routine side of the practice, such as keeping the account books, just as Rush had done for Redman, and the number of prescriptions dispensed forced Rush within a few weeks to reorder supplies from London. Out of the first money earned, he paid back the thirty guineas borrowed from Franklin—"Mrs. Franklin for a while refused to receive it, for the doctor had not mentioned the debt to her in any of his letters"—and within a year saw enough money coming in to boast of his prosperity in a stream of letters that poured out to Edinburgh classmates now scattered around the empire; the answers that flowed back attested that none of his contemporaries was doing as well.[6]

A good deal of the early success stemmed from resourcefulness. Fothergill had once confessed he himself had "crept over the backs of the poor into the pockets of the rich," and Rush, too, chose that route. His natural courtesy and kindness, his unfeigned sympathy for the distressed, won a wide following among the city's less prosperous. He soon knew the inside of virtually every hut and tenement in the city. Many times after climbing a ladder to the upper story of a waterfront hovel he returned home to shake the vermin from his clothes. He never hastened "from these abodes of poverty and misery" but "often remained in them long eno' to administer my prescriptions, particularly bleeding and clysters with my own hands." He charged only when it appeared a patient could pay; one morning he prescribed for sixteen visitors to his office and "charged but one of them." This semicharity satisfied his impulse to do good, but it also had more practical virtues. The poor's susceptibility to sickness gave him a familiarity with every disease that pervaded the city. Furthermore, his "unfettered prescriptions"—even then the poor served as guinea pigs—gave him a sound "knowledge of the doses and effects of medicine." Rush soon found he labored not in vain. "The reputation ascribed to some cures I had performed, and the faithful attendance I was said to give to my patients where no reward was expected, in a little while begat other business."[7]

Though the Presbyterians may have been a small, divided sect, Rush used them shrewdly to help build his practice. Earlier he had attacked Francis Alison for "his most virulent, bitter temper" and "as an enemy to vital religion." But Alison preached to the well-to-do Old Side congregation of the First Presbyterian Church, and Rush visited it often enough for at least one member to observe his "decent behavior" there and choose him as his physician. His praise brought in other patients. William Marshall, another Presbyterian divine who had just arrived in the city and, lacking a church, preached in a vacant store, complimented Rush so heartily that he was soon "employed by nearly every family in his congregation," which though "small and poor" brought in business that was "useful to me." A Scotsman who sold merchandise to Rush's mother was also rather artful in promoting the young physician's reputation among Presbyterians. "If he heard of anybody being very ill, he made it a practice to inquire who was his doctor. If my name was not mentioned, he expressed his surprise at it, and added long details of my opportunities of instruction in Edinburgh and of my having been the pupil of the two Hunters in London, both of whom he knew in early life."[8]

Rush spent the mornings prescribing to patients in his office, the afternoons walking his rounds through the city. Though the number of calls was few—no more than two or three a day in the early months of practice—they took time; a ride to the country to visit Captain McPherson's wife (charge: 7s. 6d.) absorbed an afternoon, and such trips came at least once a week. Still, Rush found time to mix "freely in female society," which meant occasionally stealing part of an afternoon from work to call upon the current favorite for tea or a sociable ride along the Schuylkill. Once in a while he gave a dinner or supper party to which he usually invited some of the young Scottish merchants in the neighborhood who provided a night of good talk. Generally, however, he spent the evenings studying and writing. He rarely went to bed before midnight, "and many, many times have I heard the watchman cry 3 o'clock before I have put out my candle." Rush had confidence in himself and believed "that a more easy situation was before me." Toward the elite, those who set the tone of the city and ran its affairs, he held a dislike that bordered on hatred, but he disciplined himself to bear "the insolence of office and the proud man's contumely in silence."[9]

2

Rush had come back from Europe a doctor of medicine and, he hoped, a soon-to-be professor of chemistry. No doubt he took time during the first days in the city to repair relations with Redman and Morgan, and probably only after consulting with them did he visit the college to present Thomas Penn's gift of a chemical apparatus and to apply formally for the still vacant post. On 1 August 1769, the day Rush saw his first patient—a Miss Lydia Hyde, whom he charged 3s.—the board of trustees unanimously chose him as the College of Philadelphia's professor of chemistry; Rush was the first in America to hold this post. He now joined Morgan, Shippen, Kuhn, and Bond (professor of clinical medicine), as the fifth and, at the age of twenty-three, the youngest member of the medical faculty. The position brought in a small income from fees paid by the students and, of greater personal importance, much prestige, for it ."held me up to public notice now and then in the newspapers and made my name familiar to the public ear much sooner than it would have been."[10]

As at Edinburgh, the medical school term did not begin until November 1. Rush had three months to prepare his course. In a day when men worked to prevent a gap between science and society, Rush announced in a newspaper advertisement that "the whole will be taught in such a manner as to be intelligible to the private gentleman, and inquiring artist, as well as to the student of medicine," adding the practical note that "the price of a ticket is SIX POUNDS."[11] Bent on making the introductory lecture brilliant, Rush jotted down ideas, testing phrases as he went, in a pocket-sized notebook. The chemist, he observed, "broods over the facts of nature" and "calls forth order out of confusion," but his work differs from the natural philosopher in that he examines "the texture and composition of bodies." A definition of chemistry gave trouble, for one could no more "detach its parts" than define the beauty of "a fine woman's face" by singling out her features. Rush reminded himself to emphasize the usefulness of chemistry and to enliven the lecture by illustrating "a few of the principal phenomena of mixture by experiments, such as effervescence [and] the conversion of fluids into solids."[12]

Rush worked to present his own views in the inaugural lecture but ended, like most first-year professors, giving the course he had taken. The outline he printed in 1770 under the title *Syllabus of a Course of Lectures on Chemistry* revealed a program of instruction that differed only slightly from Black's. The lectures, if published, would have been condemned as plagiarism. The opening remarks on the origin and history of chemistry and its usefulness to the physician were Black's. The definition of chemistry—"that science which teaches the effects of heat and mixture, to improve our knowledge in nature and arts"—only abridged Black's.[13]

Rush began with a long discussion of heat, Black's special interest. "I shall not risk your being put out of conceit with our science," he said when it came time to discuss Black's principle of latent heat, "by delivering it to you," a face-saving device that he had used once before to mask confusion. (The ingenious Dr. Black, he had written from Edinburgh, "has lately discovered *absolute levity,* a principle in nature which . . . . it would be too tedious to acquaint you with. . . .") The lectures on mixtures were illustrated with several experiments: marble dropped into a jar of sulphuric acid effervesced, then dissolved, leaving a homogeneous liquid; oil poured on water remained separate until shaken, then, unlike marble and acid, reseparated when left standing; camphor dissolved in wine; sulphuric acid produced a gas in the process of dissolving ammonium chloride; water became warm when sulphuric acid was added and cold when niter was poured in. The lectures on salts, earths, inflammables, metals, water, vegetable and animal substances led to a concluding talk on pharmaceutical chemistry, where Rush developed a common assumption of the day—"that the mineral kingdom contains an antidote to every disease with which the human body is liable to be afflicted."[14]

Each year Rush tinkered with the syllabus. At one point he added a section on airs and pushed the material on animal and vegetable substances into an appendix. But during the twenty years he taught chemistry, the course remained to the end largely Black's. Chemistry never intrigued Rush. He fulfilled professional responsibilities diligently but without enthusiasm. For the most part, he kept abreast of current findings but seemingly without comprehending the great work being done in Europe. When Franklin forwarded Joseph Priestley's paper "Observations on Different Kinds of Air," wherein the discovery of nitric oxide and hydrogen chloride were first announced, Rush gave no sign he understood what Priestley had done. He shared none of Black's or Priestley's interest in basic research in chemistry. Only the practical side, that side that could directly benefit the physician, concerned him; the pure scientist was a breed of man Rush did not understand and with whom he had virtually nothing in common. Chemistry had attracted him as a means to promote his career, not as an end in itself. It had, as Morgan promised, found him a seat on the medical faculty of the college; once that had been achieved, Rush lost what little interest he may have had in any thorough pursuit of the subject.[15]

3

The medical department of the College of Philadelphia had survived its shakedown period when Rush joined it and had settled into a pattern that would vary little during the remainder of the eighteenth century. The majority of students took a bachelor of medicine (B.M.) degree, which was granted after passing examinations in anatomy, chemistry, the materia medica, and the practice of physic. "The examinations were, first, private before the professors only and, second, public before the trustees of the college and as many strangers as pleased to attend," Rush once explained to a curious friend. "Between the private and public examinations the candidate produced to the professors specimens of his abilities by writing an answer to a physiological question and by giving the treatment of such a case as should be described to him." If the student wished to obtain a doctor of medicine (M.D.) degree, he must within three years produce "a Latin dissertation upon some medical subject . . . defending it publicly against such objections as should be made to it by any of the professors." At commencement the usual "orations and disputes upon medical subjects were introduced and conducted in the same way as in commencement in the arts. A charge was always delivered to the graduates by one of the professors." After a man had received his M.D., he was "taken by the hand in a formal and solemn manner by each of the professors as a sign of his being admitted to an equality of rank with them."

By the time Rush joined the faculty, commencement had become something of a social affair for Philadelphia. At the one in June 1771, the Twenty-first Regiment of the Royal North British Fusiliers provided the music. Jonathan Potts, Rush's former roommate who had abandoned Edinburgh for the arms of his fiancée, received his M.D. Nicholas Way, who was to become one of Rush's "most intimate and worthy friends," had his dissertation *De Variolarum Insitione* "impugned by Dr. Rush." At the commencement of 1773, Rush gave the charge to a graduating class that included David Ramsay, another student who would become a lifelong friend; Ramsay's contribution to the festivities was "an humorous piece on the extravagant pretensions of *empirics* to extraordinary cures. . . ."

Rush compensated for his lukewarm commitment to chemistry by using his college post as a podium from which to launch an attack against professional doctrines cherished by almost all the older, established physicians in Philadelphia. With his indiscreet "zeal for truth, justice, and humanity," he managed to find a place somewhere in the syllabus to pause and laud the virtues of the Suttonian method of inoculation against smallpox. Rush would have angered few colleagues if he had chosen to plump for the new method on its practical merits. He preferred, however, to use it as a test case in the battle between the Boerhaavian system and that of Cullen. At a dinner party attended by a number of medical students, he offered the toast, "Speedy interment of the system of Dr. Boerhaave, and may it never rise again." From that moment on, the lines were drawn.[16]

The issue revolved around the preparation of the patient for inoculation. Boerhaavians called for "an entire alteration of the blood and juices and the removal of inveterate obstructions" to insure "a person going thro' the disorder safely." To this end, a week before inoculation the patient was each day purged two or three times, then dosed with thirty or forty grains of mercury to promote salivation. This sufficed, according to the Boerhaavians, to remove obstructions in the blood, discharge "all superfluous juices and fluids," and "to free the more open passages from impurities." The Suttonian method, as Rush propagated it, discarded the use of mercury and *added* fluids through a diet that leaned heavily to liquids. Instead of justifying this regimen on the ground that "this is the way Sutton does it in London," or even that "this is what Sydenham recommended," he insisted on coupling it with Cullen's doctrine of disease. Cullen held that disease did not center in the body's fluids, as Boerhaave believed, but in the nervous or vascular system. As a result, the symptoms of disease were either a laxness or a tension in the body. The problem, put simply, was not to relieve the body of impurities but to overcome laxness (by diet) or tension (by bleeding). Rush had already become an ardent proponent of bleeding. "You tell me you used the lancet freely, and never lost one patient," a Charleston correspondent wrote after hearing of a successful bleeding treatment by Rush. "You quoted *Sydenham* as a voucher for this practice, and bled your patients to advantage when the cough was troublesome even after every other symptom had ceased. The truth is *that* most sagacious and observant physician *Sydenham* was too profuse with regard to the use of the lancet."[17] Rush thought otherwise.

Rush lectured so effectively on the virtues of Cullen's doctrines that when students went out on their own they considered themselves in the vanguard of medical reform. One, after inoculating some of the Negroes on Charles Carroll's plantation in Maryland by the old method and some by Sutton's method, wrote Rush that he was now "so far prejudiced against the Boerhaavian system that if . . . the greatest orator in physic the world ever afforded was now suffered to rise from the dead [he] would not convince me of its propriety."[18]

Thomas Bond, who had popularized the use of mercury in Philadelphia, assumed Rush attacked him personally. He complained bitterly to Franklin about the extraordinary novelties Edinburgh was inculcating in its students. No doubt Rush did nothing to disabuse Bond of his assumption. Never one to still a controversy, Rush seemed to go out of his way to present his views in such a manner that none of the faculty—not Shippen, Kuhn, nor Morgan, all Edinburgh graduates—supported him. From Charleston a former classmate said that to hear that "Morgan particularly and Kuhn should not join you in supporting Cullen's system vexes me and makes me hate them heartily." The stream of grievances, which Rush poured out to classmates and acquaintances alike, for the most part brought back a reassuring batch of condolences. "I am not at all surprised that the old doctors with you are not pleased with Cullen's doctrines, as old practitioners have prejudices," one wrote. "Don't be disheartened at the insincerity of human friendships, nor grieve because villains are permitted to walk the world in the garb of honesty," his cousin Coombe replied from London. From New York Samuel Bard reminded him how "we always fared the better at Edinburgh when our masters quarreled."[19]

By early 1771 the friction had deepened. Rush reported that Shippen was keeping students from attending his lectures. Jacob Rush told his brother to see the bright side of the dispute. "Better, infinitely better, is it to be at eternal variance with a man of his cool malice and treachery, than to have any connection with him," he wrote, adding as a warning to a brother he knew so well. "By the way, since you are come to a rupture with him, suffer me to put you upon your guard against letting a rash or imprudent expression escape from you."

By the end of the year Rush had convinced himself that the shafts of animosity Shippen and other colleagues directed toward him had injured his practice. Through the latter half of 1770 it had increased steadily—from fifty-three patients in June to sixty-one in October; then, just as steadily, the number dipped—from forty-four in November to thirty-five in April 1771. From London, Huck did his best to console Rush. "I am sorry to find that you are not quite contented with your present situation," Huck wrote. "The beginning of business is always unpleasant. You must not expect to fall into great practice at first setting out. No one ever did. Numbers of us starve in practice here." Huck ended with news of a college classmate of Rush's, Thomas Ruston, who had abandoned medicine and become a broker, "in which I dare say he will make more money and with more ease of mind."[20]

Rush continued discouraged into 1772, so much so that he put out a feeler to Huck about the chance for a profitable career in London. Huck gently suggested Rush had been overly impressed by the success of the half dozen London physicians he had met. "You never heard of the number who starve, or who do not gain the bread they eat." Huck doubted that more than fifteen physicians in all London made more than a thousand pounds a year. Rush, he said, lived comfortably among friends; coming to London would put him among strangers. He ended by promising to help if Rush persisted in the plan to come to London, but added: "There is an old proverb which one should carry in mind, viz., if you are well keep so."[21]

4

Rush believed in the doctrine of publish or perish. He left behind in London a manuscript that Huck returned unread, having been unable "to overcome my natural indolence." He softened the blow by sending along the fourth volume of the *Medical Observations and Enquiries,* "in which you will find your communication upon the effects of wort," said Huck. "I wish to do you every piece of credit in my power, and therefore urged the publication of that paper, in which I took the liberty of changing some of the expressions and in particular that where you accuse the surgeon of ignorance, in whose care the patient first was."[22]

Rush's first medical publication in America appeared in the Bradfords' *Pennsylvania Journal* on 14 December 1769. It discussed the cause of and cure for "hives," a corruption of "heaves," which described the heaving action of the lungs as the patient fought for breath. The *Journal* gave four full columns to what still ranks as a model essay on croup—a combination of research based on bedside observations, autopsies, and the available literature. It managed at once to be comprehensible to the public and a contribution to contemporary medicine. Rush felt proud enough of the effort to sign his name to it, though for some reason he used the pseudonym "Philopaidos" in a brief follow-up piece four months later.[23]

He sent the essay everywhere. The reaction from London heartened him. Coombe said he understood little of it but did "like the conclusion of it very much, which was unaffected and moral." The Dillys promised to try to "get the same printed in the *London Magazine* as soon as possible." Dr. John Millar, an English physician whose writings on spasmodic asthma had prompted the essay on "hives," found it ingenious and also promised to see it "republished either in some collection of medical observations or in some other way in which it might be more extensively circulated." Either through the Dillys' or Millar's efforts it appeared within the year in London under the title of *Dissertation on the Spasmodic Asthma of Children.*[24]

Seven months after the first piece, the *Journal* printed another by Rush, a lightweight effort on the ill effects produced by drinking cold water. This one came forth under the by-line "XYZ." Here he preached preventive medicine: "Obviating diseases is the business of physic as well as . . . curing them." Since no certain remedies had been found for those laid low by drinking cold water, he suggested holding the cup in one's hands until the chill had diminished, or, better yet, mixing some spirits with the water, for "this infallibly prevents the water doing any harm."[25]

On 2 November 1770, Rush read before the newly organized American Philosophical Society, of which he had been chosen a charter member and one of its first curators, "An Account of the Effects of the Strammonium or Thorn-Apple," a short paper of four pages but one of his most important for revealing the reasons for the heroic brand of medicine he practiced. The paper emerged from an experience with a child of three or four who "appeared to be ill with a violent fever, delirium tremors in her limbs, and a general eruption on her skin, accompanied with a considerable swelling, itching, and inflammation." The case had puzzled Rush. He prescribed a mild bleeding, followed by a laxative and a warm bath, but none of these alleviated the child's distress. When from the mother he learned that stramonium, more commonly called jimsonweed, grew in the family garden, he responded by giving the child "a puke of two grains of tartar emetic." This brought up nothing but phlegm. He then administered a strong laxative that "brought away a great number of the stramonium seeds"; the delirium abated but left her "stupid and blind" and the tremors continued. Rush thereupon doubled the dose of emetic, which produced "above eighty of the seeds the second time it puked her." One further puke carried up more seeds, and "upon this all her complaints vanished, and in a few days she appeared perfectly well." Rush used the case to make a subdued attack on Boerhaavian medicine. "Eruptions upon the skins are generally attributed to an acrimony in the blood," he said, referring to Boerhaave's doctrines, but the eruptions in this instance were "occasioned by acrid substances irritating the stomach and bowels." He also concluded that Philadelphia physicians might be practicing too mild a brand of medicine. Perhaps "it should be our practice to increase the doses of our vomits, or to give substances as will destroy the life, or virus, of those things we would wish to expel from the stomach." Clearly, the powerful pukes and massive bleedings Rush called for in the yellow-fever epidemic of 1793 originated out of doctrines that had begun to take form in his mind more than two decades earlier.[26]

Virtually every spare moment during these first years of practicing medicine went into writing. Early in 1771 Rush told the Dillys of a plan to do something on gout, a subject on which the English physician William Cadogan had recently published a successful book. He wanted also to do a piece on inoculation. The Dillys thought the topic "almost exhausted, but," they added, sounding like all publishers in every age, "if you have something new and curious, it may do." They went on to encourage another project Rush had mentioned, one that will extend "your fame over the Continent and will be a useful work to mankind in general. It will no doubt take you up some years before it can be finished," they said, "but the sooner you accomplish your design the better." What the Dillys were referring to is not known, although it may have been "the work which you are upon on *Digestion of Food in the Stomach, etc.,*" that they wrote about in a letter three years later.[27]

The essay on gout appeared in the *Pennsylvania Gazette* for 26 December 1771 prefaced by a headnote signed with the initials of a mythical preacher, "G.S."

> As Dr. Cadogan's excellent differentiation on the gout has turned the conversation of the public a good deal upon the abuse of wine, your publishing the following SERMON upon that subject in your gazette will oblige several of your readers. It was found among some loose papers in the study of a clergyman, who died a few years ago in a neighboring province, who, among other things, had paid considerable attention to the animal economy. It was preached about Christmas."

"G.S." opened with hope: not all imbibers get gout. Wine may be given to the sick, the inhabitants of low, marshy countries ("The moisture of such places obstructs perspiration, and brings on a general laxity of the system"), and to old people (it "prolongs the strength and powers of nature"). Wine should not be given to children (they need no stimulus), studious people ("Thinking is a stimulus to the constitution, and wears out the springs of life beyond the most laborious exercise of the body"), nor to those under forty. "G.S." drove home the moral with a bedroom scene. "Be not alarmed at the groans," he admonished, leading the reader into a gout sufferer's chamber, where "death, the last friend of the wretched, refuses to come at his call."

A week later the *Gazette* printed a second sermon, "found in the same bundle with the last"—this one on intemperance in eating. "G.S." now objected to highly seasoned foods for those "in the full vigor of health and youth." The old might partake of spices and also those living in tropical lands like the West Indies, where such foods "obviate the relaxing powers of heat and moisture." But the diet for most Americans should be simple. It should also be moderate and contain only one large meal daily. Custom called for the main meal at noon, but Rush risked censure by demanding it come in the evening. "Sleep is always natural after eating," he said. "Nature calls loudly for it." But a more cogent reason for late dining is "that digestion has been lately proved to be carried on chiefly by FERMENTATION, to which rest, everybody knows, is so essentially necessary that it cannot take place without it."

A third essay found in the preacher's papers dealt with exercise. "G.S." praised among the active forms walking, running (though it is "too violent to be used often"), dancing ("a most salutary exercise" that "inspires the mind with cheerfulness," but should not be practiced more than once a week), and, finally, "TALKING, which also includes reading aloud, singing, and laughing." Among the passive forms of exercise—chiefly for those "with a weakness of the nerves, such as the hysteric and hypochondriac disorders"—he favored sailing and riding, either in a chariot or on horseback. He recommended long journeys in order to enliven the mind and body of the ill—to cold climates for those who suffer from hysteric or epileptic disorders, to warm climates for hypochondriacs and consumptives.

The *Gazette* declined the third sermon, but the *Pennsylvania Packet* took the concluding portion. Soon after, the three sermons appeared as a small book. Rush dropped the coy headnotes and admitted "they never were preached," and that "the title and style of [the] sermons were chosen for no other purpose than to excite the attention of the public to subjects highly interesting to everybody." The author kept his name from the volume, for "he seeks nothing from his countrymen but the pleasure of doing them good."[28]

The anonymity seemed well-advised. One physician praised the essays, then "abused them extravagantly when he discovered that they came from my pen." A lady, perhaps a friend who wrote in jest, censured them in the press for not mentioning women and for demanding the main meal at night; Rush answered lightheartedly, no doubt delighted at the free publicity for the book. A copy went to the Dillys in London, who printed it "on a neat type and on fine writing paper, and a size handy for the pocket," changing nothing but the title. *Sermons to Gentlemen* now became *Sermons to the Rich and Studious, on Temperance and Exercise* "as it is more applicable to such persons than to gentlemen in general."[29]

Rush kept London posted on all he did. He even made certain that the *London Chronicle* carried an announcement of his appointment to the professorship of chemistry. He especially hoped the essay on "hives" would win his election to the Royal Society—after all, Morgan had been admitted on a record less distinguished—but Huck refused to submit his name. "I asked Dr. Franklin's advice first, who saw no objection to it," Huck wrote, but since "some others have been lately blackballed" it was thought better to wait. "There are among the members such as think that the society have not been chaste enough in their elections; that it is wrong to elect a very young man who has neither communicated anything to the society nor is known to the world by any other publication. You told me in your last that you would send me a paper for the Royal Society. Something of this kind would give an opening for hanging up your name, which I think I will venture to do next autumn, and will pay the fees, etc."[30]

The subject matter of the paper Rush hoped would win his election was intestinal worms. He had found through experiments that sugar, salt, honey, and summer fruits worked as a poison on them, a discovery he broadcast to friends everywhere. One, in Charleston, complimented the "commendable turn to medical investigation," but ended with a warning: "Before you publish anything of much consequence to the welfare of mankind . . . be fully assured of the principles you go upon. For should your work not be nearly sterling, there will not be wanting some who will controvert your positions, more especially as you already hold a respectable rank in your university."

Huck dismissed the experiments on worms as worthless, reminding Rush that research had already shown that earthworms lived longer in "solutions of bitter substances and infusions than in syrups." Though it seemed wasted effort to publish "what is already well known," he promised to lay the findings before the Royal Society, "but not before I have taken the opinions of competent judges upon it, because I wish that everything you do may turn out to the advancement of your reputation." As 1772 ended, so, too, did Rush's interest in intestinal worms. A quarter of a century later he published the essay in a collection of his medical papers, perhaps out of a stubborn conviction that his research had made a contribution, perhaps as a monument to the long dead hope that worms might yet gain admittance to the Royal Society.[31]

5

Rush wrote much as he talked—from compulsion and constantly. Between patients' office visits, he used the free moments to dash off a letter or the lead to an essay. Few men of the day carried on a larger correspondence. Through the mails, he kept track of friends in Edinburgh and London and traded shoptalk with ex-classmates in Maryland, Virginia, the Carolinas, Georgia, and the West Indies, sometimes puffing his achievements, sometimes requesting medical information, but always writing to keep alive old friendships and develop new ones. The departure of Jacob for London left a gap—he hinted as much by marking down the date of Jacob's sailing and the date he received his first letter—that was to be filled by stepping up the outbound flow of letters.[32]

Jacob went to London armed with letters of introduction to Franklin, the Dillys, Huck, and other London friends. These gentlemen, plus Hazard and Coombe, also still in London, eased Jacob's arrival in the fog-bound city, whose weather "he but ill-digested," got him settled near the Temple, where he would study law, and posted Rush on his daily life. Huck had Jacob to dinner and found him "very shy." Hazard wrote warmly at first, saluting "my worthy friend," but soon the letters opened with a cold "my dear sir," and for no clear reason an old friendship began to wane. Coombe kept Rush informed of both Jacob and old London friends ("The *exhibition* opens tomorrow when our friend Mr. West will figure high. His

Quebec scene, which you may remember to have seen in dead colors, cannot fail of being universally admired"), while Rush for his part passed along his cousin's love letters to a Miss Ord, whose parents disapproved of the romance.[33]

With an eye on success, Rush could occasionally forget those who had helped him, and Coombe at one point reprimanded his neglect of Franklin, who "constantly inquires of me about you, and I am sure has a sincere regard for you." Rush wrote at once, and the two doctors soon talked across the ocean about Priestley and chemistry and the common cold. The discussion of colds led Rush into a theory about "a predisposition of the body to produce a disorder in it" (which came close to the modern conception of allergies) and several generalizations about the dangers of night air (Franklin slept with a window open and believed he thrived for it). It also prompted a paper on "An Enquiry into the Methods of Preventing Painful and Fatal Effects of Cold upon the Human Body," which he read before the American Philosophical Society in September 1772. Fifteen years passed before this casual production reached print, and even then it came forth anonymously.[34]

Among nonmedical friends, Rush carried on a lively correspondence with Mrs. Coxe, his confidante aboard the *Edward* on the trip home from England, who now lived in Trenton, New Jersey. Books passed back and forth—he sending an Italian grammar and dictionary, she returning a history of China—and also some cutting remarks. When Rush apologized for careless ways, she told him to mend his habits "instead of contriving excuses," adding: "Truly, your vivacity will run away with you if you do not curb it a little." Mrs. Coxe refused to truckle to his political views. He should desist giving the American people an exaggerated impression "of their own importance." Moreover, she went on, "patriotism and patriots begin to grow stale both at home and abroad." It surprised no one who had known Abigail Coxe that when the Revolution came she and her son set sail for England.[35]

Rush had a low tolerance for forthright, opinionated ladies, and the correspondence with Mrs. Coxe lasted no more than a year. A more enduring friendship was established when Elizabeth Graeme, nine years his senior and the daughter of a respected, well-to-do physician, invited him to join "her circle of friends." She had toured England as a guest of the elite wherever she went, become friends with Lawrence Sterne—perhaps it was she who introduced Rush to *Tristram Shandy,* a favorite of his—and been honored by a special audience with the king. Soon the two were exchanging journals. She sent Rush long poems and he, whenever free, attended the Saturday evening social and literary gatherings at her home.[36]

Rush never hesitated to make older women privy to his love life. Doubtless Miss Graeme, like Mrs. Coxe and Rush's proxy mother while in London, Mrs. Jeffries, also heard in detail of Lady Jane Leslie's charms. He had left England knowing she "must now be banished forever" and determined when he came to marry "to drive a bargain in that matter." But he could not erase Lady Jane from his thoughts. "Do not offer to marry at all, if the Edinburgh lass has still hold of your heart and you feel yourself tremblingly alive," Mrs. Coxe advised. Rush sent a proposal across the sea; a rejection came back, and Mrs. Coxe commiserated that "the poor Caledonian, she shines no more to you." Rush proposed again, was rejected again. A friend said not to "be discouraged by two or three denials," but Rush, understandably, was. By early 1773 he had given up hope of acquiring a Scot for a wife, and a friend congratulated him that July "on your recovery from your late passion. Pray what is become of your fair Quaker Miss ——? From some former circumstances I strongly suspect she had made some impressions on your heart which might ripen into love." By then, however, another girl—Sarah Eve, a lively redhead, daughter of a sea captain who lived two miles out in the country on a farm—had seemingly brought Rush once again "tremblingly alive."[37]

6

The opportunity for a romance with any Philadelphia girl to fare well looked slight at one point, for momentarily it seemed as though he might leave the city. By 1772 Rush had spread the story of his troubles with medical colleagues to all his friends. A by-product of this publicity was the offer of a lucrative practice in Charleston. Dr. Alexander Garden, the city's if not America's most distinguished physician, talked of retiring because of ill health. Letters from Charleston friends hinted that his practice would devolve on Rush if he settled in the city. He was told that though a Presbyterian the city's Anglican elite would welcome him, and he would soon be making from a thousand to fifteen hundred guineas a year, well over twice his current income. Only Lionel Chalmers among Rush's Charleston friends urged him to stand his ground in Philadelphia. The promise of a large income, Chalmers cautioned, failed to take into account the thirty-odd physicians in Charleston, most of whom "have not much to do" and who would scramble for what they could get of Garden's practice. Rush, he said, would one day "take the lead in our profession, wherever you choose to reside." Why, then, abandon connections, relations, and an "honorary and profitable appointment" as professor of chemistry for a pie in the sky? Chalmers ended apologetically with some professional advice: "Whenever you consult with a person of long standing, behave with modesty and reserve, and give way in some things to his opinion, when no immediately dangerous consequences are to be expected from his prescriptions." Such tact will ease life with colleagues and at the same time carry with it practical advantages. "For in such cases, should the patient die, your reputation would not suffer, seeing you were backed by a gentleman of established skill."[38]

Rush rejected the Charleston offer with a variety of reasons. To some he said the city's muggy weather would complicate his pulmonary condition. To others he admitted being "too attached to my own country, this dear province where one owes one's ease to free and honest toil, to be tempted to exchange it for a country where wealth has been accumulated only by the sweat and blood of Negro slaves." Despite this sentiment, he urged David Ramsay, the recently graduated medical student, to accept what he rejected, and five months later Ramsay departed for the city where he would live out his life as one of its most prominent citizens.

To few did Rush admit the most convincing reason for remaining in Philadelphia—his practice in 1772 had again begun to expand. "My business has increased greatly within these two years, so much that I have much less leisure than formerly to promote my studies," he wrote in 1774, and the assessment is borne out by his ledgers. From a low of forty-three patients in February 1772 it rose to ninety-nine in October; a slump for two months followed, then in January 1773 he saw seventy-eight patients and in February eighty-six. His monthly cash income now averaged about £35, which, with other sources, gave him enough to be judged prosperous and allow him for the first time to think realistically of marriage.[39]

6

Politics Intrude

1773–1774

1

TAKE CARE how you *commit yourself* to your new correspondent," Ebenezer Hazard once said of Rush to a mutual acquaintance. "Neither his stability nor prudence are to be depended upon."[1] Hazard's churlish appraisal ignored all that had once attracted him to Rush—his lively, intelligent mind, his humanity, his curiosity about man and his affairs. Rush could be self-righteous and impetuous, but never a bore. He offered no side to the world. He was without affectations, and though he could be calculating no one ever called him devious. Hazard's censure, if he had known of it, would have produced a smile. Prudence, Rush was fond of saying, "is a *rascally* virtue." As for instability, he might have agreed that prior to 1773 he had exhibited signs of it but surely not after that date.

During that year, his practice nearly doubled; each month he saw some eighty patients, exclusive of those visited in the almshouse. He turned out two medical papers in 1773, neither of which provoked dissension with colleagues. Both were read before the American Philosophical Society, of which he was now secretary—one in June on mineral waters in and around Philadelphia, the other in November on the efficacy of laudanum as a remedy for those overcome by drinking cold water. The piece on laudanum, a slight affair, the society judged unworthy of publication; it saw print sixteen years later in the collected medical essays. That on mineral waters, then thought to be a cure for nearly all that ailed man, had a wider appeal and quickly came forth as a pamphlet.

The essay had been occasioned by the discovery of a mineral well in Philadelphia late in May 1773. Rush and Sarah Eve, one afternoon after tea, visited the well to sip its murky water. Miss Eve found it "excessively disagreeable," but the taste apparently deterred no one, she said, for it was being "drunk for almost every disorder, and is looked upon as an universal nostrum." Rush saw a chance to capitalize on a fad and at the same time promote his reputation as a scientist, and within a few days of his first sip from the well he had carried out tests on other supposedly therapeutic waters in the neighborhood of Philadelphia and written up his findings. Rush displayed a commendable laboratory technique in the analyses, but a concern for scientific accuracy led him to repress common sense when it came to explaining the "slight fetid smell" of the water from the Philadelphia well. The odor "increased by rest" and had "a strong ferruginous taste," he observed, but gave no further explanation of its unusual quality—which soon emerged. As a reader of the pamphlet noted on the margin of Rush's copy, "the water lost its virtue within a few months after investigation owing to the contents of a neighboring necessary. The well being exhausted on account of the quantity drunk it was found the well communicated with the necessary which gave the smell and sediment."[2]

Rush did little in the essay to diminish popular faith in the healing qualities of mineral waters. He found them proper to use for a variety of nervous diseases—hysteria (a disorder common among females and "accompanied with flatulences, contractions of the muscles of the belly, and a sense of something resembling a ball riding in the throat"), palsy, epilepsy, "an old obstinate diarrhea," loss of appetite, and "in all those colics which arise from mere weakness of the bowels." In addition to relieving these nervous disorders, the waters were useful "in all obstructions of the liver and spleen," in cases of chronic rheumatism, and in piles. He found them of little aid in any "hypochondriac disorder," in hemorrhages, or in most cases of gout. After telling the reader how to take the waters, he ended with a paragraph that summarized both his medical and religious philosophy at the time:

> After all that has been said upon this subject, we must acknowledge that mineral waters, like most of our medicines, are only substitutes for temperance and exercise in chronic diseases. An angel must descend from heaven, and trouble these chalybeate pools, before we can expect any extraordinary effects from

their use alone. There is a great resemblance between the fate of medicine and religion. In every age and country, an article of faith, or a mode of worship, have usurped the place of the precepts of morality. Thus, in medicine, we find a variety of remedies, such as mercury, bark, steel, wood lice, tar, lime, and mineral waters of all kinds, pine buds, ginseng, etc., have been put in the place of temperance and exercise. The fashion of the former passes away, but the effects of the latter, like the obligations of morality, endure forever.[3]

By the time this pamphlet appeared, Rush had published more on medical matters than perhaps any physician in America. Little of it, except possibly the essay on asthmatic children, did much to advance medical knowledge. Nor, for that matter, had it done much to advance his career. It may have hindered it. It was hard to begrudge a man of Rush's ability and open-faced charm success, but colleagues must have resented this constant appearance in print. At twenty-seven he was probably more widely known throughout the colonies than John Morgan, who had produced little of the much once expected of him. Up to now, however, any feeling against Rush had been confined to professional colleagues. The resentment boiled over and spread among the public when it became known, about the time the pamphlet on mineral waters appeared, that he had been the anonymous author of another, more controversial, pamphlet then circulating about the city. In this one he had dared to attack slavery.

2

Rush, until 1773, confined his zeal for reform largely to medical matters. He sought, for instance, to shed the burden of concocting prescriptions in a less obtrusive way than Morgan—by offering to set up a young man in an apothecary shop and agreeing to advance half the expenses for half the profits. He abandoned the project only when his candidate declined the offer "as a very uncertain undertaking." At another time he urged the artist Charles Willson Peale to create "a gallery of portraits of sick people laboring" under various diseases in the hope of advancing the study of medicine as well as exciting "the benevolent sympathies" of those ignorant of the miseries encountered in a sickroom.[4] He signed on as a physician of the almshouse in 1772 in order to bring better medical care to the poor. To the

same end, he became one of eight physicians who agreed in 1774 to participate in A Society for Inoculating the Poor, which had been formed when
statistics revealed that of the three hundred who had died of smallpox the
preceding year, most "were children of poor people who could not afford
the expense of inoculation." He became a member of the Hand-in-Hand
Fire Company, and he joined the Sons of Saint Tammany, a society that
met, so it said, "more for the purpose of promoting charity and benevolence
than mirth and festivity." The twenty-one toasts drunk at a Sons dinner held
1 May 1772 suggests that the purpose, temporarily at least, got lost in wine.[5]

It took a request from a friend to widen his scope for reform. In 1773
a bill came up before the Pennsylvania Assembly that called for doubling
the importation tax on Negro slaves—from seven pounds to fourteen—an
increase that would make it almost prohibitive to bring in new slaves. The
Quakers, who for a decade had worked against slavery, had initiated the
bill, but they lacked the votes to get it passed. Where once they had
dominated the legislature, they now shared power with the Presbyterians.
Anthony Benezet, one of the most respected of the Quakers and a leader
in the fight against slavery, had already enlisted Franklin's aid in England.
He now came to Rush for help in bringing over the Presbyterian vote. Rush
must have received the request with a degree of uncertainty, for his was a
slaveholding family. His mother owned a Negro girl who helped about the
grocery store and he a Negro youth named William Grubber. Nonetheless,
he agreed to help Benezet's cause, and "in a few hours" spread over several
evenings produced an essay, published anonymously under the title *An
Address to the Inhabitants of the British Settlements in America, upon
Slave-Keeping. By a Pennsylvanian.* Though Rush admitted "few of the
arguments are new" and that he only "endeavored by their conciseness to
give them new force," he had produced a remarkable pamphlet, one that
appealed both to the mind and to the heart, and for a half century few
attacks on slavery surpassed the power of its emotional appeal and logic.[6]

Rush opened with the statement that "slavery is so foreign to the human mind, that the moral faculties, as well as those of the understanding,
are debased and rendered torpid by it." He went on to develop a view that
Benezet had advanced a decade earlier when he said that the "abject condition" of black men in America had created among the whites "an idea of
superiority over them, which induces most people to look upon them as an
ignorant and contemptible part of mankind." Remove the black man from

servility, Rush now said, and you will find him equal to the white in all ways. He argued that the vices charged against Negroes—idleness, theft, treachery—"are the genuine offspring of slavery" and not the result of their blackness or any natural inferiority. Some, he went on, justify slavery as a way of bringing Christianity to heathens, but that "is like justifying a highway robbery because part of the money acquired in this manner was appropriated to some religious use." Slaveholders who refused to let their Negroes become Christians showed they knew that "a Christian slave is a contradiction in terms." He dismissed the argument that the Bible justified slavery as unworthy of consideration.

What steps, then, "shall we take to remedy this evil?" First, cut off the importation of slaves. What about the slaves already here? he asked, thinking no doubt of Grubber. Since slavery had corrupted the Negro and made him unfit for immediate liberty, those adults already enslaved should remain the property of their owners, but the young Negroes should be taught to read and write. Let them be educated "in the principles of virtue and religion," and, in time, let laws be passed to limit their "time of servitude, and to entitle them to all the privileges of freeborn British subjects."

Rush now moved from a reasoned argument into an emotional account of a slave's life that often came close but never quite slid over into bathos. The picture drawn in *Uncle Tom's Cabin* seems tempered in comparison with the one Rush offered. He focused his report on a West Indies plantation. Since he knew nothing of the islands firsthand, he must have drawn many of his lurid details from conversations with Lettsom, who had been reared there and had freed his Negroes before going to London. It may also have seemed politic to center the attack on West Indian slavery in order to soften any offense to friends in South Carolina and Virginia.

In the peroration Rush urged all legislators—"ye ADVOCATES for American liberty"—to work for the Negroes' liberty as they fought for their own. Why had the issue of slavery suddenly become crucial? "Remember," came the reply, "the eyes of all Europe are fixed upon you to preserve an asylum for freedom in this country, after the last pillars of it are fallen in every other quarter of the globe." Finally, he appealed to the clergy, reminding them that "slavery is a hydra sin," and no one dares to temporize with sin; it must be exorcized at once. Rush concluded by warning the clergy: "Remember that national crimes require national punishments." God will make America suffer until slavery is abolished.[7]

The pamphlet was published early in January 1773. The bill he hoped it would help push through the assembly passed soon afterward, and Rush told friends his work had "produced the desired effect." His involvement in the crusade against slavery, however, had only begun. Richard Nesbit, a West Indian planter currently living in Philadelphia, answered Rush's essay with one of his own, drawing heavily on the Bible to justify slavery, censuring the exaggerated account of cruelty to Negroes, and condemning abolition as a utopian scheme. Nesbit went further. It is probable that the Negroes "are a much inferior race of men to the whites, in every respect," he said. "We have no other method of judging, but by considering their genius and government in their native country. Africa, except the small part of it inhabited by those of our own color, is totally overrun with barbarism."[8]

Rush rebutted the charges with *A Vindication*. Abolition was "not a utopian scheme," for already movements were afoot to hasten its end in Virginia, Pennsylvania, and Massachusetts Bay. "Great changes have often been brought about by slender means," he said. "It shall be our business to collect materials. The next generation, we hope, will behold and admire the finished TEMPLE OF AFRICAN LIBERTY IN AMERICA." As for the argument that the barbarism of African tribes exemplified the innate inferiority of all blacks, Rush had a ready answer. "The heat of the climate in Africa," he said "by bringing on indolence of mind and body, exposes them at all times to slavery, while the fertility of the soil renders the want of liberty a less evil to them than it is to the inhabitants of northern, or less warm and fruitful, countries."

In *A Vindication,* Rush blamed Britain for injecting the evil of black slavery into the colonies, as Thomas Jefferson would a few months later in *A Summary View of the Rights of British America,* and he said it was "high time for Britain to change her conduct and to adopt some safe and equitable means of abolishing slavery in her colonies." But once again he reminded Americans they must clean their own house before attacking British mismanagement. "Where is the difference between the British senator who attempts to enslave his fellow subjects in America, by imposing taxes upon them contrary to law and justice, and the American patriot who reduces his African brethren to slavery, contrary to justice and humanity?"[9]

Whether he knew it or not, both these essays revealed that Rush had, through the ideas and events he had been exposed to during the past several years, become an environmentalist. The pattern of his thinking had been

in part shaped by John Locke, whose psychology held that men were fashioned by sensations received from the outside world. Sydenham's view that
diseases varied from climate to climate reinforced Rush's notion that men's
surroundings made them what they were. During the months Rush was
writing his essays, the Philadelphia press was filled with two serialized accounts that further strengthened his belief—one of Captain Cook's latest
voyage, completed in 1771, on the natives he had met in the South Pacific,
the other a detailed report of the life and people on the island of Tahiti, or
Otaheite as contemporaries called it, which had been discovered by an English navigator in 1767. "Human nature is the same in all ages and countries," Rush, having read these accounts, could write midway in *A Vindication,* "and all the differences we perceive in its characters in respect to virtue
and vice, knowledge and ignorance, may be accounted for from climate,
country, degrees of civilization, forms of government, or accidental
causes."[10]

The implications of this line of thought were, for Rush at least, enormous. It left him open to a basic change in his ideas about the struggle with
Britain. Up to now he, like most Americans, had argued only for the rights
of Englishmen. When the time came to broaden the struggle into one for
the rights of mankind, he was intellectually prepared to shift into the new
channel. There was a further implication in his arguments against slavery
that would have an even greater effect upon his life. The black man had
been corrupted by slavery, Rush had said; free him and he would blossom
as the white man did. Later he would extend this assumption. Change the
form of government and a corrupt society would become reformed. Alter
the penal code, improve the prisons and bad men would become good. In
short, change the environment in which men lived and society would move
swiftly toward perfection.

3

As Rush admitted, not one of his antislavery arguments was new. The
novelty of the two pamphlets stemmed from the verve of his style and from
the fact that no one before him had incorporated *all* the arguments against
slavery into two brief essays. By April the first one had been reprinted in
New York and Boston. In September it was combined with *A Vindication*

in a single pamphlet, which by the end of the year had been reprinted as far away as the village of Portsmouth, New Hampshire.

Months earlier word had leaked out that Rush had written both essays, and "the most virulent attack that was ever made upon me" burst forth. This hardly jibes with the boast he made in May that "now three-fourths of the province as well as the city cry out against" the evils of slavery. Nevertheless, people told him he "had meddled with a controversy that was foreign to my business." A friend from Virginia reported that "in a very sober conversation of some gentlemen from your province I yesterday heard you condemned for a late controversy relative to slavery in which you have been engaged." At the height of these attacks Rush received an affectionate but, considering the timing, ironical note from Ramsay. "I copy your example," he wrote, "which is in your own words to 'covenant with my tongue and reply to nothing,' and to revenge myself no other way than 'by visiting my patients three or four times a day.' "[11]

Rush believed the two essays affected his medical practice, and the account books seemed to bear him out. From an average of eighty patients a month he dropped to about fifty, then to a low of thirty-seven in January 1774. But the consequence "was but transitory," he said later. In May 1774 he treated eighty-two patients, in June ninety-eight, in July eighty-three, and in August a hundred and six. For the year from August 1773 through July 1774 the cash income from his practice, the apothecary shop, and the lectures at the college totaled £463.4.3. Unpaid billings on the books amounted to £828.9.0, giving a total income on paper of nearly £1,300. Few physicians in the colonies could have been doing much better.[12]

The involvement with slavery carried with it a pleasant side effect, for out of it developed a correspondence with Rev. Granville Sharp, a liberal Anglican clergyman and one of the leaders of the antislavery movement in Britain. Rush thought that an introduction to his pamphlet from Sharp might increase the chance for republication in England. Sharp replied with praise for the essays and condemnation for the Dillys, who refused to reprint them on the ground that the public was finding the subject tiresome. Thereafter the correspondence branched into other topics. In one long letter Rush expounded on the moral faculty as an innate part of the soul that leads men instinctively to avoid evil unless some physical cause such as disease weakens it, all of which prompted the thought that it might eventually "be as much the business of a physician as it is now of a divine

to reclaim mankind from vice." Sharp replied to these musings perfunctorily; he made it plain that he preferred to talk about politics. In one letter
he said that Britons and Americans must join to defend the colonies'
"unalienable right to the same privileges by which the liberties of the mother
country have been maintained," but adding also that "we should strictly
maintain our *loyalty to the crown* at the same time that we steadily assert
our legal and constitutional rights." Later he spoke of "the natural rights
of the British American subjects" at a time when Americans still argued
only for their rights as British citizens. Sharp may not have propelled Rush
toward an advocacy of independence—indeed, in an early letter Rush went
out of his way to say "there is not a *man* in America who wishes for the
independence of the colonies"—but he certainly did little to bank the fires of
republicanism.[13]

4

Years later Rush singled out 1773 as the date when "I took an early
but obscure part in the controversy between Great Britain and the American colonies." In 1770, when one of his old Parisian friends, Dubourg,
wrote praising the high spirit of the colonies, he had translated the letter
and inserted extracts in the press. From London, Coombe kept him alerted,
and on occasion agitated, about the doings of Parliament. But not until
1773 did he feel stirred enough to take an active role. Shortly after the
second piece on slavery appeared, he began to write a series of inspiriting
essays for the newspapers which were interspersed with another series by
Thomas Mifflin. Mifflin was a successful Quaker merchant and currently a
friend of Rush's, though years later Rush would dismiss him as a man
"known to be of a very immoral character" who "lived in a state of adultery
with many women." Mifflin wrote under the pseudonym "Scaevola," while
Rush chose "Hamden." (It was "Hamden" on the first essay, but this was
probably a printer's error for the name of John Hampden, a popular hero
in Cromwellian England. Further essays, presumably by Rush, spell the
name correctly.)[14]

The new stream of propaganda was provoked by Parliament's passage
in June, after diffuse debate, of the Regulating Act; Americans were soon
to call it the Tea Act. It was designed to rescue the foundering East India

Company by, among other things, giving the company a monopoly on the American tea market. The crown would profit in several ways: by undercutting the price of the cheap Dutch tea Americans had been drinking, an embarrassing hole in colonial smuggling activities would be plugged; the income from the threepence per pound duty would offset the cost of a loan that had been made to the company; and payment of the duty would vindicate Parliament's right to levy taxes on Americans. Americans should be charmed by the act, for the new setup would give them cheaper tea—cheaper, indeed, than in Britain. The government did not bother to send instructions to royal governors regarding its enforcement. By September the company had readied 600,000 pounds of tea packed in some 2,000 chests for the American market.

News of this great shipment had sped ahead of the tea ships to America. Rush's contribution to the turmoil that followed was an essay "On Patriotism." The article was constructed on a theme Samuel Davies had been partial to—that "the Amor Patriae is both a moral and a religious duty." Clearly, Rush sought to refute Samuel Johnson's definition of patriotism "as the last refuge of knaves and scoundrels." He groped to describe "the horror of our situation" if the East India Company landed tea and sold it in the colonies. "Then farewell American liberty! We are undone forever." Those chests of tea, he said, "contain something worse than death—the seeds of SLAVERY. Remember, my countrymen, the present era—perhaps the present struggle—will fix the constitution of America forever. Think of your ancestors and of your posterity."[15]

Two months later Rush doubled as physician and propagandist to condemn tea as slow poison to the body, drawing on Lettsom's dissertation for much of his material. "The great *Boerhaave* strongly opposed tea," he said, and the even greater Cullen "considers both tea and coffee as deleterious, and having mischievous effects on the nervous system." He urged readers to replace tea with milk, but if they must have something closer to their favorite beverage he offered any of seventeen tasty substitutes. Typical of the suggestions was number six:

> A very few small twigs of white oak, well dried in the sun, with two leaves and a half of *sweet myrtle*. This so exactly counterfeits the India teas that a good connoisseur might be mistaken in them.

> These are drying and very strengthening in all wasting diseases
> and fluxes, suitable to woman with child and good against
> agues.[16]

Rush's persuasiveness, however, was not notably effective; a year later a correspondent to the *Journal* remarked that Rush's nourishing substitutes had not been "generally accepted with that resolution which becomes the lovers of their country."[17]

These essays on slavery, patriotism, and tea—and others lost under numerous pseudonyms—gained Rush a new circle of acquaintances. He became friendly not only with Mifflin but with John Dickinson, Charles Thomson, and particularly with George Clymer. Thomson's public activity would within the year win him the title of "the Sam Adams of Philadelphia"; as the Continental Congress's permanent secretary he would be privy to all its transactions throughout the Confederation but to the end of his long life would refuse to write a history of what went on behind the closed doors, for "I shall not undeceive future generations." Rush liked him. A closer friend was Clymer, whom he found always "a cool, firm, consistent republican who loved liberty and government with equal affection"; though outwardly "cold and indolent," his "flashes of wit and humor often relieved a tedious conversation." Rush wrote often under a variety of pen names, but in his own mind he served most usefully as a sampler of public opinion. "My profession gave me opportunity of discovering the errors and prejudices which hung over the minds of the middling class of our citizens, upon subjects of liberty and government. These were communicated to some of the above gentlemen, by whom they were combatted and refuted."[18]

5

Politics intruded but did not dominate the early months of 1774, and as late as July he confessed "my profession confines me from many of the duties of a good citizen at the present juncture." He still found time to turn out medical papers and still hoped one of them would gain him admission into the Royal Society. Under the heading "Hints toward the Natural History of Pennsylvania," a subject he deemed likely to appeal to a British audience, he one day scrawled fifteen pages of notes. The outline began routinely with mention of Pennsylvania's location, its climate, and its products. The common diseases among children and adults were also listed. He attributed the colony's prime importance to its mixed breed of settlers, out of which had come several "illustrious men," among them astronomer David Rittenhouse, Benjamin West, and Jacob Duché, the Anglican clergyman who would shortly serve as chaplain of the First Continental Congress. (Franklin's name was not given.) Rush moved on to discuss the "natural history of the Indians"—their origin ("from the Jews?"), their manners, their diet—perhaps remembering that this had been a subject that fascinated Oliver Goldsmith.[19]

A chance to air these thoughts in public came unexpectedly early in 1774. Thomson, scheduled to deliver a paper before the February meeting of the American Philosophical Society, fell ill and Rush was asked to fill the gap. He narrowed down the broad topic of Pennsylvania's natural history to something more manageable—the natural history of medicine among the Indians. The audience gave the talk lavish praise. It is not unlikely that Rush took the praise to heart, for he obviously disallowed the comments of a friendly critic who later reminded him that "a discourse well spoken may captivate the auditors, and yet not bear a critical examination in a closet." During the ensuing months he snatched time from politics and medicine to polish the lecture and encase it with a multitude of erudite footnotes; on July 4 it was published as a small pamphlet which Rush considered his best piece of writing up to that time. Even years later, when it should have been apparent the piece was flawed, he touched it up once more for republication.[20]

The flaws were principally the result of thin material. Rush had never lived among the Indians and knew virtually nothing about them from direct observation. Most of his information came from histories of Canada by Lahontan and Charlevoix and from Edward Hand, a surgeon in the British army who had made a hobby of studying Indian life during several years at Fort Pitt. Hand returned to Philadelphia early in 1774 to be mustered out of the army, and Rush pumped him dry of his accumulated lore. He then patched out his fabric by weaving through the footnotes irrelevant material on medicine and medical philosophy and by adding, for a conclusion, a political tract. The merit of the essay—the substitution of the fashionable "noble savage" sentiment for a balanced account of the Indian and his way of life—was lost amid irrelevancies.

The footnotes must have enraged medical colleagues who bothered to read this latest production, and most of them must have done just that; Rush later commented that at the college the essay had "met with the usual fate of my publications" for, of course, it was "full of the new and unpopular doctrines that I taught in my lectures." In one footnote Rush ridiculed the idea that urine, which physicians examine "with the same scrutiny as if it was the book of fate," reveals anything of a patient's disease—which, true enough, it did not in the eighteenth century when the eye rather than chemical analysis judged its quality. "In diseases which are of a mixed nature, or altogether artificial, so many circumstances from diet, drinks, exercise, passions of the mind, and temperature of the air, alter the color, consistency and quality of urine, that the wisest physicians of the present day have agreed that neither the diagnosis or prognosis of diseases can be improved by the nicest observations that can be made upon it." This footnote was deleted in a revised version of the essay.[21]

In another footnote Rush took his colleagues to task for hoodwinking the public. "Physic, like religion, will not suffer by undeceiving the common people," he said. He derided the Boerhaavian doctrines, which, "like the hot regimen in the smallpox, have slain its thousands." We must acknowledge "the imperfections of our science" and overcome our prejudices "in our researches after truth." "It becomes us, therefore, by a modest skepticism in our opinions, to deprecate the censure and ridicule of posterity. The late successful inquiries into the laws of the nervous system, and the theories we have built upon them, will probably appear like the outlines of a picture, compared with that COMPLETE SYSTEM of physic which remains to be unfolded hereafter, when we arrive at a full knowledge of the structure and economy of the brain." Throughout the footnotes, he worked in opinions on a variety of subjects—a short lecture on temperance; a defense, which disappeared in later editions, of ladies' keeping "up their color with carmine"; and, in a long one on teeth, the view that the French owe the excellence of theirs to sleeping in large woolen caps.

Rush saved some political observations for the conclusion. True, America is racked with disease. But there is still hope, for, he reasoned, it "has advanced but a few paces in luxury and effeminacy." To assure greatness, the common people "must be preserved from the effects of intemperance," not by increasing the price of liquor, for "this is a remedy as unequal to the design as it is destructive to liberty and commerce," but by "the force of severe manners." We must eliminate "the ravages which TEA is making upon the health and populousness of our country." These remarks also disappeared in later editions.[22]

The final pages had nothing to do with Indians. They were lifted from a contemplated essay on population. They reveal a striking consistency in Rush's thought in the years before and after the Revolution. To judge by the ideas expressed, they could have been written as easily in 1784 as when they were, in 1774:

> The population of a country is not to be accomplished by rewards and punishments. And it is happy for America, that the universal prevalence of the Protestant religion, the checks lately given to Negro slavery, the general unwillingness among us to acknowledge the usurpations of primogeniture, the universal practice of inoculation for the smallpox, and the absence of the plague, render the interposition of government for that purpose unnecessary.
>
> These advantages can only be secured to our country by AGRICULTURE. This is the true basis of national health, riches, and populousness. Nations, like individuals, never rise higher than when they are ignorant whither they are tending. It is impossible to tell from history what will be the effects of agriculture, industry, temperance, and commerce, urged on by the competition of colonies united in the same general pursuits, in a country, which for extent, variety of soil, climate, and number of navigable rivers, has never been equaled in any quarter of the globe. America is the theater where human nature will probably receive her last and principal literary, moral, and political honors.[23]

Despite obvious signs of slipshod work, Rush also sent this essay everywhere. Extracts were published in the *Pennsylvania Journal* June 22 and in the *Packet* July 4. Ramsay reported from Charleston that it had not yet appeared in the local paper but that it was on sale, along with the piece on "mineral experiments." A copy drifted to Germany where it was translated and published in 1777. But it was to England that Rush turned expectantly for news of its reception. The Dillys replied that they would do nothing about publication until they heard what Franklin and Huck thought of it.

Rush had already sent them copies of the manuscript. Franklin found "the piece had in many respects a great deal of merit, yet as there was some particulars that would be excepted to by the medical people here, many of whom are in the Royal Society, and have great weight there," he and Huck "thought it best the publication should be postponed till after the ballot for your election." Franklin ended saying "you compliment me too highly in supposing a Preface of mine would be of any advantage to it," and without agreeing to write one.[24]

Huck, to whom the pamphlet was dedicated, rifled back stronger criticisms. He found "marks of an hasty performance": an imperfect knowledge of the diseases prevailing among Indians, "inaccuracies, and some seeming contradictions, and in some places the sense is so obscured in flowery language as to be scarcely intelligible." The discourse was further marred—Franklin, understandably, had missed these blemishes—by "that universal frenzy which has overspread America. *Quos deus vult perdere prius dementat* [Whom God would destroy he first makes mad]. Do you think, let your independence arrive when it may, that your country will ever again be so happy as it has been under the benign protection of this country?" A page of gentler jabs at American politics from this genial but fervent royalist followed. Then, as if he had been too harsh, Huck ended on a cheerful note: "I hang up your name at the first meeting of the Royal Society."[25]

If Franklin and Huck did "hang up" Rush's name at the November meeting of the society, he must have been blackballed. Neither then nor ever did he gain admission. The failure in 1774 must have especially hurt, for the year previous Lettsom, after being recommended among others by Franklin, had been accepted "as a gentleman well qualified to make a useful member of the society."[26] If the rejection disheartened Rush, he kept his feelings private. Friends in neither England nor America heard him complain, so far as is known, of being misused or ill-treated. He reacted to this, the first of a string of defeats in his life, as always: by pushing on with the business of living. Some of the defeats would leave him bitter; none ever broke his spirit.

6

The Boston Tea Party came on the night of 16 December 1773. Rush's reaction to the event is not known, but throughout America it was rebuked on the ground that it would "introduce anarchy, confusion and bloodshed among the people," something patriot leaders had sought to avoid since the Stamp Act riots eight years earlier. Britain's reaction to the tea party, however, brought Boston back into favor. In March 1774 Parliament passed the Boston Port Bill which, by closing the port to all commerce, in effect sought to starve the citizens into submission. Other Intolerable Acts, as Americans called them, followed quickly. Franklin, still in London, spoke out bluntly against these acts, and this elated Rush. "He will be received and carried in triumph to his house when he arrives among us," he predicted, and if he refuses to hold any more offices under the crown, nothing "can prevent his being handed down to posterity among the first and greatest characters in the world."

After word of the Port Bill reached American shores, Boston sent a circular letter to all colonies calling for an immediate suspension of trade between the colonies and the mother country. The suggestion had a mild reception, especially among Philadelphia merchants. Their reaction disgusted Rush, and he began to doubt their firmness for liberty. "They have twice rescued America from slavery," he said, thinking of their solid resistance to the Stamp Act and the Townshend duties, "but it is reflecting on their *business* only, to add that they have little relish for the 'feast of reason and the flow of soul.' "[27]

Swiftly, however, the idea took shape that America's troubles had reached a point where a gathering of colonial leaders was required to discuss them and decide on a common plan of action. By the end of July all colonies but Georgia had by one means or another chosen delegates to meet in Philadelphia, the most centrally located city on the coast.

Rush remained a spectator, though a close and well-informed one, through the seven-week meeting of the First Continental Congress. When the news swept through Philadelphia on August 29 that the New England delegation had reached the outskirts of the city, he hurried out to meet it as one of an informal welcoming committee of Philadelphia patriots. On the edge of town he climbed into the coach that carried John Adams and Robert Treat Paine of Massachusetts. At once, so Adams said, Rush "undertook to caution us against two gentlemen particularly." One, unnamed, may have been Joseph Galloway, speaker of the Pennsylvania Assembly, a delegate to the Congress, and a determined reconciliationist. The other was Provost William Smith of the college, who, though not a delegate to Con-

gress, was the intellectual leader of those in Pennsylvania favoring reconciliation with Britain at almost any cost. Rush described him in a way that
left a strong impress on Adams—"soft, polite, insinuating, adulating, sensible, learned, industrious, indefatigable, he has had art enough and refinement upon art to make impression even on Mr. Dickinson and Mr. [Joseph]
Reed."[28]

Rush took a quick liking to John Adams, judging him a man plain in
dress and manner, cold and reserved in conversation, filled with questions
"relative to the state of public opinion upon politics and the characters of
the most active citizens on both sides of the controversy."[29] Adams admired
Mrs. Macaulay's *History of England* and listened attentively as Rush told
of his acquaintance with her and other British friends of America.

Rush carried both John and his cousin Samuel Adams, who had
ridden into the city in another coach filled with delegates from Massachusetts, to his home on Water Street, where John admired "from the
windows of his back room and chamber a fine prospect of the Delaware
River and of New Jersey beyond it." The visitors remained Rush's guests
for a few days, then moved into rooms in Mrs. Yard's boardinghouse,
where another gentleman who was to become a close friend of Rush's—
Charles Lee, a former officer in the British army—had also taken rooms.
Many at the time, Lee among them, thought that if war broke out Lee
would become commander in chief of the American forces. Since Lee had
no official tie with Congress, he may have been in town to promote his
reputation among the delegates as an ingenious gentleman skilled in the
arts of war. Mrs. Yard was a patient of Rush's and, as it happened, seriously
ill. During the first half of October he visited her almost daily, perhaps
more often than need required in order to chat with his new friends.[30]

Congress met from September 5 through October 26. Rather than be
indebted to the government of a particular colony, it rejected the Pennsylvania Assembly's offer of its spacious hall in the State House and accepted
Carpenters' Hall, knowing this would be "highly agreeable to the mechanics
and citizens in general." Peyton Randolph of Virginia was chosen president
and Thomson secretary. While procedural matters were being settled, the
delegates got to know one another and the varying traditions of the colonies,
and, as John Adams noted, "We had much conversation upon the practice
of law in our different provinces." Once the real business of the convention
got under way, the delegates turned to philosophers in search of common

principles. Locke, Vattel, Burlamaqui, and Montesquieu, the city librarian reported, were "the standards to which they refer when settling the rights of the colonies or when a dispute arises on the justice or propriety of a measure."[31]

The crucial moment in the sessions occurred at the end of September. Delegates, voting by colonies, narrowly rejected Galloway's plan of union, which called for a continental legislature to deal with internal affairs but left imperial matters in the hands of Parliament and the crown. Galloway put most of the blame for his defeat on Samuel Adams, who, he said, "eats little, sleeps little, thinks much, and is most decisive and indefatigable in the pursuit of his objects." In mid-October the members approved a Declaration of Rights and Resolves, a restrained statement that in general asked for Americans no more than what they deemed to be the rights of Englishmen—the right of assembly and petition, the right to be free of standing armies, the right to choose their own councils. Delegates then agreed to a series of "animated addresses" directed to all parts of the empire, telling Englishmen everywhere exactly what the Americans were grieved about and why.

On October 20 Congress resolved that each colony should create an "Association," a covenant under which citizens would agree not to export to nor import goods from Great Britain. The colonies were also to choose committees "whose business it shall be attentively to observe the conduct of all persons touching this Association . . . to the end that all such foes to the rights of British-America may be publicly known, and universally contemned as the enemies of American liberty."

The two months during which these momentous activities took place behind the closed doors of Carpenters' Hall counted among the busiest thus far of Rush's career—he saw one hundred thirteen patients in September, eighty-nine in October. Congress became for some an unwelcome guest. Physicians agreed soon after it convened to inoculate no more persons during the time it was meeting, "as several of the northern and southern delegates are understood not to have had that disorder," and they feared they would catch the disease from those inoculated.[32]

Rush circulated only occasionally among the delegates. He spent the evening of October 17 dining at Thomas Mifflin's with, among others, the pair of Adamses and two Virginia delegates, George Washington and Richard Henry Lee, whose brother, Arthur, he had known in London and with whom he still corresponded. After supper the company discussed the probable consequences of Congress's actions. Rush later recalled of the conversation only John Adams' certainty that Britain would not redress American grievances and the toast Adams gave to support that belief—"Cash and Gunpowder to the Yankees." The next night Washington honored Rush by dining at his house, from where after supper they went for an evening of talk at the City Tavern.[33]

For Rush, one of the high points of the session came also on October 20 when Congress not only agreed on the import sanctions against Great Britain but voted not "to import nor purchase, any slave imported after the first day of December next; after which time, we will wholly discontinue the slave trade. . . ." He saw to it friends in England learned of this great gesture immediately. The resolution "was proposed and defended entirely upon *moral* and not political principles," he told Granville Sharp. "We have now *turned from our wickedness,*" he exulted, adding: "I venture to predict there will be not a Negro slave in North America in forty years."[34]

The evening after Congress adjourned, those Philadelphians who had entertained delegates in their homes were invited to a banquet at the City Tavern. Rush remembered the conversation that night "animated by the most fervid patriotism." The only toast of the evening he could remember, however, was that of Samuel Ward of Rhode Island: "May the fire which has been recently kindled upon the altar of liberty in America enlighten all the nations of the world into a knowledge of their rights."[35]

Rush all his life recalled the members of this First Continental Congress with respect and affection. Their conversation "constituted feasts of noble sentiments," he said. "Our country was then untainted by speculation. A selfish spirit was scarcely known. The errors of the British government and the corruptions of the British court, were the common subjects of complaint and declamation in all Whig companies. Every man who acted for the public was then honest and in earnest. Benevolence was actuated by new objects. It embraced the nations of Europe, and finally the whole family of mankind, who it was daily said were interested in the issue of our struggle."[36]

He did not then share John Adams' pessimistic estimate of the chance for reconciliation. "We hope all will end well," he said after the delegates had left for home, using a phrase that would become a favorite of his.

"There are letters in this city from London which declare that the ministry are relaxing in their schemes and that a reconciliation will be offered to us in the spring upon constitutional principles. One of those letters is from a gentleman who has the confidence of Lord North." Edward Dilly reported about this time that if Americans remained "firm and unanimous amongst yourselves there is no doubt but your grievances will soon be redressed."[37]

7

Rush did not give his entire attention to Congress and the smallpox epidemic in October, for that month he watched Sarah Eve endure "a painful and lingering illness" that carried her rapidly toward death. During the early part of October he made "night and day visits in the country" to attend her, rarely missing at least one trip a day to her bedside. She died on December 4. A week later an unsigned eulogy, which has been attributed to Rush, appeared in the *Pennsylvania Packet*. Miss Eve came forth as a paragon—amiable in disposition, polished in manners, elegant in person, a girl of such "good sense, modesty, and good humor, that no one, I believe, ever left her without emotions of love or admiration." Tradition has it that Miss Eve died three weeks before she and Rush were to be married. Nothing exists to substantiate that story. Without question, the couple were good friends, if the several references to Rush in Sarah Eve's diary are any clue. That diary reveals a lively, saucy girl who mocked pretensions and had little reverence for her elders, an attractive companion but hardly the sort Rush could be counted on to marry. To judge by the girl he did wed, he preferred women to be serious and demure, and able to bring to the wedding a dowry more substantial than that to be expected from a sea captain's daughter.

Rush squired girls other than Miss Eve during 1774. And he still had not worked Lady Jane out of his system. In a letter to her on September 28, only a few days before Sarah Eve fell ill, he promised himself "to conceal and attempt to subdue my passion" for Angelina:

Subdue my passion did I say? No, I will not attempt it. When beauty, softness, sweetness of temper, a benevolent heart, an excellent understanding, amiable manners, in a word where *all*

female excellencies are united together there is both a pleasure
and praise in loving. I devote my heart therefore forever to
Heaven and Angelina. . . .

If Rush contemplated marriage with Miss Eve, he did his best to obscure
the plan from posterity. Whatever letters, if any, the couple exchanged
were burned. No scrap by or about her remained in his papers, and in the
autobiography written years later he passed over any mention of her. A
further hint that tradition may have exaggerated a friendship into love
exists: shortly after Miss Eve died, Rush submitted to her father a bill for
services rendered, an unlikely act by a physician caring for his betrothed
on her deathbed. Captain Eve paid up promptly.[38]

The same issue of the *Packet* that carried the eulogy on Sarah Eve also
ran an announcement that Dr. Rush would present to the people of Philadelphia a series of popular lectures on chemistry, beginning on January 9
at six o'clock in the evening and costing one guinea for the series. Rush
promised to explain everything from how to manufacture gunpowder to
the cause of volcanoes and meteors. It was unclear whether he had planned
the lectures for his or the public's benefit. What was clear, however, was
that he courted popular favor as well as professional distinction, and at the
age of twenty-eight he was on the way to gaining both.[39]

In the Midst
of a
Revolution

7

The Revolution Begins

1775–1776

1

MANY YEARS AFTER THE REVOLUTION Rush remarked upon the uncommon number of apoplectic fits during the winter of 1774–1775. Anxiety, he thought, provoked the phenomenon. "Every countenance wore the marks of painful solicitude for the event of a petition to the throne of Britain." Anxiety and apoplexy increased proportionally after fighting broke out in the spring of 1775, and Rush believed that the death of at least one man from an apoplectic fit in October 1775 "appeared to be occasioned in part by the pressure of the uncertainty of those great events upon his mind."[1]

If Rush diagnosed the cause correctly, it can be assumed he would have been among the last to succumb to the malady. Few in America approached resistance to Great Britain by a less tortuous route than he. Or so it seems. One can chart John Adams' self-doubts and forebodings from the record left behind. "To what object are my views directed?" he asked two years after the Stamp Act. "What is the end and purpose of my studies, journeys, labors of all kinds of body and mind, of tongue and pen? Am I grasping at money or scheming for power?" No hint of a similar self-questioning of motives and goals survives in Rush's record. He had traveled to Europe a fervent American, and the years in Scotland and London only convinced him of the corruption of Parliament and of those who surrounded the king. From 1765 on, no mental reservations caused him to hesitate in his actions.[2]

The news out of England during that winter did nothing to instill doubt in Rush about his political stand. The government had openly determined to coerce the colonies. Soon after passage of the Intolerable Acts, it decided to hold new elections, though Parliament still had a year to run. (British law required that a general election be held at least once every seven years.) Four days after the returns were in, the king, with a sizable majority in Commons that would allow his ministry freedom of action for the next seven years, pronounced the New England colonies to be "in a state of rebellion" and said that "blows must decide" whether they were to be subject to or independent of Great Britain. Parliament endorsed the king's position when it reassembled in November 1774. In January 1775 orders went out to all colonial governors to prevent the election of delegates to a second Continental Congress. In February, three generals—Sir William Howe, Sir Henry Clinton, and John Burgoyne—set sail for the colonies with reinforcements for the army already there under Gen. Thomas Gage. In March and April came the Restraining Acts, which declared that "as Americans had refused to trade with this kingdom, it was but just that we should not suffer them to trade with any other nation." It was during debate over these measures that Edmund Burke, standing before empty benches, made his memorable plea for conciliation.

As this news filtered in, the colonies were moving toward a war footing. By the end of 1774, ten colonies whose legislatures had been shut down by royal orders had erected provincial congresses—all of them extralegal and all of them composed mainly of the same men who had sat in the regular assemblies. These local congresses approved the proceedings of the First Continental Congress and elected delegates to the Second which would meet in May. All colonies but New York and Georgia adopted the Association, and local committees were soon busy with its enforcement; even in the recalcitrant colonies, self-created local committees went ahead here and there with the program of economic sanctions. It was soon apparent that nonimportation and nonexportation was working.

In all this Rush "continued a spectator only." His lack of political experience restricted the chance to act, and for those leaders who knew him well he may have had too much exuberance to be trusted. Moreover, political power still resided in the hands of those who had wielded it for many years, and these old hands were in no mood to slacken their grip for a stranger like Rush. Even if they had been, his burgeoning medical practice would have limited the time he could actively devote to the resistance movement.[3]

By the winter of 1774–1775, the public seems to have forgiven Rush the pamphlet on slavery, and his list of patients continued to grow. It also continued to be largely limited to the plain people of the city—blacksmiths, hatters, shopkeepers, silversmiths. Few names from the city's elite appear in his ledgers. He averaged roughly eighty patients a month, and during the year he took on a new wave of apprentices. The earlier ones had left to start their own practices, and now he acquired nine more, among them the sons of Gilbert Tennent and Samuel Finley.[4]

Long after both students and apprentices had left Rush, they would write for advice on difficult cases. Those practicing in country villages reported they met resistance when dispensing his concepts. One friend told him that the college's young graduates, for all their theoretical knowledge, were regarded by their country clientele "as so many apprentices just let loose." Farmers had fixed ideas about diseases, he said, and if a Philadelphia-trained lad was "not ready with reasons to justify his deviations from what they were accustomed to, he will be rejected."[5]

Rush's chemistry course—even eight years after Edinburgh—was still substantially Joseph Black's, and in the winter of '74 attracted only sixteen students. A friend in England reported that Priestley had recently carried out a set of experiments from which he procured "air six times more salubrious than common air," making Rush one of the first Americans to know that Priestley had isolated an element that would one day be called oxygen. He may have slipped a reference to the event into a lecture, but otherwise it got little attention. Chemistry still interested him only as it could directly serve mankind.[6]

The imminence of war offered the opportunity to put chemistry to practical use. In November he published under the pseudonym "Peregrinus" the results of experiments from which he had obtained an ounce of saltpeter (potassium nitrate), an essential ingredient for making gunpowder, from a half pound of dry tobacco stalks. Two months later came "An Account of the Manufactory of Salt-Petre," with a brief follow-up essay on the art of making common salt, both under the pseudonym of "A Manufacturer."[7]

As "a manufacturer" Rush fell into a new role, one he would promote with all the warmth and effusion given another time to the marvels of agriculture and at another to commerce. In February 1775 the recently organized United Company for Promoting American Manufactures chose him president. The company had a double purpose, part practical—it planned to produce the woolen, cotton, and linen cloths that up to then had been imported from Great Britain—and part humanitarian, as befitted any project with which Rush associated. It hoped to excite the "laudable spirit of industry among the poor, . . . and also to convince the public that our country is not unfavorable to the establishing of manufactories."[8]

No one expected President Rush to direct company affairs, but the stockholders did hope that as a man of words he might arouse general interest in what to many seemed a visionary project. He did his best in a speech delivered before the subscribers of the company on March 16. He declared at the outset that the optimism once held by him for reconciliation with England had now been dispelled. "I am far from thinking that the non-importation agreement will be so transitory a thing as some have supposed," he said. "The same arbitrary ministers continue in office, and the same arbitrary favorites continue to abuse the confidence of our sovereign." He expected at least two or three years of resistance would be needed before Britain came around. To assure continuance of the embargo, Americans must begin to manufacture their own cloth, once the largest item imported by the colonies.[9]

Rush assumed that the advantages of home manufacturing were too great to be ignored. The immense sum that flowed out each year to pay for British-made cloth—more than £250,000 annually from Pennsylvania alone, he estimated—would now be kept home. Cotton imported from the West Indies and the South would unite those areas with the northern and middle colonies. Manufacturing would increase local employment and at the same time draw craftsmen from Britain. Moral advantages, too, would ensue from home manufacturing. The ships that brought cloth also brought "European luxuries and vices." Now these would be blocked from American shores, and liberty would flourish as never before, for "a people who are *entirely* dependent upon foreigners for food or clothes must always be subject to them."

Resistance to Britain became in Rush's hands a holy crusade with the welfare of mankind at stake. "America is now the only asylum for liberty in the whole world," he said. Perhaps God seeks through this contest with

Britain "to show the world this asylum, which, from its remote and unconnected situation with the rest of the globe, might have remained a secret for
ages." And make no mistake, Britain clearly wants to enslave this land of
liberty. "By becoming slaves, we shall lose every principle of virtue. We
shall transfer unlimited obedience from our Maker to a corrupted majority
in the British House of Commons," and when that happens: "We shall
hug our chains. We shall cease to be men. We shall be *slaves.*"

Rush nimbly skirted arguments that had been raised against manufacturing, as if he had never spoken from the opposite side of the question. To
the criticism that manufacturing would "draw off our attention from agriculture," he answered that it would stunt the "endless variety in the geniuses
of men . . . to confine them entirely to the simple arts of agriculture." Besides, this project would draw few from the fields, for two-thirds of the
work would be done by women and children. He rebutted the argument
that manufacturing was "hurtful to population" with a perception that put
him far ahead of the times. "I believe that many of the diseases to which
the manufacturers in Britain are subject are brought on not so much by the
nature of their employment, but by their unwholesome diet, damp houses,
and other bad accommodations, each of which may be prevented in
America."

The speech—an effective blend of self-interest and patriotism, with
only a touch of bathos—ended his association with the United Company.
His name never appeared among the list of subscribers nor again among
the company officers. While the United Company moved from one crisis
to another, mainly for the lack of a good manager, Rush had joined other
flanks in the resistance movement.

2

On April 24 at five o'clock in the afternoon, news of the battle at
Lexington reached Philadelphia. The dispatch said some one thousand
British redcoats had "marched to where they found a company of our
militia in arms, upon whom they fired without any provocation, and killed
six men, and wounded four others." That news, Rush said later, "gave a
new tone to my feelings, and I now resolved to bear my share of the duties
and burdens of the approaching Revolution." From that date he favored

independence and designed his publications "to prepare the public mind to adopt that important and necessary measure." He became possibly the first prominent Pennsylvanian and among the first in America to take what looked to most citizens like a rash and foolhardy stand.[10]

Rush circulated constantly around the edges of the Second Continental Congress from the day in May when the first delegates rolled into the city to the sound of muffled church bells, Philadelphia's way of mourning the events that had occurred a month earlier outside Boston. He struck up a friendship with Patrick Henry, whom he inoculated against smallpox in July (charge: £4 5s.). He renewed associations of the previous year—with Washington, the Adamses, Richard Henry Lee. He met Washington one day at the London Coffee House, which was located on Front Street only a stone's throw from Rush's home. Philadelphia's social life to a considerable extent centered at the coffeehouse, which offered patrons a wider choice of drink than its name implied ("Some people may be desirous at times to be furnished with other liquors besides coffee," William Bradford, the proprietor and father of Rush's friend Thomas, had said when applying for a license). Merchants, farmers, mechanics, and politicians met there. Ships' captains stopped by to write up their reports, their vessels tied up at the wharves just a few hundred feet to the east at the base of High Street. It was an informal post office for itinerants and a clearinghouse for gossip, where even the bickerings behind the closed doors at the State House were often open secrets.

Rush told Washington that if he were appointed commander in chief of the Continental army it "would give universal satisfaction to the citizens of Pennsylvania." While Congress discussed its choice for the post, Rush promoted Washington by reprinting in the local press that part of Samuel Davies' 1755 sermon "in which he predicted the future services Major Washington should render to this country"; after Congress announced Washington's appointment, Rush was invited to a party honoring the general at a tavern on the banks of the Schuylkill River. After dinner someone offered a toast to the new commander in chief; Washington in a halting way gave thanks to the guests, who as one rose to honor him. "This scene, so unexpected, was a solemn one," Rush recalled. "A silence followed it, as if every heart was penetrated with the awful but great events which were to follow." Rush remembered the party for another reason, for it was there he met and became friendly with a tall, redheaded Virginian named Thomas Jefferson.[11]

His closest friends among the congressional delegates at this time were Samuel and John Adams, "who had anticipated and even cherished the idea of independence." He continued to stop by Mrs. Yard's, where they were again lodged, to chat whenever the opportunity occurred. He complained steadily to them that the Committee of Safety, a group of citizens chosen by the assembly to organize and direct Pennsylvania's contribution to the war, did not represent the people. John Adams agreed "all this is just." Rush fumed especially against Dickinson, who favored reconciliation, convinced he had been warped by Quakers and Anglicans. He thought the "Farmer's" reputation "past the meridian and that avarice is growing upon him." John Adams may have been influenced by Rush's views when he wrote in a letter home of Dickinson: "A certain great fortune and piddling genius, whose fame has been trumpeted so loudly, has given a silly cast to our whole doings." The British captured and published the letter, and in Philadelphia, Rush reported, Adams became "an object of nearly universal detestation." Rush stood by him. He passed along the news that Adams' joking reference in the same indiscreet letter to the pack of dogs that always trailed Charles Lee, the former fellow lodger at Mrs. Yard's, had caused Lee, now General Lee and a member of Washington's staff at Cambridge, to laugh.[12]

The friendship established in '74 with Lee and the Adamses made Rush in '75 something of a go-between collector of gossip from the military and legislative camps. From the Adamses he gathered congressional news which was passed on to Lee, who returned with inside reports on the progress of the siege of Boston. Washington had taken command of the Continental army there on July 3. By late summer he had collected twenty thousand men whose task was to take a city held by nine thousand trained and well-entrenched British troops with a fleet at their backs to feed them. His staff included, besides Lee, such men as Artemas Ward, "a fat old gentleman who . . . had no acquaintance whatever with military affairs"; Israel Putnam, a hard-drinking veteran of the French and Indian War known affectionately by the troops as "Old Put"; and Horatio Gates, a self-satisfied ex-British officer. Like Gates, Lee, once described by John Adams as a "great sloven, wretchedly profane," considered himself abler than Washington. He chafed at Washington's cautious approach to the job of forcing the British to decamp from Boston. "Let me communicate to you my sentiments, but at the same time I must desire you to be secret," he told Rush in September. "I think then we might have attacked 'em long before this and with success, were our troops differently constituted—but the fatal persuasion has taken deep root in the minds of the Americans from the highest to the lowest order that they are no match for the regulars, but when covered by a wall or breastwork." He had a half year longer to chafe. The British did not evacuate the city until 17 March 1776.

Lee viewed the American cause somewhat differently from Rush. "What a trial is a civil war," he wrote in one letter, "or as I find that it is not quite decent at Philadelphia amongst your wise ones to term slaughtering of men, women, and children and laying waste with fire and sword your seacoasts, a civil war—what a trial are civil contentions?" Yet between Lee and Rush a close friendship had developed; they shared similar enthusiastic temperaments as well as political views. Both detested such trappings as titles as a "barbarous, dangerous custom." "Upon my soul they make me spew," said Lee. "Even the tacking 'honorable' to the Continental Congress creates a wambling in my stomach." Each in a halfhearted way tried to reform the other. Rush reproved Lee's constant swearing ("I am afraid your intended philippic [against General Gage] will not reach him—damn him! . . . You see I have not left off swearing, but am in hopes that your reproofs and time will bring about reformation") and Lee admonished Rush's indiscreet tongue ("You ought, my friend, to be a little more upon your guard in declaring your republican sentiments to the Southern people. Virginians and Carolinians are not yet prepared for such doctrines").[13]

The inability to hide feelings or thoughts unfitted Rush for politics, as he would soon learn. But such openness had advantages: it sped friendships with men like Lee and Adams, who gave freely of themselves when they found someone who reciprocated similarly. Adams' first judgment of the physician in the privacy of his diary was restrained: "He is an elegant, ingenious body. Sprightly, pretty fellow. . . . But Rush, I think, is too much of a talker to be a deep thinker. Elegant, not great." This from the garrulous Adams! Soon, however, he was referring to Rush as "a worthy friend of mine," "a gentleman of an ingenious turn of mind, and of elegant accomplishment." He praised his handling of inoculations, telling friends back home that "several of our members have been under his hands and come out, almost without alteration of countenance." The friendship became a major event in Rush's life. John Adams, at least during the years of the Revolution, influenced him in the political sphere as profoundly as Finley and Davies had in religion and Cullen in medicine.[14]

3

In background and temperament Rush and Adams held much in common. Both sprang from families that had "lived without tumult or luster." Both liked to talk, wrote easily in a relaxed, lively style. They loved equally to argue—"he dares not dispute nor contradict me," Rush once remarked of a companion, "and this is not only the life of conversation but steel to the flint of genius"—and quarreled with all who saw the world differently from them.[15] Each was ambitious, envied the well-to-do, and yearned for rank and place. What had once been said of Adams—he "could not look with complacency upon any man who was in possession of more wealth, more honors, or more knowledge than himself"—could as easily have been said of Rush. Self-pity suffused much of what they said and wrote. Adams once observed, "I have had poverty to struggle with, envy and jealousy and malice of enemies to encounter, no friends, or but few, to assist me," a sentiment Rush had penned many times.

Differences between the two men, however, did exist. Adams had been reared outside the experience of the Great Awakening, whose tenets had done so much to shape Rush. At Harvard he was taught that an elite of New England—Harvard men, of course—was to lead and the multitude must follow; he learned to distrust enthusiasm in religion and through John Winthrop, professor of natural philosophy, he was carried into the world of eighteenth-century rationalism. After graduation Adams withdrew to the backwater village of Worcester to teach for a year while deciding what to do with his life. There he read books Rush in his youth had never been exposed to—deistic works that caused him to see Christianity retreating in "whole cartloads of trumpetry." He could no longer tolerate the doctrines of "the frigid John Calvin" and came close to discarding the concept of Original Sin in favor of John Locke's assumption that, as Adams put it, "when we come into the world our minds are destitute of all sorts of ideas." Slowly he worked back to a position where he became more of a Calvinist than Calvin. Vice and sin, he came to think, ruled the world and the chance to eliminate evil seemed slight. "Great things are wanted to be done," he said shortly before setting out for Philadelphia in 1774, "and little things only I fear can be done."[16]

It has been said that the main goal of the Revolution "was not the overthrow or even the alteration of the existing social order but the preservation of political liberty threatened by the apparent corruption of the constitution, and the establishment in principle of the existing conditions of liberty."[17] John Adams would find this premise valid but not Benjamin Rush. Rush, conditioned by Finley and Davies, and to a degree by the people he met in Edinburgh and London, saw the Revolution as a great crusade that would hasten the arrival of the Kingdom of God on earth. The corrupt and degenerate elements England had foisted on America would be eradicated. The entrenched elite would be thrown out and governments would come to be based on the consent of the governed. Established churches that forced men to worship as the state wished would be eliminated and religious liberty would prevail. Rush, in short, hoped for a real revolution, and his buoyant attitude allowed him to look forward to a break with Great Britain with slight anguish.

Adams, on the other hand, agonized for months over his decision. The effort threw him into a lethargy that left him incapable of action. He took a trip through Connecticut, hoping a change of scenery would settle his mind, but returned to confess he still moped and slumbered all day. Adams wanted wealth. Rich men, he said, "feel the strength and importance which their riches give them in the world." He had no complaints with the way Massachusetts' society and government were organized. He dreaded the thought of political innovation and believed in government by the people as a useful theory, not to be practiced if it meant leveling or other social changes. To throw in with Sam Adams and his friends would be to discard an intelligently ordered society for—what? The unknowns of a future outside the empire tormented Adams until New Year's Day 1773, when he at last made up his mind to join with his cousin Sam. "I never was happier in my whole life," he said. "I feel easy and composed and contented." But not necessarily, as he was often to tell Rush, optimistic.[18]

In spite of the gulf between their views on man and society, Rush and Adams had enough in common to establish the basis for a friendship that, with one long break, would last until death. The relationship, at least during the years of the Revolution, had a special quality. A spread in age—Adams was forty years old, ten years senior to Rush—may have generated something resembling a parent-son relationship. Adams' long experience in politics enhanced the prospects for such a tie to deepen. For well over a decade, politics—on the local, provincial, and now the continental level—had been central to his life. Colleagues in Congress regarded him as a skilled politician and also the best-read man in America on the theory and practice of government. Rush, though long a knowledgeable spectator, had prior to 1775 no practical political experience. Given his admitted weakness "to hold great men too much in veneration," he could be expected to accept, as he did, Adams' dicta on politics much as he had accepted Cullen's on medicine. Eventually Rush would break with Adams—as in time he would react against the teachings of Cullen—but during the Revolution the two men almost never found themselves on opposite sides of an issue, despite their contrasting perceptions of life.

4

Nothing that occurred in 1775 could diminish Rush's optimism. In October, he wrote an exuberant account of the state of affairs to Thomas Ruston, his Nottingham classmate, who had reported regularly on British politics in letters Rush got published in the Philadelphia press. Naturally, he expected that his own reports to Ruston would see light in some London newspaper. In one letter he lavished praise on Congress ("firm and united" and "determined to ask everything hereafter with the sword in their hands"), the invasion of Canada ("we expect every hour to hear that the standard of American liberty is planted in the heart of Quebec"), and independence ("Britain and America *will* hereafter be distinct empires. America is the *punctum saliens*—the only vivid principle of the whole world"). He glorified Washington as "one of those illustrious heroes whom providence raises up once in three or four hundred years to save a nation from ruin." Rush gave the letter to Peggy Watson, a young milliner returning to Scotland who had been a patient of his. The British intercepted it, but a garbled version, which Miss Watson may have given from memory to Ruston, appeared in the London *Morning Post* early in 1776.[19]

Rush's praise of Washington for British ears may have disguised some private misgivings. Recently, while dining out, he had met Col. Adam Stephen, a Scotsman and former Edinburgh student, now a resident of Virginia. Stephen had been Washington's second in command of the Virginia regiment during the French and Indian War, but since then the once close

friends had become bitter enemies. Stephen had turned to Rush at the dinner table and in a low voice asked "who constituted General Washington's
military family?" "Colonel J[oseph] Reed and Major Thomas Mifflin, both
good men," Rush had answered. "I am glad to hear it," Stephen said, "for
General Washington will require such men about him. He is a *weak man.*
I know him well." He went on to say that another Virginian he knew had
found Washington "a very dull young man," so much so that "he was
unable to count some change he once saw him receive in a store." Rush,
unaware of the enmity between Washington and Stephen, was enough impressed that he asked to make a copy of Stephen's journal of the ill-fated
Braddock expedition of 1755, which the colonel allowed him to do.[20]

Rush's direct involvement in the war effort came the first week in
July. Congress gathered up his essays on how to make saltpeter and published them, together with a brief introduction by Franklin, as a pamphlet.
Pennsylvania's Committee of Safety soon after chose him with several others
to superintend the building of a "saltpeter manufactory." On the same day,
July 3, the committee also voted to build a fleet of gunboats, or row galleys
as they were called, to defend the city from any invaders who might venture
up Delaware Bay. By mid-September thirteen of the galleys were completed,
and Rush accepted the post of physician-surgeon to the fleet. The shakedown cruise for the boats came September 28, members of the Continental
Congress and the Pennsylvania Assembly being invited to participate. Rush
joined the group late in the morning, after completing his visits to patients.
He climbed aboard the *Bull Dog,* among whose passengers were John
Adams, David Rittenhouse, and Michael Hillegas, a well-to-do merchant
who, with George Clymer, had just been appointed joint treasurer of the
united colonies. As the boats drifted downriver, the men joked about sending a letter to Lord North, purporting to reveal a plot to sabotage British
arsenals. Hillegas took the fancy seriously, but the others soon laughed him
out of acting on it. The otherwise uneventful outing proved so pleasant for
these overworked gentlemen that Rush and Adams found themselves still
reminiscing about it long after the Revolution.[21]

Rush may have taken on the city's galley fleet assignment reluctantly.
At about the same time, the top medical post in the Continental army had
become vacant when Dr. Benjamin Church, director general of the hospitals, was removed from office by Congress after being accused of spying
for the British. Who better than Rush could fill the position? an ex-appren-

tice now with the army that encircled Boston asked his former master. Rush may have wanted the job, but no one seems to have seriously considered him for it. Congress on October 16 gave it to John Morgan, leaving Rush to handle more modest assignments in Philadelphia. This probably suited him, for he rarely exaggerated his talents as an organizer or as a leader of men.[22]

5

Early in 1775 while browsing in Robert Aitken's bookstore Rush met a man named Thomas Paine, whom Aitken had hired at the modest salary of fifty pounds a year to edit the *Pennsylvania Magazine*. Paine had arrived the previous year from England carrying a letter of introduction from Benjamin Franklin and hoping to open a school for young ladies. Rush, a proselytizer for female education since the visit to Paris, approved of Paine at once. The two chatted amiably and then parted. In March Rush read an essay in the *Pennsylvania Journal* that attacked slavery, and, learning Paine had written it, he became eager "to be better acquainted with him." The two met off and on through the year. Rush liked Paine's social ideas—apparently they steered clear of religious topics in their talks—but disapproved of his "desultory life, his intemperate habits," and also his political views, for, if as an old man he recollected right, Paine at this time "was unfriendly to the claims of America."[23]

Apparently it took the battle of Lexington to change Paine's views on independence and to bring the two closer. Rush wanted to disabuse the public of the "mass of prejudice and error" it held in regard to the idea of independence, but after attempting an essay on the subject, he "shuddered at the prospect of the consequence of its not being well received." Part of the trouble was that Rush had set himself an impossible task, for when he abandoned the project to Paine he warned him "that there were two words which he should avoid by every means as necessary to his own safety and that of the public—*independence* and *republicanism.*"

Rush urged Paine to write on the subject and for reasons that Paine, if he had been so inclined, should have found humiliating. "I suggested to him," Rush recalled, "that he had nothing to fear from the popular odium to which such a publication might expose him, for he could live anywhere, but that my profession and connections, which tied me to Philadelphia, where a great majority of the citizens and some of my friends were hostile to a separation of our country from Great Britain, forbade me to come forward as a pioneer in that important controversy." Having been burned once by the pamphlet on slavery, Rush was not about to be burned again, especially not now with his practice prospering.[24]

Paine "seized the idea with avidity." As the essay progressed, he brought the pages around to Rush's house to be read. When he had finished, Rush urged him to show the work to Benjamin Franklin, Samuel Adams, or someone else who "held the same opinions that he had defended." Franklin saw the manuscript, making only one or two minor changes, and possibly Sam Adams did, too. Paine planned to entitle the pamphlet "Plain Truth," but Rush objected to that title. He suggested instead "Common Sense," and "this was instantly adopted." Now, only a printer was wanting, and Rush supplied that, too. He spoke to Robert Bell, a Scotsman "whom I knew to be as high-toned as Mr. Paine upon the subject of American independence," and Bell agreed to take the risk. Rush brought author and printer together "and *Common Sense* burst from the press of the latter in a few days with an effect which has rarely been produced by types and paper in any age or country."[25]

The shared experience of *Common Sense* did not strengthen the rapport between Paine and Rush. The two never became more than acquaintances, though Paine would have liked to make more of the relationship; as late as 1790 he was sending Rush notes when the occasion arose, the last one of record being a glowing account of the progress of the French Revolution. "I met him now and then at the tables of some of our Whig citizens," Rush once said, "where he spoke but little but was always inoffensive in his manner and conversation." Perhaps Rush was jealous of Paine's "wonderful talent of writing to the tempers and feelings of the public." Perhaps Paine's personal habits—he was "intemperate and otherwise debauched in private life"—and certainly later his deism put Rush off. (To the end he believed *The Age of Reason* "probably perverted more persons from the Christian faith than any book that ever was written.") Perhaps they looked at humanity from divergent angles; Paine was said to love mankind but hate men, where Rush tended to love men but regard mankind with suspicion.[26]

Despite the distance the two kept in later years, they had much in common, in some ways more than had Rush and Adams. Both saw the

Revolution as something greater than a war for independence. They broke over the Pennsylvania Constitution of 1776, but goodwill persisted between them through the Revolution. The reform movements that later engaged Rush's energy had, with the possible exception of the drive against spirituous liquors, Paine's support. They shared so many views in the 1780's that Rush found himself, consciously or not, borrowing from Paine for his own essays. When Paine died in 1809 Rush censured his vanity—"He once said he was at a loss to know whether he was made for the times or the times made for him"—and dismissed his writing as "always adapted to the common capacities," two judgments equally easy to make about Rush. An earlier estimate, unvarnished by his reaction to *The Age of Reason,* came closer to his true feeling. It was made during the Revolution, when *Common Sense,* and also the series of *Crisis* papers, each of which was published at a low point in the war when the cause seemed lost, had done so much to rouse the spirit of the people. "We have seen the wonderful effect of the pen properly managed in America in the publications of 'Common Sense,' " he wrote in 1781. "I believe his 'Crises' did as much mischief to the enemy and as much service to the friends of liberty as it has been in the power of any one man to render this country with any other weapons short of the sword."[27]

6

Through the latter half of 1775 Rush was simultaneously concerned with totally different matters—independence and marriage. In August, he visited Princeton and stayed at Morven, the estate on the edge of town where his friends the Richard Stocktons lived. There he saw again their daughter Julia, whom he had once, when she was a child, carried home in his arms after a college commencement. Now she came to greet him as a handsome young lady of sixteen, the very age of Lady Jane when he had fallen in love with her. She had a generous mouth, a high forehead, and she wore her brown hair swept up from the neck. Her eyes were dark, and she had "a complexion composed of white and red, a countenance at the same time soft and animated, a voice mild and musical, and a pronunciation accompanied with a little lisp," Rush observed. He later told his children that their mother's engaging manners and correct conversation had first caught his eye, but when she said Dr. Witherspoon "was the best preacher she had ever heard," he knew he had come upon someone with "a soundness of judgment and correctness of taste seldom to be met with in a person of her age."[28]

At another time he confessed she had originally charmed him by singing a Scottish tune "the first evening I was introduced to her, with the same air and lisp that I once heard Angelina sing the same sweet song in Nicholson's Square." Apparently Lady Jane and Julia Stockton resembled one another in other ways, for Rush years later admitted to Angelina that there were "some family shades of likeness between you and Mrs. Rush." Miss Stockton had one further virtue—she would bring "a pretty little fortune" to the marriage, a practical side of the bargain that Rush kept always in mind.[29]

Soon after the brief holiday at Morven he determined to offer his hand to Miss Julia as quickly as possible. He wrote from Philadelphia asking the Stocktons' permission to see their daughter. Once visiting rights had been granted, weekly trips to Princeton began, and "after several visits my suit was blessed with success." Courtship may have interfered with but did not suspend Rush's other activities. He attended his practice more assiduously than ever, only now with closer attention to collecting bills from patients. In the three months before marriage, he brought in more than three hundred pounds in cash, an ample enough sum for a young man to begin married life with.[30]

During the courtship Rush came upon a handbill passed out by a young man named Charles Willson Peale, who had recently come to Philadelphia. Peale, after presenting his compliments to the ladies and gentlemen of the city, offered "his services to paint their portraits in miniature or large, if most agreeable at their own houses." Rush chose to honor his coming marriage by accepting Peale's offer.[31]

The wedding took place at Morven on 11 January 1776, two days after the publication of *Common Sense* and exactly a week after Rush's thirtieth birthday. ("The rule he generally laid down," a friend said, "was that no female should marry before she was sixteen, nor male before he was twenty-one; and the longer they both delayed matrimony after these periods the better; provided the delay in a female did not exceed twenty-four, or in a male thirty."[32]) John Witherspoon officiated at the ceremony. There is no indication that the couple took a honeymoon. Rush's daybook shows he visited four patients on the day of the wedding—possibly, though, an apprentice made them—and carried on his practice throughout the week as if nothing out of the ordinary had occurred.[33]

Rush stepped into marriage suffused with love for his bride. "I did not know till since we parted how much you were a part of myself," he wrote a few months later when she was visiting her parents, "and I feel some abatement of my affection for my country when I reflect that even she has deprived me of an hour of my dear Julia's company." He ended another note a few days later with: "Adieu, my sweet Julia. My heart glows with an affection for you at this instant so tender, so delicate, and so refined that I want words to express it. Once more adieu . . . I have a thousand things to say to you. I think, write, talk, work, love—all, all—only for you."[34] Years later he still wrote to her as "My Loveliest Girl," and the letters continued in this vein through the marriage whenever his wife, however briefly, absented herself from home.

Mrs. Rush bore her husband thirteen children, nine of whom lived to maturity. She was a devout, self-effacing woman who appears to have accepted her husband's view that with marriage "subordination of your sex to ours is enforced by nature, by reason, and by revelation." She remained for Rush until his death what he, a man of exacting standards, considered "a perfect wife," or, as he once put it, what "would pass for a *good woman* even in Scotland and for what the world calls a *fine woman* even in England."[35]

8

Pennsylvania Politics

1776

1

A FRIEND congratulating Rush on his marriage said, "I really think this step is not only a mark of your confidence in our general cause but a mark of confidence in the security of your situation." He used the word "security" in a double sense—to note Rush's solid financial situation and also Pennsylvania's relative safety from attack; invaders would have to travel either across New Jersey or up the hundred-mile funnel of Delaware Bay to reach Philadelphia. The friend went on to denounce Pennsylvania politics. "I am told your people are most unequally represented in assembly. Do not the choice spirits think of correcting so essential a defect in every free constitution? Why have you not had a convention or fallen upon some plan to get rid of that damned nonresisting Quakerism that prevails so much in your assembly?"[1]

By the time this letter arrived, Rush had begun to do something toward answering the questions it raised. On February 16, a month after his marriage, he was elected to Philadelphia's Committee of Inspection and Observation, an event that marked his formal and public entrance into politics. This committee, one of a network that spread throughout Pennsylvania and all the colonies, had been created to implement the regulations of the Association that the first Congress had designed in 1774. The Philadelphia committee originally consisted of forty-three members; it soon expanded to sixty-six, and then to an even hundred. Influence increased with size. Under the guise of executing the resolves of Congress, it began to usurp more and more authority, even to the point of interfering in citizens' personal affairs and private opinions. By 1776 it regulated or attempted to regulate the price and sale of scarce items, such as salt. It checked ship cargoes for contraband, padlocked shops of merchants who ignored its regulations, publicly reprimanded those it judged disloyal, and imprisoned those it considered traitors.

The February election that put Rush on the committee had been carefully planned. In January several self-styled "friends of America" had met at the Fountain Tavern "in order to consult and consider of proper persons to be elected" to the committee; they held a further caucus in early February, and then, two days before the election, settled on a ticket that included Rush's name. These actions were taken not by the gentlemen of the city, who for a half century had controlled its politics, but by men who up to that time had wielded little influence: the shoemakers, the shopkeepers, the blacksmiths. The key manipulators in this new power bloc were such men as James Cannon (schoolteacher), Timothy Matlack (brewer), Christopher Marshall (druggist), and Thomas Young (physician), with Thomas Paine and Benjamin Rush working on the periphery.

Zeal for an independent America united these men. But there was also something more: all to a degree were outsiders. Matlack and Marshall had both been read out of their Quaker meetings. Young, who had been one of the leaders in the Boston Tea Party, had become during his wanderings from Albany to Boston to Newport to Philadelphia something of a professional maverick in politics. Paine, with a wreck of a life behind him, had floated into Philadelphia slightly more than a year ago at the age of thirty-seven, full of animosity for the England he had just left. Cannon had emigrated to America in 1765, the same year that a fellow Scotsman, James Wilson, had. Both began teaching at the College of Philadelphia. Wilson had gone on to become one of Pennsylvania's most respected lawyers; Cannon, still at the college, tried to survive on the poor pay of an instructor in mathematics. Rush continued to consider himself ostracized by his colleagues, and the fact that he was the only member of the college medical faculty who had not been appointed to the staff of the Pennsylvania Hospital did nothing to give him the feeling of being accepted. All these men shared a strong desire to remake America, to purge it of ills that they had diagnosed. They had not yet got around to specifying what the ills were nor whether they agreed how they should be exorcised. At the moment they were obsessed by the issue of independence.

When the ballots were counted on February 14, thirty-two new members, virtually all men who were warm for independence, were placed on the inspection committee. Most of the new members were tradesmen and craftsmen, the sort of people Rush had for patients, and they wasted little time in broadening their mandate. Twelve days after the election, the Philadelphia group requested its local counterparts in the counties to choose delegates for a Provincial Convention to meet in Philadelphia. The purpose of the convention was, deliberately, phrased in vague terms: it would take "into consideration the present state of the province." Members of the Pennsylvania Assembly, who up to now had worked closely with the committee, suddenly found themselves "thwarted in their measures by a body of men from whom they expected to derive the firmest support." When word of the proposed convention first leaked out, one gentleman in the city wrote: "Tim. Matlack and a number of other violent wrongheaded people of the inferior class have been the chief promoters of this wild scheme; and it was opposed by the few *gentlemen* belonging to the committee—but they were outvoted by a great majority."[2]

The instigators of the convention aimed at one thing: to force Pennsylvania to accept the idea of independence. "The scheme of the convention was principally to get Andrew Allen and a few other good men removed from Congress," one man said. "They have stood forth and dared to expose the designs of the cunning men of the East [New England], and if they continue members of Congress will prevent this province from falling into their favorite plan of independency."[3] The men behind the "scheme" had petitioned the assembly earlier to change the instructions of Pennsylvania's delegation in Congress so they might vote for independence if the question came up. The assembly had refused. The proponents of independence then took a subtler tack. The sentiment for independence was assumed to be strongest in the back counties of Pennsylvania. These counties, along with the city of Philadelphia, were notoriously underrepresented in the state legislature. The three eastern counties of Bucks, Philadelphia, and Chester had long controlled Pennsylvania politics. Complaints about their extensive influence turned up occasionally, and even moderate men in the three counties thought the situation unfair. But no outraged populace tried to improve its political position; Pennsylvanians did not care that much about politics. Still, the discrimination existed and the Independents, as those who favored separation from England were now being called, decided to use it to further their designs. They sounded out the assembly about revising the representation along more equitable lines. They hoped that once the city and back counties got their share of seats, the Independents would be able to manipulate the legislature. But again the assembly balked. This second rebuff had resulted in the call for the Provincial Convention.

The committee's decision stirred up a great noise through the city, at least among the "thinking people." These people, according to one report, said "that when they elected a committee it was for a particular purpose but by no means as a legislature in the room of the assembly. If they had imagined that to be the case, there would have been ten times the number of electors."[4]

Public pressure may have influenced the committee to back down. A more decisive reason would seem to have been the assembly's willingness to compromise. Dickinson and Reed, members of both bodies, worked out an acceptable proposal, and on March 8 the forty-one-member assembly reluctantly agreed to enlarge its membership by seventeen seats—four to go to the city and thirteen to the back counties. The eastern counties, understandably, received nothing. Like most workable compromises, this one satisfied both sides. It stopped the "mouths of those violent Republicans belonging to the committee. . . ." They were appeased because they were convinced that the people would fill all seventeen seats with men who shared their views on independence. It pleased the assembly because it righted a long-known wrong and at the same time fended off, for a while at least, the most serious threat to its existence that the legislature had faced. The question of amending Pennsylvania's instructions to its delegates in Congress had been bypassed. The decision was left up to the men the people would send to the enlarged assembly.

Rush's hand in this maneuvering remains hidden. He once said without elaborating that from the time he joined the committee he "took an active part both in [its] debates and business." His reputation as a writer may have caused him to help in drafting the circular letter sent to all county committees explaining why it was rescinding the call for a convention. "As the present unequal distribution is the ground of every other complaint," it stated, "the committee had this principally in view." When the assembly amended its stand on the matter, the letter continued, "further need for a convention ended."⁵ Had overconfidence in its ability to elect Independents led the committee into a tactical mistake? What if the people failed to give the Independents control of the assembly? The assembly had generously gratified the committee's greatest wish; in admitting this, the committee had left itself with no sound excuse for complaining, regardless of the assembly's future action.

2

  The assembly designated May 1 for the election. The date had hardly been set when a Moderate faction, standing for reconciliation, and an Independent faction took form. The Moderates, on the defensive for the first time, began to campaign at once. Many wrote letters to like-minded friends in Lancaster, York, Carlisle, and other parts of the backcountry, urging them to run for one of the open seats in their counties. But their efforts centered on Philadelphia. They now realized, belatedly, that to lose control of Philadelphia meant to lose control of Pennsylvania.

  The Reverend William Smith, a Church of England divine and the college provost Rush had warned John Adams about in 1774, became the Moderates' chief publicist. Rush said he "possessed genius, taste, and learning," excelled as a speaker, but also swore and drank. Years earlier Dr. Smith had sold himself and his ideas on education—less Greek and Latin, more emphasis on practical subjects—to Franklin, who drew him to Philadelphia to head the college. Rush liked his ideas on education but little else about the man. "It was a favorite maxim with him," Rush once said, "that to gain mankind it was necessary not to respect them." Neither man, in fact, wasted much love on the other. Years after both had died, an old-timer recalled a story about them. "About the commencement of the Revolution of 1776 the gentlemen of Philadelphia were in the habit of meeting every day in the old City Hall, in Market Street below Third," he wrote. "One day the meeting had taken place, and after a while Dr. Smith entered the hall. Dr. Benjamin Rush was there, and, walking up to the doctor, said: 'Dr. Smith, we have come to the conclusion that you are the author of _____' (*Publius,* I think, an article which had appeared in one of the newspapers). The doctor regarded Rush with a glance of dignified contempt, and said: 'Ben Rush, I knew you when you were *so* high,' holding his hand about three feet from the floor. 'You are no higher yet, mon.' No more was said on that subject."[6]

As "Cato," Smith squared off at the Independents in a series of newspaper articles, the first one appearing on March 13, only five days after the assembly had agreed to compromise. In the opening article he unmasked what he thought was the inspection committee's misleading invitation: that the calling of the Provincial Convention would serve to give rule to all the people of the colony and not just the privileged few in the eastern counties. If the convention did meet, he wrote, "and could succeed in assuming the powers of government, they must all at length be vested, for the sake of execution, in the hands of a *few men,* who consider themselves as leaders in the city of Philadelphia; and the province in general have but little to say in the matter."[7]

From this point Smith moved to the merits of reconciliation. He approached the issue by two routes. He began by unfolding the first full-scale, intelligent attack made on *Common Sense,* elaborating on the advantages of the tie to Great Britain, then concentrating on Paine's theories of government. This, in turn, directed him into extended praise for the glories of Pennsylvania's government. And so far as he could see, the Independents had coupled the idea of independence with political revolution. To vote for them was to risk overturning Pennsylvania's constitution. None of the moderate-minded men among the Independents, such as Benjamin Rush, who would soon mourn the passing of the assembly, attempted to answer this side of Smith's argument.

"Cato" provoked some of the ablest penmen among the Independents into public replies. None of the rebuttals, however, can definitely be traced to Rush, who appears for once to have allowed others to speak for him. If this seems unlikely, then possibly he suppressed his contributions out of respect for his later conservative views on government. The scurrilous attack by James Cannon, writing under the name "Cassandra," suggested that Cannon's position on Smith's faculty influenced his judgment. Cannon emptied his invective upon Smith's personal failings, then turned to answer the criticisms of the committee by saying in essence that it represented the people more truly than the assembly. "The Forester," whom the city promptly and correctly took to be Thomas Paine, concentrated on replying to "Cato's" attack on *Common Sense.* Another·writer lampooned the Moderates' campaign, which John Dickinson, now standing resolutely for reconciliation with England, had joined. "How many poor men, common men, and mechanics have been made happy within this fortnight by a shake of the hand, a pleasing smile and a little familiar chat with gentlemen. . . . This year their humility is amazing; for they have stooped to the drudgery of going from house to house to circulate election lies about division of property. . . . Do you think ever Mr. J_____ _____ would ever speak to you, if it were not for the May election? Be freemen then, and you will be companions for gentlemen annually."[8]

The Independents lost their light touch as the campaign advanced, and the issue of suffrage qualifications came to the front. Pennsylvania law, like that of most colonies, required that for a man to be entitled to vote he must be over twenty-one, white, a Christian, and swear or affirm that he was worth fifty pounds currency or owned fifty acres of cleared land. Actually, the law deprived few who really wanted it of the right to vote. "The only end this answered was that of tempting men to forswear themselves," said Paine. "Every man with a chest of tools, a few implements of husbandry, a few spare clothes, a bed and a few household utensils, a few articles for sale in a window, or almost anything else he could call or even think his own, supposed himself within the pale of an oath, and made no hesitation of taking it."

The appearance of "associators" on the scene, however, introduced a new element into the voting question. Years earlier the pacifist Quakers had prevented the creation of a militia organized and supported by the province. But under Benjamin Franklin's initiative, informal associations of able-bodied men in each county had eventually been formed. These associators were Pennsylvania's equivalent of the militia in other colonies. Two days before the election, one who called himself "Elector" came forth with a novel suggestion: that all men in the armed forces, regardless of age, length of residence in Pennsylvania, or amount of property owned, deserved the vote. "Elector" was immediately reminded that "a great number of the associators in this city are minors and apprentices, a great number of them new men lately arrived among us, who know not the happy form of the government of Pennsylvania. . . ." "Elector's" radical ideas may have seriously hurt the Independents' chances, for voters were cautioned by another that his *"novel system* . . . may teach us what we are to expect, should we suffer men, professing such principles, to get the direction of our affairs." Once again, no moderate man among the Independents attempted to separate the "Elector's" rash proposal from the drive for independence.[9]

3

The election was a tumultuous affair, with both sides canvassing the city for votes from sunup until the polls closed at midnight. The Independents went to bed certain they had won, only to find the next morning that the Moderates had swept the city, winning three out of the four new seats. A more painful disappointment hit the Independents later in the week when results from the eight western counties rolled in. A final tally of the backcountry vote showed that even if the Independents had won all Philadelphia, they still could not have gained control of the assembly.

The election affected Congress. Pennsylvania was America's economic keystone, or, as one man phrased it, "what the heart is to the human body in circulating the blood." America could not move toward independence until Pennsylvania was persuaded to go along. The May election results demonstrated that the Moderates reflected rather than lagged behind public opinion in that colony. Since Pennsylvania set the pace for the Middle Colonies, her faith in reconciliation only bolstered the faith of moderate men in New York, New Jersey, Delaware, and Maryland.

This seemingly settled situation, however, changed abruptly. First came news that instead of sending peace commissioners in response to Congress's last petition for "harmony," the king had dispatched foreign troops to American shores. "You will see by the papers," one man said, "what a formidable armament we are daily to expect—45,000 *commissioners*, at least, of different nations, that is to say Hessians, Hanoverians. . . ." This news fixed the minds of many for independence. Rush all his life decried "the absurd and frivolous reasons" that led many Americans to favor independence. Of the man who told him he was ready for it now that he knew Hessians were coming to "assist in subjugating us," Rush said: "Foolish man! As if there was any difference between being killed by a Hessian and a British bayonet!"[10]

As this news reverberated, word arrived in the city on May 6 that the *Liverpool* and *Roebuck*, two British men-of-war, had left their patrolling stations at the mouth of the Delaware and were coming "up our bay and river sounding and filling water and it is thought were making themselves acquainted with the channel for no good purpose." Early in the afternoon the "alarm guns," which were fired only when an attack was imminent, echoed through the city. They "put the town into some consternation for a short time."[11] Congress continued in session, for after the first flush of excitement people realized the ships still lay several miles downriver and if they planned to attack the city it would not be that day. John Adams, hoping perhaps the alarm guns might panic timid members, asked Congress to recommend that all colonies that had limited the power of their delegates to vote for independence "repeal or suspend those instructions for a time." The motion was defeated.

May 7 passed quietly, though through the day the muffled boom of firing cannons could be heard from downriver. The news next evening was good. The *Roebuck* had been forced aground and the city's armed row galleys had her surrounded. During the night the *Roebuck* drifted free on the high tide. The firing resumed once again May 9, this time farther up the river, closer to the city. Thousands of citizens turned out along the shores to watch the galleys cautiously lob their shots from great distances toward the slow-moving warships. The battle was carried on half-heartedly during the early afternoon; toward sunset the tempo picked up and the "firing was very heavy; we counted distinctly sixty in seven minutes." The firing ceased around seven o'clock, then, admitting to a draw, the warships slowly swung about and sailed back down the river to their patrolling stations. Rush, as the fleet's physician-surgeon, no doubt spent the evening visiting the crews of the galleys and attending to casualties. Thus began his direct participation in the war.

The retreating warships left behind an undamaged but changed city. One man canceled his planned tour of the county courts, for "my family are too much alarmed to make it eligible for me to be absent." Another put his house up for sale. A visitor paying calls found his friends absent because "the appearance of the king's ships so far up the river made them hurry their families out of town." The feeling of all was that "a larger force will come against us."[12]

On May 10, shortly after the news that Hessians were on their way had been substantiated and less than twenty-four hours after Philadelphia had been jarred from complacency by the sounds of battle, John Adams made a bold move in Congress. He offered a resolution requesting all colonies "where no government sufficient to the exigencies of their affairs have been hitherto established" to erect such governments immediately. The resolution was designed to promote a change of government in Pennsylvania. John Dickinson, doubtless to Adams' astonishment, approved of the measure, adding that of course it did not apply to Pennsylvania, which already had a government "sufficient to the exigencies of their affairs" and one to which the voters had just given a mandate. The liberties and rights the colonies now fought to preserve, he argued, were amply protected in Pennsylvania by the Charter of Privileges of 1701, which, among other things, gave the assembly the right to initiate all legislation; moreover, the assembly functioned so smoothly that Pennsylvania's contribution to the war in men and materials exceeded that of any other colony. With Pennsylvania's unexpected blessing, the measure passed easily.[13]

John Adams refused to be outmaneuvered. All important resolutions of Congress were dignified with a high-sounding preamble before they reached the public. Adams used this device effectively to block the loopholes in his measure. His preamble stated in essence that "it appears absolutely irreconcilable to reason and good conscience, for the people of the colonies now to take the oaths and affirmations necessary for the support of any government under the crown of Great Britain, and it is necessary that the exercise of every kind of authority under the said crown should be totally suppressed. . . ."[14]

The target of the preamble was unquestionably Pennsylvania, where the assembly still took oaths of loyalty to the crown, where the king's justice was still practiced in the courts, and where the general official tone of the colony still approved the king's authority. James Wilson dispelled any doubts about the purpose of the preamble on May 15, the day Congress debated it, by saying: "In this province if that preamble passes, there will be an immediate dissolution of every kind of authority; the people will be instantly in a state of nature. Why, then, precipitate this measure? Before we are prepared to build a new house, why should we pull down the old one, and expose ourselves to all the inclemencies of the season?"[15]

The preamble came up for vote in the early afternoon, the ballots being cast as usual by colonies. Six colonies (the four of New England, plus Virginia and South Carolina) voted for the measure, and four (North Carolina, New York, New Jersey, and Delaware) voted against it. Georgia was absent; Pennsylvania and Maryland abstained. "Most of those here who are *termed the cool considerate men* think it amounts to a declaration of independence," Caesar Rodney of Delaware said shortly after the vote had been taken.[16]

4

Rush convinced himself—correctly—that the success of the drive for independence in Pennsylvania depended on a select few, among whom he was one. "General Mifflin and all the delegates from the independent colonies rely chiefly upon me . . ." he wrote at one point to his wife, then visiting her parents in Princeton. Rush paused over the boast, then lined out "me" and continued: ". . . Colonel [Thomas] McKean and a few more of us for the salvation of this province."[17]

By "salvation," Rush meant, of course, independence. And to achieve that objective he and the "few more of us" boldly plotted to bring about nothing less than a revolution in the state government. Their chances of success had improved greatly since the May 1 election. The river battle had bolstered the confidence of Philadelphians; "British ships of war will not be thought so formidable," one Independent wrote.[18] More than that, it forcefully brought home to the city's inhabitants, as they heard the thundering guns and faced the threat of bombardment, that whether they liked it or not they were engaged in a shooting war in which their lives and their property were at stake.

The river battle, augmented by news of foreign troops, provided the combustibles which, if ignited, might swing Philadelphia into the independence column. Yet the city only two weeks earlier had voted down the Independents' candidates. In 1776, the tradition had already developed that regardless of the ill will generated in any campaign, regardless of how wide the split between contending factions, the results of an election were accepted by both sides. The loser did not cease to oppose, but he opposed from within the prevailing political framework; he did not threaten to overthrow the government because he had lost the opportunity to run it. After May 15, Philadelphia's Independents chose to ignore this tradition. They were convinced that the drive for separation would fail if Pennsylvania could not be forced into line. These otherwise cautious, prudent men, therefore, suddenly and willingly began using dubious means to achieve their ends. They were, after all, locked in a crusade. "The hand of heaven is with us. Did I not think so, I would not have embarked in it," Rush told his wife; then, knowing she "had all the timidity of her sex as to the issues of the war and the fate of her husband," he added: "You have everything to hope and nothing to fear from the part which duty to God, to my country, and to my conscience have led me to take in our affairs. The measures which I have proposed have hitherto been so successful that I am *constrained* to believe I act under the directions of Providence."[19]

The exact measures Rush proposed to push Pennsylvania toward independence are lost in the covert strategies he and his cohorts carried out through May. On May 14 he sat on a committee that met "to take into consideration and to concert a plan necessary to be adopted on the meeting of our assembly next second day," and it may have been he who suggested the idea of a mass meeting to put pressure on the legislature. Rush became so involved in revolutionary activity that on May 18 he saw only one patient and on May 19, the day before the mass meeting, he saw none.[20]

The meeting was well planned. By ten o'clock in the morning, May 20, some four thousand people had crowded into the brick-walled yard behind the State House, where Congress was meeting on the first floor and the assembly was about to convene on the second. Rain fell steadily, but the crowd did not leave. From a rickety platform Daniel Roberdeau, moderator of the gathering, read Congress's resolution of May 15 "in a loud stentorian voice that might be heard a quarter of a mile." The people cheered the measure mightily. Roberdeau then read aloud several resolves that had been carefully prepared by leaders of the Independents before the meeting. The first said that the assembly's instructions "have a dangerous tendency to withdraw this province from that *happy union* with the other colonies, which we consider both as our *glory* and *protection*." The crowd passed it unanimously. The second said that since the assembly lacked the authority of the people it would be assuming arbitrary power if it sat this session. One man dared to vote against this; he was "abused and insulted," reported an observer, and he thereupon "thought it prudent to vote with the multitude." Next, it was agreed unanimously that the present government was not "competent to the exigencies of our affairs." Finally, the crowd voted as one to call a Provincial Conference of county committees to draw up plans for a constitutional convention.[21]

One of the delegates who watched these proceedings was impressed by how neatly the intent of Congress had been distorted. The compelling argument in the preamble's favor had been the necessity for regular governments. The throng at the mass meeting had voted to demolish their regular government. "By their mode it will be impossible for them to have any government for three months to come, and during that time much confusion," Caesar Rodney observed. "If the present assembly should take order in the matter, the work would be done in one quarter of the time." But the Independents were careful to maintain that they were not demolishing their regular government. Roberdeau ended the meeting reading aloud a "Protest" against the assembly. Buried within the document was this tortuous but revealing sentence:

> In thus protesting against the authority of the House for framing a new government, we mean not to object against its exercising the proper powers it has hitherto been accustomed to use . . . until such time as a new constitution originating from and founded on *"the authority of the people"* shall be finally settled by a Provincial Convention to be elected for that purpose, and until the proper officers and representatives of the people shall be chosen agreeable thereto and qualified to succeed this House.

The assembly, then, would continue to function while the source of governmental power was transferred from the crown and proprietors to the people. The transfer, supposedly, would be orderly. Those who had written the "Protest," however, failed to see in their political innocence what a politician like Rodney knew from instinct: you cannot destroy confidence in an institution and expect it to continue functioning with public support.[22]

5

The Pennsylvania Assembly convened May 21, and one legislator, shortly thereafter, suggested that Congress be asked to clarify the meaning of John Adams' measure. If Congress agreed that the assembly, after eliminating all vestiges of royal authority in Pennsylvania, was qualified to run the colony's affairs, the revolution would be stopped in its tracks. Rush got off a hasty note to Richard Henry Lee of Virginia, at the time one of Rush's closest friends in Congress and the leader of the southern contingent pushing for independence. The note warned Lee that the assembly's seemingly innocent request "shows a design to enslave the people of Pennsylvania." He continued: "I conjure you . . . not to desert us in this trying exigency. Four-fifths of the inhabitants of our colony will fly to the *ultima ratio* before they will submit to a new government formed by the present assembly. Please to circulate the papers you will receive herewith among *all* the Southern delegates tomorrow morning."[23]

The brace of Adamses took a hand in helping the city Independents block the assembly's request for clarification. On May 23 Christopher Marshall visited Samuel and John Adams at their lodgings before breakfast. In the afternoon, after Congress adjourned, the two Adamses visited Marshall at his home. After they departed, Marshall, briefed by the experts, dropped over to James Cannon's place where they were joined by Rush, Matlack, and Paine. The next day they had completed a "Memorial," which went to Congress on May 25. The "Memorial" sought only to discredit the assembly further. "This situation of our province," it said, "requires vigor and harmony in the direction of both civil and military affairs, but these can never be obtained when a people no longer confide in their rulers." It parried the assembly stratagem for clarification by flattering Congress. "The committee have too much confidence in the wisdom of your body, to believe (when informed of the true situation of the province) that you meant not to include the assembly thereof in your recommendations to 'assemblies' to form new governments."[24]

The Moderates refused to be silenced. The day after the mass meeting, May 21, they were circulating a "Remonstrance" that reminded citizens Congress had no business interfering in Pennsylvania politics and therefore "the representatives of the people are left as the sole judges whether their governments be 'sufficient for the exigencies of their affairs.'" It pointed out, too, that in Pennsylvania "courts of law are open [and] justice has been administered with a due attention to our circumstances. . . ." The "Remonstrance" was "carried by numbers two by two into almost all parts of the town to be signed by all (tag, longtail, and bob), and also sent into the country and much promoted by the Quakers." Some six thousand people eventually signed it.[25]

Despite these efforts, the effects of the "Remonstrance" gave the Moderates little to gloat about. "It gives me great pleasure to inform you,"

Rush told his wife, "that our cause continues to prosper in nine out of ten of the counties in our province. Two emissaries . . . were detected at Lancaster and York with the 'Remonstrance.' One of them fled; the other was arrested by a county committee and obliged to go off without gaining a single convert to Toryism. The 'Remonstrance' was burnt as treasonable libel upon the liberties of America in Reading in Berks County. Many hundreds who signed it in Philadelphia county have repented of their folly and scratched out their names. A German we are told in Oxford township (a spot watered with the Tory dew of the Reverend Dr. Smith's ministry) came up to the man who had by direct falsehood prevailed upon him to sign the 'Remonstrance,' and begged him to erase his name. The man refused it. The German in a passion took the paper out of his hands and tore it into a thousand pieces, saying at the same time, 'Now, sir, you tell me d____d lies again.' The 'Remonstrance' had eighty-six names subscribed to it." Rush's enthusiasm did not outrun the facts. The Germans took space in the press to say that "being imposed upon by misrepresentations" into signing the "Remonstrance," they now "publicly disclaim against the sentiments therein contained." Rush especially exulted over Provost Smith's situation. "Poor Dr. Smith is half distracted. You would hardly know him. The party that once protected him in his insolence and villainy are now in the situation that we are told the rocks and mountains will be in at the last day. They can no longer hide him from the impending wrath of an insulted people."²⁶

Rush gave his wife, whom he missed terribly while she visited at Morven, a day-by-day account of Philadelphia affairs during her absence at the end of May:

> May 24: "Mrs. [John] Hancock called to pay her compliments to our Aunt Boudinot. I waited upon General Washington. Dined at two o'clock *most luxuriously* upon cold ham and salad. Spent all the afternoon at home. Had a visit at five o'clock from Colonel Lee, who drank tea with me. We talked of nothing but the base defection of the Maryland Convention from the late resolve of Congress. The colonel said he should hate hereafter to breathe the contaminated air of that province in his way to Virginia."
>
> May 25: "Was called up at six o'clock to visit a patient near Frankford. Came home before nine and was favored with

a visit from Dr. [Samuel] Treat of Burlington and Mr. Rittenhouse. The latter breakfasted with me. Had the pleasure of my
mother and Adam Gordon's company to dine with me."

May 26: "Awoke!—but no Julia near me. I wafted a sigh
after her to Morven. Inoculated a New England officer recommended to me by General Mifflin. Dined with James [Finley]
and Adam at home. Was just preparing to go to church when I
was sent for to pay another visit to my patient near Frankford.
Met Mrs. Bache [Franklin's daughter] this evening in the street,
who told me she called upon you yesterday but did not leave her
name. Came in at nine o'clock and sat down at the southeast
corner of our common parlor to write the above letter to you."

May 27: "General Washington is to review all our city
battalions. The design of this is to give the Indian ambassadors
now among us an august idea of the military strength of our
province."

May 28: "Had a levee of clergymen to breakfast with me.
Had a visit from Mrs. Stamper, who took Adam home with her
after leaving much love for you. Had the pleasure of an old
schoolmate's company to drink tea with me. We spent two years
in Edinburgh together."

May 29: "Entertained Mr. Rittenhouse, Colonel Trumbull,
and Major Mifflin (cousin to the general) with a plain family
dinner. Expected General Gates and General Mifflin, who disappointed me. Spent the evening in company with five of the
backcountry assemblymen—*all* firm independents. Heard from
my brother that seven thousand men has risen in arms in Maryland to compel their convention to declare independence. *All's
for the best."*

June 1: "I hope, my dear, we shall see many happy days
in Philadelphia together, notwithstanding we have precluded
ourselves from the society of a few Tory families. 'I should have
blushed,' says 'Cato,' 'if "Cato's" house had stood secure and
flourished in a civil war.' I should have blushed much more to
have heard it said at such times as these that I shook hands or
drank madeira with men who would have sacrificed their country
to ambition or avarice. No, my dear, the spirit of my great an-

cestor [John Rush], who more than once dyed the sword which
hangs up in our bedchamber with the blood of the minions of
arbitrary power, *now* moves me to declare—the spirit of my ancestor did I say?—nay, I trust the spirit of God himself moves
me to declare that I will never desert the cause I am [embar]ked
in till I see the monster tyranny gnash [its] impotent teeth in
the dust in the province of Pennsylvania. This I think will be
the case on the eighteenth of next June, the day appointed for
the Provincial Convention."[27]

6

The news pouring into Philadelphia from all sections of the continent
during the spring and early summer of 1776 had been mixed. In mid-March
came word that the British had evacuated Boston. This raised the spirit of
Congress to a point where on April 6 it dared to declare the ports of all
America open to the world, which was its most defiant step yet toward taking the colonies outside the empire. In mid-May came what John Adams
called "the dismals from Canada"—news that the American forces there
had been routed and that the invasion commanded by Richard Montgomery,
who had been killed, and Benedict Arnold, who had been wounded, had
ended in disaster. The gloom this news evoked among the delegates did
not, however, retard the drift toward independence, which "every day rolls
in upon us . . . like a torrent," said Adams. On June 7 Richard Henry Lee,
as the senior delegate of his colony, rose and, in line with instructions from
his government, introduced a three-part resolution that asked Congress to
declare "that these United Colonies are, and of right ought to be, free and
independent "states," that measures should be taken "for forming foreign
alliances," and that "a plan of confederation" should be drawn up at
once. Aware that Congress was now traveling across treasonable ground,
Thomson noted in his congressional journal only that "certain resolutions"
had been "moved and discussed." The upshot of the discussion was that
all decisions on the issues raised should be postponed for three weeks.
    Meanwhile, on June 14, the Pennsylvania Assembly adjourned, hav-
ing achieved almost nothing during its three-week session. On the same
day Philadelphia's Committee of Inspection and Observation chose twenty-

five delegates for the Provincial Conference which was to meet four days later. Among those selected was Benjamin Rush.

Most of the deputies hoped that Benjamin Franklin would preside over the conference, but an attack of gout had immobilized Franklin, and the post went to McKean, a lawyer who had been in politics for twenty of his forty-two years. Though McKean was a man of talents, he was also a man "of great vanity, extremely fond of power and entirely governed by passions, ever pursuing the object present with warm, enthusiastic zeal without much reflection or forecast."[28]

The main job of the conference was relatively simple: to draw up rules for the constitutional convention soon to follow it. The conference sat for seven days straight without a break, meeting even on Sunday, for a delay might create an "unhappy circumstance" that would let the Moderates retrieve power. The conference went about its business in "a spirit of harmony," according to Christopher Marshall, who dismissed as trivial "some small bickering between Colonel Smith of York County and the members of Chester County, in which dispute Elisha Price of Chester got so beside himself so far that he run in the yard, jumped over the fence, so into the street, where he was pursued, took to his lodgings and continued, so as not to be capable to attend again."[29]

The conference had first to decide who could vote for deputies to the constitutional convention. A group of German associators submitted a petition asking that all who were taxable be entitled to vote. If a man— or boy—could fight for his country, so the reasoning went, he should be allowed to share in its political affairs. The conference agreed. It did not go to the lengths that "Elector" had urged during the election campaign, that *all* associators, regardless of age, deserved the right to vote. It decided that any member of a military organization who was twenty-one or older, had lived in Pennsylvania one year, and had paid either provincial or county taxes could vote in the election for convention delegates.

The conference widened the voting population to include those who favored independence, then narrowed it to exclude those who opposed it. Test oaths were required of all voters to prove that they would "support a government in this province on the authority of the people only." Next, it was agreed that an oath of religious conformity should be required of all who would stand for election to the constitutional convention. Every deputy must "profess faith in God the Father and in Jesus Christ His eternal Son, the true God, and in the Holy Spirit, one God blessed for evermore; and . . . acknowledge the Holy Scriptures of the Old and New Testament to be given by divine inspiration."

Rush was "the chief and zealous opposer" of the religious oath. He spoke at length to the conference against it, arguing that there were many good men who did not believe in the divinity of the Son of God. "I am not one of that class," he hastened to add, but no man, he went on, "whose morals were good should be exempted because he would not take that declaration." But the deputies wanted the oath, and it passed almost unanimously. Of late the war had revealed a growing amount of dissoluteness in Pennsylvania, and this breakdown of virtue had begun to worry some. "But are we not a sinful people?" asked one man. "Has not God a controversy with us? Where is the piety of our military men? I think the swearing and all manner of profaneness and confidence in our own strength, which are found among our undisciplined soldiery, promise no very good events."[30]

The rebuff on the religious oath did not squelch Rush. On Sunday, June 23, he urged the conference to publish an address favoring independence. The deputies chose him and James Smith, lawyer and member of Congress, to draw up an appropriate paper, which they had ready the following morning and which was adopted by the conference at once. The address resembled in several ways Thomas Jefferson's Declaration of Independence, which had been laid before Congress a few days earlier. It opened with a list of charges against the king: he has ignored our "petitions for a redress of our complicated grievances," he has "purchased foreign troops," he has "excited the savages . . . [and] also the Negroes." The king having done all these things, the compact between him and his colonists was now dissolved. The address ended with a brief appeal to the world:

> We do further call upon nations of Europe and appeal to the Great Arbiter and Governor of the empires of the world to witness for us that this declaration did not originate in ambition or in an impatience of lawful authority but that we were driven to it in obedience to the first principles of nature, by the oppressions and cruelties of the aforesaid King and Parliament of Great Britain as the only possible measure that was left us to preserve and establish our liberties and to transmit them inviolate to posterity."[31]

On June 25 the conference ended. The next day a broadside written by James Cannon appeared on the streets about a constitution for Pennsylvania. This new government, it declared, should be one founded on more than the people's authority; it should be controlled by the people. "Would it not be prudent," it asked rhetorically, "to instruct your deputies, when chosen, to reserve an annual return of all power into your hands." It took a strong view on the suffrage question: "Trust no man but such who is determined to extend the principle of a free annual election by ballot to all possible cases. . . . He who would incline to restrain it in any case whatever, where it can be conveniently exercised, loves not liberty." What sort of men should be chosen to create this constitution? "A government made for the common good should be framed by men who can have no interest besides the common interest of mankind . . . great and overgrown rich men will be improper to be trusted." Obviously, if the electors do not take care they will, as before, "have an aristocracy, or government of the great." Is training, intelligence, or learning needed for this job of making a constitution? Not at all. "Honesty, common sense, and a plain understanding, when unbiased by sinister motives, are fully equal to the task."

Cannon and his friends, among whom Rush up to now had been one, here gave fair warning of the kind of government they planned for Pennsylvania, if they could keep control of affairs for only a few weeks longer. For the times, it would be a radical republican government. In June of 1776, Rush said nothing in opposition to the points contained in Cannon's broadside or to the trend of events being shaped by members of the Provincial Conference. But years later he would write of these weeks: "The time is remembered with shame and indignation when the people of Pennsylvania were called upon to 'reject men of learning' in choosing a body of legislators to form a system of government of the state."[32] Rush's republicanism would have its limitations.

9

In and Out of Congress

1776–1777

1

THE THREE WEEKS' DELAY Congress had imposed on discussion of Richard Henry Lee's motion for a declaration of independence sufficed to effect a shift in the vote of several delegations—most notably Pennsylvania's. On July 1, as Congress sat informally as a committee of the whole, the vote had gone nine to two in favor of independence, with Pennsylvania and South Carolina opposed. Tuesday morning, July 2, the delegates walked through a heavy rain to cast their votes formally. A glance at the Pennsylvania delegation indicated a change would come there. Dickinson, who yesterday had stood "slender as a reed, pale as ashes" condemning the action Congress was about to take—all avenues for reconciliation had not yet been explored; the measure was ill-timed, precipitate—had absented himself from the chamber. So, too, had Robert Morris, who opposed independence because "it was an improper time" and because it "will neither promote the interest nor redound to the honor of America." James Wilson was there, but he had announced yesterday that having sensed a change in sentiment among the people of Pennsylvania during the past weeks he would vote for the measure. When Secretary Thomson, calling the roll, reached Pennsylvania, Benjamin Franklin, John Morton, and Wilson voted aye, and Thomas Willing and Charles Humphreys voted nay, thus placing the colony's vote in the affirmative column.

After the roll call had ended, Congress President John Hancock announced that the colonies—now states—had unanimously declared their independence of Great Britain. Every delegate present knew that the unanimity was more apparent than real. New York had abstained, on the ground it lacked instructions. In Maryland, Delaware, North and South Carolina, as well as Pennsylvania, the delegations had been bitterly divided.

Benjamin Rush preferred to emphasize the appearance rather than the reality of the vote. For him that great "leap in the dark" almost immediately "produced a new era" in Pennsylvania. Some two thousand of the state's troops soon after marched to New York, which momentarily expected to be invaded, and "the cry of them all is for BATTLE." The Tories were now silent, though "very surly," and "the spirit of liberty reigns triumphant in Pennsylvania." Rush thought Howe's campaign to take New York City would fail, that Horatio Gates would manage to hold off any British attack from Canada southward down the Hudson, and that Charles Lee would preserve the South from capture. But he saw a long war ahead, for the Declaration would certainly "produce union and new exertions in England in the same ratio that they have done in this country."[1]

On July 15, while Congress worried about continental affairs, Pennsylvania's constitutional convention convened in Philadelphia. This event, too, pleased Rush. "The proprietary gentry have retired to their country seats, and honest men have taken the seats they abused so much in the government of our state," he said. For Rush a long dominant elite had at last been cast out—the initial step required to make the Revolution a real revolution. Nor could he fault the convention's first major decision in usurping the power of the Pennsylvania Assembly. On July 20, it voted for a new delegation to represent the state in Congress; it chose Benjamin Rush as one of the eight members.[2]

Hours after hearing the news, he met John Adams on the street. Adams offered congratulations and Rush, glowing with pride and political innocence, said the new delegation would act with uncompromising honesty on the issues that it would confront in Congress. Adams smiled and said that to praise a politician's honesty "is saying a great deal of a public character, for political integrity is the rarest virtue in the whole world."[3]

Rush resigned as physician-surgeon of the galley fleet, a post he had held for ten months, and took his seat in Congress on July 22. A few days later—the day remains uncertain but probably came early in August—"I

subscribed a copy upon parchment of the Declaration of Independence."
He never forgot the scene—"the pensive and awful silence which pervaded
the house when we were called up, one after another, to the table of the
President of Congress to subscribe what was believed by many at that time
to be our own death warrants." Only once, as he remembered it, did anyone
break the silence. Benjamin Harrison of Virginia, a large, heavy man,
turned to Elbridge Gerry of Massachusetts at the table and said: "I shall
have a great advantage over you, Mr. Gerry, when we are all hung for what
we are now doing. From the size and weight of my body I shall die in a
few minutes, but from the lightness of your body you will dance in the
air an hour or two before you are dead." As Rush recalled, "this speech
procured a transient smile, but it was soon succeeded by the solemnity with
which the whole business was conducted."[4]

When Rush took his seat he already knew most of his colleagues.
Some, like John Witherspoon and his father-in-law Richard Stockton, now
representing New Jersey, were friends of long standing. Some he had
tended in sickness, some he had met in homes about the city, and some he
had entertained at his own table. But it was one thing to know these gentlemen socially and another to see them operating behind the closed doors of
their chamber in the State House. And it was one thing, he soon saw, to talk
politics and another to be a politician. "I find there is a great deal of difference between sporting a sentiment in a letter or over a glass of wine upon
politics," he said after taking his seat, "and discharging properly the duty
of a senator. I feel myself unequal to every part of my new situation except
where plain integrity is required."[5]

The fury of debate may at first have shocked Rush. He had scarcely
joined Congress when he heard Samuel Chase of Maryland insinuate from
the floor that New England troops had caused the failure of the Canadian
invasion. The failure, John Adams ripped back, emanated solely from "the
impudence of the gentleman from Maryland," and if Chase could only see
his failings he would beg from his knees for Congress's forgiveness, then
"afterwards retire with shame, and spend the remainder of his life in sack-
cloth and ashes, deploring the mischief he has done his country."[6]

Rush up to now, from his outside view, had venerated Congress and
most of the delegates. A short while after becoming one himself, he saw
"how little of the spirit of [the Declaration of Independence] actuated

many of the members of Congress who had just before subscribed it."
Whatever scathing judgments he made of colleagues at the time have disappeared, but something of his disillusionment shines through the temperate sketches composed many years later for his children. Robert Treat
Paine "opposed everything, and hence he got the name of the *Objection-
Maker.*" Samuel Chase "possessed more learning than knowledge, and
more of both than judgment," and "his speeches were more oratorical than
logical." A fondness for ceremonies and a want of "industry and punctuality in business" marked John Hancock, whose manners were "much influenced by frequent attacks of the gout, which gave a hypochondriacal pee-
vishness to his temper." Richard Stockton, though he favored independence,
revealed timidity "where bold measures were required."

Rush complimented while he censured—Hancock was "a disinterested
patriot" and even Chase admittedly "rendered great services to his country"
—but he had unreserved praise only for John Adams. "He saw the whole
of a subject at a single glance, and by a happy union of the powers of reasoning and persuasion often succeeded in carrying measures which were at
first sight of an unpopular nature," he said. "He was equally fearless of
men, and of the consequences of a bold assertion of his opinion in all his
speeches." Rush watched him only a few days on the floor and then knew
why all Congress "acknowledged him to be the first man in the House."

Of himself as congressman, Rush said only: "He aimed well."[7]

On the first day in Congress, Rush may have thought himself unequal
to his new situation, but on the second he spoke for ten minutes on the
proposed Articles of Confederation. The relatively small size of the State
House chamber encouraged audacity. "I felt that I was not thundering like
Cato in the Utica of our Committee of Inspection," he told his wife, recalling the Tuesday night committee meetings in the Philosophical Hall,
where sometimes all one hundred members showed up. "The audience is
truly respectable. Dr. Franklin alone is enough to confound with his presence a thousand such men as myself. I hope, however, in a little time to
experience the same freedom and confidence in speaking that I observe in
other members. I find even our illustrious body is marked with features of
human nature. We can talk nonsense now and then as well as our neighbors.
This reconciles me to myself."[8]

Rush found his confidence ten days later when he dared to give a full-fledged speech, again on the proposed Articles. The job of creating a fundamental law for the new nation revived divisive forces that had been dormant while Congress armed the country for war. The draft of the Articles before the delegates did little more than crystallize an informal arrangement that had taken form during the past two years. Among other things, it left the voting procedure as it was: each state would cast only one vote regardless of its size. This, particularly, Rush, as a member of a populous state, objected to. The first Congress in 1774 had been nearly ripped apart by the issue; yet the one-state, one-vote procedure was finally accepted as an expedient in a time of crisis. Now that the proposed constitution sought to formalize what had been considered temporary, Rush, for one, spoke up.

Congress represents the people, not the states, he said, and to destroy the idea of equal representation destroys part of our liberty. Moreover, voting by states "will tend to keep up colonial distinctions," and "it will promote factions in Congress and in the states. It will prevent the growth of freedom in America. We shall be loath to admit new colonies into the confederation." Finally, he said, "the voting by the number of free inhabitants will have one excellent effect, that of inducing the colonies to discourage slavery and to encourage the increase of their free inhabitants." Rush knew that delegates from the small states suspected his views were conditioned by the state he represented, and he tried to disarm their suspicion in his final words. "I would not have it understood," he said, "that I am pleading the cause of Pennsylvania. When I entered that door, I considered myself a citizen of America."[9]

No doubt colleagues praised the maiden speech, though some may have wondered about the remark that "China is not larger than one of our colonies." It was erudite—quotations from Abbé Raynal and Montesquieu, among others, buttressed points when needed—occasionally eloquent, and, as time would show, prescient. But it swayed no votes. The decision that states should cast ballots as single units was fixed in the Articles. It did, though, bring Rush to the delegates' attention. Five days later, on August 6, he was assigned to a committee investigating the defective powder made for the army. On August 7 he was added to the medical committee, whose current job was to expedite the flow of medicine to army hospitals.[10]

2

Word came from the South that summer that a British attempt to take Charleston had been successfully resisted. Meanwhile, the British, with a new army aboard, had sailed in with the largest fleet yet to invade the New World. Under the command of Admiral Lord Howe, brother of Sir William, it dropped anchor off New York City and sat there ominously as the month of July drifted to an end. Washington, with the Continental army brought down from Boston and reinforced by militia from Connecticut, New York, and Pennsylvania, worked to build up the defenses of the city.

The strategy of the British seemed obvious. They would take New York City, then move up the Hudson to join forces with Gen. Sir Guy Carleton in Canada, thereby isolating New England from the war. Washington sought to meet the expected attack on the city by spreading three of his divisions along Manhattan Island, one across the East River on Brooklyn Heights, and another further out on Long Island under Gen. John Sullivan. He expected General Howe to strike first at Manhattan. Howe surprised him by committing the bulk of his forces to a landing on Long Island on August 26. Skillfully, he outmaneuvered and surrounded Sullivan's forces, and fourteen hundred Americans were killed, wounded, or made prisoner. Among the prisoners was Sullivan. Only by luck and ingenuity did Washington extricate the men stationed on Brooklyn Heights and bring them across the East River onto Manhattan. "I am obliged to confess my want of confidence in the generality of the troops," Washington wrote Congress after the retreat. "Till of late, I had no doubt in my own mind of defending this place," he said, meaning New York City, "nor should I yet, if the men would do their duty. But this I despair of." Worse news followed. The militia were deserting in great numbers, "in some instances," he said, "by whole regiments." Pressed by the superior British forces, Washington abandoned New York City early in September and retreated northward toward Harlem Heights.

It was at this point that General Sullivan came on parole to Congress with a request from the British "for a committee of Congress to meet Lord Howe in their private capacity to confer upon peace with Great Britain." John Adams listened to the proposal, then turned to Rush in the next chair and said he "wished the first ball that had been fired on the day of the defeat of our army, had gone through [Sullivan's] head." Adams blunted that view only slightly when he rose to speak, calling Sullivan "a decoy duck, whom Lord Howe has sent among us to seduce us into a renunciation of our independence." Rush, too, spoke against the proposal. We have only lost a battle and a small island, he said, but New York still retains her independence. But suppose the state, suppose half the states, "nay, suppose all the states in the union except one had been conquered—still let that one not renounce her independence," he went on. "But I will go further: should this solitary state, the last repository of our freedom, be invaded, let her not survive her precious birthright, but in yielding to superior force, let her last breath be spent in uttering the word *independence.*"[11]

Neither Adams' brusqueness nor Rush's emotion swayed Congress, which voted to send a committee to hear Lord Howe's proposals. "It would seem as if mankind were made to be slaves," Adams told Rush as they walked home that afternoon, "and the sooner they fulfill their destiny the better." For all his bitterness, or perhaps because of it, Congress prevailed on Adams to join with Benjamin Franklin and Edward Rutledge as a committee of three to visit Howe. The committee returned a few days later with word that Lord Howe had no power to make any overtures until America renounced its independence. That ended talk of peace. Rush passed along to his wife a couple of the "many clever things" said during the interview with Howe. When his lordship had asked in what capacity he should receive the committee, Adams had answered: "In any capacity your lordship pleases except in that of *British subjects.*" When Howe remarked that America's defeat would mortify him, Franklin said: "I hope your lordship will be saved that mortification. America is able to take care of herself."[12]

Rush's mood in the early fall of 1776 varied somewhat with his correspondents. "No difficulties discourage us, no losses depress us," he wrote Dubourg at the time Congress talked of sending Franklin to Paris to negotiate an alliance. "We look only to heaven and France for succor, being resolved if we are subdued that our last breath shall be 'Independence upon the Court of Britain.'" To his wife he dismissed "the melancholy aspect" some wore for the loss of Long Island. Indeed, he even wished Howe might capture New York City, which would draw there all the Tories for miles around (as happened), much as molasses spread on a board attracts all the flies in a house, leaving America "purged of those rascals whose idleness or perfidy have brought most of our present calamities upon us." To Col. Anthony Wayne Rush talked of the "melancholy accounts of the distresses of our troops from wants of every kind" and worried about the torpid spirit of America. "I apprehend we have overrated the public virtue of our country."[13]

Rush wrote to Wayne, a fellow Pennsylvanian, because Congress, on September 24, had made Rush chairman of a committee of five to devise ways and means of furnishing provisions, medicines, and general supplies to the northern army, an anomalous force with two bickering commanders in chief, Philip Schuyler and Horatio Gates. Gates was taking one wing of the army into Canada, with Wayne as one of his field commanders. Wayne, who would soon be called "Mad Anthony" by his troops, and Rush shared similar temperaments, which may help to account for the friendship that developed between them. Washington, using phrases he might have applied to Rush, said of Wayne that he was "more active . . . than judicious and cautious. . . . Open to flattery, vain, easily imposed upon, liable to be drawn into scrapes."

The letters to Wayne asked for a listing of "all your wants," but Rush had no desire to be hedged in by his committee assignment, as indicated by his request for detailed accounts of "those who stand highest with you" in the army. "Duty and inclination will prompt me to do everything in my power to remedy abuses, correct delays, and reward merit of every kind in the army." Rush got along well with army officers. Since the outbreak of hostilities, he had become friends with not only Charles Lee but also Gates, and he continued to pass along to them any compliments picked up in Congress. But it was Wayne's career, perhaps because Wayne was a Pennsylvanian, that he worked hardest to promote. "Merit like yours will weigh heavily with Congress, but it must be held up in a pointed light to their view," he told Wayne as Congress prepared to appoint new brigadier generals. "Upon this account I beg leave to suggest to you that your friends in Congress (among whom I desire to be classed) will derive great support from a few words in your favor from General Gates. You must not omit improving this hint to your advantage." Wayne, the same age as Rush, continued through the war and after to accept his friend's advice with good humor.[14]

Though military problems preoccupied Congress during the fall of

1776, as the British drive pushed Washington off Long Island, out of New York City, and from one vantage point after another, it could not sidestep several lengthy debates about the army's medical department. Every discussion eventually focused on the raging antagonisms among the three key medical officers: Doctors Samuel Stringer, John Morgan, and William Shippen, Jr. Doubtless Rush played a large part after his appointment to the medical committee in attempting to resolve conflicting authorities among the three temperamental physicians, but whatever his role it remains lost in the unrecorded discussions around the committee table. It would seem, however, that the influence he exerted did not promote Morgan's authority.

The dissension between Director General Morgan and Stringer, the director of hospitals of the northern army, came before Congress in mid-August. The line of command set down by Congress had put Stringer under the director general. During the summer Morgan sought to use his authority to improve a miserable situation in the northern department's hospitals, which were then being flooded with sickly soldiers returning from the disastrous attempt to capture Canada. Stringer rebuffed all efforts to help, insisting he alone would run his department's hospitals. After listening to the recommendations of the medical committee on which Rush sat, Congress reversed its original organizational plan and in effect made Stringer autonomous by resolving that all directors of hospitals "possess the exclusive right of appointing surgeons and hospital officers of all kinds."[15]

This settlement was followed almost immediately by an outburst between Morgan and Shippen. About the time Rush entered Congress, Shippen had accepted an appointment as director of hospitals for the "flying camp," a collection of ten thousand troops from the Middle States to meet any emergency that might arise in protecting that region from a vantage point on the west bank of the Hudson River. With little to do, since all the fighting was occurring across the river, where the "flying camp" refused to venture, Shippen kept up a lively correspondence with friends in Congress, among them Rush. "The satisfaction you have given in your department will induce Congress to continue you, if possible," Rush wrote in September. He went on to suggest how Shippen could continue as director of hospitals while keeping up his private practice and lectures in Philadelphia, then ended: "I wish the same simplicity and economy were used in prescribing everywhere as we hear are used in the hospitals under your care," which might be construed as a dig at Morgan.[16]

In October, as the wounded from the battles on Long Island and Manhattan were moved to New Jersey, Congress sliced away more of Morgan's authority by specifically giving Shippen autonomy over all hospitals on the west side of the Hudson. Morgan objected, quite rightly, to the authority granted Shippen inasmuch as he, Morgan, had been assigned control over all Continental army hospitals. Nevertheless, he lived with the division of power until a few weeks later when Washington moved the army across the river. It seemed illogical that the director general should be subordinate to one technically under him, but thus it would be, to judge by Congress's last order on the matter. In November Shippen asked Congress to clarify the chain of command. He also wrote Rush. "Would not a new commission be necessary, describing the sphere of my action?" he asked. "I can't with propriety say what I know, least it look like finding fault with a man I have not had a good understanding with." Rush read the letter to Congress, which "immediately produced" a resolution giving Shippen full charge of all sick and wounded on the west side of the river and Morgan those on the east side. Rush did little or nothing to build a case for Morgan; perhaps his currently close friendship with Richard Henry Lee, Shippen's brother-in-law, swayed him to Shippen's side in the controversy. When in December Morgan came before the medical committee requesting more authority and more supplies, the most he got from the man whom he had done so much for as a youngster was sympathy. "I would not for ten times the consideration go through the toils and difficulties of your station," was all Rush had to say.[17]

Rush's cavalier attitude toward Morgan may have owed something to exhaustion. In addition to attending the sessions of Congress daily—so many members had absented themselves that the few still in town made a point of being on hand for each meeting—he continued his medical practice and at the same time met regularly with five congressional committees besides the medical committee. The committee on intelligence, created in mid-October with Rush as chairman, required the reading of all reports sent to Congress, for its purpose was to publish "authentic accounts" on the progress of the war. The committee on prisoners required Rush, among other duties, to visit the city jails where captured soldiers were being housed to make certain they were in good health and being well treated. As if this were not enough, he appears also to have acted as liaison between the Board of War and Pennsylvania's Committee of Safety, a group one congressman judged "a set of water gruel sons of b_____s," in the effort to work out jointly a set of defense plans for Philadelphia.[18]

A few months in Congress had shown that Rush had the energy, the instinct, the ruthlessness, and even a certain Machiavellian talent to become a superb politician. He lacked, it would soon be seen, patience. Also, with a living to earn, he lacked the time.

3

Rush did not cease to be a practicing physician upon his election to Congress. He saw patients every morning, then from nine until two or three in the afternoon he sat with the delegates in the first-floor chamber of the State House. After Congress broke for the day he had dinner, saw more patients, and, if required, attended a meeting of one of his several committees.

The timing of his election could not have been worse so far as his domestic life was concerned. His wife, as usual eager to avoid the heat of a Philadelphia summer, had gone again to her parents' home outside Princeton. She had hardly left when the congressman-physician pled for her return. "I cannot support the burden of public and private business which now lays upon my shoulders without you," he wrote. He promised that once she had his life back on an even keel she could "go to Morven again with your Papa when he goes to take charge of the government of New Jersey, an event which all parties say is inevitable." (It was not inevitable; William Livingston became New Jersey's first governor.) As with all summertime bachelors, Rush's life became steadily more disheveled, and his letters were filled with daily disasters—William, his Negro slave, "fell asleep as usual this evening"; Betsey, the maid, fled the moment she was needed. "My business suffers from the want of you," he pleaded. "Do come home as soon as possible, or I tremble at the consequences."[19]

Mrs. Rush returned, brought order back into her husband's life, and once again left, hoping for a lengthy rest at Morven. But again troubles descended. "My extreme hurry continues," Rush wrote almost immediately. "I was called up and obliged to go out last night. I am just now sent for to visit a family four miles in the country. What shall I do for horse, carriage, and William? Betsey is hunting a barber. My prentices are as irregular in their attendance upon the shop as ever. What a pretty figure will a life of forty or fifty years with a fine agreeable wife spent in this manner make in the history of a man! Oh dear! The Romans educated slaves only to the profession of physic for six hundred years. A wise nation! and a most suitable employment for slaves!" Another note four days later found Rush still lamenting. "I begin to sicken for your company. What will become of me a fortnight hence?" He refused, however, to beg for his wife's return. "I flatter myself that you will soon be infected with homesickness and that you will tease me in less than a fortnight to send William for you."[20]

For a time Rush's practice, while he served in Congress, flourished as never before. He saw sixteen patients on August 1, twelve the next day, including one who called him out of bed, twenty-six the next. So it continued through the month and into September. The character of the practice changed as it increased. In July he made nine visits for Congress to prisoners of war and soldiers stationed in the city. In August he billed Congress £7 6s. for twenty-six such visits and saw eighty-nine private patients. In September Congress paid him £138 14s., a month in which he also treated fifty-seven of his own patients. "I was willing to be poor, that my country might be free," he said. "The latter I hope will be granted, and contrary even to my wishes I find I am growing rich."[21]

As the news spread of Washington's precipitous retreat across New Jersey late in the autumn of 1776, Rush began to wind up his practice, either because he planned soon to join up with the army or because he wanted his affairs in order when the British invasion of Philadelphia that everyone now expected took place. In November he cut down on visits for Congress and treated only forty-one of his own patients. In December he saw a mere fifteen patients. During these months he made an effort to clean up his books and by the end of the year had gathered in the considerable sum of £458. He tried whenever possible to get paid in gold, for already a mild inflation had set in, with £5 in gold, he noted, now worth £6 in continental money.[22]

In Congress and out, Rush worried over large matters and small that had anything to do with the health of soldiers. One day he came upon a prisoner of war whose hair "was cut short all round by General Howe's orders." Rush immediately advocated for the army what eventually would be called the "G.I. haircut." "It saves time and trouble and prevents lice," he said. "It moreover prevents a soldier from suffering from rain, which often keeps the hair wet for hours afterwards."[23]

On November 22 Congress asked the medical committee to investigate the condition of a number of soldiers who had come into the city from the "flying camp" sick with what was variously called putrid or camp fever and what was quite likely typhoid. They had arrived in wagons without officers or surgeons, and along the way, according to Rush, "many died in the open air with hunger and cold." No arrangements for their care had been provided. By the end of December a gravedigger said the soldiers were dying "so fast that he cannot dig graves for them all, and so digs a large hole fifteen feet square and ten feet deep and so buries them two tier, and that the highest coffin is about five feet underground." On one day more than fifty soldiers were buried and by the end of the month the fever had spread to the civilian population, this at a time when smallpox had begun to be "much about" the city. All told, Rush later said, "there were buried in potter's field from November 1776 to March 1777, betwixt a thousand and eleven hundred soldiers, the chief of whom belonged to the flying camp." Three and a half years later Rush irrationally placed the blame for this catastrophe entirely on Shippen's failure to anticipate it, forgetting that six days after Congress called for an investigation of the soldiers' condition, he had written Shippen: "I am bound in justice to your fidelity, to inform you, that every person who comes from the camp, speaks in the most respectful terms of your conduct towards the sick and wounded under your care."[24]

While physicians coped with the camp fever and smallpox, the city learned that Washington was ferrying his harried army across the Delaware, beyond, he hoped, General Howe's reach. "The city alarmed with the news of Howe's army . . . proceeding for this place," Christopher Marshall reported in his diary on December 2. "Drums beat. A martial appearance. The shops shut. . . . Our people begin to pack up some things, wearing and bedding, etc." By the tenth, the panic, like the fever and the pox, had become epidemic, with "all ranks sending their goods out of the town into the country." In the evening of December 12, a bellman went "through the city, ordering every person to go this day and assist in entrenching the city."[25]

It was also on December 12 that Congress voted to adjourn and meet again twelve days later in the village of Baltimore. Samuel Adams, who rarely talked from the floor, ended the session with "a short but very animating speech," Rush recalled. "There was nothing very oratorical in his manner, but what he said infused a sudden vigor into the minds of every member of the House."[26]

Soon after Congress left town, Rush moved his furniture and books to a friend's house in the nearby village of Darby and then carried his wife to a relative's home in Maryland. His mother and sister, Rebecca, settled in at Rush Hill, the small house outside the city that Susanna Morris had bought to retire in when she felt the time had come to give up her business. With family and property as safe as possible, he joined a Philadelphia regiment ordered out to reinforce the Continental army, for "I was then resolved to stand or fall with my country."[27]

4

Rush left Philadelphia about December 20, the streets virtually empty, the shops shuttered, and so many of the inhabitants gone that to one observer the city seemed "as if it had been plundered," with only "a dark and silent wilderness of houses" left standing. After joining the Pennsylvania militia, then bivouacked at Bristol, a village just north of the city, Rush a few days later rode out with Joseph Reed to visit Washington at his headquarters above Bristol. Reed, at thirty-five, had begun to thicken about the middle. After graduating from the College of New Jersey he had read law in the office of Rush's father-in-law, Richard Stockton, then gone on for further study at the Middle Temple in London, returning to establish a prosperous practice in Philadelphia that carried him into politics while still in his twenties. He had traveled to Boston in 1775 as Washington's military secretary and since then had been advanced to the post of adjutant general. He talked discouragingly of the war as they traveled along. He praised the British soldiers' bravery and condemned the cowardice of the American troops, especially those of New England. Of John Dickinson he said: "Damn him, I wish the devil had him, when he wrote the Farmer's letters. He has begun an opposition to Great Britain which we have not strength to finish." He revealed a low regard for Washington as a military leader and put most of the blame for the calamities of the war on him. In his opinion Washington "was only fit to command a regiment," and he now despaired of success.[28]

Reed's gloom, though excessive, reflected the anxiety of all close to the war. Rush knew the war only secondhand and reacted to the crisis with the enthusiasm of a recruit. In the days that followed the talk with Reed he sent a stream of letters to Richard Henry Lee, then with Congress in Baltimore, begging "leave to suggest such things as have occurred to me" to expedite victory.[29]

Naturally, a multitude of imperative reforms occurred to Rush. Worried about so many matters that touched the war effort, he advised on virtually everything. He wanted to counter those who balked at accepting inflated continental currency by having Congress recommend state laws "to *fine* the person who refuses it, *severely.*" He worried about enlistments from New England, where an "excessive rage for privateering" then prevailed. He put forth for promotion acquaintances like Adam Stephen, who, though he drank to excess, had "genius as well as knowledge," and Hugh Mercer, a Scotch physician serving with the Virginia militia. He lamented over the suffering he saw among the troops, most of whom lacked proper winter clothing. He worried about the lack of funds to pay for spies.

Rush did more than worry, more than urge, suggest, or recommend. He demanded immediate action on his proposals. "Pray don't let this matter be neglected," he said of the currency problem; "our salvation hangs upon it." The forwarding of money to compensate spies should be "done in an *instant,*" not "debated and postponed in the usual way for two or three weeks." Congress should also deal instantly with the "clothing and officering of the army." Mercer's promotion "must not be neglected." "We must have an army," and "it must consist of seventy or eighty thousand men, and they must be fit for the field before the first day of May next."[30]

The peremptory tone of these letters owed something to natural impatience but more to his sudden exposure to Washington's vagabond army that had been whittled down to a mere twelve hundred regulars. While Reed sank further into despair, Rush worked feverishly to save what looked lost. Now that he saw the war from the soldier's point of view, he decided the time for caution had passed. "The *vis inertiae* of the Congress has almost ruined this country," he said. The situation called for swift, extreme measures, and to that end he made rash demands on Congress. "General Washington," he said, perhaps thinking back to an earlier crusade and the authority that had been given its leader, Oliver Cromwell, "must be invested with dictatorial power for a few months, or we are undone."[31]

5

Rush spent the night of December 23 at a farmhouse near Washington's headquarters. The next morning the general gave an hour to the congressman-physician. He seemed "much depressed" to his visitor "and lamented the ragged and dissolving state of his army in affecting terms." Rush assured him that despite "present difficulties and distresses" Congress backed him to a man. During the conversation Washington, with a preoccupied air, doodled constantly on slips of paper. One accidentally dropped to the floor and Rush, leaning to pick it up, saw the words Washington had been writing—"Victory or Death," the countersign, it turned out, when the next night Washington led his troops across the Delaware to Trenton.[32]

Rush missed the chance to share in that victory. After the talk with Washington, he left to rejoin Gen. John Cadwalader's regiment of Pennsylvania militia, which was to cross the river near Bristol and cut the enemy's line of retreat and reinforcement. Great blocks of floating ice frustrated Cadwalader's crossing, and after several tries the dejected, freezing army returned to Bristol in a swirling snowstorm, only to learn soon after that Washington had found a way over the river and surprised the Hessians at Trenton.

Cadwalader got his troops over the next day. The army camped at Burlington the following night, then on December 29 marched to Bordentown, and from there to Crosswicks. Rush felt himself part of a glorious enterprise. "There is no soil so dear to a soldier as that which is marked with the footsteps of a flying enemy—everything looks well," he said. "Our army increases daily, and our troops are impatient to avenge the injuries done to the state of New Jersey; the Tories fly with precipitation of guilty fear to General Howe."[33]

On New Year's Day Rush rode to Trenton to visit army friends—Generals Arthur St. Clair and Mercer and Col. Clement Biddle. They regaled him with details of the victory, and as the evening wore on noble assertions filled the air. General Mercer said solemnly that "he would cross the mountains and live among the Indians, rather than submit to the power of Great Britain in any of the civilized states." The talk died with arrival of news that the British, then at Princeton, apparently planned to move against Trenton. Washington called a council of war, and Mercer and St.

Clair took their leave of Rush. The staff could not agree whether to draw up Cadwalader's regiment from Crosswicks or leave it there as a diversion against the British. Gen. Henry Knox suggested asking Rush whether the Pennsylvania troops would mind serving directly under Washington temporarily. Rush was called into the room and the question put to him. He said Cadwalader and his men "would be very happy in being under his immediate command, and that I was sure they would instantly obey a summons to join his troops at Trenton." Later in the evening Washington handed Rush sealed orders for General Cadwalader which, after a three-hour ride through a damp, cold night, he delivered at one in the morning.[34]

Cadwalader's detachment of eighteen hundred men reached Trenton at seven in the morning, January 2. Rush went to St. Clair's quarters "and begged the favor of his bed for a few hours." He had barely fallen asleep when a gunshot startled him awake. A Negro woman, whose presence Rush left unexplained, entered the room wringing her hands, soon followed by St. Clair, who said the British had begun their advance. "What do you intend to do?" Rush asked. "Why, fight them," St. Clair said, taking down his sword "with a calmness such as I thought seldom took place at the expectation of battle." A short while later, as Rush marched with his own group toward the enemy, he asked a companion how he felt. "As if I were going to sit down to a good breakfast," came the reply. Rush's failure to volunteer his own thoughts suggests he felt like any normal man on the way to battle, more in the mood to lose than eat a good breakfast.[35]

Rush remembered what followed through a mist of fleeting impressions. He recalled Washington and his aides pounding past "in all the terrible aspect of war." He recollected General Mifflin, wearing a blanket coat, galloping at the head of a body of Pennsylvania troops and shouting at them to quicken their steps. General Knox stuck in his mind as "active and composed." At one point he passed Rush and shouted, "Your opinion last night was very fortunate for us. You have. . . ." Rush let the sentence hang unfinished when telling the story to his children, "for a man deserves no credit for an accident in which neither design nor judgment are discovered."[36]

These things Rush saw and heard as he moved about searching for the wounded. The first man he tended, a New Englander, had come stumbling up with his right hand shattered by a cannonball and hanging to his arm by a piece of skin. Rush did what he could for the soldier, then had him carried to a house outside Trenton that had been appropriated for a hospital. By nightfall the cannonading dropped off, and only the popping sounds of muskets echoed in the air. By then Rush had collected some twenty seriously wounded in the makeshift hospital located along the Delaware. There he and Dr. John Cochran—"he possesses humanity as well as skill and is dear to all who know him," said Rush—worked through the night. Finally, when the chance came to drop on some straw for a few hours' sleep, the horrors of war dawned on Rush. "I want words to describe the anguish of my soul, excited by the cries and groans and convulsions of the men who lay by my side," he said.[37]

Early on January 3, before the sun rose, Cochran slipped from the house and "went up to Trenton to inquire for our army." He returned to report that it "was not to be found," that the hospital appeared to be in a no-man's-land that might soon be occupied by the British. Rush and his assistants rounded up wagons and horses, piled in their patients, and started toward Bordentown, seven miles southeast of Trenton, where they supposed Washington had taken his forces. Along the way they heard firing but "we were ignorant from whence it came." They next learned Washington had traveled by way of Quaker Road, a little used route suggested to him, so Rush thought, by Colonel Reed, surprised the British at Princeton, and defeated them. "What do you think of Col. Joseph Reed's name not being mentioned in the histories of our Revolution as the person who suggested the retreat and escape of our army by the Quaker Road after the second battle of Trenton?" Rush asked years later. (Many other officers claimed the credit.) "That wise measure gained the victory at Princeton, saved our army from annihilation, and perhaps, considering the desponding state of the public mind at that time, it saved our country."[38]

Part of the way to Bordentown Rush trudged alongside Charles Willson Peale, the two of them "making speculations on what would be the issue of our struggle for independence," Peale later said. Rush seemed to think that the nation's affairs were not being handled as well as they could be. While patients and staff rested at Bordentown, news came of the victory at Princeton. Rush's reaction was mixed—with praise for "our brave troops for the patience with which they have undergone cold, hunger, and all the usual distresses of a winter's campaign"; with sadness over the reported death of General Mercer, a man whose "character was marked with all the traits of one of the heroes of antiquity"; with fury at the Hessians "for plundering the inhabitants of New Jersey." His feelings about the supposed abandonment by Washington of his hospital outside Trenton were temperate, given Rush's low boiling point, especially when under stress. His

strictures passed on to Richard Henry Lee were directed at "our commanders" and against their lack of "economy." "They confine their care
principally to military abuses, and too much neglect to inspect the quarter-
master, commissary, and medical departments," he said. "A general should
be great in minute things." Buried within this mild censure of George
Washington's leadership was the seed of disillusionment planted months
earlier by Adam Stephen.[39]

Rush moved his perambulating hospital from Bordentown to Princeton on January 6. On the outskirts of the town he crossed a battlefield "still
red in many places with human blood" and still populated here and there
with wounded men—among them General Mercer, whose rumored death
now proved to be false, and Capt. John McPherson of the British army.
Both were being tended by a British surgeon's mate, who turned them over
to Rush's care. (Technically Mercer was a British prisoner, having been
"obliged to give his parole in order to procure a surgeon from the enemy.")
Mercer suffered from several bayonet wounds, the worst in his belly, but
Rush thought, mistakenly, that he would survive. "He is in good spirits,
drinks plentifully, sleeps tolerably well, and talks cheerfully on all subjects,
as usual."[40]

Captain McPherson, who had been wounded in the lungs but would
recover "in consequence of the loss of 140 ounces of blood," asked if the
Dr. Rush who attended him had in Edinburgh been a friend of William
Leslie. When Rush nodded, McPherson revealed that Captain Leslie had
died at Princeton at the head of his company. Rush "wept for the first time
for a victory gained over British troops." Later he learned that Leslie's body
had been tossed in an American baggage wagon and carried to the village
of Pluckemin, some twenty-five miles north of Princeton. There a letter
found in his pocket identified him as a friend of Rush. Washington, on
learning this, had the Scotsman buried with military honors, "a mark of
respect to an enemy at that time very uncommon in our army," Rush later
told Leslie's sister, his once beloved Angelina. He was interred in the village's Presbyterian graveyard, and Rush eventually placed a tombstone over
the plot as testimony "of my affection for him and his worthy family."[41]

Distress over Leslie's death soon gave way to Rush's mounting enmity
toward the British. He found Princeton in ruins—a deserted, desolated
village with Nassau Hall damaged, the church burned, and nearly all the
homes plundered. Morven Hall, where he had courted and married his

wife, had been stripped of its furnishings, its barns emptied of grain, its livestock driven away. Rush estimated his father-in-law's loss at not "less than five thousand pounds." He heard tales of incredible barbarity on the part of British troops—of a chaplain murdered in "cool blood" after he had surrendered, of a wounded lieutenant who, though "he begged for quarters," was bayoneted thirteen times, "all the while crying for mercy."[42]

On Saturday, January 11, after four days in Princeton, Rush judged his patients—among them General Mercer, who died four days later—out of danger and left for Philadelphia, from where after a brief rest he planned to push on to rejoin Congress in Baltimore. Three weeks earlier, as Rush rode from Philadelphia toward Washington's headquarters, Paine had published the first of his *Crisis* essays. This one opened with the lines: "These are the times that try men's souls. The summer soldier and the sunshine patriot will, in this crisis, shrink from the service of their country; but he that stands it *now,* deserves the love and thanks of man and woman." Rush had responded before Paine's great appeal had come forth. Now, for the time being at least, the crisis appeared past. Rather than idle about camp tending wounded men others could car. for just as well, he must get back to Congress.

Before ending his informal tour of duty—officially Rush had served without pay as a civilian physician—Rush sent off two more practical suggestions to Richard Henry Lee. The first dealt with the treatment of prisoners by the British. When he had complained about their "hard fare," the British had replied: "Why do not the Congress appoint a commissary and send provisions to them?" That seemed reasonable to Rush, and he urged Congress to rouse itself "in behalf of our poor fellows." Six months later the delegates got around to appointing a commissary general for prisoners.[43]

The second concerned the medical department, which, he told Lee, "must undergo a revolution." He had just heard that Congress had solved the bickering between Morgan and Stringer by dismissing both from the service. Rush did not grieve over the decision nor question it, but he did hope nothing would be done about filling the vacant posts or tampering with the organization of army hospitals until his return. He knew "several worthy characters who should immediately be placed on the medical staff in our army." More important, he had seen enough of the excellent care the British gave their wounded to suggest some basic changes in the Ameri-

can medical setup before a new director general was appointed. He only
hinted at his strong feeling when he told Lee that as the British had abandoned Princeton, General Lord Cornwallis had seen to it that a surgeon
and five assistants were left to care for the wounded remaining on the battlefield. "I am sorry to say nothing of this kind was done by our generals."
The American army, he saw now, must adopt the British hospital system
if the wounded were to receive adequate care. Rush conveniently forgot
that three months earlier Morgan had urged on Congress "the plan of the
British establishment, which I am persuaded is more complete than any
that will be substituted in this place." At the time he had displayed no
enthusiasm for Morgan's proposal—perhaps because it was Morgan's, perhaps because it seemed wrong to ape the British. Now, after a few weeks'
active duty, he saw its merits and what had once been John Morgan's conception now became his.[44]

6

Rush left for Baltimore sometime around January 20. His wife saw
him off from Mount Welcome, cousin Elihu Hall's Maryland farm where
she now stayed, with the hope he would enjoy much "pleasure and frolick-
ing" in that town. He reported soon after arrival that life without her left
him miserable. "In this state of banishment from *home* and *you,* the music
of Corelli would serve only to increase my melancholy," he wrote her. "To
exchange a *whole* house for a *single* room—to *request* instead of *commanding* when the most trifling favor is wanted—and above all to give up a most
affectionate wife for the society of strangers—to lay aside freedom, ease,
and unbounded confidence in conversation for constant restraint and formality, are circumstances that illy agree with a man of my age and disposition."
    Rush not only now lived amid strangers but in a village he detested
at first sight. Rain turned the streets to mud. The well water tasted of salt.
Living costs were incredibly high, at least a hundred per cent higher than
in Philadelphia. He promptly urged the return of Congress to civilization,
which meant, of course, Philadelphia. Baltimore could not handle both
Congress and "the constant accession of strangers who have business with
Congress," he said. Moreover, "our return there will have the same effect
upon our politics that General Washington's late successes have had upon
our arms." Though only something like half the delegates had followed

the exodus south, Congress preferred misery to the possibility of capture
and voted to continue in Baltimore until Philadelphia seemed safe from
invasion.[45]

Rush complained more on paper than among his friends. While in
Baltimore, Matthew Thornton, a delegate from New Hampshire, found
himself abed and in the care of two physicians he called "Dr. Cash" and
"Dr. Surly." Rush, who as a friend stopped by two or three times a day to
chat, he nicknamed "Dr. Gay." "Dr. Gay," Thornton wrote home after one
visit, "tripped round, sung a tune, and told me 'all would end well.'"[46]

When John Adams arrived on February 4, Rush once again settled in
a chair next to him. Curiously, the Pennsylvania Constitution, which had
been promulgated the previous September, had brought the two men closer
together than ever. When he first saw the finished document, Rush had
reacted temperately. "It is thought by many people to be rather too much
upon the democratical order," he said, "for liberty is as apt to degenerate
into licentiousness as power is to become arbitrary." This guarded optimism
soon faded, to some extent because of John Adams' appraisal of the document. "You were my first preceptor in the science of government," Rush
admitted years later. "From you I learned to discover the danger of the
Constitution of Pennsylvania." When Adams had first read a printed copy
of it, he commented, according to Rush's recollection: "Good God! the
people of Pennsylvania in two years will be glad to petition the crown of
Britain for reconciliation in order to be delivered from the tyranny of their
constitution." Rush later told Adams he repeated that remark only "to
friends I can trust," failing to mention that he had inserted it in a brief
paragraph in the *Pennsylvania Evening Post* for 2 November 1776.[47]
Adams had little to lose from the indiscretion except his temper, but Rush,
whose presence in Congress depended on the sufferance of a Pennsylvania
Assembly controlled by gentlemen who favored the new constitution, risked
his political career by making it known, as he did, how he felt about the
document.

Among the first things he told Adams in Baltimore was of Reed's
despair of victory—not, he hastened to add, to injure Reed, whom he still
respected, but as "an instance of a man possessing and exercising military
spirit and activity and yet deficient in political fortitude"—and then leaned
over and, in a whisper, asked Adams if he thought America would win the

war. "Yes," said Adams, "if we fear God and repent our sins, I will see it out or go to heaven in its ruins." At another time Rush asked his friend if Americans were qualified for republican government. "No," said Adams, "and never should be till we were *ambitious to be poor.*" At still another time, when Congress discoursed on who should be sent as ambassadors to Europe, he asked what Adams now thought of that "piddling genius," Dickinson. "Mr. Dickinson is the most unfit man in the world to be sent abroad," came the answer. "He is such a friend to monarchy that he would prostrate himself at the feet of every throne he saw. I would prefer Dr. Witherspoon to him." Neither man ever received a foreign assignment.[48]

On every matter that came before Congress during Rush's month in Baltimore, he and Adams argued from the same side of the question. A debate over the propriety of a New England "congress" that had met to regulate prices found them both refusing to sanction the action. Adams' speech revealed a conception of the central government's powers that would one day make him a Federalist. The New England states, he said, "bore the same relation to the Congress that four counties bore to a single state." The counties could regulate local but not state affairs. Similarly, states could meet to discuss matters to which Congress was indifferent, "but they have no right to touch upon continental subjects." Rush followed Adams' lead to the extent that he even borrowed the county-state analogy. The New England gathering had usurped the power of Congress, he said, "as much as four counties would usurp the powers of legislation in a state should they attempt to tax themselves."[49]

In a later debate Rush and Adams each arose to oppose price controls by Congress, though inflation had become a serious problem throughout the colonies. Rush spoke at length on the subject, for price control had been tried and failed in Philadelphia when he served on the Committee of Inspection and Observation. How, then, he asked, could it be expected to succeed on the continental level, where the problem of enforcement seemed insuperable? Congress will diminish its authority and prestige by attempting to impose an unworkable law on the people. "The continent labors under a universal malady," he said, this time drawing on medicine for his analogy. "From the crown of her head to the sole of her feet she is full of disorders. She requires the most powerful tonic medicines. The resolution before you is nothing but an *opiate.* It may compose the continent for a night, but she will soon awaken to a fresh sense of her pain and misery."[50]

The analogy offended Richard Henry Lee, who favored price controls. "The learned doctor," he said with a sarcasm that suggests the friendship with Rush may have been drowned in the stream of letters from the front, "has mistook the disorder of the continent. He labors under a spasm, and spasms he knows require *palliative* medicines." Rush gave a temperate answer to the retort. "The gentleman from Virginia has miscalled the malady of the continent," he said. "It is not a spasm, but a dropsy. I beg leave to prescribe two remedies for it. First, raising the interest of the money we borrow to 6 per cent; this like a cold bath will give an immediate *spring* to our affairs. And second, *taxation;* this like *tapping* will diminish the quantity of our money, and give a proper value to what remains."[51]

The question of surrendering to Washington the power to appoint general officers, debated on February 19, again saw Rush and Adams allied. Rush, without referring to Washington, argued that such a move would undermine "the virtuous principles of republican government." The people's representatives must control the army. "If the motion," he said, "is passed, I shall move immediately afterwards that all the civil power of the continent may be transferred from our hands into the hands of the army, and that they may be proclaimed the highest power of the people." Once again Lee rose to the attack. "I wish the learned doctor would distinguish between the practice of children and men," he said. "Our generals would certainly make a judicious choice, and would not be governed by the principles which actuate boys at school."[52]

Adams, no doubt to the consternation of many, centered his objections to the plan unmistakably on Washington. "I have been distressed to see some members of this house disposed to idolize an image which their own hands have molten," he said. "I speak here of the superstitious veneration that is sometimes paid to General Washington. Altho' I honor him for his good qualities, yet in this house I feel myself his superior. In private life I shall always acknowledge that he is mine. It becomes us to attend early to the restraining [of] our army."[53] Rush and Adams had spoken out with equal force against the right of the commander in chief to appoint the army's general officers, but Adams had managed shrewdly to do what Rush forever would fail at when discussing Washington—to distinguish between the man and his office. Rush's failure helped to ruin him politically and would blot his reputation with historians into the twentieth century.

On February 20, Congress discussed a letter from Gen. Charles Lee, now a prisoner of war, who had written of Lord Howe's desire for another peace conference. Rush and Adams both spoke against the proposal but Rush at greater length. He attacked the timing—now, with Britain "alarmed with the fear of a French war," was no time to negotiate—and, surprisingly, the character of Lee, who, "with all his great qualities, possesses the weakness of being easily imposed upon" and whose judgments are "dictated by caprice and passion." Adams praised Lee's talents as a general but condemned his vanity. Congress vetoed the proposal unanimously.[54]

That same day, after weeks of discussion, a motion to raise the interest rates on loan certificates (government bonds) from 4 per cent to 6 ended in defeat, to the joint disgust of Rush and Adams. The first issue of these certificates, $5 million worth, had come in October 1776. The public's response was phlegmatic. "Very little was procured" from this issue, said Rush, and further ones proved harder to sell. By the end of the year citizens were preferring to put their spare cash in business enterprises, where the higher returns had become more attractive, especially in view of the mild form of inflation that had set in.[55] Objections in Congress to raising the interest rate came from delegates like Richard Henry Lee who feared the certificates would be snapped up by the mercantile North; the nation's debt would become concentrated in that section, thereby giving it after the war a grip on the financial policies of the central government. Still, up to the final vote Rush had thought the motion would pass, for a private count had shown eighteen members for and only ten against it. But the vote by states brought defeat, one more proof to Rush "of the impropriety of each state having a separate vote." Those for the motion had represented two-thirds of the nation's population; seven members representing five small states had defeated it. "This unjust mode of representation I hope will be altered in the Confederation," Rush said. "If it is not, it will end sooner or later in the ruin of the continent." Congress diluted these forebodings a few days later when it reversed itself and voted to raise the interest rates to 6 per cent. "This resolution brought immense sums of money into the treasury," Rush later boasted.[56]

On February 27, the medical committee, now chaired by Rush, submitted its revised version of a plan drawn largely by Shippen for reorganization of the medical department. Normally, in the covering letter that accompanied such proposals from his command Washington simply acknowledged without comment what was being sent. This time he had gone

out of the way to urge Shippen's plan on Congress. True, the plan called
for higher pay for physicians and surgeons, but Washington saw no other
way to attract able men into the service. Moreover, "it will in the end not
only be a saving to the public, but the only possible method of keeping an
army afoot," he said. "For my part, I am certain that if the army which I
hope we should have in the field this year is suffered to smolder away by
sickness, as it did in the last, *we must look for reinforcements from some
other places than our own states.*" These were strong, even threatening,
words. The plan, which was similar to Morgan's, owed much to the British
hospital system, but "we should not hesitate a moment in adopting their
regulations, when they so plainly tend to correct and improve our former
want of method and knowledge in this important department."[57] Congress
ordered the plan to lie on the table, for on that day the legislature held its
last session in Baltimore and voted to reconvene in Philadelphia on March 4.

February 27 also marked the end of the legislative team of Adams
and Rush. Earlier in the month the first Pennsylvania Assembly under the
new constitution had chosen a new delegation for Congress in which Rush's
name did not appear. The past few months, privately and in print, he had
attacked the state's new constitution; now his opposition had been rewarded.
"Welcome this storm of popular rage!" he told his wife when he heard that
the assembly intended to dismiss him. "I shall kiss the rod that smites. I
never was so weary of public life and never languished more for the sweets
of domestic life than since I parted last from you."[58]

10

"Here Ends the Chapter"

1777

1

EVERY MAN who perseveres when cut down deserves respect. Benjamin Rush seldom in a long life of battles took defeats with great grace, but he always endured them, repaired briefly to a corner, and soon returned to the strife. The dismissal from Congress—his worst humiliation to date—hurt deeply. Rush said little privately and nothing publicly that revealed his inner feelings, though the abrupt retirement from politics left him for once wondering where to go and what to do. Other factors compounded his uncertainty. He wanted to be with his wife, already five months pregnant with their first child, but he could not carry her to Philadelphia, for furniture had been moved from the house. Besides, the British might mount an attack on the city in the coming summer, and a harassing trip at that time could injure his wife or the baby, which was expected in July. The sensible thing to do would be to stay with Mrs. Rush at Mount Welcome until the child was born. But four months in the country was probably more than Rush could stand, especially at this moment in his nation's life.

Rush inched rather than jumped toward a decision. In the days of confusion after Congress adjourned in Baltimore, he appears to have gone to Hall's farm, then sometime in March carried his wife up to Rush Hill, eleven miles outside Philadelphia, to which his mother and Rebecca had retreated. John Adams visited the place later in the year and as a farmer himself admired its sixty acres, its two orchards and fine garden, and called it "the most airy and at the same time the most rural place in Pennsylvania," adding that it had "a charming brook, beautiful meadows, and clover in abundance."[1]

Rush passed the month of March marking time until he determined the next move. Perfunctorily, he submitted his accounts for service in Congress, listing £143 for the first period, £34 for the second, and adding £10 for traveling expenses to and from Baltimore.[2] Rusticated, with no patients to fill his days and only a family of women to talk with, he was driven in upon himself. The romance of revolution had waned, and now he began to ruminate about the affairs of men and the course of politics in a republic. He wrote an essay, signed only "S" (for Staunch Whig?), that the *Pennsylvania Packet* published March 18. For Rush it was a notable piece, the first from his pen for public consumption reflecting a disillusionment born of his weeks in Congress. The idea for the article had been suggested by Thomas Paine, who in his second *Crisis* essay had said that at a later time "I intend to distinguish between the different kind of persons who have been denominated Tories; for this I am clear in, that all are not so who have been called so, nor all men Whigs who were once thought so. . . ." But it was Carter Braxton, as the first draft of the essay reveals, who triggered Rush into writing it. Braxton, a delegate from Virginia, had proclaimed in Congress that he abhorred all New Englanders, their laws, their manners, their governments, and their religion. Distaste for Braxton's views led Rush to divide Americans into five classes, four of them uncomplimentary to those who fit the specifications. At the top of the list, but lowest in virtues, stood the Rank Tory, who loved slavery, hated liberty, Congress, and Continental money, and favored "unconditional submission to Great Britain." Next came the Moderate Man, who yearned for the status quo ante bellum. His views were shaped, like those of Braxton, by "a connection with men who held offices under the old government," by ties with the Church of England, and by an insatiable fondness for luxuries. He loved the Rank Tory and hated everything about New England and its people.

The Timid Whigs rated little better. As men of little faith, they exaggerated British power and underestimated America's capacity to survive. What the Timid Whigs by their doubts did to undermine the war effort the Furious Whigs did by violence. They hated Tories more than

British and wanted to suspend justice in order to root out and punish them, holding they "should be tomahawked, scalped, and roasted alive." Worse, they were "all cowards and skulk under the cover of an office, or a sickly family, when they are called to oppose the enemy in the field."

The Staunch Whigs alone, those "friends to liberty from principle," won praise. No misfortune dismayed these implacable foes of Great Britain. They favored "order and good government," they ruled with justice and mercy, and their faith in victory could not be shaken. "They esteem virtue and wisdom as the principal qualities in legislators," Rush wrote in an early draft, but on reflection he revised the sentence to read: "They esteem the loss of property, of friends, and even of life itself as nothing when compounded with the loss of liberty." Also in the published version he dropped a sixth class of men, Neither Whigs nor Tories who "have no principles of any kind," and a conclusion that credited the Declaration of Independence for cleansing the dross from America and leaving only Staunch Whigs in power.[3]

On March 24, six days after this essay appeared, Rush left his wife at Rush Hill and returned to Philadelphia. He took a room in a boarding-house run by a Miss Leonard, then, still marking time, made a halfhearted effort to revive his medical practice. He saw four patients on March 25, two the next day, but from then on only occasional entries appear in the daybook. He collected something on bills to old patients—an average of about £30 a month from March through June—but mainly he fretted about other things. Early in April, Howe put his army in motion. Rush thought for sure it headed toward Philadelphia—what better way "to chastise the people of America" than by taking its greatest city?—and that success would crown the drive. "There is a false confidence in the situation and strength of the city, and in the spirit and number of our troops," he said. The refugee problem that capture would precipitate distressed him. "Few of them I believe will fly for safety into the back parts of our state, owing to the difficulty of procuring tolerable accommodations, so much have the country families been crowded with refugees from this and the neighboring cities." These private views of the situation put him within a hairsbreadth of his public definition of the Timid Whig.[4]

Rush had further reason to be dispirited. About this time Horatio Gates passed through the city. During a conversation with him Rush men-

tioned Joseph Reed's comment that Washington "was only fit to command
a regiment." Gates remarked that Patrick Henry "had said the same thing
of him when he was appointed commander in chief." Rush liked and respected Henry and his judgment of a fellow Virginian impressed him. Also
at about this time, his friend Mifflin went out of his way to disparage Washington, saying "he was totally unfit for his situation, that he was fit only to
be the head clerk of a London countinghouse."

The only encouraging news Rush picked up in those early weeks back
in the city came out of Congress. In March the delegates had begun to consider the reorganization plan for the army's medical department that Rush's
committee had put before it on February 27. The plan looked perfect on
paper. It eliminated the chance for such bickering that had developed under
Morgan's leadership by creating a more centrally controlled department; it
increased the powers of the director general, and his authority over deputies
was spelled out; and it provided for generous financial support for paying
physicians and surgeons, procuring medical supplies, and establishing hospitals. The plan failed, however, to create the post of commissary general
for the department, which would have relieved the director general of
housekeeping chores over a large organization and left him free to concentrate on medical matters.

Time would reveal other flaws not the fault of the new plan. Congress, for example, refused in the ensuing months to stop meddling in the
department's business; it kept tight control over appointments and never
hesitated to undermine the director general's authority by countermanding
orders it disapproved. Two further reasons for the continuing ineffectual-
ness of the medical department could be blamed on neither Congress nor
the reorganization plan. America lacked a physician of sufficient stature and
character to impose his views on the department and Congress. Yet even if
a Washington had been unearthed among the nation's physicians he would
have been swamped and defeated by the illnesses that pervaded the army
in 1777. A head count in July revealed 3,745 sick in the Continental army
and nearly every hospital bed occupied—this, several weeks *before* Howe
unleashed his attack on Philadelphia.[5]

When Congress reconvened in Philadelphia early in March, Rush no
doubt talked over with former colleagues on the medical committee and
among the delegates generally the virtues and defects of the reorganization

plan. It surely would have won his vote if he had been in Congress when it was finally approved on April 7. Four days later Congress chose Shippen to be the new director general—if the selection dismayed Rush, he kept the thought to himself—and, among other staff appointments, approved Benjamin Rush as surgeon general for the middle department, the region where all expected the coming campaign to center. Except for the physician general of the department, he would have only Shippen and his deputy, Thomas Bond, Jr., over him, and nothing up to now suggested he did not expect to work smoothly with his former teacher and colleague. The token support given Morgan earlier makes it seem he may even have preferred to work under Shippen.[6]

Rush regarded the appointment as a turning point in his life. The day after it came he saw one patient, and after entering the name in the daybook he wrote, "Here ends the chapter."[7]

2

Rush evidently made it plain that while willing to go on active duty at once, he wanted to stay something of a free man until the birth of his child. He had planned to bring Mrs. Rush into Philadelphia, but "as everything is now turned topsy-turvy in town," he wrote to her at Rush Hill, "I fear you will not spend your time very agreeably here." Nonetheless, on April 19 she came in. Rush allowed her to stay only briefly, then packed her off to Elihu Hall's farm. Once again he became a summertime bachelor.[8]

Rush momentarily relaxed his concern over his wife to write an essay "To the Officers in the Army of the United American States: Directions for Preserving the Health of Soldiers," to which the *Pennsylvania Packet* on April 22 gave over its entire front page.[9] Nothing he wrote during the Revolution had more lasting influence. A few passages, such as those that spoke of the foul air of marshes and swamps sowing "the seeds of bilious and intermitting fever," reflected eighteenth-century medical opinions. A few others, like those on temperance and the virtues of a vegetarian diet, had their origin in pet projects or theories. But for the most part his strictures hold up well after nearly two centuries.

At a moment when thousands of soldiers lay dying in army hospitals from ills unconnected with the battlefield, Rush dared to argue against all apparent common sense that "the mortality from the sickness in camps is not necessarily connected with a soldier's life." He held that bad diet, incorrect dress, and lack of cleanliness in the camps account for most of these deaths. He counseled officers never to crowd too many men into tents, never to let them lie in wet clothes after a march. Camps should be kept "clean of the offals of animals and of filth of all kinds." He warned against exposing troops "to *unnecessary* fatigue," which only invited disease. In a supposedly unwashed century he urged baths for soldiers at least twice a week. They should change their underclothing frequently. They should wash their utensils after every use.

Knowing that much of this rubbed against the grain of the time, he drew from the past to justify his argument. The healthiness of Roman armies owed something to the flannel shirts they wore; Rush believed that linen shirts promoted perspiration, which was "disposed to form miasmata which produce fevers." Roman troops took cold baths regularly, and this "contributed much to preserve their health." So, too, did the fact that "spirituous liquors were unknown to the armies of ancient Rome"; they carried vinegar in their canteens, which among other things calmed "the inordinate action of the solids which is created by hard duty." The addition of what would later be called wheat germ to the soldier's diet seemed sensible because "Caesar fed his troops with wheat only in his expedition into Gaul."

"If it be criminal in an officer to sacrifice the lives of thousands by his temerity in battle," Rush asked at the end of the essay, "why should it be thought less so to sacrifice twice their number in a hospital by his negligence?" The implied censure stirred up action among some officers in the army to whom he sent his piece. Gen. Nathanael Greene urged Washington to carry out some of the reforms. "Your own reputation, the protection of the country, and the success of the campaign are dependent upon the health of the army," he said. Soon afterward orders went out to place latrines and slaughter pens with more care. Soldiers were told to bathe more often and to eat more vegetables. Unfortunately, the improvements were nullified by the quickened tempo of the war. The most that could be said was that a start in military hygiene had been made.

The day the essay appeared Rush was deep in work at what had once been the House of Employment but had now become converted into a military hospital. He had been on duty only a few weeks when early in May "a fatal hospital fever," or putrid fever as he called it at another time—probably either typhus or typhoid fever—swept through the wards. "Several of the attending surgeons and mates died of it, and most of them were infected with it," Rush said, failing to note that among the physicians who died was his onetime friend Thomas Young. Rush had broken with Young over the Pennsylvania Constitution, but he retained enough respect for his professional ability to borrow a prescription that in 1793 he would offer as an "infallible" cure for the yellow-fever epidemic then raging through Philadelphia.[10]

Rush blamed the epidemic on severe overcrowding and demanded of Shippen "more room for the sick." Shippen refused the request; no doubt he had no other choice, for the number of empty public buildings were few and to disperse the infected soldiers among families in the city would have risked too many additional lives. Rush returned to his hospital to watch the soldiers "shivering with cold upon bare floors without a blanket to cover them, calling for fire, for water, for suitable food, and for medicines—and calling in vain." Three years later, Rush would blame the deaths that followed on Shippen's refusal to expand hospital facilities or to allow "a sufficient quantity of wine (one of the most powerful medicines in the above fever) to the sick"; later still, in a calmer mood, he tended by implication to exonerate the man and put the blame on a system that left little authority or discretion to the physician on the scene. "No order," he wrote in 1800, "was given or executed for food, medicine, liquors, or even apartments for the sick without the consent of the director general, who seldom went inside of a hospital, and whose business as purveyor was sufficient to employ all his time."[11]

The immediate bitterness toward Shippen in 1777 momentarily evaporated with the onset of summer, which "lessened the evils which were experienced from the want of air in our hospitals," for it was easy to ventilate them by means of open doors and windows. But this short, sharp encounter with death en masse unnerved Rush. Previously a single patient's death had left him disconsolate for days. Now he had been forced to watch men, most of them young men, die by the score, and the experience, together with worse ones to come, eventually proved more than he could take.[12]

3

At the height of the "hospital fever" epidemic, Rush—still as much politician as physician—put himself into the middle of the battle against Pennsylvania's new constitution. Others opposed the constitution as violently as he did, and those for it defended the document with equal passion. This first effort to implement the abstractions embedded in the Declaration of Independence suddenly revealed to Pennsylvanians—and the citizens of all states, for that matter—that they had been at odds without knowing it over what those abstractions meant. Phrases like "consent of the governed" and "governments of our own choice" now took on new, more specific meanings, and with the clarifying arguments over precisely what these phrases did mean, the state's leaders split into two factions, Constitutionalists and Republicans, with Rush among the latter.

The constitutional convention that had sent him to Congress the previous summer had also devised the state document. Rush had had nothing to do with creating it, nor had he worried about what the delegates would produce. Two friends—Cannon and Matlack, both *"good* men"— were members of the convention, as were, too, Benjamin Franklin and David Rittenhouse, "gentlemen distinguished for their uncommon abilities, and deservedly dear for their virtues to every lover of human nature."[13]

Cannon, as Rush knew, held exceedingly democratic views. In June 1776, he had published the broadside detailing his ideas on a new constitution. "Trust no man," he had written, "but such who is determined to extend the principle of a free annual election, by ballot, to all possible cases."[14] Cannon's appointment by the convention to the drafting committee allowed nearly every suggestion advanced in his broadside of June to become incorporated into the new constitution. It extended the vote to all men over twenty-one who had lived in the state one year and paid taxes. No special property qualifications hindered any voter from holding public office. The unicameral assembly was supreme in all legislation, and all members had to stand for reelection annually. If the aristocracy captured control of the executive, it would do little harm; it was a plural executive, called the Executive Council, and its twelve members had relatively little power. Judges no longer held office for good behavior; the Executive Council appointed them for seven years, the assembly appropriated their salaries, and they could not be reappointed. As a final protection against any faction or class getting control of the government, every seven years the people would choose a Council of Censors to check on violations of the constitution. The document also called for a system of free schools, restriction on high bails or immoderate fines, religious toleration, and the abolition of imprisonment for debt.

The constitution was not submitted to popular ratification but went into operation once the convention approved its own handiwork. Voters were required to take an oath not to act in any way "prejudicial or injurious" to the new government, and assembly members had to swear they believed in one God and that the Old and New Testaments were "given by divine inspiration." There was no provision for amending the constitution. Change in the fundamental law was possible only if two-thirds of the Council of Censors voted to call a new constitutional convention.[15]

Rush's initial criticism of the finished document was rather reserved. He would have preferred the governor and Executive Council to have a veto on legislation, and he hoped that the Council of Censors would "remedy this defect at the expiration of seven years." It was John Adams' caustic comments on the document, however, that may have changed Rush's assessment and caused him to begin publishing denunciations of both the constitution and those responsible for advancing it.

Opposition to the constitution put Rush in an odd position. Old friends like Cannon and Matlack, who favored this "rascally government," now became enemies, as evil as they had once been *"good* men." Old enemies acquired virtues hitherto lost from sight. Early in December he wrote warmly to the formerly censured John Dickinson, who had demonstrated his contempt for the constitution by retiring from politics to his farm in Dover, Delaware. Rush urged him to return to the assembly, for new members "will turn the scale in our favor as soon as they come to town." In the face of a possible invasion, "it becomes us to unite heart and hand in repelling the common enemy," he said. "The eyes of the whole city are fixed upon you."[16]

Opposition to the constitution waned as Howe's expected attack on Philadelphia appeared certain in December 1776. It revived, however, once that danger seemed removed with Washington's victories at Trenton and Princeton, and Rush's attacks "against our domestic tyranny" made him one of the first casualties in the war over the constitution: he lost his seat in

Congress. Now nothing could curb his invective. The assembly became "the only *unaccountable body of men* that ever existed in a free country." Even the people had become corrupted, or as he put it, "intoxicated with the *must or first flowings of liberty.*" By May, while contending with army red tape, with Shippen, and with the hospital fever, he had turned vitriolic. He even castigated his coreligionists. "A majority of Presbyterians," he said contemptuously, "are in favor of the constitution." He saw Pennsylvania in a delirium—"she has lifted a knife to her own throat"—an exaggeration possibly prompted by his anguish over the soldiers then dying around him. Exactly a year ago he had maneuvered against a tyrannical assembly. Now he found that "a mob government" had replaced "one of the happiest governments in the world," and he wanted to weep "over the dear nurse" of his youth. Pennsylvania's experiment in government had hardly got under way, yet Rush, with his bent for hyperbole, was already saying he "had rather live under the government of one man than of seventy-two," for "a *single* legislature is big with tyranny."[17]

Rush's denunciation of the Pennsylvania Constitution must have stunned those friends with whom he had worked to promote independence. Nothing he had said earlier hinted at the views now expressed. What had caused the sudden switch? Admittedly, Adams had helped considerably to condition his views. Rush had given so little thought to the form government would take after independence that when Adams instructed him on the subject he was as easily primed in political thought as he had been on other matters by Finley, Davies, and Cullen. Moreover, the high hopes he had for America—"our virtue . . . will know no bounds," he had told Patrick Henry a few days after independence had been declared—were bound to be dashed; his dreams could never quite fit reality. Perhaps of greatest significance in the alteration of his views was that his old animus against the elite of Philadelphia had died, for as an ex-congressman, as a signer of the Declaration, as a friend of Dickinson, Wilson, and Robert Morris, all of whom opposed the constitution, he now numbered among that elite. Wealthy Quakers and Anglicans were also his friends; no longer did he pass "unknown or neglected" among those in Philadelphia "who called themselves great." Further, his dismissal from Congress by the state party in power—the party of Cannon and Matlack—helped to ease the transfer of allegiance. And finally, events of the past year had taught Rush something about himself that he might not have been persuaded to rec-

ognize previously—that basically he was a conservative gentleman. He did
not want to overturn society but only, as he had told Patrick Henry, to
purify it of the "British customs, manners, and ideas of government"
America had been contaminated with.[18]

More extraordinary than Rush's opposition to the constitution was the
excellence, for one whose political experience had been limited, of the
arguments he advanced against it in the press. At the very time in May that
Rush privately excoriated the constitution, he submitted to the *Pennsylvania
Journal* a toned-down version of his remarks in the form of four letters,
which ran under the pseudonym "Ludlow."[19] The letters gave Pennsylvanians one of the most thoughtful, even judicious, critiques of the constitution that had, until then, been published. The first one briefly pointed
out numerous instances where the assembly had already violated the "unworkable" document. Half the deputies had not taken the required oath of
allegiance; the speaker had issued writs that were supposed to come from
the Executive Council; and, contrary to the constitution, laws had been
passed and put into operation without "giving the people an opportunity of
seeing them."[20]

The second and longest of the letters attacked the concept of a single-
house legislature. It opened with a long quotation from John Adams'
Thoughts on Government, written in 1776 as a rebuttal to Thomas Paine's
conception of an ideal government. Paine favored a single legislature, an
elected judiciary with limited terms, and a weak executive. Adams argued
for two legislatures that could check one another's excesses, a reasonably
strong executive that worked with the legislatures and had a limited veto
over their acts, a strong judiciary appointed for good behavior, and the
usual property qualifications for voters. *Thoughts* appeared anonymously,
and though a few were in on the secret—Paine learned who wrote it, said
Adams, and "he came to visit me at my chambers at Mrs. Yard's to remon-
strate and even scold me for it, which he did in very ungenteel terms"—
the author was not generally known until Rush revealed it in his second
letter. Adams told his wife that Philadelphians were "making a factious
use of my name and lucubrations," adding: "Much against my will, I assure
you, for altho' I am no admirer of the form of this government, yet I think
it is agreeable to the body of the people, and if they please themselves they
will please me." Unaware that "Ludlow" was Rush, he went on: "Besides,

it is not very genteel in these writers to put my name to a letter from which I cautiously withheld it myself."[21]

Rush, like Adams, called for a government of checks and balances. He noted that while "it has often been said that there is but one rank of men in America," the inequalities of property have "introduced natural distinctions of rank in Pennsylvania, as certain and general as the artificial distinctions of men in Europe." Ignoring these distinctions by creating an all-powerful legislature in which any man could serve did not give power to the poor and middling sort but only opened the door for the rich to capture control of the government. "Where there is wealth, there will be power," he observed in an effective phrase, and "the rich have always been an overmatch for the poor in all contests for power."

Rush, in advocating an upper house in the state legislature, did not urge an Americanized version of the House of Lords. That body possessed special privileges and derived its power from the crown. The upper house he and his friends conceived of would have *"no one* exclusive privilege" and all its power would be "derived from the *annual* suffrages of the people." He dismissed as ridiculous the idea that an upper house, or "Council" as he called it, would lay the foundation for aristocratical power. The source of the power of those in the Council would be the same—the people. "Who would believe," he asked, "that the same fountain of pure water should send forth, at the same time, wholesome and deadly streams?"[22]

Here Rush had gone far beyond the proposal advanced by Adams in *Thoughts on Government*. Adams had called for the lower house, not the people, "to elect by ballot, from among themselves or their constituents or both" the upper house. Rush in effect held America to be "blessedly different from all other nations." He accepted the argument of those who had made the Pennsylvania Constitution—"having no rank above that of freeman," one of them had said, "she has but one interest to consult," that is, the people—and turned it upside down to build his own case for a bicameral legislature.[23]

In the third letter, Rush objected to the Executive Council and the judiciary as conceived in the constitution. Neither offered checks to the unbridled assembly. Together the council and its president presented an "insignificant figure," because they lacked a veto over laws passed by the assembly. Additionally, the fact that their salaries were determined by the legislators "will necessarily render them dependent upon them." The judges not only were paid by the legislature but held their tenure at the will of its members. "In vain do they hold their commissions for seven years," said Rush. "This is but the shadow of independence."

He went on to condemn those provisions that allowed common soldiers to elect all militia officers below the rank of brigadier general and also those that called for the people to elect all justices of the peace. Truly, "all power is *derived* from the people," but it is not *"seated* in the people," he said. "Government supposes and requires a delegation of power; it cannot exist without it. And the idea of making the people at large judges of the qualifications necessary for magistrates, or judges of laws, or checks for assemblies proceeds upon the supposition that mankind are all alike wise and just, and have equal leisure."

Rush found it particularly infuriating that the constitution could not be amended. "Must we groan away our lives in a patient submission to all the evils in the constitution which have been described?" He decried the power given the Council of Censors, which after the constitution had been on trial for seven years would meet to determine whether there had been any infractions of its provisions by anyone in the government. "Where," he asked, "is the man who can insure himself a moment's safety from a body of men invested with absolute power for one whole year to censure and condemn, without judge or jury, every individual in the state?"[24]

He rounded out his assault in a brief fourth letter demanding that a new convention be called in order to revise the constitution immediately. He made the proposal in the face of the strong likelihood that the British would invade Pennsylvania during the ensuing summer. "The liberty of the whole world is the price for which we fight," he admonished. "Human nature looks to us to avenge the mighty ills she has suffered from the tyrants of the world."[25]

In June, as the last letter appeared, all four were collected and published as a pamphlet under the title of *Observations Upon the Present Government of Pennsylvania. In Four Letters to the People of Pennsylvania.* The moderation displayed in his public pronouncements on the constitution was absent in a note that accompanied a copy of the pamphlet to Anthony Wayne. "In my opinion the government of Turkey is not more to be dreaded than the government of Pennsylvania," he said. "If it should finally be established, I shall bear my testimony against it by quitting the state."[26]

Fortunately, no one ever asked Rush to eat those words. The new government under the constitution became so well entrenched that thirteen years passed before moderate-minded men like Rush, as he now judged himself, could force the kind of constitution on Pennsylvania that struck them as sensible.

Rush, nonetheless, had not labored in vain. Eventually it became apparent that he had produced the most comprehensive single attack that would be made against the Pennsylvania Constitution of 1776. His task had been formidable, for the constitution had brought about a most unexpected revolution in the state's government. Swiftly, without fanfare or public discussion, the state's radicals had imposed on Pennsylvania a government that obliterated the distinction between power derived from the people and power seated in the people. It was Rush who found the rebuttal to this view. Power is seated in the people "only on the days of their elections," he said. "After this, it is the property of their rulers, nor can they exercise it or resume it, unless it is abused." It was Rush who first showed that the unchecked power given to the Pennsylvania Assembly violated the principles of the American Revolution. The colonists had warred against a king and a Parliament that, unrestricted in their power, were infringing on the rights of their subjects. The power the constitution gave the assembly was as potentially dangerous to the people as that which the crown had formerly held over them.[27]

One of the most effective ways of rounding up support for the single-house legislature had been to spread the rumor that the elite of Philadelphia hoped to revise the constitution in order "to introduce a House of Lords, hoping to become members of it." Rush demolished the rumor in a way that helped to change the nature of constitutional discussion from 1777 onward. The upper house, like the lower, would derive its power "from the *annual* suffrages of the people," he said. This, Gordon Wood has pointed out, was "a startling new conception of the people's relationship to the government." Wood goes on to say: "Picturing the people as partaking equally in both branches of the legislature not only destroyed the conventional theory of mixed government but it necessarily involved a major adjustment in the conception of representation; for it was now somehow possible for the people, simply through the electoral process, to have two different agents speaking for them at the same time."[28]

The ideas Rush advanced in his *Observations* became the foundation for the attack that thirteen years later resulted in the rejection of the state constitution of 1776. He has received slight credit as a political theorist largely because he abandoned the subject almost as he embraced it. *Observations* was his first and last extended contribution to the discussion until the eve of the Constitutional Convention. His contribution in 1777 was submerged in the flood of pamphlets that followed during the ensuing decade and its importance virtually forgotten until recently.

Rush's interest in politics diminished as summer approached. On July 1 a vacancy on the army medical staff allowed his promotion by Congress, with Shippen's implicit approval, to physician general of the middle department. With the imminent campaign bound to center in his district, this, in effect, made Rush a key officer in the medical department, second only to Shippen and Bond. Further good news came a few days later: Mrs. Rush's pregnancy was nearing its end. Rush left for Mount Welcome on July 14. Shortly before one o'clock in the morning of July 17 his wife gave birth to a son. Three days later Rev. John Ewing, pastor of the First Presbyterian Church and then Rush's friend, later an enemy, christened the infant John, after Benjamin Rush's father. Leaving his wife behind to recuperate, Rush returned to Philadelphia on July 24 and shortly thereafter left to join the army in the field. Now, rather than in April, he should have written in his ledger, "Here ends the chapter." Politics would continue to occupy and enrage him, but now it would no longer be central to his life, though years would pass before Rush realized this. Any hope of achieving eminence as a politician had ceased to exist. The months of army duty directly ahead would produce one of the most embittering experiences of his life and would come close to breaking his spirit. Now, for the first time, Rush was launched on an adventure that would compel him to make decisions where no shadow of a Finley, a Davies, a Cullen, or an Adams hovered close by to guide him.[29]

11

In and Out of the Army

1777–1778

1

JOHN ADAMS had joined the revolutionary movement with modest hopes for the future, and a year after the Declaration of Independence little had occurred to disillusion him. He had not expected men to suddenly shed vice and flock to the banner of virtue. Sloth, corruption, and stupidity had not vanished from the world, and he had never assumed that separation from Great Britain would cause them to. Benjamin Rush, on the other hand, had banked on the Declaration to bring about a real revolution in America—a purified people marching as one in a glorious crusade while the world looked on. A year with the reality of independence had darkened the dream. Rush still hoped for a revolution in the hearts of the people, still dreamed the war would introduce "among us the same temperance in pleasure, the same modesty in dress, the same justice in business, and the same veneration for the name of the Deity which distinguished our ancestors." But by the summer of 1777 hopes were tarnished with doubts, and he saw "a gloomy cloud hanging over our states." He once feared Tories would subvert the cause; now he saw the corrosiveness of internal danger. "If we are undone at all," he said early in August, "it must be by the aristocratic, the mercenary, the persecuting, and the arbitrary spirit of our own people—I mean the people who are called Whigs."[1]

Others shared Rush's dejection, for out of the long hot summer Philadelphia patriots found little to refresh their spirits. Frustrated for good news, they celebrated July 4, the first anniversary of independence, with more abandon than the normally sedate city allowed itself. At noon the vessels in port, their yardarms fluttering with varicolored flags, unlimbered their guns. Speeches and toasts followed at the taverns about the city, then at four in the afternoon every available cannon opened up with a roar that to one sensitive lady "was terrible to hear." At six came a parade of the troops, "with great pomp, tho' many of them were barefoot and looked very unhealthy, and in the evening were illuminations, and those people's windows were broken who put no candles in."

That glad day highlighted the summer. In mid-July citizens learned that Ticonderoga had been surrendered to "Gentleman Johnny" Burgoyne by General St. Clair. His apology, published in the Philadelphia press, was that his troops "were not half supplied with arms and had less ammunition." At six in the morning on July 31 the alarm guns boomed through the city and soon after "an express came in which says that about 280 sail appeared at the Capes standing in for our bay." The express erred. General Howe was moving his army by water round from New York but not up Delaware Bay. The fleet was continuing down to Chesapeake Bay. There at the north end he planned to disembark the army and march overland from the south toward Philadelphia.[2]

Rush at this point rejoined the army medical department. Early August found him at Morristown, where Washington currently had his headquarters. As physician general Rush was the third-ranking man in his department, with only Shippen and Bond, the assistant director, his superiors. He liked Bond, who, though the son of a colleague who had opposed Rush's medical theories, could not "be too much commended for his humanity and zeal in doing his duty." When the army was not on the move, Rush's station was Princeton, although he was expected to travel among the military hospitals scattered through New Jersey to supervise the attending physicians and their staffs. His main tie to the director general was through a weekly report on the number and conditions of the hospital sick.

The return to duty pleased Rush, momentarily. He found "that great order, cleanliness, and the most perfect contentment prevail in our hospitals." Rush's enthusiasm here is curious, for he later declared that "the dysentery prevailed in the summer of 1777 in the military hospitals of New Jersey. . . ." Dysentery, or "the putrid diarrhea" as it was then called, "was the most intractable disorder of any we had to deal with," according to another physician, who went on to describe the disease and the attempted cure for it. "The patient would often be able to move about, with little or no fever, his skin remarkably dry and dusky, and constant drain from bowels. Various attempts have been made to force the skin by warm bathing, ipecac mixed with opium, etc., and by that means to divert the current of humors from the bowels; but all to no purpose. . . . Multitudes melted away, as it were, of this miserable complaint, and died. The only expedient I ever found effective for their relief was to billet them in the country, where they could enjoy pure air and a milk diet; or to furlough them to their own homes, if within reach."[3]

Rush was with the army when Washington put it in motion in mid-August, after ascertaining that Howe's objective was Philadelphia. The troops, numbering some ten thousand, trudged through the dusty streets of the city on August 24, were ferried across the Schuylkill, headed southward, and on September 11 met the British at Brandywine Creek. Through the battle Rush tended casualties "in the rear," but at one point when he went to the front to assist corpsmen he nearly fell "in the hands of the enemy by my delay in helping off the wounded." He saw enough of the battle from his hospital tent to realize that Howe had inflicted another severe defeat on the Americans, of whom more than three hundred were killed.

Two days after the battle, Washington arranged for a flag-of-truce party of physicians and surgeons, Rush among them, to care for wounded Americans who had been captured by the British. The discipline and order found inside the British lines at first astonished, then infuriated, Rush. Sentries spoke, stood, and looked "like the safeguards of the whole army." The commissary, staffed by able men, took "great pains" to feed the troops fresh vegetables, "and I observed everywhere a great quantity of them about the soldiers' tents." "Order and contentment" prevailed in the hospital. "You must not attribute this to their humanity," he told John Adams, who had supplanted Richard Henry Lee as the favored correspondent in Congress. "They hate us in every shape we appear to them. Their care of our wounded was entirely the effect of the perfection of their medical establishment, which mechanically forced happiness and satisfaction upon our countrymen perhaps without a single wish in the officers of the hospital to make their situation comfortable."[4]

The return to the American lines only intensified Rush's depression.

He approached a general's headquarters "without being challenged by a single sentry." He heard that two thousand troops had "sneaked off with the baggage of the army to Bethlehem," and because sergeants rather than officers made the daily head count there was little chance they would be missed for several days. He watched soldiers wander casually about the lines exposed to easy capture by the enemy. He saw "languor in all the branches and extremities of the army." These sights carried Rush deep into the "slough of despond."

The course of military events carried him deeper still. At ten in the morning on September 26 British troops marching smartly to the music of "God Save the King," tramped into a Philadelphia empty of nearly all but those sympathetic to the crown. For more than a week citizens who favored the American cause had been pouring out toward the homes of friends and relatives in the countryside. Lancaster, the largest inland town on the continent, overflowed with refugees. Congress had decamped on September 18, heading first for Lancaster, but finding the place too crowded and still uncomfortably near the British if they took it in mind to move inland, traveled on to the village of York. Meanwhile, Washington once again engaged the enemy, this time on October 4 at Germantown, just north of Philadelphia, and though momentarily on the edge of victory, confusion during the predawn engagement produced in the end one more defeat. He retreated to leave the British firmly and comfortably lodged in Philadelphia as winter approached.

"My dear friend, we are on the brink of ruin," Rush wrote Adams at this time. The virus of his own Timid Whigs ("The loss of a few riflemen in a skirmish, or of a fort, or a village, induce them to conclude that the contest is over and that America is subdued") seemed to have infected him. He now thought "new measures and new men alone can save us." The army needed overhauling, especially at the top. "Good general officers would make an army of six-months men [short-term enlistees] an army of heroes," he said.[5]

A visit to Washington's perambulating headquarters on October 10, six days after the battle of Germantown, hardened these feelings. He found Washington, "at this time the *idol of America*," surrounded by incompetents—Col. Alexander Hamilton, "a young man of twenty-one years of age"; Nathanael Greene (soon a good friend), "a sycophant to the general, timid, speculative, without enterprise"; General Sullivan, "a proud, vain, lazy, ignorant drunkard"; and the once-admired Adam Stephen, who had turned up drunk at the battle of Germantown, now "a sordid, boasting, cowardly sot."⁶ These judgments, particularly of Greene, reveal Rush in an agitated state. And the agitation lingered. Three weeks after visiting Washington's camp he still complained of "the ignorance, the cowardice, the idleness, and the drunkenness of our major generals." If the army could not be purged of these sots, he told Adams, then Congress should go on record with two resolutions:

> 1. Resolved that if any major or brigadier general shall drink more than one quart of whiskey, or get drunk more than once in twenty-four hours, he shall be publicly reprimanded at the head of his division or brigade.
> 2. Resolved that in all battles and skirmishes the major and brigadier generals shall not be more than five hundred yards in the rear of their respective divisions or brigades upon pain of being tried and punished at the discretion of a court-martial.⁷

A single staff officer won Rush's approval—Thomas Conway, a brigadier general then threatening to resign if Congress failed to promote him. Conway had served in the French army and was an able soldier, but his attractiveness to Rush stemmed from a major failing: indiscretion. "Some people blame him for calling some of *our generals* fools, cowards, and drunkards in public company," he told Adams, when urging his promotion to major general. "But these things are proofs of his integrity and should raise him in the opinion of every friend of America."⁸

Up to now Rush had attacked those around Washington but never "the idol" himself. Gates's decisive victory over Burgoyne at Saratoga, which he learned about in mid-October, changed the focus. He liked Gates, to begin with; one evening before the general had taken command of the northern army they had "feasted upon schemes and plans of national happiness." The victory at Saratoga strengthened Rush's respect for Gates and, conversely, a long-maturing disrespect for Washington. Gates, he heard, ran "a well-regulated family" compared with Washington's "unformed mob." "Look at the characters of both!" he implored Adams. One had "planned with wisdom and executed with vigor and bravery," while the other had been twice outgeneraled, twice beaten, and in the process lost Philadelphia. "If our Congress can witness these things with composure and suffer them to pass without an inquiry, I shall think we have not shook off monarchical prejudices and that like the Israelites of old we worship the work of our hands." These words, perhaps the severest censure yet handed Washington, Rush wrote to Adams, who had the sense and good taste to keep them to himself. Rush would have less luck with his next indiscreet attack on Washington.[9]

2

While attacking Washington and his generals, Rush simultaneously waged a bitter campaign against the army medical establishment. His censures were, at best, impractical, at worst, irresponsible. Before Howe began to press Washington, the army hospitals were filled with dysentery cases and soldiers down with the various, unspecified "fevers" that plagued the military, plus several hundred men who had been inoculated against smallpox and had to be cared for in strict isolation. The battle of Brandywine handed Director General Shippen six hundred wounded to deal with. Three weeks later, the engagement at Germantown brought in more than four hundred more. The original plan had been to move the majority of these casualties by wagon to Trenton, where preparations had been made to receive them; the overflow would be dispersed to outlying New Jersey villages such as Mount Holly, Bordentown, and Burlington. The loss of Philadelphia convinced Washington that it would be unwise to leave the wounded in these exposed towns. Almost overnight, then, Shippen arranged to open hospitals in villages throughout the relatively secure Pennsylvania Dutch countryside—at Easton, Allentown, Bethlehem, Reading, Lancaster, Lititz, Ephrata. A courthouse here, a church there was taken over by the medical department, and as rapidly as possible beds and blankets, food, wine, and other supplies were moved in. Patients were trundled to these makeshift hospitals in open, springless wagons, much worse off by the time they arrived. At the end of October overcrowding had reached a point where Shippen felt the need to inform Congress about "the pressing necessity of the hospitals, which begin to feel the effects of cold and dirt." It was for the medical department a time of unspeakable chaos, and it was in the midst of this chaos that Rush began his diatribe against the department in a series of letters to John Adams.[10]

First, he called for adoption of the British hospital system, where military guards were detailed to the wards. One night shortly after returning from the British encampment, his staff contended with more than a hundred drunken patients, something unheard of in the British army, Rush said, where a captain's guard was assigned to every two hundred patients in each hospital. "Besides keeping their men from contracting and prolonging distempers by rambling, drinking, and whoring, guards keep up at all times in the minds of the sick a sense of military subordination," he said.[11]

Next, there should be a clear separation of duties between physicians and surgeons and the administrative staff under the director general, who, as Rush saw it, should be mainly a purveyor of supplies and equipment. "We see, we feel the distresses of the sick, and therefore are better capable of directing everything necessary for their convenience than men who never go into a hospital but who govern them by proxy," he said. The director general's authority disturbed Rush because it defied the theory of checks and balances that Adams' pamphlet on government had illumined for him. "Such unlimited powers and no checks would have suited an angel," he wrote Adams. His duties should be confined to furnishing the medical staff with medicines, wines, and stores, and to prevent fraud these should be requisitioned in writing."[12]

Rush's censures were based in part on obvious flaws in a medical department ineptly conceived by Congress—a conception he himself had shared in—and in part, despite later disclaimers that he attacked only the system, on a dislike of Shippen, a dislike that perhaps originated with Shippen's criticism of certain material the young Rush had offered students in his chemistry course. But there was more to it than that. Shippen, together with his father, counted among the most distinguished physicians in Philadelphia, and it hurt to be corrected from that corner. Then, too, Shippen, ten years Rush's senior, had failed in the younger man's eyes to help him get established when he returned from London. Finally, Shippen looked and acted like an aristocrat; appearance alone may have overawed Rush to the point of jealousy. "Possessed of a lofty stature, and an open, animated, and manly countenance, his personal appearance was dignified and commanding," Shippen's eulogist wrote years later. "In addition to an imposing figure, and a graceful deportment, he was deservedly ranked among the handsomest of men." Shippen had married Richard Henry Lee's sister;

Rush no longer got along well with Lee, after the contretemps in Congress over raising the interest on loan certificates. Shippen was a close friend of Washington's; Rush at the moment had scant regard for Washington.

In August, when Rush had praised the "great order, cleanliness, and the most perfect contentment" that prevailed in the hospitals, Bond had won the credit. By October, mounting anger had flushed his resentment of Shippen into the open. While Bond might deserve praise, Shippen, he emphasized in a letter to Adams,[13] "is both *ignorant* and *negligent* of his duty."

Rush always claimed that he judged on the evidence, not from personal antipathy. Early in September he visited the army hospital at Trenton. He found no coffee, tea, rice, wine, or sugar in the commissary stores, and the doctor in charge said medical supplies came through in "such small quantities and so out of time that they did the sick but little good." In October, after leaving Washington's headquarters, he traveled to Reading, and in the hospital there "found the wounded soldiers in the most distressed condition" and so in want of essentials "that most of them lay for several weeks in the same shirts in which they were wounded." When he prescribed madeira wine for one of the patients, an orderly said only port was available, that the several pipes of madeira in the hospital stores belonged to Shippen.[14]

At that point, Rush lost all sense of proportion. In the Reading hospital's commissary room he proposed to three staff members that they join in signing an affidavit against Shippen. "We will bring the Shippens down; they are too powerful and have reigned long enough," he was heard to say. And in a letter to Adams he warned that if the medical department were not soon reformed "I shall trouble you with my resignation, and my reasons shall afterwards be given to the public for it."[15]

A week or so of rest or a long face-to-face talk with Adams might have helped calm Rush down. Neither was to be had. On November 9, he toured the hospital in Burlington, New Jersey, and the next day left for Red Bank, a New Jersey hamlet opposite the mouth of the Schuylkill, "in order to fix a hospital in the neighborhood of our forts on the Delaware." These garrisons—Fort Mercer and Fort Mifflin—guarded Philadelphia. The British shelled the forts mercilessly for a week before they fell. Rush watched the barrage for a day and "found it impossible to exaggerate the sufferings" of the troops within. He returned to Burlington on November

12, then five days later traveled to Princeton to visit his wife and, for the first time, his newborn son. ("He spends his whole time in sleeping, eating, and pulling his mama's caps and handkerchiefs to pieces.") He had planned to stay in Princeton only briefly, checking the hospital there, then move out to join General Greene, who expected soon to engage the British army led by Cornwallis. Cornwallis in mid-November came out of Philadelphia with two thousand troops to take Fort Mercer, that bastion at Red Bank that was blocking the British fleet from sailing further up the Delaware. Greene was dispatched to attack the British but bad timing prevented an engagement; Fort Mercer had to be evacuated and Rush, with no place to go, lingered in Princeton for the next six weeks.[16]

Those weeks could have been the tonic to restore Rush's spirits, but involvement with hospital affairs offset the satisfaction of being with his wife and child. Some five or six hundred patients—the total varied from week to week—were quartered in Nassau Hall and the Presbyterian Church. He hoped soon to commandeer the Quaker meetinghouse and the palatial home of a decamped Tory, but nothing came of the plans. He relieved the overcrowding slightly by billeting ambulatory patients with farmers on the outskirts of the village. "The air and diet of a farmer's kitchen are the best physic in the world for a soldier worn down with the fatigues of a campaign," he said, and the farmers did not mind "taking the poor fellows into their houses, especially when they were indulged with the soldiers' rations of beef and bread in exchange for the milk and vegetables they gave them."[17]

The problem of discipline more than of space harassed Rush. Many of his patients had "complaints so trifling that they do not prevent their committing daily a hundred irregularities of all kinds." "The sick cannot be governed without military authority," he told General Greene, whom he no longer considered a sycophant to Washington but an understanding friend. As matters now stood, a month in the hospital washes away "the discipline of a whole year." Moreover, the presence of military authority to enforce physicians' orders would hasten cures. It could not be accidental that Howe had only one thousand sick in his hospitals while the Americans currently had nearly four thousand. He urged Greene to create a post similar to the British army's inspector general, whose business would be "to appoint guards, have a roll called, visit the wards, and finally to report all deficiencies to the commander in chief."[18]

In another letter the same day, December 2, he repeated the suggestion to Shippen. The calm, even friendly tone of the letter's early paragraphs—the Princeton hospital seemed in fairly good shape; Maj. Robert Stockton, the commissary officer and a cousin of Rush's father-in-law, "cannot be too much commended"—receded as Rush turned to matters none of his business. "Is not this the time to lay in stores for next year?" he asked. Would it not be a good idea to send Bond to New England to buy wine, sugar, and molasses and to pick up linen and sheets from the hospitals there? This should be done quickly, for "every day increases their scarcity and high price." Shippen already believed Rush carped only because, as Rush put it in a letter six days later to his congressional friend William Duer, "[I] intended to displace him." Certainly such advice, part of a glossary of suggestions offered Shippen since May, hinted who could handle the job better. But the director general misjudged Rush; Rush was ambitious, but never for power. He had deep faith that institutions "mechanically" could force "happiness and satisfaction upon our countrymen," but he had no desire to run such institutions. "On the contrary," he said, to underscore his contention that he struck at Shippen for selfless reasons, as he no doubt did, "I am resolved to retire as soon as the campaign is closed, since I cannot act agreeable to the dictates of my conscience and judgment."[19]

In his long letter to Duer, a delegate from New York, Rush put aside the quarrel with Shippen and gave the congressman a judicious comparison of the American medical department with that of the British, "which is said to be the most perfect in the world." He censured the conception of the director general's office rather than the man who held it, and suggested that Congress had given the post more power with fewer checks than General Washington held as commander in chief. He stressed the point that he was not attacking Shippen. "All I shall say is that if he possessed the abilities of a Bacon, the industry of a Boyle, and the integrity of Aristides, he could not execute one half of the extensive powers you have given him."[20]

In a second letter sent to Duer five days later, however, Rush's criticism of Shippen was unrestrained, which raises wonder about what had occurred in the interim. "For God's sake, do not forget to take the medical system under your consideration," he now wrote. "It is a mass of corruption and tyranny and has wholly disappointed the benevolence and munificence of the Congress." He attacked Shippen directly, hinting he has never entered a hospital nor been exposed to the fevers that last spring killed six surgeons and struck all staff members "in a greater or lesser degree." He went out of the way to praise Shippen's assistants. And to make certain these complaints were aired on the floor of Congress he told Duer: "You may make any use you please of this letter and *my name* with it." At last the fat was in the fire.[21]

During the two weeks after this letter went to Duer, Rush gave Gov. William Livingston a tour of army hospitals in New Jersey. On December 25 Livingston wrote Washington on what he had seen in a way that reflected Rush's influence. The next day Rush also sent a long letter to Washington, explaining that he was bypassing his superior only because he thought Washington had not been told by the director general of the inadequacies of the hospital organization. The letter was a carefully edited second draft with all intemperate remarks excised. It rehearsed old complaints about overcrowding, scanty stores, and the want of military guards, but phrased them tersely and effectively and without undercutting Shippen.[22]

On January 2, not having heard from Washington, Rush left Princeton determined to put his complaints and his resignation before Congress ("I thought it only my duty"), which was still meeting in York. He could not have known that Congress the day before had heard his letters to Duer read aloud and that a committee headed by John Witherspoon, who could be expected to be friendly to Rush, had been appointed to look into the issues raised. But he may have known that Washington had answered Governor Livingston's letter on December 31 without bothering to respond to his own. The letter Washington finally wrote to Rush on January 12 said he had ordered "a discreet field officer to visit the principal hospitals," and that he would do all he could to make army patients "as comfortable as possible." This vague but conciliatory answer came ten days too late.[23]

3

Rush took a leisurely six days to reach York. The first night he stayed with his mother at Rush Hill, the next at the encampment at Valley Forge, where he found the same confusion, waste, and filth that had tormented him in the hospitals. "Sir, this is not an army—it is a mob," General Sullivan told him over the breakfast table. If Shippen stood responsible for the condition of the medical department, who else but Washington, Rush wondered, should be blamed for the state of the army? He moved on to Lancaster on January 5 and remained two days, doubtless taking time to check on the situation at the army hospital. The town was filled with friends who had retreated westward when the British occupied Philadelphia. One afternoon he and George Bryan, a former political ally with whom he now differed over the state constitution but still remained on friendly terms, took tea with Christopher Marshall and spent the evening in talk. *"By the conversation with those gentlemen* tonight there appears to be a general murmur in the people about the city and country against the weak conduct of General Washington," Marshall reported in his diary. "[They say] his slackness and remissness in the army are so conspicuous that a general languor must ensue, except that some heroic action takes place speedily." Marshall had listened skeptically. "But it's thought by me," he said, "that G.W. must be the man to put such a scheme into practice, notwithstanding a cry begins to be raised for a Gates, a Conway, a De Kalb, a Lee. But those men can't attain it."[24]

Rush reached York, ninety miles west of Philadelphia, on January 8. He found it a "noisy, crowded town" of some five hundred houses and populated entirely by the Pennsylvania Dutch, though a sprinkling of displaced Philadelphia families relieved the somber tone they gave to the village. Twice he dined with Gen. Daniel Roberdeau, now in Congress but a friend dating from the days of '76 when he and Rush had worked to carry Pennsylvania toward independence. Rush wrote his wife that "I was struck in a most agreeable manner with the resemblance between you and Miss Nanny Roberdeau, and kissed her over and over for your sake." The letter bubbled with confidence that all would end well, and Rush, with a righteous cause in hand, at this point had no reason to doubt that it would. Congress, which currently sat in the town's dingy courthouse, had dwindled to twenty-one members, most of whom he knew from his previous service. Among the absent was John Adams, who was at home preparing for a diplomatic mission to France.[25]

It must have delighted Rush to learn that on January 6 the medical committee had urged Congress to supply the sick with clothing and blankets, to order an inspector to visit the hospitals, and to request Shippen and Rush to attend Congress on January 26 "to be examined touching certain abuses said to prevail in the hospitals." The apparent disposition of Congress to reform the medical department made Rush yield "to the solicitation of my friends in suspending my resignation." He did not relish a public confrontation with Shippen, but "the obligations I owe to my country" and "the dictates of my conscience" forbade retreat. Besides, "if the system is altered and Dr. Shippen can be restrained by proper checks from plundering the sick, I shall not resign my commission but shall serve another campaign."[26]

Rush may also have been cheered to find the low opinion he held of Washington shared by several members of Congress. His friend Gates had been placed at the head of the newly created Board of War, designed, as Rush saw it, to bring about "a reformation of every department of the army." He doubted much improvement would result, for Gates and Washington were at loggerheads, to a certain extent because of an insulting comment General Conway had made in a letter to Gates (a comment Rush had relished and passed on to John Adams), which, when Washington heard it, created an unpleasant atmosphere at headquarters for both Gates and Conway. Washington's coolness toward two of the men in the army Rush thought most highly of convinced him of "a continuation of all the calamities under which we have groaned for these two years in the Middle States." Congress would go on treating Washington courteously and would consult him in all matters, but "they are determined to support the authority and influence of Gates and Conway," he said, speaking, it turned out, for himself, not Congress.[27]

On January 12 Rush made the fateful mistake of airing his melancholy thoughts about the war in a letter to Patrick Henry. "America," he said, "can only be undone by herself"—by a Congress satisfied with "partial remedies" for a major disease, by an army where one finds "discipline unknown, or *wholly* neglected," by a corrupt, ill-run medical department. But all was not lost. The northern army under Gates "has shown us what Americans are capable of doing with a GENERAL at their head." That oblique shot at Washington became direct a few sentences later when Rush repeated the observation by Conway that had already achieved underground fame: "A great and good God hath decreed America to be free, or the _____ and weak counselors would have ruined her long ago." Henry, like others who had previously heard the remark, would automatically fill the blank space with "commander in chief"—Washington. It was one thing to quote Conway's remark to John Adams, a close friend and a New Englander; it was another to pass it along to Patrick Henry, a casual friend and a Virginian. In doing so he perpetrated if not the most indiscreet act of his life, certainly the most harmful in the long run to his reputation.[28]

Though Rush was never permitted to forget this letter, he never explained why he wrote it to Henry nor why he cloaked his authorship by failing to sign it. There are several possible explanations why he directed it to Patrick Henry. He regarded Henry as a friend.[29] Also, in March of 1777 Gates had told him that Henry had a low opinion of Washington's military ability, and thus, presumably, he would be sympathetic to any criticism of the general. Rush, too, knew Henry now lived on the periphery of continental events and might like to know the current views of those close to Congress. Finally, as governor of Virginia his influence might help to undermine Washington's reputation in his own state. In leaving the letter unsigned, Rush did not hope to hide his identity, for he could have disguised his hand or had the letter copied by another. (Nor was this the only unsigned letter he sent during the war. "Your letter of no date and signed with no name, ought certainly either to make me laugh or make me cry," Charles Lee wrote him in August 1778. "Who the devil is, what the devil is it you are so all damnably afraid of?"[30]) More likely, he assumed Henry, who had received other letters from Rush, would recognize the handwriting but could circulate the letter among friends without worrying about the author being known. That Rush expected the letter to be published by a local newspaper was apparent, and that may have been the compelling reason he did not sign it.

Regardless of why he acted as he did, Rush miscalculated. Henry, like Washington, was a Virginian, and though he had three years earlier said he was above all an American, Virginia remained his "country," and no man dared insult one of its leading citizens. Moreover, as governor of the state and commander in chief of its armed forces he may have felt both a responsibility to and kinship for Washington that had been lacking the previous year when he disparaged the general. For whatever reasons, Henry sent Rush's letter on to Washington, who immediately recognized the handwriting. Enough of Rush's censorious reports had crossed his desk to make identification an easy matter. "This man has been elaborate and studied in his profession of regard for me," he told Henry, some four months after Rush penned his letter, "and long since the letter sent to you."[31] His fury at Rush's duplicity was increased by the timing of the letter, which came when he and his staff believed—perhaps incorrectly, as it turned out—that a group of congressmen, working with Gates and Conway, planned to push him from the post of commander in chief.

The outpouring to Patrick Henry did little to relieve Rush's unhappiness over Washington's leadership. Ten days later he wrote the absent John Adams: "I am daily looking out for some *great* military character to start up, perhaps from the plow, to save this country." But there was still hope for the nation. Gates at least had "rescued this country in a degree from its idolatry to *one* man." These juxtaposed sentiments revealed Rush at his confused worst. Translated into his own terms, they meant: America needs a Cromwell, but a Cromwell brings evil in the wake of salvation.[32]

4

On January 19 Congress listened to a letter from Shippen that denied all Rush's charges. In passing, Shippen wondered who had authorized Rush's visit to York, for "there may arise some cause of complaint at Princeton from his long absence from his duty without leave at this important period." The observation may have registered with some delegates, for Rush, who had denounced the lack of discipline in Washington's army, had taken it upon himself to visit Congress without asking the permission of his superior, William Shippen, Jr.[33]

As the date for a confrontation with Shippen neared, Rush grew uneasy. He prepared his mind for defeat and made plans to retire to Princeton, "secluded from the noise and corruption of the times and spending my time in the innocent employments of husbandry on a farm in Jersey with an amiable wife and rosy boy." A note of self-pity materialized as he balanced his integrity against Shippen's peculations. "One of my marks you know of a good Whig is that he must not grow rich during the war," he told a friend. "One of yours is that he cannot be a good Whig unless he grows poor during the war. I shall be a Whig of the first magnitude if measured by your scale."[34]

On January 25, conforming to the required formalities of the occasion, Rush wrote a short note to Henry Laurens, president of Congress:

As the Director General of the military hospitals has contradicted the assertions contained in my letter to General Washington in a *public* letter addressed to the *whole* body of Congress, I shall esteem it a particular favor if Congress will indulge me with the privilege of a *public* hearing, in order that I support the complaints I have made of the abuses which prevail in our hospitals.[35]

Congress heard Rush's letter on January 26. The next morning it denied the request for a public hearing but turned the file of the Shippen-Rush correspondence over to a committee of five chosen to investigate the charges. The members of the committee were: Witherspoon, chairman; John Penn of North Carolina; James Lovell and Elbridge Gerry, both of Massachusetts; and Roberdeau of Pennsylvania. Rush considered all five friends and anticipated a sympathetic hearing. The committee convened promptly after it had been created, listening to Rush detail his charges on the afternoon of January 27 and to Shippen's rebuttal on the next morning.

Rush disclosed nothing new for those who had heard the catalogue of complaints. He made the same points incorporated in his letter to Washington, only at greater length. No doubt he had the committee on his side until, toward the end of the presentation, he moved from a critique of the hospital system and the unfettered powers of the director general to a personal attack on Shippen. This tactical error undercut much of that said earlier, making it seem he spoke only out of hostility toward his superior. He said of Shippen "that while our sick were suffering from the want of madeira wine at Reading, he had sold six pipes upon his own account which he had transported thither among hospital stores in public." He assured the committee he struck at Shippen not out of "personal resentment" but "from the purest affection to my country." Some in Congress held that the root of the trouble lay in "a want of harmony" between Shippen and himself. Not so, said Rush, adding with heavy sarcasm that he begged pardon for having lived "so long in harmony" with him, "and that to have harmonized any longer with him would have been high treason against my country."[36]

Shippen denied almost all the accusations. Overcrowding in the hospitals could not be prevented, especially at the height of a campaign when casualties poured in. Scanty or insufficient supplies were to be expected in wartime, and those shortages confronting the medical department were no worse than the ones Washington contended with on the military front. Shippen did admit selling six pipes of wine, but, according to Rush, "pled as a precedent for his making money by the directorship" that the director general of British hospitals during the French and Indian War had "made a large fortune" in the same way. Lovell thought Rush made much of little. In Rush's view, he *"palliated* the crime of transporting wine in *public* wagons by saying it was common in all the staff departments, and added that the suspicions which fell upon the doctor's integrity fell upon everybody in every age and country that was trusted with public money."[37]

Witherspoon asked for proof of the general charges of maladministration and of the specific accusations against Shippen. Rush somewhat disingenuously answered that he had not come to Congress "to detect rogues." He only wanted the hospital system reformed and the purveying business taken out of Shippen's hands, but if Congress wanted to investigate the situation, he would prove true all the facts he "had related and of many more of the same heinous nature."[38]

Rush emerged from the hearings momentarily confident. He told a friend "he imagined the favorite system of Shippen's would be essentially altered in consequence of it," for General Roberdeau had afterward assured him so, and with that assurance he had got Rush's promise to return "with cheerfulness again to my duty in the hospitals." Shippen, meanwhile, set about puncturing Rush's buoyant mood by telling several delegates that Congress had to choose between him and Rush. Obviously, Witherspoon must calm the storm stirred up by these two sons of Nassau Hall, and he reported back to Rush the ultimatum Shippen had handed Congress. Witherspoon's earlier uneasiness with the volatile young man who had a decade earlier persuaded him and his wife to come to America came to the fore, and he now told Rush that he and Shippen could never work well together, that one of them must resign, and that Rush should be the one. Rush insisted he could work with Shippen once the promised changes in the director general's authority had been made. Witherspoon repeated "that one of us *must* leave the department," and added that since Rush had made so many enemies in Congress he should resign.[39]

Acquaintances found Witherspoon a "coldly observing" man, "shrewd," not "much melted to compassion." He faced a messy situation that demanded a quick resolution, and although he may have exaggerated the number of Rush's enemies to terrify him into a speedy resignation, Rush refused to be coerced "by the fear of being dismissed by the Congress." "You have suffered enough in the opinion of the public by dismissing Dr. Morgan without a trial," he said. "I dare you to dismiss me in the same manner." Witherspoon tried another tack. Rush had been misled if he thought the hospital system would soon be reformed. He could promise "that no material changes would be made in it, and that the purveying business would not be taken out of Dr. S.'s hands." That news, coming from the chairman of the committee that would report on the charges against Shippen, convinced Rush the cause was hopeless. Witherspoon's defection cut deeply. "The doctor had witnessed the sufferings of the sick soldiers at Princeton," Rush wrote years afterward, only months before he died, "but he was notwithstanding the friend of Dr. Shippen upon this occasion."[40]

An hour after the shock delivered by Witherspoon, Rush wrote out his resignation to the president of Congress.

> Finding it impossible to do my duty any longer in the department
> you have assigned me in your hospitals in the manner I would
> wish, I beg the favor of you to accept of the resignation of my
> commission.[41]

The resignation was dated January 30; it was accepted unanimously, "without a word said by any person upon the subject." Not one of his former colleagues, none of the friends who only a few days before had promised their support, spoke up in his defense. And yet only fifteen days earlier Rush had told his wife he had determined to take the case against Shippen before Congress "not only from a sense of duty and a love for my country, but in consequence of the advice of some very worthy members of Congress, who assure me that a contrary step will be ascribed to a want of perseverance or to downright disaffection."[42]

One wonders what would have been said if John Adams had been present to speak for his friend. The moment Adams had heard from Rush that he had come "to Yorktown [that is, York] to lay down my commission," he had written urging him to hold on to his post. "Men who are sensible of the evils in the hospital department are most likely to point them out to others, and to suggest remedies," he said. "Patience! Patience! Patience! The first, the last, and the middle virtues of a politician."[43]

5

Rush left York immediately after his resignation had been accepted and arrived in Lancaster the same day. A righteous man had been spurned by the leaders of a cause to which he had given three years of his life, a cause from which he had expected a resplendent revolution in the affairs of men. Now stunned by the course of events, he wondered what to do next. Before leaving York he had confided to Witherspoon the thought of joining a proposed expedition to invade Canada under the joint command of Conway and the Marquis de Lafayette. Shortly after he reached Lancaster, Witherspoon advised him that several members of Congress "seemed to be at a loss what station or character you could sustain" in the expedition. Rush absorbed that rebuff and decided after a few days' thought that when Washington mounted a new campaign in the spring he would serve as a volunteer with the Pennsylvania militia.[44]

During the early part of what became a two-week visit in Lancaster, he prepared "my last legacy to my countrymen in the line of my profession"—a revision of the essay on soldiers' health, which the Board of War had asked to be republished in an edition of four thousand copies with "such additions and alterations" as the author thought proper. Rush polished a few awkward sentences, inserted a paragraph on idleness as "the bane of a soldier," and added some remarks about the virtues of discipline.[45]

Other less literary matters occupied him during the stay in Lancaster. On February 1 he wrote Shippen, justifying his actions at York, repeating his lack of resentment toward him, and insisting "I have no revenge in me." Actually, a desire for revenge did indeed obsess Rush, and he lingered in Lancaster in order to achieve it more swiftly. A check of Shippen's records showed that only twelve patients had died at the Lancaster hospital in December and a similarly low number in January. From a carpenter, however, Rush obtained an affidavit that thirty-two coffins had been delivered to the hospital in December and thirty-three in January. Rush visited the hospital and inspected the coffins. "From their weight and smell," he reported, "I am persuaded they contained hospital patients in them," adding, in an ill-disguised slur on Shippen's obviously phony records, that "if they were not dead I hope some steps will be taken for the future to prevent and punish the crime of burying the Continental soldiers alive."[46]

While at the hospital he also talked with a surgeon who told him that Shippen had "ordered him to make use of *one* of the pipes of madeira for the sick in the hospital under his care," but that when he sought to use the wine he found it had been all set aside as "private property" and two pipes from the stock had been sold for £800, which Shippen had pocketed.[47]

Rush left for Reading on February 12 to collect further material on the director general's peculations from the hospital there. Dr. Jonathan

Potts, his friend from Edinburgh days, said Shippen had "sold several hogs-heads of brown sugar to a person in Reading." A few days later Rush moved on to Allentown, then to Bethlehem, where from the physicians and surgeons he collected more incriminating facts. Shippen's records showed that in December the hospital had held 320 patients, of whom only twenty-one died; Samuel Finley, one of the resident physicians, swore the hospital in that month admitted "420 patients, and there died within the said month above 40 patients."[48]

Back in Princeton Rush spent a few days relaxing with his wife and son, visiting the hospital to gather further information, and then, after collecting his thoughts, sat down on February 25 to write another letter to George Washington which he hoped would suffice to start court-martial proceedings against Shippen. He presented Washington with a variety of damaging statistics and suggested that between seven hundred and eight hundred patients had died in army hospitals during a period Shippen said "no *fatal* disease prevails in the hospitals, very *few* die, and the hospitals are in *very* good order." (Rush added his own emphasis to Shippen's remarks.) Normally a letter such as this from a former physician general would have been answered promptly and its charges investigated thoroughly. Washington did neither. He had received the anonymous letter sent to Patrick Henry and now regarded Rush as part of a "faction" created to overthrow him and raise Gates to commander in chief "on the ruin of my reputation and influence." He turned the letter over to Shippen, who dismissed Rush as a troublemaker, then nearly a month later forwarded it to Congress with a note that gave implied approval of Shippen's judgment.[49]

Rush waited for Washington's reply, and when none came he carried the attack back to Congress in mid-March by sending his friend Roberdeau a dossier against Shippen. Shippen alone was now the target, for on February 6 Congress had passed a series of resolutions that embodied nearly all the reforms Rush had urged a month and a half earlier. He made clear to Roberdeau that if he had known these reforms were in the offing he would not have resigned his post, which he had done only because Witherspoon had said the committee would recommend only *"very trifling* alterations" in the hospital system.[50]

Throughout March and into early April, an obsessed Rush traveled about the countryside gathering more material on Shippen. He visited the army at Valley Forge, where he still found "men dirty and ragged" and

Washington and his generals living "in houses out of camp." He conferred with an investigatory committee from Congress and visited hospitals missed on the earlier tour. In mid-April he learned the letters to Roberdeau and Washington had been read aloud to Congress and then referred to a special committee, which now asked him "to ascertain with precision" his charges against Shippen. Rush replied that he had expected and preferred the army to court-martial Shippen. But if Congress insisted on carrying out its own investigation, Rush would cooperate fully with its requests for facts, figures, and names. There the matter rested until six weeks later John Morgan returned to the fray with his own attack on Shippen.[51]

During these weeks Rush lived "an inactive and, of course, disagreeable life" in Princeton. Friends of '75 and '76 and events of '77 had left him disillusioned. He again sought to revive the friendship with John Dickinson. "Dr. Young is dead, Cannon is gone to South Carolina, and Paine has lost all his popularity, so that Matlack alone remains in power and influence, of all the authors and pillars of the constitution," he wrote Dickinson in late March. "I have no doubt but what that large and respectable body of men who have been driven into retirement by the violence of the times will at some future day step forth and form a party that will shake the influence and temper the violence of the present rulers of Pennsylvania." It was a long letter, filled with forebodings, but Rush found a spot to drop in his favorite phrase: "All will end well."[52]

Rush by now had abandoned any thought of returning to the army. He went further and decided to abandon medicine, for "Princeton afforded no prospects of business in my profession, and I had no desire by changing my place of residence to enter into country practice." He determined instead to study law. His father-in-law approved the decision "and promised his influence to have me admitted to practice in a year, or in two years at the furthest." The British saved Rush from beginning at the age of thirty-two a new career. As he was about to start legal studies, he learned that Clinton had sent out orders to evacuate Philadelphia. "This suspended my new enterprise," he said, no doubt for once with silent thanks to the British. At the end of May he drove away from Princeton with his wife and son, carrying them out of the expected path of the retreating British and back to the isolated and relatively safe farm in Maryland. He left them there on June 17, and four days later returned to Philadelphia to begin life once again as a civilian physician.[53]

12

Back in Philadelphia

1778–1780

1

RUSH returned to Philadelphia to find the streets piled high with filth, and though he judged the city partly purified, now that a good many Tories had decamped with the British, it still resembled "too much the ark which preserved not only the clean but unclean animals from the deluge." He brought his wife back to their old home in late July, but the effects of her second pregnancy, the summer heat, and the arrival in the city of a "malignant bilious fever" soon combined to send her on to Princeton.[1]

Rush's practice revived slowly in July. He saw eighteen patients and received slightly more than £8 in cash. In August he visited sixty-two patients. Billings for the month totaled about £500, but in his ledger Rush noted that with the rising inflation £10 in paper money now equaled only £5 5s. in gold. (Two months later the rate of exchange equaled ten to one.) To keep solvent he resorted to barter. He urged his wife to bring "a dozen pounds of purging salts" when she returned from Princeton, for "I have discovered by a new species of alchemy the art of converting a pound of that saline matter into sixteen square dollars."[2]

The epidemic bilious fever kept Rush and his apprentices busy through August and on into the autumn. In a free moment he worried about his wife's health. He quizzed "my loveliest girl" about their son—"Did he know you? How many teeth has he got? Does he run alone?"—and sent along an

ointment to sooth some sores that had appeared on his body. Early in September he twice visited Dr. John Berkenhout, an acquaintance from London
days who now resided in the city jail. Berkenhout had come to Philadelphia
posing as a friend of America, but a London newspaper that turned up in
the city revealed him as a lackey of the British ministry and possibly an
agent for the Carlisle peace commission, which had recently arrived in New
York with the announced goal of seeking a way to end the war. When
Berkenhout refused to clarify his position, Pennsylvania jailed him. Rush
visited his cell "under an American mask of sympathetic feeling for my
situation," as Berkenhout saw it, expecting "to make some important discovery concerning the nature of my convention." Rush talked, as the Englishman aptly and no doubt correctly put it, "with uncommon loquacious
plausibility."[3]

Rush could afford to be loquacious without being obsequious to Berkenhout even though the commission headed by Lord Carlisle had brought
to America the most generous peace offer yet extended by the British. It was
authorized to deal with Congress "as if it were a legal body" and to yield
everything that the Americans had officially asked for prior to 1775—
that is, everything but independence. But the timing of the offer could not
have been more inept. The commission arrived shortly after word had been
received that the French, convinced by the victory at Saratoga that the new
nation had a chance to win, had signed a treaty of alliance and another of
commerce with the United States. Even as Berkenhout drifted into Philadelphia the effect of the treaty had become obvious. French troops, French
gold, a French fleet either had made their appearance or were on their way
to give a lift to the American effort. Berkenhout, who was thought to have
come to Philadelphia to seek out influential congressmen willing to promote
the Carlisle commission's offer, could well be dismissed with "loquacious
plausibility."

A few days after the second call on Berkenhout, Rush himself succumbed to the malignant fever (presumably typhoid). His physicians—
Redman, Kuhn, and Morgan—despaired for his life, so much so that Ramsay later reported from South Carolina that he had heard from one who
seemingly knew firsthand that "Doctor Rush died last week." Rush made
out a will and prepared his mind for death. However, on the eleventh day
"it pleased . . . God to break the violence of my disease." Friends said his
survival was "deemed the next thing to a miracle." The illness left him

permanently marked, for at the age of thirty-two his hair had suddenly become heavily streaked with gray. Recovery was slow—on October 24 he had not yet picked up four letters being held for him at the post office—and years later he still remembered the considerable financial loss "sustained by my long confinement."[4]

Physical exhaustion put Rush in a low mood for the rest of the year, and the public misfortunes of friends did nothing to lift his spirits. The three men on Washington's staff he respected most—Generals Lee, Conway, and Mifflin—had "all been banished from headquarters." Lee—now "poor General Lee"—had been court-martialed after the battle of Monmouth Courthouse and found guilty of charges filed personally by Washington. The sentence of a year's suspension from active duty had not for Rush "diminished my veneration nor lessened my attachment to my honored friend," whom he would always stubbornly consider "as the *first* general in America." He never abandoned Lee and the general cherished the friendship until his death in 1782. "You appear to me to be one of those very few mortals who from the beginning and through the whole course of this contest, have acted from the pure unadulterated principles of liberty and republicanism, uninfluenced by any views of avarice or ambition," Lee wrote in 1779. "Every day's acquaintance has improved your character in my opinion. For God's sake, therefore, let me have the satisfaction, every post, if it is possible, of hearing from a man I so sincerely love and esteem." Rush did his best in a busy life to keep the ostracized Lee in touch with what was going on and, in passing, to make him a good Christian. "Such is my complaisance for you that I had determined to be a very orthodox Christian," Lee wrote shortly before he died, adding that a book urged on him by Rush had only left him with "an utter detestation for the God of the Jews. You see however I am open to conviction. Pray recommend me to some able Apothecary. . . ."[5]

All three of Rush's military friends had been "sacrificed to the excessive influence and popularity of *one man*," he believed. "Monarchies are illuminated by a *sun,* but republics should be illuminated only by *constellations* of great men." But where in America did one find such constellations? Not in Congress, which Rush, his resignation having been so enthusiastically accepted, now distrusted almost as much as he did Washington. He saw it as a body of opportunists that talked only "of *state necessity* and of making justice yield in some cases to policy." Men like himself who "loved liberty for its own sake" had left Congress, to be replaced by men of "ambition, craft, avarice, and dissolute manners." Rush, as he would for the rest of his life, looked back to '74 and '75 as the pinnacle of his and America's career, when it was liberty alone that "we loved and contended for." Now he spoke as an old man, as an onlooker. "My temper and my business render me alike independent of the world," he said in March 1779, admitting he had closed himself off from the war, living "wholly for the benefit of an amiable wife and two children, and of my patients." He pretended to ask no more of life.[6]

2

Rush's melancholy was not confined to himself but reflected a general feeling of disillusionment. By late 1778 the Revolution had lost the quality of a crusade. Many who had prospered on wartime contracts now rolled about Philadelphia in gaudy coaches. While the ragged Continental army survived on half rations, slim supplies, and often no pay, the city's rich dressed their women in finery and loaded their tables with delicacies. "Speculation, peculation, and an insatiable thirst for riches seem to have got the better of every other consideration and almost every order of men," said Washington while visiting the city to confer with Congress. War profiteering coupled with the display of conspicuous consumption convinced John Adams that unless something were quickly done to revive public morality "a civil war in America" was a distinct possibility.[7]

Though Washington and Congress disappointed him, it was, above all, the people who disheartened Rush while he recuperated. Not only were the profiteers in evidence, the British evacuation had unleashed the spirit of revenge. In July, shortly after he had returned to the city, a petition demanding that the disaffected be rooted out and prevented from intimidating "the good people of this state from appearing against them" was published in the newspaper with 186 signatures. Rush's name was not on the list, which might have at first struck some as odd. Like Jeremiah, the Old Testament character he believed he resembled, Rush favored revenge; he did not grieve, for instance, over the indignities suffered by the once mighty Allen family, for "I think it no breach of charity to suppose that a family so much affected in power and property . . . were actuated only by low and interested motives." Yet while Rush could be unrelenting against personal enemies, he refused to persecute men for their religious or political beliefs. While on the Committee of Inspection and Observation, for instance, he had been "often disgusted in observing an intolerant spirit towards the persons who were opposed to the war," he once said. "I frequently advocated or palliated their conduct, by which means I lessened my influence among my Whig fellow citizens." When the state indicted for high treason a Quaker acquaintance named John Roberts, described in the press as "an infamous Tory," Rush signed a petition calling for a pardon. It did little to improve his outlook for the future when the jury in November found Roberts guilty, nor his attitude toward those who favored the constitution when George Bryan and Joseph Reed saw to it he hanged.[8]

By November Rush had sufficiently recovered from his illness to resume a full-time practice, and on December 1 he revived at the college his lectures in chemistry, for which twenty-four students signed up. He had hardly completed the first lecture, however, before another sickness in the family disturbed whatever equanimity had entered his life. Early in December his father-in-law, Richard Stockton, came over from Princeton with a cancerous sore on his lip. After consulting Rush and his colleagues, it was agreed the malignant spot should be cut out by Dr. John Jones, whom Rush regarded as the ablest surgeon on the continent. "I did not utter a sigh, or move a muscle," Stockton told his wife, from whom he had kept secret his illness until after the operation.[9]

Stockton's stoic behavior may account for a brief but strange article Rush published shortly after the operation. He entitled it *Contrast between the Death of a Deist and a Christian, David Hume and Samuel Finley,* but, curiously, neither the quotations from a letter by Adam Smith detailing Hume's death nor the excerpts from Rush's diary on Finley's demise presented much of a contrast. Hume "never dropped the smallest expression of impatience," while Finley's "truly polite behavior continued to the last." Finley expressed "an entire resignation to the Divine will," while Hume submitted with only "the most perfect . . . resignation." Rush probably intended to show Finley as "an example of that *faith* which kindles love in the heart," but he ended, knowingly or not, revealing that deist and Christian died in strikingly similar ways.[10]

Rush's efforts to make his father-in-law's recovery more comfortable only exacerbated a tense household. He opposed Jones's prescription of a spare, wineless diet, holding that the abrupt change for a man long accustomed to rich food would produce a "scrofulous tumor" in the neck. Mrs. Stockton, who had hurried to Philadelphia to be with her husband, favored the son-in-law, perhaps suspecting with him that the malignancy would soon spread through the body, but Stockton, after wavering, stuck with Jones's orders. (In April of the next year "an ugly kernel" appeared in Stockton's throat; after two years of unremitting pain, Stockton died in February 1781.)[11]

A single event occurred to lighten Rush's mood in these early months back in Philadelphia. On 1 January 1779 his second child and first daughter, Anne Emily, was born. This time Rev. James Sproat, Rush's pastor at the Second Presbyterian Church, baptized the child. But even if John Ewing had been the only minister available, Rush would have been reluctant to have him officiate, for by now Ewing, firm for the Pennsylvania Constitution, had become a political enemy.[12]

3

Rush isolated himself from politics far less than he pretended after the return to Philadelphia. In October 1778 Reed, who had forgotten his doleful opinion of Washington on the eve of the battle of Trenton, paid a visit while Rush recuperated from the malignant fever and tried to entice him back into action. Reed originally had opposed the Pennsylvania Constitution—Rush had admired the way he spoke "his mind with a manly decision"—and refused the post of chief justice when it had been offered. Now he had reversed field. Only a few days before seeing Rush he had at last taken the oath of allegiance and then agreed to stand for the post of president of the Executive Council. Reed, along with two of Rush's former political colleagues of '76—Ewing and Bryan—believed that the best way to make the constitution work was for "respectable people" to take control of the government. Bryan, now the leader of the Constitutionalists in the assembly, was a Scotch-Irish immigrant who, according to one recorder of the times, was "a well-meaning man" who "felt he was acting the patriot." He had a memory for minutia and "was a never-weary monotonous talker," who, in conversation, constantly identified "himself with the *people,* in opposition to those who were termed the *well-born.*" Reed, though among the well-born, had also by now come to identify himself with the people. When Reed appeared at Rush's bedside for a long conversation, Rush recalled, he "invited me to share with them in their premeditated usurpation. I objected to the proposal and told him that he would ruin himself by taking a part in the establishment or support of so bad a constitution."[13]

Rush's opposition to the constitution of 1776 became a central event in his life, one that engaged his passion and energy for more than a decade and in several instances determined forever his friends and enemies. At first glance his vituperative campaign against the new government seems little more than perverse. Much of the early legislation of the reform-minded assembly that should have satisfied him—"An act to prohibit, for a limited time, the making of whisky and other spirits . . . "; "An act for the suppression of vice and immorality"; "An act for the gradual abolition of slavery"— he passed over in silence. An assembly created out of an ill-begotten constitution could do no good.

Reed's election to the presidency of the Executive Council in October 1778 did not ruffle Rush. "Our new government is demolishing, and those furious patriots who have half ruined our state are now sinking into obscurity and contempt," he said in November. This optimism arose from the news that the assembly would call for a poll of the voters on the constitution. But on February 27 the assembly rescinded the resolution for the plebiscite scheduled for a month hence. The recently organized Republican Society, which counted Rush as one of its founding members, had been caught flat-footed, still preparing its propaganda against the constitution, while those for it had poured into the assembly petitions with more than ten thousand signatures opposing the March plebiscite. The timing of the scheduled vote seems to have swayed the moderate members of the legislature. Pennsylvania in the spring of 1779 writhed in the worst inflationary spiral of its history; this was scarcely the moment to get a balanced judgment from the people on their state constitution.

Inflation had hit Philadelphia especially hard, and in May mobs roamed the city in search of the profiteers they considered responsible for the enormous rise in prices, looting the shops of those they deemed guilty. Rush found himself caught in the spiral. In January 1779 he received £430 in paper money from thirty-three patients. In December only thirteen patients paid their bills, which in hard money amounted to less than £50 but in paper totaled £1,060. The phrase "not worth a Continental" was born.[14]

Rush blamed the inflation completely on Congress. It should have made an *"immediate* application of a foreign loan" to rescue the country from the deluge of worthless paper; instead, in an address to the states in May, it condemned profiteers and handed the states the problem to solve. Philadelphia, taking the cue from Congress, held a town meeting on May 25, at which a committee was chosen to find a way to regulate prices. This approach, said Rush, "resembles a violent puke given to a man in the last stages of consumption."[15]

The nation's "present distracted and corrupted state" soon carried him out of his "beloved retirement." As "Leonidas" (the Spartan king slain at Thermopylae and thus an appropriate pseudonym for one whose brief "political race" had ended shortly after signing the Declaration), he lectured Congress in July on how it could repair the financial catastrophe: stop the printing presses, resort to loans from the people, pay decent interest rates on the loans, and above all let good men dispense the money. The corruption of private virtue in public servants appalled him. "How many of your officers have been called from billiard tables and taverns to execute the most important commissions under you!" he railed. "Where are the men who filled these seats in the year 1774?" Price regulation offered only a *"palliative* remedy," impossible to enforce and an inhibition to "the springs of enterprise and industry." Liberty is the goal of our struggle, not independence, which is only the means to an end, "and you might as well think of preserving animal life in a burning volcano as to think of preserving liberty in the society or neighborhood of your money." Rush closed on a note unusually cynical for him:

> I have fears within me that I am almost afraid to utter. None of you can be unacquainted with the depravity of morals and manners that preceded the overthrow of the Commonwealth of Rome. . . . Are you sure we have no Caesars nor Cromwells in this country?[16]

A sore spot had been touched when he wondered where the men of 1774 had gone. Everyone knew that the quality of congressional delegates had slumped seriously over the past year as one after another of the old lights—Adams, Jefferson, Henry, Franklin—either returned to their states or went abroad for the nation. Rush's attack counted as the first and for long the most insulting directed at Congress, and the delegates took prompt no-

tice of it. Elbridge Gerry, one of the holdovers from 1774, rose in anger
the day after the article appeared in John Dunlap's *Pennsylvania Packet*
and moved that the printer "be directed to attend the bar of this house to
answer such questions as shall be proposed." Several members objected
that to do so would invade the liberty of the press and that "it would be
lowering and disgracing the dignity of Congress to take any notice of the
printer or author." The motion died, but only after a long debate. Rush
apparently never knew the brief furor the essay created among old colleagues, nor Gerry that his friend had caused the tempest.[17]

Inflation continued to agitate the people of Philadelphia. Craftsmen
balked at the city's proposed price schedule and refused to accept it until
all prices were controlled. Since Congress had refused to act, the Constitutionalists wanted the assembly to impose price controls. They argued that
the unchecked prices acted as a tax on the plain people. The merchants
answered that high prices resulted from, but did not cause, inflation, and
that price controls could only bring ruin, forcing them to sell below cost.
Also, they said, enforcement of such controls in a loosely knit state with a
weak government was impossible. No sane man would accept a fixed price
and American paper money for the goods on his shelf when the French,
with hard money in their pockets and thousands of soldiers and sailors to
buy food for, were willing to pay what the market demanded to supply their
people. Another mass meeting at the State House was called for July 27
"to determine the mode of choosing a new committee" for regulating
prices, this one to consist of 120 members.

The Constitutionalists, who sought controls in order to block sky-
rocketing prices, attempted to dominate the meeting first by announcing that
"no person who does not produce his certificate of having taken the OATH of
ALLEGIANCE to this or the United States [shall] be admitted into the State
House yard," then, after the audience had assembled, by stationing close to
the speakers' platform a mob of some hundred men armed with clubs and
a voice-drowning fife and drum. When General Cadwalader tried to convince the crowd that price regulation would do more harm than good, the
organized minority hooted him down. Cadwalader "and a majority of those
present" transferred the meeting to the yard of the College of Philadelphia.
They accomplished little there except to choose a committee, of which Rush
was one, to publish an account of the proceedings. The unresolved tension

led two days later to a private meeting in the morning of all the city's merchants to discuss measures for dealing with "the present alarming occasion," and of the Republican Society in the evening.[18]

Throughout these public wrangles Paine and Rush, with opposite viewpoints, had battled over every issue. Suddenly, in mid-August, they found something they once again agreed upon. Paine, in a sober, well-reasoned essay, admonished those Constitutionalists who had begun to distrust the French because a few war profiteers in flour had made fortunes selling to the French navy. He defended the durability of the Franco-American alliance, founded as it was "on the solid basis of mutual interest," and ridiculed those who saw a plot to blow up the alliance as men indulging in a "laughable piece of romance." Rush handled the matter quite differently. He opened with a shrill preface that instead of praising the French preached revenge against Great Britain. "Your hatred of that haughty nation must erect a monument of justice to deter other nations from imitating [her] example." One must hate the people, too, for "humanity to Englishmen is treason against America." After detailing British barbarities ("Let him see the lovely virgin, the pride and ornament of the village, dragged to the bed of a British or Hessian revenger"), he advised that "cruelty to Americans is now part of the natural law of England."[19]

The forced tone continued. "We should view a piece of English broadcloth as the tissues of our former chains, and even their delicious porter and cheese should appear as the poisons that lulled us into an ignorance of our strength and resources." A search for positive virtues in the new ties with France reduced Rush to such remarks as: "Those alliances are always the most beneficial and durable which are formed between nations as *unlike* to each other as possible in religion, laws, and manners." He now hoped that "the throne of France [may] never want a LEWIS the XVITH!" the same whose manners he had deplored a few years earlier when he watched him dine at Versailles.

Publication of the essay coincided with the appearance of another epidemic fever, which forced Rush to forsake politics for business. Not completely, however, for he blamed the new sickness on the British, who by their wholesale felling of trees around the city when they occupied it released noxious fumes into the atmosphere which were the source of the disease. He visited 111 patients in August, 107 in September, and confessed

in mid-October he had "not paid a single visit to anybody but sick people."
He sent his wife to the safety of Rush Hill, where, whenever he got the
chance, he wrote letters to "My loveliest girl."[20]

In the midst of the epidemic, Philadelphia had erupted with a first-
class riot that did little to boost Rush's spirits. A handbill calling for the
militia to "drive off from the city all disaffected persons and those who
supported them," passed about the city on October 4, led to a leaderless
and liquored mob marching on the house of James Wilson, who had been
the state's foremost defender in the courts of dispossessed and imprisoned
Tories. The attack on Fort Wilson, as it came to be called, resulted in seven
deaths and nineteen wounded. "Since this melancholy affair we have had
a calm in our city," Rush reported later. "But every face wears the marks of
fear and dejection. We look over our shoulders and then whisper when we
complain to each other in the streets of the times." The riot caused even
Paine to mention "the sickness which has so generally prevailed through
the city."[21]

An election the week following depressed Rush still further, for the
Constitutionalists this time captured full control of the assembly. The continuing inflation had proved a boon, for it had been easy to blame it on the
merchants, most of whom were Republicans and who had resisted the Constitutionalists' popular fight for price control. "Poor Pennsylvania! has
become the most miserable spot upon the surface of the globe," he said.
"They call it a democracy—a mobocracy in my opinion would be more
proper." His mood continued to sink as the year's end approached. The
college announced late in October that medical lectures would begin early
in December, but by then an upheaval in the school's affairs, an offshoot
of the political turmoil, saw Rush sitting on the sidelines and only Shippen
among old colleagues giving his course. The year 1779 ended with Rush
again talking of abandoning medicine. The imminence of his father-in-law's
death perhaps suggested the idea of retiring to Princeton, where he could
live off the produce from Morven's lands and thus escape inflation, politics,
and the infighting of academic life.[22]

All had appeared back to normal with the college at the end of 1778,
less than six months after the British evacuated. The doors had been reopened late in September and at the usual time the winter series of medical
lectures had begun. The first sign of new trouble came on 25 February 1779
when the assembly created a committee to look into the college's affairs.

Politics and religion both lay behind the probe, for the Anglican ties and rumored Tory leanings of Provost Smith and several of the trustees had angered some of the deputies, especially the Presbyterians. But a desire to reform the institution—to restore "its broad bottom," as one man phrased it—also motivated the assembly.[23]

The investigatory committee, headed by Rush's friend George Clymer, showed a genuine interest in improving the college. Its report pointed out that the college lacked funds to expand into the university Pennsylvania would need to train leaders in the postwar world. A second committee chosen later in the year, after the Constitutionalists had gained complete control of the legislature, emphasized the college's "evident hostility to the present government and constitution of this state, and, in diverse particulars, enmity to the common cause"; its report became the basis for an act passed by a large majority of the assembly on November 27, which transferred the college's lands, funds, buildings, and charter to the newly created University of the State of Pennsylvania. The act transformed a private college into a semi-state institution. The state guaranteed £1,500 in additional income; it required an oath of loyalty from trustees and faculty; six officers of the state, including the Executive Council president, sat on the board; and the assembly ratified all trustee appointments.[24]

Rush welcomed the plan to make the college a university. He assumed this meant only "the erection and endowment of new professorships in all the arts and sciences." And when Rev. John Ewing, baptizer of his first child, supplanted Reverend Smith as provost, Rush congratulated him. He wondered, though, if it might not "have been better to have placed an Episcopalian at the head of the university, to prevent the Episcopal society from complaining of ours." Ewing, as Rush remembered it, said no, adding, "It is now our turn to have a Presbyterian head."[25]

Presbyterian and state control brought with it a series of reforms. A Catholic for the first time in America sat on the board of trustees of an institution of higher learning. Two new professorships were created, one in astronomy, one in German classics, and a "German School" designed to bring German-speaking youngsters into the mainstream of Pennsylvania affairs was created. Ewing advertised for competent tutors to handle the expected increase in students, and the board selected a committee to study ways of establishing the medical school, as it was called for the first time, "on the most respectable footing."

Rush could find little to complain about in these changes. He did object to the assembly's "illegal" seizure of private property when it converted the college into a university, to the amount of state control over the institution, and to the loyalty oath required of the faculty. But these imperfections could be overlooked; the presence of Shippen on the faculty could not. The board in July 1780 invited *all* former medical professors to resume their chairs, and when Shippen accepted, Rush and Morgan refused the invitation. Only after it became obvious that his duties as director general would prohibit Shippen from giving his course did Rush accept his appointment. He gave the introductory lecture in chemistry on 20 November 1780.

As usual, Rush launched into his lectures with enthusiasm. Whatever feelings colleagues had about Rush, it was hard to deny his effectiveness as a teacher. "To the many obligations I am already under to Dr. Rush," a former student wrote a few months before the chemistry course was resumed, "I shall take the liberty of adding one more, 'Of making use of his name on all occasions.' I think I shall not *take* it in *vain*. It shall be my *Abracadabrara* in all difficulties."[26]

4

The year 1780 had started badly for the nation—as the war dragged into its fifth year the British continued to hold New York and gain ground in the South—but well for Rush, who in January heard that Shippen was "at last arrested." Morgan had caused this good news. In June of 1779 Congress after long deliberation had in effect apologized for its summary dismissal of Morgan with a commendation for his achievements as director general. Morgan, who also believed in revenge, promptly charged Shippen with misconduct in office, and Congress instructed Washington to initiate an investigation. Meanwhile, Morgan took his case to the public. While the *Packet* serialized his seemingly interminable *Vindication,* he set about collecting facts that might contribute to the devil's downfall, asking Rush, among others, for contributions. Rush gave congratulations for "awakening the attention of Congress," said he had little else to offer, then produced a small essay on his relations with Shippen.[27]

Washington at first refused to order Shippen's court-martial. The charges were vague and unsupported; he desperately needed the director general for the upcoming summer campaign. Morgan turned again for help to Rush, who responded with a point-by-point rendering of "matters I am willing to testify upon oath respecting Dr. Shippen." In October 1779 Washington agreed to order Shippen to trial after the present campaign, and soon thereafter charges were filed with the judge advocate. The first four—that Shippen had sold hospital stores as his own property, that he had speculated in hospital stores and adulterated hospital wines, that he had kept no records of expenditures, and that he had neglected his hospital duties and made false reports to Congress—were substantially those made by Rush. Morgan contributed the fifth alone—that Shippen had perpetrated "scandalous and infamous practices such as are unbecoming the character of an officer and gentleman"—which was based on the assumption Shippen had maneuvered Morgan out of the director general post.[28]

Formal arrest for Shippen came on 5 January 1780, with the trial set to begin early in March. Rush had "no doubt of his being broken." How could a court acquit a man who had "murdered 4,500 of our countrymen by his inhumanity and injustice," and who had in the process "amassed a princely fortune by selling wine and other hospital stores out of the hospital magazines?"[29]

Rush left Philadelphia on March 14 to testify at the trial, which was being held at Washington's headquarters in Morristown. His absence from the city came at an awkward time, for only a day or two earlier he had inoculated several children against smallpox whom normally he would have visited once, possibly twice, a day during the early, miserable stages of their long confinement. Snow-clogged roads delayed his arrival at Morristown until March 16, where he found that the court, too, had lost time "in consequence of the snowstorm," forcing a postponement of his testimony for several days.

Shippen appeared "sanguine and insolent" when Rush first saw him in the courtroom, but after Morgan had read aloud the depositions collected from men who had served in army hospitals under Shippen's command, he became "agitated and distressed." Rush was certain "all will end well" until he heard Shippen object to the depositions being read into the record on the ground that he had not been present when they were made or even under arrest at the time. The court upheld the objection. That done, the presiding officer, Gen. Edward Hand, the physician who had helped Rush with the essay on Indians, called Rush to the stand.[30]

Rush testified for an hour on March 20, but the climax of the day's activities came afterward, for General Washington had asked him "to dine with him and treated me with a degree of attention which led me to believe he had magnanimously forgotten my letter to Governor Henry," he later recalled. Rush found "the general uncommonly cheerful." The conversation centered chiefly on the affairs of Ireland. Only a few days earlier Washington had ordered the army to celebrate Saint Patrick's Day by way of thanks for Irish petitions to Parliament designed "to promote the cause of America."[31]

On March 21 he testified for five hours and on the next day for five and a half hours. He said nothing friends had not heard before. He attempted to be restrained—the 4,500 soldiers Shippen had "murdered" in 1777–1778 now became a thousand—but as he warmed to the story emotion took over. He gave lurid, heart-rending descriptions of "respectable farmers' sons" falling before the dread putrid fever in hospitals that Shippen's indifference and negligence had made "like slaughterhouses." Toward the end of the eleven and a half hours of testimony it became evident that much of what Rush had to say came from what he had been told rather than from what he had seen. Nonetheless, he left the stand convinced his testimony had toppled Shippen from power. After dining with General Greene, he left to spend the night in nearby Basking Ridge with Elias Boudinot, the president of Congress and his wife's uncle. March 24 found him back in Philadelphia, once again fully engaged with family affairs and the ills of his patients.[32]

5

Rush watched the Shippen trial from afar during the spring and summer of 1780. The melancholy of the previous year had disappeared and he suffused geniality even as he jousted with the university trustees over the Shippen appointment. He told friends he had found the army at Morristown greatly improved "in discipline, economy, and healthiness." A new scheme of Congress to beat inflation by calling in all circulating money at forty to one would, he thought, "restore to our counsels and arms the vigor of 1775." The imminence of Shippen's conviction, Washington's warm welcome in Morristown, his wife's involvement in the war effort—with other gentlewomen of the city she had solicited "benefactions for the army" with such ardor that she now reproached her husband for his "lukewarmness"— the sudden surge in his medical practice either singly or together had lifted him out of his depression.[33]

At a moment when many others around him were close to despairing, Rush, perversely, insisted on painting a glowing picture. The Continental army had indeed endured the winter, but Washington, unlike Rush, had little good news to dispense with the arrival of spring. "Every idea you can form of our distresses will fall short of the reality," he wrote at the moment Rush was purveying glad tidings. "There is such a combination of circumstances to exhaust the patience of the soldiery that it begins at length to be worn out, and we see in every line of the army the most serious features of mutiny and sedition." Those dispiriting words of Washington were followed by more depressing news. The city of Charleston had fallen to the British on May 12 and word of the defeat had seeped into Philadelphia early in June. The loss, Paine judged, correctly, "is such a formidable blow that unless some very sudden and spirited exertions be made the distress that will follow will be long and heavy."

The darkest hour of the war had come—for all but Rush. The loss of Charleston did not distress him. Rather, he told John Adams, it "has produced a new era in the politics of America, such as you and I saw and felt and admired in the years 1775 and 1776. Our republics cannot long exist in prosperity. We require adversity and appear to possess most of the republican spirit when most depressed."[34]

Rush's belief that adversity would bring out the best in Americans proved true to an extent. The loss of Charleston did inject, momentarily at least, a new spirit into the war effort, thanks in large part to Paine. It was he, knowing that Pennsylvania's currently empty treasury would make it impossible for the state to contribute to Washington's summer campaign, who suggested that if the rich of Philadelphia "have any spirit, any foresight of their own interest or danger, they will promote a subscription either of money or articles, and appoint a committee from among themselves to solicit the same in the several counties; and one state setting the example, the rest, I presume, will follow." Out of that suggestion came a meeting of the well-to-do at the City Tavern, and out of that meeting came pledges amounting to $300,000—Rush gave $2,000—"to support the credit of a bank to be established for furnishing a supply of provisions for the armies of the United States."[35]

Supplies began moving from Pennsylvania to Washington's army, but one state's contribution was not enough to put the army into action. By mid-July, when a campaign should have been under way, Washington had only about one thousand able-bodied men on hand. "I have almost ceased to hope," he said. "The country in general is in such a state of insensibility and indifference to its interests that I dare not flatter myself with any change for the better." Worse was to come. On September 25 Benedict Arnold defected to the British. He had spent thirteen months negotiating the best deal possible with the enemy and had wangled the command of West Point to make his betrayal more valuable to himself and the British. The act stunned Washington, and with great reluctance he ordered the hanging of the personable young Major André, who had served as a go-between for Arnold and Clinton and whose capture had revealed the plot.

6

Rush's practice proved modest during the first half of 1780. From January through March he averaged sixty patients a month. Few paid their bills and when they did it was in almost worthless currency. He raised the cost of a house call to £60 in an attempt to keep even with inflation. In these months he received only £3 in gold money.[36]

In April "a catarrh appeared among children between one year and seven years of age." Rush thought at first that an epidemic of smallpox was in the offing and inoculated forty-three of his young patients. He found it hard to classify the disease. Runny eyes and nose accompanied by a cough were the usual symptoms. "A few patients expectorated blood. Some had swellings behind their ears, and others were affected with small ulcers in the throat." The mysterious epidemic passed quickly. Except for one youngster whose pulse indicated bleeding, all patients "yielded in a few days to emetics, blisters, and the bark, assisted by the usual more simple remedies in such diseases."[37]

The city's children had hardly recovered when in May the adults were struck by an intermittent fever. James Wilson numbered among Rush's

100 patients that month. He had 91 patients in June—most of them recuperative—but in July the number pushed up to 122 and in August to 181. (In that same month, on the 29th, his second son, Richard, was born.) "Many have died from drinking cold water," Rush reported. The essay he had written years earlier on the dangers of cold water was printed up in the form of handbills which were tacked to the water pumps throughout the city.

The effort to enlighten the public did not stop there. Busy as he was, Rush found time to join with others during the summer of 1780 to found the Philadelphia Humane Society, modeled on a similar organization established in London some time earlier by his friend Lettsom. The society sought through educating the public in the proper methods of resuscitation to rescue "those whose animation may be suspended by drowning, breathing air contaminated by burning charcoal, hanging, exposure to choke-damp of wells, drinking cold water while warm in summer, strokes of the sun, lightning, swallowing laudanum, etc." This was the first such society created in America—they would proliferate after the war—and though the Philadelphia venture existed largely on paper for several years, its importance for Rush was that it promoted an aspect of his profession he thought received too little emphasis from colleagues: preventive medicine. As he liked to tell students, it "required as much skill to *prevent* diseases as to *cure* them."[38]

The sickness in the city did not abate with the end of the sweltry summer months. Rush saw 255 patients in September and on a single day in that month visited "upwards of sixty patients, all in different—and some in very remote—parts of the town, and most of them with one disorder, viz. the bilious remitting fever." Never before had he seen "more than half the number of people sick at one time in this city during the twenty years that I have known it in the line of my profession." The weeks preceding the outbreak had been unusually hot and the wind had blown steadily from the south and southwest over marshy land where the British had stripped away the trees for firewood; once again Rush blamed an epidemic on the noxious fumes from the denuded marshland. He also noted in passing that "the moschetoes were uncommonly numerous during the autumn, a certain sign (says Dr. [James] Lind) of a unwholesome atmosphere."[39]

A giddy feeling marked the onset of the disease, followed by chills, then pains in the head, back, and limbs, so "exquisitely severe" that the slightest touch on the affected areas became unbearable. The common and appropriate name for the disease was "breakbone fever," known today as dengue fever, a self-limiting, rarely fatal virus transmitted by mosquitoes. The fever and relentless pain lasts from three to twenty days. Modern treatment consists principally of good nursing and a "tincture of time." Rush's treatment began "by giving a gentle vomit of tartar emetic," which, he found, if induced "while the fever was in its forming state, frequently produced an immediate cure; and if given after its formation, on the *first* day, seldom failed of producing a crisis on the third or fourth day." After the stomach and bowels had been emptied, he gave small doses of tartar emetic mixed with Glauber's salts to excite perspiration, then ordered his patients to lie flat in bed ("The quickest and most effectual way to conquering a fever, in most cases, is by an early submission to it"), nourished by weak tea or punch, lemonade, wine, whey, tamarind, or apple water. The faint pulse that accompanied the disease obviated bleeding, but if the fever continued past the fourth day Rush resorted to blisters on the neck or behind the ears. He normally used opium sparingly, but the pleas of patients "for something to give them relief from their insupportable pains, particularly when they were seated in the eyeballs and head," were so insistent that he prescribed it in almost every case, "and always with the happiest effects."[40]

Patients recovered slowly. They complained of a continual giddiness, loss of appetite, and a weakness in the knees. "But the most remarkable symptom of the convalescence from this fever, was an uncommon dejection of the spirits," so severe in some cases that one of Rush's patients said it should be called "the *break-heart fever*." "To remove these symptoms, I gave the tincture of bark and elixir of vitriol in frequent doses. I likewise recommended the plentiful use of ripe fruits; but I saw the best effects from temperate meals of oysters, and a liberal use of porter. To these was added gentle exercise in the open air, which gradually completed the cure."[41]

Rush could write with feeling of the epidemic—his description has been called a medical classic—for at its height he became a victim. The fever, he said later, with no mention of the pain endured, "yielded in a few days to an emetic and the bark." He suffered the same dejection of spirits during recovery that had oppressed others. At one point, he said,

I dreamed that a poor woman came to me just as I was getting into my chair in Penn Street, and begged me to visit her husband.

I told her hastily, that I was worn out in attending poor people, and requested her to apply to another doctor.

"0! sir," said she, lifting up her hands, "you don't know how much you owe to your poor patients. It was decreed that you should die by the fever which lately attacked you, but the prayers of your poor patients ascended to heaven in your behalf, and your life is prolonged only upon their account."

He awoke from the dream in tears. Rush seldom paid much attention to dreams, for he was convinced they could be explained by physical causes—too many blankets on the bed, a fever—but this dream "left a deep and lasting impression upon my mind," he said years later. "It increased my disposition to attend the poor and never, when I could not serve them, to treat them in an uncivil manner."[42]

A psychiatrist who has probed beyond the sense of guilt Rush revealed here in sacrificing public service to self-interest has interpreted the dream this way:

As all dreams do, this one, too, has a foot in childhood. It is not too remote a conjecture to think that the poor woman in the dream represents the dreamer's mother. She was then sixty-three, a widow, either living in the Rush household or soon to be. . . . We need not doubt his filial devotion, but all such feelings have their darker side and here in the dream, by turning his back on the poor woman (his mother) he seems to be admitting this shadowy side of himself. The picture brings tears to his eyes because of his love for her and his guilt at denying her. In the dream the poor woman begged Dr. Rush to visit her husband; that is, to take care of him. Now, what of his mother's husbands? She had made three marriages. . . . During [the third one] Rush had left home to embark on his studies, but who can doubt how grievously he must have suffered for his mother because of this unhappy marriage? Now she appears in a dream in the guise of a poor woman asking him to visit her husband, perhaps to intercede for her. But Rush will have none of it; indeed, he suggests to her that she apply to another doctor. What the dream signifies about his relations with his father, we can only conjecture. We know, however, that Benjamin was five

years old when his father died—a time when the hostility of a
small boy toward his father is at its height. It is not surprising
that the dreamer has no interest in visiting the poor woman's
husband.[43]

7

The Shippen trial dragged on from March until 27 June 1780, when
the court acquitted the accused of all five charges. With respect to the
second, though, it declared "that Doctor Shippen did speculate in and sell
[privately purchased] hospital stores, . . . which conduct they consider
highly improper, and justly reprehensible." Washington sent the findings
on to Congress on July 15 without comment. Congress spent ten consecu-
tive afternoons listening to pertinent parts of the testimony from the trial
read aloud. On August 18 Timothy Matlack moved that Shippen's "acquittal be confirmed." Samuel Adams, who wanted to avoid approval of
the verdict, suggested that Congress simply order that Shippen "be discharged from arrest." Adam's version of the resolution passed ten states
to two.[44]

This noncommittal response to the court verdict became meaningless
on October 6, when Congress, in effect, accepted Shippen's acquittal by
reappointing him director general of the medical department. A day later
Rush met a delegate on the street and after passing the time of day asked
if the rumor that Shippen had been reappointed were true. When told it
was, he said he "was sorry for it, as I believed it would injure the character
of Congress." The delegate answered, as Rush recalled, "that the appointment was opposed by many gentlemen; that it was carried by a majority of
only one state; that Pennsylvania seemed to make a state affair of supporting Doctor Shippen; and that Mr. Matlack, in particular, had spoken much
in his favor."[45]

The extant evidence suggests that Congress erred in ignoring the
court's reprimand and in honoring Shippen with a reappointment to his
old post. Neither Morgan nor Rush had produced sufficient evidence to
force a conviction on criminal charges, but enough disinterested witnesses
had testified about Shippen's speculation in wine, then considered a medical
necessity, to warrant the court's reprimand and the judgment of a modern

scholar, the trial's most careful student, that Shippen's actions were "morally indefensible."[46]

Morgan once again took his case to the public when Congress refused to censure Shippen, but Rush at first stayed on the sidelines. In September, when Morgan's new attack began, Rush was being run ragged by the epidemic of breakbone fever. His case load continued heavy through October, when he had 134 patients, and only in November did it begin to ease up. On November 18 he made public peace with the university by announcing that two days hence he would give the introductory lecture in chemistry; and on the same day he wrote the most vitriolic attack yet against both Shippen and Congress. The director general's reappointment, he suggested, owed something to the madeira served to the delegates at Shippen's table. Congress had become so corrupt, he went on, addressing Shippen, "that unless you are dismissed and the delegates who voted for you discovered and charged, it will not be in the power of foreign alliances or loans to save our country." Then, carried away by this rhetoric, he spoke of women who "bedew the papers that contain the tales of your cruelties to the sick with their tears," and of children who "ask if you are made and look like other men." Rush concluded that Shippen's reappointment would "serve like a high-water mark to show posterity the degree of corruption that marked the present stage of the American Revolution."[47]

A second letter on December 2 opened with a reference to Timothy Matlack, who had recently been defeated for reelection to Congress. Matlack might be able and eloquent, "but as he was the friend of a speculator in office I rejoice in his dismission." The letter went on to raise further questions about Shippen's speculation, and then, in passing, to involve in the feud the "good-tempered" Bond, the assistant director who had praised Shippen publicly and censured him privately to Rush. Bond responded with a letter of his own, accusing Rush of being "capable of lying in the worst sense of that approbation."[48]

Through all this Shippen had been serializing his own *Vindication*, while Morgan filed a rebuttal to every installment. On December 23, when the *Packet*'s publisher at last deferred to good taste and called a halt to the affair, Rush published what he considered clinching evidence of Shippen's frauds—a series of depositions made by Patrick Garvey, a clerk who had kept the accounts of the medical department and who had found irregularities in the director general's records. If, after this latest accusation, "Shippen triumphs one day longer," Rush declared, "then virtue is a shadow and liberty only a name in the United States."[49]

On 3 January 1781, the director general resigned his commission. Americans could once more raise their heads! But victory was only momentary. Upon retiring, Shippen asked Washington for a testimonial. Washington wrote that he had been satisfied with the director general's conduct and that, so far as he could judge, "I believe no hospitals could have been better administered." Shippen published the encomium for all Philadelphia to read. Garvey's accusations still remained to be dealt with, and from these Rush believed "Shippen cannot escape." But he did. Garvey was arrested on suspicion of trading with the enemy and soon after fled from the city. He reappeared later in the year to open a grocery store, and nothing ever came of his accusations.[50]

13

"All Will End Well"

1781–1782

1

IN OCTOBER 1780 the Republicans by a slim margin at last won control of the Pennsylvania Assembly. Soon afterward word that Virginia had abandoned claim to the western territory raised hope that the Articles of Confederation, after several years wandering about the country searching for votes of approval, might soon be ratified. These changes on the political front, coupled with Shippen's resignation from the medical department of the army, contributed to the renewed optimism Rush radiated in 1781. Phrases like "let us have patience" and the favorite "all will end well" reappeared in letters.

Again there was something almost perverse in his cheerfulness: the news was not all that good. On New Year's Day 1781 the Pennsylvania Line, fifteen hundred strong, mutinied. For nearly a year the once well-fed, well-supplied Pennsylvania troops attached to Washington's army had lived on short rations. Their lack of "clothing beggars all description," said Anthony Wayne, their commander. "For God's sake send us our dividend of uniforms, overalls, blankets." While Wayne worked for "twenty tedious days and nights" negotiating a settlement with his soldiers, Congress belatedly mollified them with provisions and promises. The mutiny might have been expected to throw Rush into despair. It bothered him hardly at all. "It appears upon examination that most of them were entitled to their discharge above a year ago," he commented with rare understanding to

John Adams. "They are still devoted to our cause, and such of them as do not reenlist will add to the strength and defense of our country by entering on board privateers or other vessels of war."[1]

This fragile optimism toughened as the year progressed. Paper money became almost valueless by February, forcing it out of circulation and bringing back into the market what gold and silver existed. Maryland acceded to the Articles of Confederation, at last giving the new nation a constitution; France sent over a sizable new loan; Congress created out of anarchy the Departments of Foreign Affairs, Finance, and War; and Robert Morris, whom Rush was heralding as "a new star in our American hemisphere," became the superintendent of finance. Morris's energy gave the government a semblance of vigor during the early, trying months of 1781. He persuaded Congress to charter the Bank of North America, in which Rush purchased one share of stock.[2] He started flour, meat, and rum toward the army as well as clothing and ammunition. Washington credited Morris for a large share in the successful campaign of 1781 and said "it will soon be a matter of wonder how Mr. Morris had done so much with so small means."

That campaign Washington expected to focus on New York City, where General Clinton was ensconced with his army. But in the summer of 1781 Lord Cornwallis, with a force of 7,200 men, carried on a "country dance" in Virginia with an American army of 1,200 led by Lafayette that caused Washington to change his plans. Lafayette skillfully held his army just out of British grasp, always willing "to skirmish, but not to engage too far," he said, noting: "I am not strong enough even to be beaten." When Washington sent reenforcements to Lafayette, Cornwallis backed off toward the coast, finally settling down behind a fortified position on the Yorktown peninsula to await a British fleet to carry his troops away. Washington watched these movements from his post above New York, where his five thousand continentals had been joined by an equal number of French troops led by the Comte de Rochambeau. On August 14 he learned that the Comte de Grasse was on his way with thirty ships and three thousand French marines. Five days later Washington took the gamble of his life. He decided to move his combined armies from New York to Virginia on the long-shot chance that they could entrap Cornwallis's force before a British fleet arrived to evacuate it.

While the army trudged slowly across New Jersey, Washington pushed on ahead to Philadelphia, where he pleaded with the city to round up food, clothing, and equipment for his men. The pressure he put on Morris led to a miracle—the troops as they reached Philadelphia were given a month's pay in gold. It took a full day for the army to pass through the city. A few days after it had faded from sight, Rush wrote portentously: "The fate of Great Britain and the repose of Europe will probably be determined in Chesapeake Bay." But apathy, too, was in the air. The war had stretched on for more than six years, and Philadelphia had endured more of it than any other city on the continent. Its citizens were exhausted. Something of a detached, almost disinterested attitude was behind the good wishes shouted to the soldiers as they tramped past, and they had no sooner slipped beyond the Schuylkill when they were forgotten. Rush, for example, laid plans for resuming his tiresome squabble with Shippen. Also, he turned to politics, passing along to a friend the rumor that John Dickinson was slated to become president of the Executive Council if the Republicans won the upcoming assembly election.[3] Citizens still had no word from Washington's army when they went to the polls in early October and split their vote almost evenly between Republicans and Constitutionalists; the presidency went not to Dickinson, as predicted, but to a relatively unknown compromise candidate, William Moore, a moderate Constitutionalist. On October 22 an express rode into the city "with the agreeable and very important intelligence of Lord Cornwallis and his army's having surrendered on the seventeenth instant." When official word of the victory at Yorktown arrived two days later, the boom of guns echoed at noon through the city from every ship in the harbor. The city paused to attend divine service in the afternoon, and in the evening virtually the entire population strolled the streets enjoying the illuminated windows. Charles Willson Peale's were judged the most impressive. In each of his windows on the first two floors he had placed lighted transparencies of the battle and its heroes and stretched across the windows on the top floor in large letters "FOR OUR ALLIES! HUZZA! HUZZA! HUZZA!"[4]

With Cornwallis's defeat, Rush said, "the pride of Britain, and the pillar of all her hopes in America, is fallen, fallen, fallen!"[5] He was right.

2

Rush's medical practice in 1781 flourished as never before. He averaged 75 patients a month from January through April, nearly a hundred in May and June, and more than 130 from July through October. He made a slight effort to enhance his professional reputation with two brief publications. In April he wrote an inconsequential Preface ("The author of the following work is too well-known to stand in need of much commendation. He has produced a revolution in medicine") to Cullen's *First Lines of the Practice of Physic,* one of the few medical works that had been smuggled into the city since the war began and which Rush arranged to have republished soon after it fell into his hands.

Later in the year he also published a lecture he had delivered in February on the Suttonian method of inoculation, a model guide for students and tyro physicians. Rush gave no ground in the battle initiated on his return from Europe—he still deprecated the use of mercury, favored by local physicians—but the restrained tone made it apparent that he sought to avoid rather than start arguments. With a humbleness perhaps false, he even suggested that with so much yet unknown about inoculation he expected the future would bury his name in silence "and forget that ever I ventured to lay a single stone in this part of the fabric of medicine."[6]

Once again in 1781 his professional life was dominated by the fight with Shippen. But even the renewal of that quarrel in October could not dampen the good mood Washington's victory at Yorktown had put Rush in. The previous autumn medical students at the university had ignored the raging faculty feud and petitioned the trustees for Shippen to revive his lectures on anatomy, which he did on January 4, the day after his resignation from the medical department. Rush and Morgan waited until they had finished their own courses in late February, then jointly told the trustees that "they cannot, consistent with their own characters, and the interest of science and virtue, consent to accept their appointments in the university with Doctor Shippen." In submitting their resignations, they did not presume to "think themselves necessary to fill the places they formerly occupied," for there were many as competent as they.[7]

The trustees agreed, and the resignations were accepted. At the board meetings in June 1781, the effort to reconstruct the medical faculty produced total disorder. Morgan, among others, was nominated for Shippen's post, professor of anatomy, a course he had never taught. The elder Shippen proposed Dr. James Hutchinson, a member of the board, for the chair in chemistry, but Hutchinson, though a Constitutionalist and thus a political enemy, nominated Rush for the position. Later Trustee Timothy Matlack, still a political enemy, had the Morgan-Rush resignation read aloud, but board members Rev. William White, rector of Christ Church, and Francis Hopkinson, poet, essayist, and signer of the Declaration of Independence, stated that Rush now wanted to retrieve his old post. A vendetta could be carried so far. When the vote came, Shippen was chosen professor of anatomy "by a large majority of votes," Rush professor of chemistry "by a majority of votes" only, and Morgan, who had not rescinded his resignation, was—the minutes are vague at this point—defeated for the professorship of practice and theory of medicine. A short while later, White announced that Morgan agreed to accept the position he had occupied since 1765, and the board thereupon reappointed him.[8]

The settlement crumbled almost immediately as Morgan reattacked Shippen in the public prints. The feud sputtered through the summer, then burst into flame in late September when Morgan and Rush published their letter of resignation and again said they refused to teach while Shippen served on the faculty. In passing, they accused Joseph Reed, now president of the Executive Council, of having arranged for Shippen to retrieve his professorship in order "to shelter him from merited disgrace." Furthermore, they said Shippen's accounts while director general "have been examined in the auditor's office; and we have authority to say, *they have not, and cannot be passed,* although millions of dollars have been drawn from the public treasury."[9]

This shot provoked but one reply from Shippen—publication of Washington's commendatory letter of his tenure as director general—and the first of a series of letters from the army's commissioner of accounts, who wondered about the Rush-Morgan authorities, since no one had yet checked Shippen's records. Morgan regarded the commissioner's question as ungentlemanly and refused a direct answer. Rush dove to a new low in his reply. He virtually called Shippen a traitor: "As well might General Arnold publish the polite letter his Excellency [Washington] wrote to him after his service in the campaign of 1777, to acquit himself of the crimes of speculation in Philadelphia, or of treachery and defection at the post of West Point." He told the commissioner that it did not matter what the accounts showed, he, Rush, *knew* the records were corrupt.[10]

Shippen met the insinuation of treason with silence, but the infuriated commissioner brought a newcomer's energy to the fray. He dismissed Morgan as a "quibbling son of Aesculapius." Rush's reply he judged, quite accurately, a *"jargon of diction"*; if it "means anything at all it will only amount to *this,* that should the accounts be approved honest, and *pass muster,* the commissioners must be held out to the world as corrupted, and that Doctor Shippen (after having been charged with the plunder of millions) is actually so poor, as not to be able to bribe them."

This riposte silenced Rush and he now faded from the controversy. Morgan, however, refused to let go, and as his attacks continued, Philadelphians, in what one of them called "this *truly hackneyed subject,*" joined in demanding that Morgan produce his evidence or shut up. The affair took a nasty turn in mid-November when one writer accused Morgan of treasonable flirtation with the enemy during the British occupation of Philadelphia. Morgan dismissed the accusation as absurd, but with that reply he, too, dropped from the fight.[11] Nevertheless, the feud with Shippen continued to obsess Morgan; failure to break his opponent ended by breaking him. His interest in the medical school—he never again taught at the university— withered, and his medical practice from that time on sagged. Rush, on the other hand, had too many obsessions, too much energy, to be overwhelmed by a single defeat.

As a free-lance professor, temporarily at least, Rush advertised in the fall of 1781 that his lectures in chemistry would begin November 19— place unannounced. The advertisements also noted that a course in the practice of physic would be offered as well. The course in general medicine, according to a student's lecture notes, reveals Rush's views on diseases toward the end of the Revolution:

> *Consumption:* This disorder is more frequent in this country than formerly and this is owing to the change in the manner of living and dressing. The constitution [of the people is] still getting worse, . . . the climate being considerably changed—our winters being damper than usual.
>
> *Neuroses:* The nerves are not alone affected in these two ideas—*comata—apoplexy.* More frequent than formerly—'tis artificial—the child of luxury—more frequent in Europe than here owing to their high living and indolency. 'Tis peculiar to short-necked and corpulent people. Tho' this is not a rule without exceptions. . . . It most attacks those turned of forty.
>
> *Cholera:* Opium is an infallible remedy in this disorder. . . . Nature generally clears the stomach and bowels. Opium must be given in great quantities.

Rickets: Less frequent here than in Europe. . . . *Cure:* give plenty of steel and bark . . . generous food. Fresh air and cold baths. This alone cures.

Syphilis: This disorder and the gonorrhea are different, tho' they sometimes appear in the same person at once. *Cure:* Mercury alone is to be depended on, as it is a sovereign remedy in all climates and stages of the disorder. Mercury was first made use of in this disorder under the form of an ointment.[12]

Teaching and his regular practice occupied only part of Rush's time from one day to the next. As in the past, political affairs continued to intrigue him, particularly after the arrival of David Ramsay in the city in March 1782.

3

Ramsay came to Philadelphia to serve as one of South Carolina's delegates in Congress. He stayed with Rush. Also visiting the family at the time was Elias Boudinot's daughter "Sukey," who overnight had become one of the city's most popular belles. She immediately began to "humanize" the bachelor Ramsay. "With a little more attention to his hair and the seam of his stockings," said Rush, "I think the doctor might engage to carry back with him to Carolina a Jersey or Pennsylvania beauty."[13]

No doubt Ramsay and Sukey numbered among the several friends with whom Rush and his wife attended "a most splendid entertainment" in July given by the French ambassador to celebrate the birth of the dauphin of France. More than a thousand invitations had been issued, and some ten thousand citizens turned out to watch the arrival of an assortment of guests—Whigs and ex-Tories, politicians and soldiers, the learned and those who knew not "whether Horace was a Roman or Scotchman." "The company was mixed, it is true, but the mixture formed the harmony of the evening," said Rush. "Washington and Dickinson held several dialogues together. Here were to be seen men conversing with each other who appeared in all the different stages of the American war. Dickinson and Morris frequently reclined together against the same pillar." Even Mifflin and Reed, though political enemies, "accosted each other with all the kindness of ancient friends." Thomas Paine alone among the multitude of guests elicited a snide comment from Rush. "The celebrated author of *Common*

Sense," he said, "retired frequently from the company to analyze his thoughts and to enjoy the repast of his own original ideas."

Philadelphia never before had experienced such sumptuous entertainment. A lavish display of fireworks interrupted the dancing, then the party resumed until midnight, when a supper prepared by thirty cooks borrowed from the French army was served. The awed crowd, reduced to near silence, "looked and behaved more as if they were *worshipping* than *eating,*" someone remarked. The party broke up about one in the morning, with the Rush entourage among those leading the way home. "Everybody felt pleasure, but it was of too tranquil a nature," said Rush of the evening.[14]

The complexion of the Congress David Ramsay now sat in differed considerably from the one Rush had joined six years earlier. Then, weighed down by the job of directing a great war for thirteen infant states, there had been time only in passing to argue about the division of power between the states and the central government. Rush, even then a nationalist, had missed no chance during his short tenure in office to urge strengthening of the bonds of union, but out of step, as he so often was, he had been one of the minority that went unheeded. Now, after several years of existing precariously, never certain where it would get the money to pay its bills, Congress had come to be dominated by men convinced the union could survive only if the central government were made stronger. The reforms inaugurated in 1781—creation of separate administrative departments, for example—reflected the changed attitude. That same year, having been forced at last to suspend payment of interest on loan certificates, Congress took a crucial step that it hoped would lead to increasing its powers: it asked the states for permission to levy a permanent 5 per cent duty on all imports, the money collected to be used by Congress as it saw fit. Morris, who had prodded the delegates into making this request of the states, held that the measure was needed to win the war. The victory at Yorktown undermined that argument. Morris thereupon shifted ground: the measure was needed to discharge the accumulated war debts, he now said, which Congress, not the states, was responsible for paying off. To distribute the debt among the states would be "ruinous" to a strong union, he insisted. An innovation as fundamental as an impost required unanimous consent from the states, and in the summer of 1782 the recalcitrant legislature of tiny Rhode Island rejected the proposal and thereby defeated it.[15]

With his good friend Ramsay in Congress, Rush now had fresh, daily reports on what went on behind the closed doors in the State House. This pipeline to the fountainhead of government may have helped persuade Rush to write the series of nine essays—three under the pseudonym "Retaliation" and six as "Leonidas"—on continental affairs that appeared in the press from late May to mid-August. Something more personal, however, could have driven him into his study. The death of his second daughter, four-month-old Susanna, in late May, about the time the first essay appeared, suggests he sought to escape from grief not only through keeping busy professionally—he averaged more than ninety patients a month during the period the series ran—but through writing.[16]

The early pieces were brief, discursive, and only reworked old material. Indeed, one was a reprint of an essay he had published three years earlier on the French alliance. Not until the fourth article, published in mid-June, did Rush find a theme worth exploring, one that nicely tied into the burgeoning nationalism among the delegates in Congress. America, if it expects to become a great nation, must have a strong navy, he said. "The man who looks forward to peace as the proper time to build and equip a navy is as absurd as the man who refuses to go into the water until from lectures and books he has learned to swim. A war is the hotbed of seamen, who form the soul of a navy."[17]

These thoughts were not new with Rush. He had heard John Adams expound on the need for a navy years earlier when sitting beside him in Congress. In 1779 he had written General Lee on the subject. "You observe, I think justly, that the sea appears the proper element of the Americans," Lee had replied. "It behooves 'em therefore, in time, to lay the foundation of a formidable navy, . . . for no man of common sense can suppose France or Spain have taken the part they have done merely pour les beaux eyes des Americans. . . ."[18] The time had now come to publicize these views. When France entered the war, Congress let the might of the American navy wash away—from thirty-four ships in 1777 to seven in 1781—on the assumption France would thereafter handle the war on the sea. The recently created Shelburne ministry in England had announced "the plan of a naval war" against America, and the first results of this new strategy became painfully apparent on 12 April 1782—only six months after Yorktown—when Adm. George Rodney defeated a French fleet commanded by de Grasse in the West Indies, a victory, said Rush in his fifth essay, that leaves Britain "as powerful and insolent upon the ocean" as ever.

In this fifth essay Rush rested his argument on a shaky assumption. "The man who expects peace in less than seven years (without a miracle)," he said when peace was less than a year away, "looks for an event as contrary to the fixed principles of nature as for a stone to ascend against the laws of gravity." But *if* the war did last seven years, and *if* it was "to be carried on by sea," then to win America must have a strong navy. And to build one presents no formidable problem, he said lightly. A navy "consists of nothing but oak and pine, kept together by hemp and iron. And what do we see on yonder shore? Why, forests abounding with oaks and pines, mountains abounding with iron ore, and a soil capable of producing all the raw materials of sails and ropes. Then let not the oaks and pines and iron of America be afraid of the oaks and pines and iron of Britain."[19]

Not too long after these observations appeared, a member of Congress said to Rush: "The ideas contained in these papers are just—but what can Congress do? We want money."

"Yes, sir," Rush replied, "you want money, but you want something of much more importance, that is CREDIT."*[20]

That exchange gave Rush the theme for his next two essays, or, to put it more accurately, moral lectures. Honesty, he advised Congress, is the best policy. "We must be honest, or we shall be undone." Suspension of the interest payments on loan certificates, Rush said, has done more to injure the nation's public credit, "the principle hinge of government, than it is in the power of language to describe." Resumption of the interest payments

---

*Credit, his own as well as the state's, was much on Rush's mind in 1782. Near the end of the year Charles Willson Peale wrote him a brief dunning note. Peale had built a gallery onto his house where he planned to display his collection of portraits. Now he wanted to collect a debt, possibly for the portraits he had painted of Rush and his wife in 1776.

> When a person is in cash, the people of Maryland use the phrase, such a one is in blast. If he is without money, then he is out of blast. I don't know from whence the phrase came, but throughout that state it is expressed.
> I am out of blast. My building has made me miserably poor. If it is convenient to you to assist me into blast you will very much oblige your very
> Humble Servt.

Rush, too, appears to have been out of blast, for in 1782 he borrowed £150 from his friend William Bingham, reputed to be the richest man in Pennsylvania, at six per cent interest. He still had not paid the debt thirteen years later when the interest alone amounted to £101.[21]

will reestablish credit and allow the government to resort to further loans from the people, "to enable us to finish the war with vigor and safety." Rush here did not argue from self-interest. At the time, the face value of the loan certificates he owned amounted to only $1,341.

The huge debts the nation was acquiring, Rush continued, were nothing to be disturbed about. Debts are a cement to the Union, he said. "The interest which the individuals of each state have in the redemption of these certificates will render the perpetual Union of the states no less dear to them than their liberties and independence." Here Rush only rephrased what Robert Morris had been telling Congress for some time. Thomas Paine had put the thought better and earlier than either man. "No nation ought to be without a debt," Paine had written in *Common Sense.* "A national debt is a national bond."[22]

In the next essay on the need for a navy, Rush glanced ahead in order to judge America's role in the postwar world. Gone is the enthusiasm for manufacturing expressed earlier in the Revolution. Factories, it now appears, corrupt men's health. "The manufacturing towns in Britain resemble convalescent hospitals," Rush wrote. "They are at best large machines, of which the principal instruments and wheels are men." Agriculture alone is "most conducive to health and population, and most favorable to the practice of virtue." Moreover, the vast, vacant continent has destined Americans to the agricultural way of life, just as the immense ocean that separates the nation from Europe has destined it to commerce, an enterprise upon which Rush lavished praise. Commerce "forms the only barrier that can be contrived to check the aristocratic tendency of a monopoly of land," he said. "It opens the door to power, rank and influence to everybody. It is the magnet of talents and the cherisher of virtue. It is calculated to restore men to their original equality, and to expel tyranny from the world." Trade ties all nations together, now that America has escaped the restraints of England's exclusive commercial system, and teaches men they are "children of the same father, and members of one great family."[23]

Midway in the series, which by now dealt only tangentially with the need for a strong navy, Rush went out of his way to eulogize Congress. "The present Congress I believe is composed of men of as much integrity and abilities as ever met together for the government of this, or perhaps of any other, country." This extravagance seems only to have egged Rush on.

"I insist upon it," he continued, "that the difficulties which our rulers have surmounted within these two last years, are proofs of a *stronger* and purer virtue than any that were exhibited in the beginning of the war." Now came a singular confession. "So far am I from admitting that the patriots of 1775 or 1776 monopolized all public spirit or wisdom that I believe most of the evils in government, with which we are now contending, have been bequeathed to us by the disaffection of some of them, by the timidity of others, and by the ignorance of them all."[24]

Rush, who all his life glowed with pride for the part he had played in the events of '75 and '76, appeared here, consciously or otherwise, to censure himself as much as his compatriots of those years. He compared the early patriots with the light infantry of an army: they gave the first warning of the approaching enemy, but then "fell back when the battle thickened, and made way for the heavy troops," who by "their strength and steadiness have turned the battle from our gates." He does not wish to demean those early zealous patriots, but only to honor "those men who have distinguished themselves in *every* stage of the controversy." The steadfastness of these men has won the day, and "they deserve encomiums beyond the conceptions of my heart or the expressions of my pen." Rush concluded the passage with this sentence: "We have sinned beyond repentance or forgiveness." Then, after begging pardon for the digression, he added: "It was necessary. It is of consequence for us to know ourselves."[25] No dream he recorded, nothing he ever wrote, revealed more of Rush's uneasiness about his retreat from the war and from public life than this oblique confession of "Leonidas" in 1782. Not surprisingly, he commenced to pour his energy into a variety of projects designed to reform American society, as if to compensate for his momentarily slack devotion to the cause.

Rush never, as long as he lived, reverted to censuring the men of '75 and '76, but throughout the remainder of 1782 he continued to be agitated by the issues raised in these essays. He accepted the imminence of peace with the remark that "whatever is, is right," but continued to wish it had been possible to "have bequeathed at least a naval war to my children." The fact that in the first nine months of the year Philadelphia had "lost at a moderate computation eight hundred thousand pounds by capture" testified to the danger British naval power presented to America's permanent independence. The threat of parties and factions dominating postwar politics did not upset him, for such divisions would preserve rather than undermine liberty. "It will be by opposing the pride and ambition of the great families and officers of government to each other that the common people will find safety and freedom among us," he said. He did fear that unless the power of "our states can be limited" the Republic's future was uncertain. A strong union of the states was central to his vision of a great and powerful America.[26]

4

While Rush expounded on continental matters during the summer of 1782, he also promoted the publication of a book that had recently become a favorite of his, Rev. John William Fletcher's *An Appeal to Matter of Fact and Common Sense.* The enthusiasm for Fletcher's work signaled a break in his religious views. He had from youth adhered to the Westminster Confession, with its emphasis on predestination and Calvin's wrathful God, and publicly appeared as an orthodox Presbyterian—"but without affection" —until he met Rev. Elhanan Winchester. Winchester, a Baptist from New England, had come to Philadelphia in 1780, only to find that his liberal views on salvation did not sit well with the congregation. After Winchester was eased from his pulpit, the hall of the University of Pennsylvania was made available to him, and it was likely there that Rush first listened to him and first heard of Fletcher.[27]

Fletcher, an Anglican clergyman from a backwater parish in England, had over the years produced a stream of works that rejected predestination for the doctrine of universal salvation. After reading the *Appeal,* Rush became convinced "of the salvation of all men"—though he continued to believe in future punishment after death "of long, long duration"—and so eager to have the unenlightened share the message that he took steps to have the work published in Philadelphia. The proposal for publication that appeared in July 1782 may well have been written by him. If so, Rush made the *Appeal* sound like orthodox fare. It has "little or nothing to do with the controverted points of doctrine," said the announcement, "but treats the essentials of religion (wherein all Christians agree) in a close, energetic, and masterly manner."[28]

Rush's religious change came at a time when others he knew were also shifting. James Wilson, born and reared a Presbyterian, moved to the Episcopal Church in 1782. Samuel Blair, a friend from youth and a Presbyterian minister, also came to accept the idea of universal salvation. Perhaps to these and others of the day the doctrine of predestination seemed unsuitable for a republic based on the idea that all men are created equal. As the Revolution approached a successful conclusion, it seemed possible that neither men were so evil nor God so wrathful as pictured by Calvin.[29]

The summer of 1782 saw Rush confess that he had "sinned beyond repentance or forgiveness." This admission, coupled with a new faith in the eventual salvation of all men, may have persuaded him that the time to start saving them—and himself—should be now, not in the afterlife. The principles of universal salvation and final restitution "have bound me to the whole human race," he told his English friend Price a few years later; "these are the principles which animate me in all my labors for the interests of my fellow creatures."[30]

In 1782 Rush became involved in the first of the multitude of reforms that would engage his energies for the next seven or eight years. In June he found time to sandwich between the string of essays on public matters a lecture on the evils of drinking spirituous liquors. It was a brief piece, the first shot in a long battle. The increasingly heavy consumption of spirits among all classes perturbed Rush, but in this essay he chose as the target the Pennsylvania custom of serving such refreshments to harvest workers. The custom cost farmers dearly in money and lost time; it produced no good, many quarrels, and much intemperate language. Rush prescribed in lieu of whisky such substitutes as water, milk, buttermilk, or, especially recommended, "vinegar and water sweetened with molasses or brown sugar." All these "are cooling and grateful to the stomach," he said. "They invigorate the appetite and obviate that disposition to putrefaction in the humors to which excessive heat and labor naturally dispose them."[31]

During these same months Rush perfected plans for a new backcountry college at Carlisle to be named after his now honored friend Dickinson. He also revived a long-dormant interest in the abolition of slavery. "For God's sake," he wrote Nathanael Greene, who planned to settle in South Carolina after the war, "do not exhibit a new spectacle to the world, of men just emerging from a war in favor of liberty, . . . fitting out vessels to import their fellow creatures from Africa to reduce them afterwards to slavery." As he had before the Revolution, Rush still objected to immediate emancipation. "They are rendered unfit by their habits of vice (the offspring of slavery) for freedom," he added. "Make their situation comfortable by good treatment. Time may unfold a method hereafter of repairing to their posterity the injustice that has been done to the present generation."[32]

The letter to Greene exemplified Rush's new faith in "the eventual salvation of all men," a faith that would in the next few years direct him down a wider road toward regeneration than the one posted by Finley and Davies. Those gentlemen, coming out of the Great Awakening, held that only men spiritually reborn through the church could be among the saved. Rush did not reject their teaching; he broadened it and to an extent secularized it. Moral reform of the individual remained central to his beliefs, but he now saw that the church offered only one route among many to that goal. Other institutions—schools, newspapers, governments, prisons, even hospitals—could, if suitably contrived, also help hasten men toward salvation. The "road to glory"—a phrase Congress had cut from Jefferson's draft of the Declaration of Independence—now became a many-laned avenue. During the next five years Rush would work relentlessly to open up every lane, driven by the thought that only by reforming every American could the nation itself become virtuous.

5

The state election in October 1782 gave reason for Rush to continue to be in good spirits. The Republicans increased their hold on the assembly, with Jacob Rush now one of the deputies. On November 7, they used their new strength to install Dickinson as president of the Executive Council. The time had come to purge the state "of tyrants, fools, and traitors," Rush said. "I have pledged myself to my friends that I will never relinquish the great object of a good constitution."[33]

A single sad note marred the election results: the defeat of his friend from Carlisle, John Montgomery, with whom he was working to establish Dickinson College. But Rush did not despair. "Your friends," he told Montgomery, "I believe will if possible show your country the sense they entertain of their treatment of you by putting you into Congress next

month." The prediction came true on schedule, when later in the month the
assembly chose Montgomery, along with Thomas Mifflin, Thomas Fitzsimons, James Wilson, and Richard Peters (all friends of Rush's) to represent the state in Congress.[34]

Rush's high spirits continued through the year. More and more he
again involved himself in public affairs. In November, as a member of a
committee of nine, he signed (and may have written) a petition to the
assembly that asked in moderate tones for "the speedy adoption" of a plan
to pay the interest on the loan certificates purchased by the public and to
create a sinking fund for paying off the principal. Little came of the plea;
the assembly turned the matter over to Congress, which launched a debate
that was still rambling on when news arrived in March 1783 that the preliminary articles of peace had been signed.[35]

14

The Spirit of Peace

1783–1784

1

O N 30 NOVEMBER 1782 the United States of America and Great Britain signed a preliminary treaty that went into effect a short while later when Britain made peace with France and Spain. Congress ratified the treaty exactly eight years after the war had begun at Lexington, on 19 April 1783. Thomas Paine that day published the thirteenth *Crisis,* the last of a series of papers of which the first, opening with the words "These are the times that try men's souls," had been read aloud to Washington's soldiers the night before they descended on Trenton. Now Paine wrote: " 'The times that tried men's souls' are over—the greatest and completest revolution the world ever knew gloriously and happily accomplished."

The war may have ended but not the Revolution. And even jubilance over the war's end was dulled on Saturday, June 21, when some three hundred Pennsylvania soldiers picketed the Pennsylvania Executive Council, then sitting in the State House; they demanded that the state produce their back pay before demobilizing them. The soldiers had selected with care their day to demonstrate, not wishing to embarrass Congress, which normally did not convene on Saturday. Unfortunately, Congress happened to meet that particular Saturday, and it chose to believe that "the dignity and authority of the United States" had been offended by the soldiers' presence. It asked the Executive Council to arrest the ringleaders, but Dickinson refused. The soldiers had public sympathy behind them, and the state militia would balk if ordered to quell the demonstration. The Congress that Rush less than a year earlier had lavishly praised took flight from the city on June 24, coming to rest in the village of Princeton.[1]

The hasty departure left Rush aghast. "Our papers already teem with scandal against you," he wrote a delegate in one letter, and in another he attempted to cajole the members back with sarcasm. "Some wicked folks here say that the air of Princeton used to be famed *only* for curing consumptions, but that it has lately been very efficacious in curing a species of *madness* called Congo-mania." The shrill tone of these and other letters about Congress's departure may have owed something to the death in July of Rush's third daughter, a four-and-a-half-month infant who had been named after his friend Elizabeth Graeme Ferguson.

While behind the scenes Rush sought to promote a quick settlement of the back-pay issue by serving as an intermediary between Dickinson and the soldiers, he dispatched conciliatory pleas to friends in Congress. "Come and spend at least a few months in Philadelphia to heal the breach between us," he wrote to Montgomery. "Afterwards I wish you may never spend another month in any of the large cities of America." He even offered to donate to Congress ten acres in the center of Princeton, plus one hundred acres of woodland outside the village, if it decided to settle there permanently.[2]

Meanwhile, Congress President Boudinot had asked Washington for troops to quash the uprising. Washington responded with a detachment of fifteen hundred that had orders to march toward Philadelphia on the double. This news staggered Rush, for it came when the assembly was about to consider whether or not it should grant Congress the right to levy an impost duty. "For God's sake! as you value all that we have gained by the Revolution, consider what you are doing," he wrote Montgomery. "If you remain one week longer at Princeton feeding one another with ideas of insulted and wounded dignity (all *stuff* in a republic) you may lose Pennsylvania forever from your wise plans of Continental revenue."[3]

Rush at last found himself on the popular side of an issue and allied once more with his friends of '75 and '76. Paine, who had heard of his efforts to draw Congress back to Philadelphia, sent him a brief but friendly note and as his contribution to the campaign he enclosed a "Memorial" urging Congress to return to Philadelphia. He told Rush that he preferred not to claim authorship of it in order that those who found Paine's writing suspect would not be deterred from signing. The subterfuge worked to the degree that when the "Memorial" appeared in the press early in August it carried the signatures of citizens from both Republicans and Constitutionalists.[4]

The threatened arrival of Continental troops sufficed to end the uprising. But Congress, a petulant child in the eyes of Philadelphians, continued at Princeton. On August 2 Rush gave vent to his forebodings in a letter to Boudinot. He said all Pennsylvania had turned against Congress; that the assembly, soon to meet, would no doubt take measures "that will separate us forever"; and that possibly it might even "put a stop to our taxes being paid into the federal treasury." "For God's sake, be wise," he said, "and let not those words *dignity of Congress* produce the same fatal effects upon our Union that *supremacy of Parliament* has produced upon the British Empire. The house is on fire—it is no matter *where* it kindled or *who* blew the flame. Buckets—buckets should be the cry of every good citizen." At the end he apologized for an unbridled tongue, then added: "I am zealous above all things for our Union, and I place all my hopes of the safety, perpetuity, and happiness of our government in the success of the late wise and benevolent resolutions of Congress upon the subject of finance."[5]

The plea was lost on Congress. "You know the man and can make proper allowances," Charles Thomson observed to Rush's friend Richard Peters, doubtless summing up the reaction of most other members. Congress endured the bucolic atmosphere of Princeton four months longer.[6]

2

The catastrophe envisioned by Congress's flight never materialized, and within a few weeks Rush had forgotten—or at least put out of mind—fears about the Union's future. He turned instead, in the time he could spare from his practice, to Pennsylvania affairs. He decided to ask John Penn, Jr., Pennsylvania's last colonial governor who was returning to retire on his estate along the Schuylkill, to donate a tract of land to the proposed college in Carlisle. Montgomery, to whom he revealed the plan, approved the idea but deplored the timing. In October, the people would vote not only for a new assembly but for the Council of Censors; the council, to which Montgomery was seeking election, could propose any needed constitutional amendments and call a convention to deal with these issues. Any candidate associated directly or indirectly with a Penn before such a crucial election courted certain defeat. Rush agreed, but by then his proposal had leaked out. The accusation that the Republicans planned to let the Penn family collect old quitrents and to restore its lands in unsettled parts of Pennsylvania circulated throughout the state.[7]

The election proved even more vituperative than previous ones. Jacob Rush kept his seat, but only after enduring a scathing attack on the eve of balloting by "Clarendon," who called him "a needy practitioner of the law, who has been long gaping with rotundity of belly, vacant, and open mouth, for an office." "Clarendon" condemned Jacob for his slanderous pen, but perhaps, he added, he was only "the imputed father, compelled by a busy and overbearing brother to stand midwife to the ebullitions of his own violent and distempered fancy." Even if he were defeated, President Dickinson would see to it he was taken care of.[8] "Clarendon" was on the mark; early in 1784 Jacob Rush was appointed a justice of the state supreme court.

The Republicans held their grip on the assembly and won control of the Council of Censors, though not by the two-thirds majority needed to call a constitutional convention. Montgomery, however, lost by fifty votes his bid for the council, largely because of, even Rush admitted, "the old story of the restoration of the proprietary estate." The disheartened Montgomery said he would never again serve the people, but Rush refused to listen. "This madness will soon be over," he wrote. "All will end well." And it did. The assembly renamed Montgomery to Congress, along with Mifflin and Peters, adding as new delegates Edward Hand and Cadwalader Morris, merchant and ironmaster.[9]

Rush ended 1783 in a high mood. The Republicans dominated Pennsylvania politics. The Council of Censors he thought certain would call a convention that would repair the evils of the old constitution, and if that body refused to do the right thing, "it may easily be brought about by an appeal from the assembly to the state." Massachusetts had accepted Congress's plan for an impost, and a friend representing that state told Rush that "Rhode Island must follow that great state." Even the continued absence of Congress failed to depress him. "Their enmity to Pennsylvania and their attempts to check her progress in wealth and power is as absurd as if a man should refuse to receive food by his mouth least his head grow too big for his body and should consent to be nourished only by clysters," he told Montgomery. "They are the ridicule of our whole city. . . . Poor creatures. Don't be angry at them. They are only proper subjects for pity—and blisters." As he had begun the year, so he ended it—with the phrase "All will end well."[10]

3

Rush had professional as well as political reasons to be hopeful for the future in 1783. Not only did his practice continue to thrive, but the Pennsylvania Hospital honored him with the offer to become a staff member, a post that paid nothing in money but much in prestige. The hospital's physicians were automatically considered among the city's most distinguished members of the medical profession.[11]

The honor emerged out of John Morgan's mounting lack of interest in the world around him. He had begun to withdraw from professional affairs soon after he realized that he could not annihilate Shippen. His decision to leave the hospital's staff marked the first of a series of retreats. It pivoted on an incident seemingly so trivial that it left the hospital's board of managers stunned. Late in April the board had voted, with the approval of two of its staff physicians, to cease charging for the treatment of venereal patients referred to the hospital by the House of Employment. After a month of brooding over the matter, Morgan wrote the board that he had not expected, when asked to join the hospital staff, to devote "time and attention to the cure of diseases brought on by concupiscence, without fee or reward, which in my humble opinion tends rather to the growth than diminution of immorality." More important, the decision to change accepted practices had been taken "without any regard paid to the judgment of the rest [of the staff] on what regards the honor and interest of each other."[12]

The board must have sensed Morgan would not reverse his stand, that if it retreated on this issue some other equally minor matter would provoke his resignation. "The doctor resigned his place," a note in the board minutes read, "to the grief of the patients and much against the will of the managers, who all bore testimony to his good abilities and great usefulness in the institution as a physician."[13]

Surely, some on the board would have preferred even an apathetic

Morgan to the presence on the staff of the amiable yet contentious Rush, but it was hard to blink the fact that at the age of thirty-seven Rush ranked in ability and reputation among the foremost physicians in the United States. The vacant post was offered to him, and Rush, promptly and with delight, accepted the honor.

Success appeared on another front during the fall of the year. The board of the university made one more effort to entice back to the fold the entire prewar medical faculty. On November 22 a rump meeting of the board—less than half of the twenty-four members showed up—was held to vote for new professors. With the dissident members' absence no doubt prearranged, Rush, Morgan, and Kuhn were reelected to their former posts. The vote only made formal a decision that must have been worked out earlier, for the day previous to his reelection Rush began the lectures in chemistry.[14]

The course continued to be what it had from the beginning. Seven years' isolation from Europe prohibited any chance to incorporate in the lectures the most recent findings of European scientists. One change, urged by the university, was introduced. In order "to lessen the expense to young gentlemen who may come from other states," the university had asked the professors to lecture daily, thus shortening the time students would have to spend in the city.[15] Rush met his class six days a week from the end of November until mid-January, with only Thanksgiving and Christmas off. During these two months, he continued to carry on a full practice. Fortunately, he resumed teaching as an epidemic of scarlet fever, or scarlatina anginosa as it was then called, began to taper off.[16]

The fever first appeared at the end of July, striking chiefly among children. In September it became epidemic among adults. ("I am so *wholly* taken up with my business that I can do nothing," Rush told Montgomery.) It continued through October and the early days of November, "but with less alarming symptoms." On November 29 at ten in the evening an earthquake tremor shook the city, but Rush noted no change "in the disease in consequence of it." At the end of December and into January, as he was winding up the chemistry lectures, the disease revived "with great violence," and three of Rush's patients died.[17]

He took special care to observe the disease's symptoms. Knowing it would soon spread beyond the city into neighboring states, as it did during the spring of 1784, he wanted to be sure country doctors were posted on its characteristics. Usually it came on with a chill and vomiting, and the patient's throat swelled, making speaking, swallowing, and breathing difficult. Eruptions on the skin accompanied the fever, their location varying from the chest and the limbs to the outside of the throat. In its later stages "the disease frequently went off with a swelling of the hands and feet."[18]

Something like panic gripped the city during the epidemic. Anyone with a sore throat but "without any other indisposition" *knew* he had the disease. Some physicians recommended a bag of camphor hung about the neck as a preventative, but Rush put no faith in this. "I have reason to entertain a more favorable opinion of the benefit of washing the hands and face with vinegar," he said, "and of rinsing the mouth and throat with vinegar and water every morning, as a means of preventing this disorder."

Rush's treatment generally followed that recommended by Cullen. He prescribed tartar emetic or ipecac to force the patients to vomit, for besides "evacuating the contents of the stomach, it cleansed the throat in its passage downwards." He gave calomel continually, but "to restrain its purgative effects, I added to it a small quantity of opium." This regimen was followed by one more benign and, by later standards, more appropriate. "Detergent gargles" were prescribed to keep the throat clean, and, for patients who had trouble breathing, "steam of warm water mixed with a little vinegar, through a funnel into the throat." Rush held that this routine, if imposed in the early stages of the disease, "never failed of completely checking the disorder, or of so far mitigating its violence, as to dispose it to a favorable issue in a few days." If the disease did not yield to this medication by the third day, Rush "applied a blister behind each ear, or one to the neck, and I think always with good effects."[19] He rarely questioned the efficacy of his treatments, and doubtless as he left patients' bedsides he reassured them, as he so often reassured his friends and himself, "All will end well."

4

"Heaven has blessed me not only with domestic happiness but with unexpected and even unsought-for degrees of external prosperity," Rush said in the first year of peace. "My business is still extensive and profitable." The account books bear him out. His income from his practice, from the apothecary shop, from students and apprentices, and from his wife's estate was substantial enough for Rush to say, "I have not a wish now to gratify with respect to the honors and emoluments of my profession."[20]

Except for the death in 1783 of his infant daughter, Elizabeth Graeme, little else marred a placid family life. His mother continued to run the dry-goods store near the city market, while his sister Rebecca operated the china shop across the street. With Richard Stockton's death, he had begun to share responsibility for his wife's family. He took Susan Stockton, Mrs. Rush's younger sister, into his home.[21] Despite a slight tension over financial matters—to save money, Rush wanted his mother-in-law to rent Morven and move into Princeton, something she refused to do—he got along reasonably well with his wife's "truly amiable" family. Mrs. Stockton doted on her grandson Richard, named after her late husband, and kept him at Morven as long and often as the parents would permit. Rush still adored his wife after eight years of marriage. "I have had a dull time of it since you left me," he wrote during her regular summer visit to Morven. "To *your* honor and the honor of matrimony I can truly say, the longer I live with you the more unhappy I am in a separation from you." The three children nettled him when they rampaged through the house and garden or invaded the sacrosanct parlor, but when they traveled with their mother to Princeton the "melancholy silence which reigns through every apartment of the house" unsettled him.[22]

Anne Emily, the only surviving daughter, at five and a half was "a pleasant, sweet-tempered girl." Richard at the age of four already puzzled his father. One moment Rush saw him as "a rough, boisterous fellow"; at another he seemed so sedate in the way he talked and behaved, "so much like a gentleman, that I cannot treat him like a child." John, the oldest child, "a handsome, promising boy" of six and a half years, was his father's favorite. Rush hoped one day to see him off for Edinburgh to study medicine, and as a confirmed romantic he even dreamed of the boy falling in love with Lady Jane's daughter. He envisioned John approaching the lass as his father may have approached Lady Jane—"in the meadows or in the park with his hat in his hand, bowing respectfully to her and afterwards gallanting her home all the way."[23] But reality someday would turn the dreams for John to anguish.

Politics alone blemished an otherwise agreeable life. Republicans throughout 1783 and into 1784 continued to control the assembly and the recently elected Council of Censors, but they also continued to lack the necessary two-thirds majority to impose reforms or to call a constitutional convention. Rush saw a convention in the near future as inevitable—"the wealth and the sense of the state, together with a great majority of the people" favored it, he said in mid-1783—and it distressed him to see the opposition centered among Presbyterians. Their stubborn adherence to the constitution only added "fresh vigor to the prejudices against us."[24]

He tried through friends in the backcountry to increase the pressure on the council for a convention, but with no success. Gen. John Armstrong, for instance, said that the tempers of all were at the moment too short, jealousies too sharp, and that Rush and his cohorts demanded too much. True, the constitution had flaws, but why should the Republicans expect those for it to act reasonably while their opponents carried on a vituperative campaign against it? Belatedly, Rush realized that the Republicans had pushed too hard. "Our friends," he said, putting the blame on others, "have not conducted matters with the prudence or consideration that was expected of them." He asked Armstrong to urge the Council of Censors to amend at least the most egregious flaws in the constitution. If he could not have an upper house to check any outrageous decision of the assembly, then what about strengthening the executive or, at the very least, having the judiciary appointed for good behavior rather than seven-year terms? The general promised to strive "as prudently as I can to convince and persuade a few of the most tenacious of my acquaintances of each side."[25]

The efforts at compromise came too late, for the censors refused to consider even "a few essential amendments." Rush, with that peculiar optimism of his, saw this as "all for the best." He preferred to wait until Pennsylvania had "recovered from the fumes of democracy" before reforming the constitution. "Besides," he added, "the worse it is, the more certainly it will mend itself. We are apt you know to neglect a trifling toothache, but fly to a physician for relief from a fever."[26]

The Republicans abandoned hope of effecting change through the Council of Censors in September 1784. They decided instead to use their legislative majority to secure revocation of the test or loyalty oath, which excluded a third to a half of otherwise eligible citizens from voting. The test act ostensibly disfranchised only loyalists, but in practice it made second-class citizens of all who objected to oaths on principle, of pacifists, and of those who refused to swear full support to the 1776 state constitution. In

effect, it deprived all Quakers and a large segment of the German population of the vote. The Republicans assumed these nonjurors, as they were
called, would favor a new constitution, thus their eagerness to have the test
act repealed.

Anthony Wayne, whose loyalty no one questioned, headed the campaign in the assembly. Despite the Republicans' solid majority, the Constitutionalists defeated the attack by absenting themselves from the hall,
thereby preventing a quorum and making it impossible to vote on the decision to repeal the test act. The frustrated Republicans made the act the central issue of the October election, and the voters responded by dealing the
party a humiliating defeat; Republicans not only lost control of the assembly
but were reduced to a smattering of seats. Rush reacted furiously. No longer
were things "all for the best." He suggested to friends that now might be
the time for demagogic tactics. "We shall never vanquish our adversaries
till we treat them like savages, by carrying hostilities into their country," he
said. "We must attack them for their public abuses and private vices."[27]

The debacle brought "fragments," as Rush put it, of the party to a tavern to decide on future battle tactics. It was agreed they must organize
nonjurors to petition the assembly for repeal of the test act, but "Republicans must appear in this maneuver as little as possible," Rush explained
to a friend. "It is most probable the petitions will have no effect upon the
present assembly," he went on. "But their refusal will serve to show their
inconsistency, to rouse and irritate the sons and friends of the nonjurors,
and above all to fix the dye of their infamy in such a manner that neither
time nor repentance will ever be able to wipe it away."[28]

To this campaign Rush contributed a pamphlet entitled *Considerations upon the Present Test-Law of Pennsylvania,* an effective piece of
propaganda and also one of the ablest and most eloquent of his political
essays. He condemned the test act as unconstitutional, impolitic, and tyrannical, buttressing each charge with facts and illustrations. He argued first
from principle. "The spirit of the nonjurors was hostile to nothing but
war," he said. They committed no crimes, created no insurrections during
the Revolution. "Why then should we inflict the heaviest of all punishments upon them—not banishment—not death—but SLAVERY." Such a spite-
ful law contradicts Pennsylvania's generous heritage from the Quakers, who
when they created the colony gave "power and offices . . . alike to men of
every nation and sect with themselves." A law that strikes out at people

"principled against war," becomes "an invasion of the rights of conscience, and a direct act of persecution for conscience sake." A war fought for liberty has ended enslaving a large part of the state, he said at one point, then came this striking sentence: "Liberty differs from almost everything else that is precious, in this, that the more your neighbors possess it, the more you will enjoy it yourselves."

There were also practical considerations. Why should nonjurors, who pay two-thirds of the state's taxes, continue to support a government that won't let them vote? The test law deprives Pennsylvania of the service of some of its best-educated citizens. Foreigners after one year's residence can vote, and to judge by the present rate of immigration "men with European ideas of government will soon occupy the seats of our present rulers." Remember, Rush warned, "Rome was undone by strangers getting her government into their hands, and introducing foreign prejudices, customs, and vices among them." If none of these arguments is convincing, he concluded, then let charity alone condition your attitude toward the nonjurors. "If they have erred—nay more, if they have sinned during the late war, we shall consult the freedom and prosperity of the state by forgiving them. If we are wise, we shall do more—we shall protect and cherish them as the surest resources of the wealth and independence of the state."[29]

Rush saw to it that, as with all his works that pleased him, this one circulated widely, especially through the backcountry where the feeling against nonjurors ran highest. He sent a copy to Montgomery with a note that it had been written "by that turbulent spirit Dr. Rush, who I hope will never be quiet while there is ignorance, slavery, or misery in Pennsylvania." Col. Thomas Hartley, an old friend from '76 who had served with Rush on the Provincial Conference, wrote from York County asking for several more copies, adding that in his opinion the county would soon produce petitions favoring revision of the oath.[30] In mid-1785 portions of the essay were reprinted in the *Pennsylvania Gazette.* The pamphlet helped speed the flow of petitions against the test law toward the assembly, but not until March 1786, when the Republicans regained control of the legislature and Benjamin Franklin, the state's new president, put his prestige on the line, was the test law revised in a way that deprived only outright, active loyalists of the vote.

The confirmation of "equal privileges upon every citizen of the state" pleased Rush immensely. "The success of friends of humanity in this business should encourage them to persevere in their attempts to enlighten and reform the world," he told a friend following passage of the revised law, and a few years later he remarked to John Adams with pride that his enemies had confessed publicly that it was Rush's pamphlet that had "repealed that impolitic law."[31]

5

Rush's forgiving nature had not suddenly sprung forth with the arrival of peace. The conviction for high treason of his Quaker acquaintance John Roberts in November 1778 had convinced him that the time had come to help others accused of disloyalty. In October 1779, while on a professional visit to several jailed Quakers, he urged one of them, Mathew Johns, to apply for a writ of habeas corpus. Johns did and won his freedom, which inspired a companion, Thomas Story, to follow suit, with the same success. In December of that year Rush negotiated with the Executive Council to obtain the freedom of John Potts, Jr., brother of his Edinburgh roommate, and Phineas Bond, a local lawyer. In June 1780 he returned to the council asking indulgence for Mrs. Daniel Coxe, daughter of John Redman but married to a Tory, the son of the irrepressible Abigail Coxe. A few months later he helped get accusations lifted against his colleague Adam Kuhn, who soon rejoined the university faculty as professor of botany. Though Rush later fought with Kuhn, he never traded on his act of kindness or used it against his colleague in any way. In 1781 he helped Elizabeth Graeme Ferguson retrieve the family estate of Graeme Park, which had been taken from her when her husband turned loyalist.[32]

Rush suffered for these acts of clemency. Years later he said Ewing had slandered him as an "enemy of Presbyterianism" for aiding oppressed Quakers and Episcopalians, and that "he reduced my business by it *among the Presbyterians* in the course of two years from near one hundred to only ten families." Even Rush's "friends of order and justice" failed to support him. "Some of them avoided me at the time I was most persecuted, as if I had been bitten by a mad dog." Memory exaggerated the persecution endured in the 1780's but not the sense of disassociation. "I have lamented often that my political principles and conduct have separated me from the friends of my youth, and above all from those whose religious principles and mode of worship are most agreeable to me," he wrote in 1783. "My heart is still with them, and I think the time is not very distant when they will think as I have done for seven years past upon the subject of the politics of our state."[33]

6

Peace in 1783 ended a long isolation from Europe, which for Rush had been a privation harder to endure than for most Americans. For seven years he had been without the latest medical news and cut off from friends who meant much to him. Once the old lines of communication reopened, he again recognized how tight his associations with Great Britain were.

Rush found the war had altered neither the character nor opinions of old friends. Dr. Huck—now Huck-Saunders, for he had tacked his wife's name onto his own—proved as ardent a royalist as ever, calling the Revolution a "rascally rebellion" caused by "worthless and wrongheaded men of both countries." Mrs. Coxe remained friendly toward Rush but not toward Americans, for "the milk of human kindness flows not so spontaneously among you as *us*," she said with asperity. "But what ails me," she remarked in a later letter, "I am slipping into politics unawares. Yet you provoked it by touching on the subject, tho' as you are no longer tremblingly alive in these matters, I hope you will only coolly laugh at my strange opinions."[34]

Generally British friends, not Rush, made the first friendly gestures. "After a very long and very disagreeable silence, permit me to renew our correspondence," one letter began, setting the tone for letters from other friends that soon followed. Dr. Cullen numbered among the first to revive old ties, sending word by an emigrant from Scotland "that you and I have never been at war with one another" and that it delighted him to have once again "free and friendly intercourse" with those "in America I have always esteemed and loved." Lettsom soon afterward forwarded from London a package of medical books, several pamphlets, and a long letter filled with the sort of advice Rush preferred to give rather than receive: the Philosophical Society ought to broaden its interests; the medical school should add a course in natural history; perhaps it would be well to "establish a society for the recovery of the drowned [and] the frozen. . . ."[35]

Rush's response to these letters revealed the relief he felt that all would be as it had been. He thanked Cullen·for reviving "in me all the enthusiasm for science with which you inspired me in the years 1766 and

1768." An essay of Lettsom's on Dr. Fothergill "has attached me more to my profession than ever," he said. "Let heroes pursue glory and happiness in arms; I wish for no greater share of both than are to be derived from imitating Dr. Fothergill." Lettsom, too, was relieved to find still flourishing in Rush a "commendable thirst after knowledge and a desire to improve the healing art."[36]

Previously his closest ties abroad had been with Edinburgh, and these also were quickly reestablished. "I cannot describe to you how much pleasure your letter gave me," he told the banker Thomas Hogg. "It seems as if we had both been dead and buried for eight years, and that your letter was the first signal of our resurrection." Lady Jane Leslie, now Lady Jane Belsches, wrote asking about her brother's death, and Rush replied with a full account. When Charles Elliott, a bookseller with whom he began again to place orders, wrote that he had "a great many of your pupils now about me," the former close relationship with Edinburgh had been fully rebuilt on old foundations.[37]

Some British friends reembraced Rush for reasons other than affection. Timothy Bevan renewed an old association by filling an order for opium, calomel, Glauber's salts, jalap, and other pharmaceutical supplies, then tacked onto the bill the nearly £60 Rush had owed before the Revolution plus £26 accumulated interest, a debt "I flatter myself thou wilt take the earliest opportunity of making [good]." The Quaker's "business as usual" attitude for once reduced Rush to silence, and two years later Bevan was wondering why he had not been "favored with a few lines from thee." The old man died with the debt unpaid, and years later Rush was still complaining to the son, Joseph Bevan, who had taken over the business, about being charged compound interest during the Revolution. The problem had been worked out by the 1790's and Rush was soon happily corresponding with Joseph about penal reform and the French Revolution.[38]

Correspondence with Charles Dilly, the London bookseller, reopened affably with news about mutual acquaintances, but gossip quickly swerved to business. Was Rush writing anything? If he knew of any good books being printed in America, please send the "sheets in part as they issue from the press" so Dilly could get the jump on other London publishers. He had heard Thomas Paine was writing a history of the Revolution; if so, he would like to publish it, for anything "from the pen of so able a writer as Mr. Paine will be well received." Finally, he wondered about payment of a £35 bill (no interest charged) for law books purchased by Jacob Rush before the war. Rush directed the bill to his brother, who refused to answer the dunning letters from London until mid-1786, when Dilly turned the matter over to a Philadelphia lawyer. The embarrassed Judge Rush finally replied he was hard-pressed for cash but would pay up by Christmas, which he apparently did.[39]

Dilly gave as much as he asked of Rush. He kept him posted on the latest medical publications, sent over gratis a new edition of Cullen's *First Lines,* gave advance notice of Mrs. Macaulay's proposed visit to America (she came in 1785, but Rush never met her to revive their old friendship), and made sure he was informed about the doings of all his London friends. Dr. Richard Price, for instance, had "grown quite infirm and sees little company and has left off visiting among the families he has been accustomed to see."

Dilly continued to serve as before the war as Rush's literary agent and publisher. He rejected the essay on inoculation but forwarded it to Edinburgh with the hope it might receive notice in a medical journal there. He arranged for the tract on spirituous liquors to appear in the *Gentleman's Magazine* in 1786 and later in the year he published Rush's long essay on the moral faculty and physical causes of disease.[40]

Rush used not just Dilly but all his British friends as they used him. A collection of medical essays he hoped to have published in London would be "under your inspection and patronage," he told Lettsom. When James Wilson became mired in debt through land speculation, Rush did his best to raise loans for him among friends like Lettsom and other well-to-do Londoners. Affection and gratitude for their early support of the American Revolution motivated the new stream of letters to Granville Sharp and Price, but so, too, did self-interest, for Rush confessed to a friend that he hoped "to draw from them at a future day supplies of books and other articles for a college."[41]

7

Paine's history of the Revolution that Dilly had wondered about proved a false rumor—though Paine deluded himself for years to come that he would one day complete it. But other of Rush's friends had done more than dream of such a project. Rev. William Gordon was well into his *History of the Independence of the United States*. Ramsay, having finished his *History of the Revolution in South Carolina* by the end of 1784—Rush, with his "talent at drawing characters," had been asked to contribute sketches of the military men he had known—had moved on to write an account of the entire war. Rush himself planned to do a political history of the revolutionary years in Pennsylvania. He tested the idea on Dilly, who doubted such a book would sell well in London. "But as you are requested by your friends to undertake the work," he added diplomatically, "there cannot be a doubt but it would answer by the sale in your country sufficient to return expense of paper and print." Rush talked about the volume the rest of his life but never wrote it. He incorporated sketches in his autobiography of those he had known in Congress and in the army; he helped others, particularly Gordon and Ramsay, with their works, but other than the reminiscences that filled his letters, he had little to say in print about the war's political or military events.[42]

The single essay he wrote on the Revolution, aside from those that dealt with medical matters, centered on the psychological effect it had upon men's minds and their actions. For reasons he could not comprehend, the war restored to health "many persons of infirm and delicate habits," in particular hysterical women. "It may help to extend our ideas of the influence of the passions upon diseases to add," he suggested tentatively, "that when either love, jealousy, grief, or even devotion, wholly engross the female mind, they seldom fail, in like manner, to cure or to suspend hysterical complaints." Despite the miseries and hardships war brought, he noted, without attempting to account for it, "an uncommon cheerfulness" prevailed everywhere, even in the face of defeats, death, or loss of property. ("All will end well.") He was also struck by the incredible increase in the birthrate, greater "than it had ever been in the same number of years since the settlement of the country." (Five of Rush's children were born during the Revolution.) He thought possibly the increase might be attributed to prosperity, which, though built on the uncertainties of paper money, "favored marriages among the laboring part of the people." Regardless of the reason, he knew for certain "that marriages were more fruitful than in former years, and that a considerable number of unfruitful marriages became fruitful during the war."[43]

He also believed the war produced variations on old forms of insanity. Among the Tories appeared a form of hypochondria that he called *Revolutiona.* "In some cases," he said, "this disease was rendered fatal by exile and confinement; and, in others, by those persons who were afflicted with it, seeking relief from spirituous liquors." Rush remarked, too, on another variation of derangement that came forth just after the war, "a species of insanity, which I shall take the liberty of distinguishing by the name of *Anarchia.*"[44]

8

Distress over the prevailing Anarchia was soft-pedaled, if mentioned at all, in letters sent across the sea. "Upwards of six thousand souls have arrived in this city since the peace, all of whom have been kindly received and comfortably accommodated," he told an English acquaintance in 1783 in an effort to counter a British press report that the new nation foundered. The following year he reported that "the spirit of peace and good government begins to diffuse itself through every part of the United States." Any fear of a military dictatorship had dissolved. Washington had returned to Mount Vernon to resume the life of a farmer, and "our army has quietly melted away into peaceable citizens."[45]

British exaggerations of the "factions and riots" oversweeping America provoked Rush into fashioning some exaggerations of his own. "Funerals are such uncommon things in our new countries that they are resorted to as a kind of spectacle," he told one friend in 1784. "The human mind here is like soft clay," he told another who thought of emigrating. "It has as yet received but few impressions but what are derived from nature. Our love of liberty is the effect of instinct rather than education. Religion and science will have no prejudices or errors to encounter among us. You may cast us into any mold you please." And to still another prospective emigrant, he predicted: "America seems destined by heaven to exhibit to the world the perfection which the mind of man is capable of receiving from the combined operation of liberty, learning, and the Gospel upon it." Occasionally he admitted to British friends that all was not perfect, that the scum of the nation had been "thrown upon the surface by the fermentation of the war." But such confessions were always followed by the glad news that the scum was also "daily sinking, while a pure spirit is occupying its place," that "the means of subsistence here are so easy, and the profits of honest labor so great, that rogues find it less difficult to live by work than by plunder."[46]

Much of this cheerfulness was forced out to rebut British slander. With some friends he dared to be honest. "I lament the decay of the American character . . . and wish I could say something in defense of it," he told Lettsom. "War tends to loosen the bonds of morality and government in every country; the effects of it have been greatly increased by the people of America handling for four or five years a depreciating paper currency." But even when events confounded his expectations, the optimism of these early postwar years remained intact. America was the world's last hope. Europe is in a state of torpor, he told one person. "Europe resembles an old garment that has been turned," he wrote to another. "The habits of your people forbid every species of improvement in human happiness. In America everything is new and yielding. Here genius and benevolence may have full scope. Here the benefactor of mankind may realize all his schemes." Looked at from this angle, Anarchia resembled the harmless obstreperousness of a child. "Remember, my dear sir, that we are at present in a *forming* state. We have as yet but few habits of any kind, and *good* ones may be acquired and fixed by a good example and proper instruction as easily as *bad* ones without the benefit of either."[47]

A Multitude
of Causes

15

The Birth of "Our Brat"

1783–1784

1

SOMETIME in the early summer of 1782 Rush sat visiting on the front porch of William Bingham, of whom it was later said that his wife as well as his house numbered among the two handsomest sights in Philadelphia. During the Revolution Bingham had served as an agent of Congress in the West Indies, a post he used to promote his own as well as the nation's welfare. While still in his twenties, Bingham returned to Philadelphia with a sizable fortune, married the beautiful Anne Willing, then sixteen, and settled down to a life in business that would soon make him one of the richest men in America.

With Rush on the porch that afternoon was John Montgomery, whose son had recently been his apprentice. Montgomery, now nearly sixty, had emigrated from northern Ireland when in his teens. He had settled in the backcountry village of Carlisle, where his early and warm support for the Revolution had been rewarded by election to Congress. This particular afternoon he carried in his pocket a petition from the citizens of Carlisle requesting a charter from the assembly to expand the local grammar school into an academy. He hoped Rush would support the petition by using his influence among the legislators. Rush, it turned out, would do more than that. Montgomery's petition would launch him on a project to which he would be dedicated for nearly ten years. The phrase "remember Bingham's porch" would become an incantation, uttered whenever it looked as though all might not end so well.

At the time Rush and Montgomery rocked away the afternoon on Bingham's porch, rumors of peace were flowing in from Europe. Rush insisted "we are not ripe for it." Others shared his anxiety. The states of America were not united, despite the title they had given themselves. They were thirteen disparate, antagonistic sovereign bodies. They were riven by factions. "Religious bigotry has yielded to political intolerance," said Rush. "The man who used to hate his neighbor for being a Churchman or a Quaker now hates him with equal cordiality for being a Tory."[1] There were external problems as well. America had been the first settlement in the New World since Columbus discovered it nearly three centuries earlier to defy successfully the mother country. Now it was about to step forth as a new nation in a world of empires, each of which would covet the magnificent real estate that had once been Great Britain's. Could it survive?

The uneasiness this question raised in Rush was linked to another anxiety, one that had worried him since the days of '76: how could America exorcize the corruptions Great Britain had imposed on Americans' manners, morals, and opinions? It was not enough to form new governments based on republican principles. The people themselves must be changed. They must be converted, Rush thought, "into republican machines." And how was this to be done? Through education. It was up to the schools to reshape the American character, to form a diverse people into a single mold that would give them a national character. A nation of educated "republican machines" would bring to the country a unity out of diversity. A United States that existed now only in name would become a reality. Schools, in short, would indoctrinate the nation with the wonders of republicanism, and thereby unite the country.

This conception of the role of education in America was not solely Rush's. Jefferson shared it. So, too, did Noah Webster and Jeremy Belknap, two conservative New Englanders who would soon be Rush's good friends. Washington in time would call for a federal university because he believed it would instill the proper "principles, opinions, and manners" in Americans. "The more homogeneous our citizens can be made in these particulars, the greater will be our prospect of permanent union," he said. Jefferson expressed the same thought similarly. "Cast your eye over America: who are the men of most learning, of most eloquence, most beloved by their country[men] and most trusted and promoted by them?" he asked. "They are those who have been educated among them, and whose manners, morals, and habits are perfectly homogeneous with those of the country . . . . the consequences of foreign education are alarming to me as an American." Rush, too, favored the word "homogeneous," when he proposed "one general and uniform system of education" which would "render the mass of the people more homogeneous, and thereby fit them more easily for uniform and peaceable government."[2]

None of these gentlemen sensed the paradox they had raised. "Having fought a war to free the United States from one centralized authority, they attempted to create a new unity, a common citizenship and culture, and an appeal to a common future," David Tyack has noted. "In this quest for a balance between order and liberty, for the proper transaction between the individual and society, [they] encountered a conflict still inherent in the education of the citizen and expressed still in the injunction to teachers to train students to think critically but to be patriotic above all."[3]

If Benjamin Rush is to be censured for the views he promoted in the months and years that followed his conversation with Montgomery on Bingham's porch, it is only because he wrote more often and more fully than perhaps any American of the day on education. Others, notably Jefferson, contemplated colleges, but Rush was the first to create one after the Revolution. Others talked about a free public-school system, but Rush alone developed a detailed plan for one. Others spoke of educating women, but only Rush prepared a syllabus. The first six presidents of the United States called for a federal university, but only long after Rush had advanced the idea.

2

On Bingham's porch, Rush turned the conversation away from the grammar school Montgomery's petition called for. Why dream modestly? Rush wondered aloud. Why stop with an academy? Why not create a college? A decade earlier he had proposed a college for Presbyterians to John Ewing, who had agreed that "the time is not very far distant when our increasing numbers will render another college to the westward, in Virginia or Carolina, absolutely necessary."[4] Carlisle, located 125 miles west of Philadelphia, just beyond the Susquehanna River amid the soft hills of the Cumberland Valley and deep in Scotch-Irish country, seemed the perfect

locale for another Presbyterian school. It lay outside the orbit of the College
of New Jersey and close enough to the Great Wagon Road, which cut
southward to the Carolinas, to draw students from a backcountry saturated
with Presbyterians. Backcountry farmers had been deterred from sending
their sons to the University of Pennsylvania by the expense and by the effect
of the city on young men's morals. A college at Carlisle would be convenient, healthy, and free of Philadelphia's temptations.

Originally Rush envisioned a theological seminary or, as he put it,
"a college for the education of ministers of the Gospel in a part of the state
where our society is most numerous and reputable." He planned to call it
"The School of Prophets." The University of Pennsylvania could never
serve as a nursery for Presbyterianism: less than half its trustees were Presbyterians, most of them being Episcopalians. To Rush, the university's
"extreme catholicism" meant that "as no one religion prevails, so no religious principles are inculcated in it." Rush saw great virtues in sectarian
education. "Instead of encouraging bigotry, I believe it prevents it by removing young men from those opportunities of controversy which a variety
of sects mixed together are apt to create and which are the certain fuel of
bigotry."[5]

A college would enhance the backcountry. By diffusing knowledge
and eloquence through the region, it would "make the only possible balance
that can exist to the commerce and wealth of our city." By educating those
who might otherwise never get to college, it would "soften the tempers of
our turbulent brethren, to inspire them with liberal sentiments in government and religion, to teach them moderation in their conduct to other sects,
and to rescue them from the charges of bigotry and persecution that are so
often brought against them."[6]

The accusations of bigotry and persecution made against Presbyterians
had long perturbed Rush. True, in the past they had not received the share
of power their numbers—something like a third or more of Pennsylvania's
population—entitled them to. But now with the test law or loyalty oath
disfranchising numbers of Quakers, Episcopalians, and, to a lesser degree, Pennsylvania Germans who had been either neutral or opposed to the
Revolution, the Presbyterians controlled the state government. They now
held more power than, from their numbers, they deserved. Moreover, they
were misusing it and exciting powerful opposition. "To prevent the effect
of these combinations against them reducing them to their ancient state of

oppression and insignificance, it becomes them above all things to entrench themselves in schools of learning," he argued. "These are the true nurseries of power and influence. They improve talents and virtue and these by begetting wealth form the ingredients that constitute power in all countries. In the present plentitude of power of the Presbyterians, let them obtain a charter for a college at Carlisle in Cumberland County."[7]

These arguments, together with his conception of the curriculum and other details of the college, Rush embodied in "Hints for Establishing a College at Carlisle," written in early September 1782—shortly after the last of his nine essays on continental affairs had been published—and circulated among friends in the city and backcountry. He then initiated a heavy correspondence with prominent clerical and lay leaders in the backcountry to build up grass-roots support, for public airing of the project had released considerable opposition: Carlisle was too difficult to reach; a new college would split the church; the church risked public disfavor by establishing a sectarian school at a time when sentiment favored a nondenominational approach to education. Why, asked one man, relinquish hold of the university until forced to, "for if the Episcopalians make an attack on that institution that will be time enough to secure a new charter." It will "be called a party business," a man from Baltimore charged. "We have hitherto lived in great harmony with the people of every denomination in this place and are unwilling both as Presbyterians and members of the state of Maryland to risk the interruption of this social intercourse we at present enjoy."[8]

A good deal of the opposition centered among supporters of the College of New Jersey. General Armstrong, for one, a member of the college board of trustees as well as an assemblyman, did not wish to see a competitor rise against Witherspoon's school, though he was willing in time to have a college in the backcountry at some distant location, such as Pittsburgh. This argument sounded familiar to Rush, who a decade earlier had heard Ewing, then in London on a fund-raising trip, say that "friends of Harvard College have wrote against Dr. Wheelock's Indian School [Dartmouth] as hurtful to that college and have induced many here to believe that the money collected for it had been misapplied."[9]

Despite the number and power of those opposed, a college at Carlisle had much to recommend it. First, Rush had determined to devote his energy, persuasive skills, and political connections to promoting it. A majority of the backcountry leaders, lay and clerical, favored it. The assembly was now controlled by Republicans, many of them non-Presbyterians and Rush's friends, who would welcome the chance to reward a dissident wing of the church with a college charter. The clause in the state constitution that encouraged the government to promote education would win votes from Constitutionalists. Finally, backing came from a powerful corner when Rush proposed to name the school John and Mary's College, in honor of President Dickinson and his wife. Rush assured the uneasy Montgomery he had "nothing to fear for the character of Mr. Dickinson. His conduct is highly approved of by all classes and parties. I think the Constitutionalists give him most credit for his behavior."[10]

Rush missed no opening to advance the college. In mid-March 1783, he sought to undermine General Armstrong's opposition with a long, well-argued letter that appealed to his religious, regional, and, finally, pecuniary interests. "The value of land in the neighborhood of Princeton before the college was erected there was from 30 to 40 [shillings] an acre," he concluded. "It has risen in the space of five and twenty years to £8.0.0 and £10.0.0 per acre, which is £5.0.0 an acre more than land sells for in the neighborhood of most of the villages of New Jersey." Armstrong did not capitulate to this or follow-up letters, but Rush's persistent reasonableness eventually disarmed him, especially when on the political front Rush attempted to work out a conciliation in regard to a constitutional convention between his friends among the Republicans and Constitutionalists like Armstrong.[11]

A critical juncture in the campaign was reached in April when the Carlisle presbytery met to judge the project. Rush assigned Rev. John King, a backcountry resident, to handle negotiations, assuring him before the meeting that "firmness and decision will carry all before them." Apparently they did, for the presbytery approved the design, selected a board of twenty-four trustees—all Presbyterians—and proceeded with arrangements to circulate a petition through the backcountry asking the legislature to grant a charter. Everything appeared to be going well. Dickinson had promised the college a good part of the valuable library of his late father-in-law Isaac Norris, and Rush had already begun to promote books for the college from clerical friends in Britain. A plan to attract students from among the Dutch Reformed and Lutherans raised the hope "of seeing our sister churches in Holland contribute towards the advancement of their own doctrines and mode of worship in this new country." Rush now saw the college uniting the dissident elements within Presbyterianism and becoming "a kind of Mount Zion to which all our tribes will look up and which will prevent our being hereafter the wandering Arabs of America."[12]

Optimism at the moment, however, seemed unwarranted, for also in April resistance toward John and Mary College intensified. "A strong party is forming against it," King reported. Some say it is "a *Tory scheme,* a plot entered into to subvert all order in the state." Ewing led those who censured the plan, and Rush seemed dazed by the hornet's nest that had been overturned. In one breath he could write that "the opposition to our scheme has sunk into insignificance from Dr. Ewing & Company," and in another, in the same letter, wonder at length about the "strange mixture of folly and absurdity in the opposition of Dr. Ewing and his junto to our college." He pretended to be puzzled by the attacks. "They say our plan is too *contracted.* Then they accuse us of an attempt to *divide* the Presbyterians, thereby tacitly confessing that they consider *their* university as a *Presbyterian* institution." Then, harking back to the split that had occurred among Presbyterians during the Great Awakening, he added: "They say our college is to be a nursery for the Arminianism of the Old Lights, [while] with the Old Lights they accuse us of a design to spread the enthusiasm of the New Lights through the state." Montgomery wondered if they ought to abandon the plan and revert to an academy. No, said Rush, all our work has been "expressly for a *college*"[13]—for "Our Brat," as he would one day call it.

The opposition came to a head early in June when the Philadelphia synod met. Arguments against the college by Ewing & Company "much staggered" the prospective trustees, and several returned to the backcountry "but half converts to the right" and at least two as "outright opponents." Rush tried to delude friends into believing Ewing's attacks should be cause for satisfaction: every educational project Ewing had fought—notably the Colleges of New Jersey and Philadelphia in their infancy—had succeeded, and the one he had backed—an academy at New Ark, Delaware—had failed. But Rev. John Black, one of the college's backcountry supporters, was not to be hoodwinked. He convinced Rush that he exaggerated Ewing's personal pique, that many objected to the school's narrow denominational base, and that the project would collapse unless concessions were made. It was agreed the board of trustees must be enlarged from twenty-four members to forty, and that among the additions should be some "Covenanters and Creeders"— that is, members of the German Lutheran and Dutch Reformed churches.

These changes would bring the number of denominations represented to thirteen, thus giving the same "broad bottom" that Rush had found objectionable about the University of Pennsylvania. The plan for a School of Prophets was also forfeited. Rush could bend when he had to.[14]

While these changes were being negotiated, Rush stepped up the campaign for a charter. "Let us be up and doing," he said, fearful about the complexion of the assembly after the October elections. A petition by Rush went to the legislature with sixty-four signatures. Wilson, the state's ablest lawyer and with a "perfect knowledge of all the charters of the American colleges," agreed to draw up the charter, though it appears another lawyer, Miers Fisher, actually did the job. A plea went out to Montgomery to head for Philadelphia, for "I can do nothing without you." The behind-the-scenes efforts through July and August to win a favorable hearing in the assembly were rewarded on 1 September 1783. "The ice is at last broken," Rush wrote to the absent Montgomery, "and leave has been obtained to bring in a bill to found a college at Carlisle," but only, he added, by the slim margin of four votes. Deputies from Carlisle's own county of Cumberland spearheaded opposition to the bill. They condemned the proposed college site as being too near "the sickly banks of the Susquehanna, where the youth would enjoy fogs and the society of boatmen, wagoners, and such like companions for half a century to come." Montgomery must "come to town *immediately,*" read one urgent message. "Everything hangs upon the next *two* weeks." The legislature toyed with a decision while the beleaguered Rush coped with the epidemic of scarlet fever, then at its height.[15]

Rush was convinced, perhaps correctly, that "if we fail this session, you will see petitions (*composed* in Philadelphia) next year from Harrisburg, Chambersburg, Shippen's Town, and even Pittsburgh against the town of Carlisle." The assembly, however, finally eliminated these fears and honored Rush's strivings of the past year on September 9, when Dickinson College, as it was now to be called, the first Pennsylvania college outside Philadelphia, received its charter of incorporation.[16]

3

In an early letter to Cullen after the war, Rush complained that "the practice of physic still continues to be laborious and by no means profitable in proportion to our labor in this new country." He no longer talked of abandoning medicine for law—it was too late at the age of thirty-eight to shift. But he did decide to ease his burdens by taking on a partner. The move was not predicated on a sudden surge in the size of his practice. During the first six months of 1784 he averaged approximately the same number of patients that he had in previous years, about seventy-five.[17] Perhaps his old mentor, John Redman, helped convince Rush he should begin to ease up, for it was about this time that Redman retired from practice.

Redman long ago had moved from the center to the periphery of Rush's life, but he never moved out of it. He was sixty-four years old in 1784, and though his odd dress made him look like a relic out of the past, no one thought of him as a sedate old gentleman. He wore "his hat flapped before and cocked up smartly behind, covering a full-bottom powdered wig, in the front of which might be seen an eagle-pointed nose, separated by a pair of piercing black eyes, his lips exhibiting, but only now and then, a quick motion, as though at the moment he was endeavoring to extract the essence of a small quid." In fair weather he could be seen almost daily "on a short, fat, black, switch-tailed mare, and riding for his amusement and exercise in a brisk racking canter, about the streets and suburbs of the city." Rush's son James all his life held a vivid recollection of Redman and his mare. "I remember him well hitching her to the turnbuckle of the mansion shutter, so that she always stood on the foot-pavement, when he visited my father, which he made it a point to do once or twice a year."[18]

Life for Rush, as for Redman, was something to be enjoyed, not just endured, and he may have reasoned in 1784 that a partner to share his practice would give him more leisure. But other factors brought about the decision. For one thing, said Rush, "this connection was the more necessary, as frequent attacks of a pulmonary affection rendered it unsafe for me to go out in the night and bad weather." For another, attendance at the hospital now occupied part of what had already been full days, and the work there, especially with the mentally deranged, intrigued him. He began to keep a private record on the lunatics, noting the reasons for their mania. Twenty-four cases, for example, were listed as "induced by spirituous liquors," five by disappointed love, five by grief, five by religious melancholy. He also marked how many "were cured," how many "were relieved," and how many "received no benefit." Rush here, quietly and casually, was easing into a field of medicine that in time would earn him the title of "father of American psychiatry." He never explained why, in 1784, the mentally ill began to engage his interest.[19]

Rush could afford the new interest, for though the size of his practice remained steady the quality had altered; more patients paid for their care. During the first half of 1784 cash income exceeded £800, more than enough to satisfy the needs of a man who had never set out to garner a fortune. Rush could see little sense in enduring the drudgery of a large practice when Dickinson College called for attention and a host of other projects—medical, civic, social, and educational—needed to be set in motion if Pennsylvania were to become the beacon to guide the world to reform. All these matters had to be attended to by one who no longer had the energy of youth and often complained to friends of "great fatigue."[20]

Rush chose to share his practice with a young man named James Hall, whom he had accepted as an apprentice in 1779. Hall was the son of Elihu Hall, at whose Maryland home, Mount Welcome, Rush and his wife had stayed on and off during the war. In 1783 Rush financed his trip to London for fifteen months to attend "lectures . . . and the practice of the Saint Thomas Hospital." When Hall returned in the summer of 1784 the partnership became formal. Rush was very fond of the young man, called him Jamey, and enjoyed the fact that he "loves to tease." Two years later Rush was both pleased and uneasy when Hall fell in love—pleased because the girl was the daughter of his old friend of '76, Thomas Hartley of York County; uneasy because Hall would be "marrying into an intemperate family" and might "learn to drink." (He did and died of it in 1801.)[21]

Hall's sharing of the professional burden gave Rush a chance to indulge himself in other interests, "for you know," he once confessed, "I love to be in the way of adding to my stock of ideas upon all subjects." The tales of a friend recently back from Canton led to a page in his journal on the oddities of the Chinese—they never get angry, are ingenious rogues, produce vegetables of a vapid taste, "manure their ground only with human ordure. . . ." The first ascension of a balloon in Philadelphia drew forth a long and vivid account of the crowd of some ten thousand, "all gaping with impatience to see the new phenomenon," of the fall of the astronaut from his seat as the great air bag smacked against the wall of the House of Employment, of the continuing slow, majestic ascent of the balloon until it caught fire and its charred fragments scattered over the city. "Philosophy, curiosity, and even wit and humor are all at work in our city upon the subject of balloons," Rush said. "There is little else talked of—they furnish metaphors, similes, and hyperboles upon all subjects. Some people expect a new era in politics, war, and commerce from these balloons, while others treat them as an invention calculated only to amuse gimcracks in philosophy and to terrify children."[22]

Another day the round of calls was interrupted to attend a Jewish wedding to which he had been invited by Jonas Phillips. Rush seems to have been the favored physician of the city's Jewish community, for the Phillips as well as the Franks family were patients of his. He was fascinated by the strange ceremony and even more by the reactions of the participants, especially the bride, whose face mirrored a blend of "innocence, modesty, fear, respect, and devotion." Facial expressions intrigued Rush; in the countenance of the fallen astronaut he had seen "not fear or terror, but emotions far beyond both—it expressed the last degree of *horror* and *despair.*" He carried away from the wedding ceremony, along with his affection for the Phillips family, the hope that some day the benighted Jews, that "once-beloved race of men, shall again be restored to the divine favor" and be reunited with Christians. For him only one nation, the United States, and only one religion, Christianity, could save the world. Hope for the future lay in the universal acceptance of the principles of both.[23]

4

Hall's presence did not bring about any fundamental change in Rush's professional life. He continued to carry on a large correspondence with physicians throughout the world, and many used him as a clearinghouse for information. A doctor from New York wrote of curing venereal patients "by the use of *opium* alone," and wondered if the treatment was worth a report in the American Philosophical Society's *Transactions;* Ramsay asked from South Carolina about the worth of the opium cure. A physician on Tortola referred a patient to Rush and mentioned in passing that "any medical intelligence will be thankfully received," and Rush, no doubt recalling similar requests of his own to London and Edinburgh friends, sent along copies of his most recent pamphlets. He regularly passed out the latest medical news to correspondents—"I cannot forbear mentioning that we have lately found common salt a very efficacious remedy in a spitting of blood in this country"—and welcomed all that came in. The generosity went further. Every student he could persuade to study at Edinburgh carried with him a warm letter of introduction to Cullen. Apprentices were still watched over as if they were sons; he observed their morals, kept parents posted on their progress, and continued after they had set out on their own to advise and help them whenever he could. The same solicitousness carried over to students who attended his lectures in chemistry and in the practice of physic.[24]

Rush continued to give the course inaugurated in 1781 on the practice of physic, either at the university or informally in some loft about town. The extant notes of students indicate no fundamental revision of his ideas. Chemistry, on the other hand, engaged his thoughts more than ever. To judge by references in the lectures, Rush, now that the Revolution had ended, was spending considerable time catching up on the small mountain of research published in the eight years that American ports had been closed to European learning. He read or glanced at the work of almost every important chemist of the day, incorporating their findings in lectures as swiftly as possible. Richard Kirwan, whose *Elements of Mineralogy* was first published in 1784, was recommended to the class the following autumn as the first writer to bring chemistry to the aid of natural history. Antoine François Fourcroy's *Chemistry* came forth in an English edition in 1785, and Rush had read enough of it by that fall to recommend it to his class as a useful work.

Time and new discoveries had forced a readjustment in several once cherished judgments. Macquer's *Elements of Chemistry,* which in 1771 he had urged on students, fourteen years later was found "faulty in points of system and, sorry am I to say it, I shall frequently have reason to mention his name only to point out his errors." His old teacher Black, once pictured as a satellite of Cullen, in 1785 deserved "to be considered as the father of chemistry and [the] first [who] taught it as a regular science." He continued, though, to teach the phlogiston theory, which more advanced scientists were discarding in favor of Lavoisier's theory of oxygen. He followed Priestley's work closely, summarizing it for the classes and emphasizing when he disagreed with such radical statements as that oxygen "was the pablum of plants."[25]

As a chemist Rush deserves no laurels; as a professor of chemistry he must be recognized as a distinguished teacher of the subject. Four of his students—Caspar Wistar; James Hutchinson; John Redman Coxe, Redman's grandson; and James Woodhouse—succeeded in that order to the chair he first held, and one of them—Woodhouse—was among the outstanding chemists of his time. John Penington, a favorite student, in 1789 organized the first known chemical society in America and a year later published the first book on the subject by an American. "If any man deserves to be called the father of American chemistry that man was Benjamin Rush," a scholar on this aspect of his career has written. That judgment seems strong for one whose involvement in the science was marginal from start to finish. His postwar spurt of interest, for instance, soon faltered, and students' notes after 1785 reveal no substantive changes in the content or style of the lectures.[26] Accident made him the nation's first professor of chemistry—Morgan had taught the first course but only as a sideline to his main interest, the theory and practice of physic—and in that post Rush served as a pipeline to transmit word of the work being done in Europe. As a teacher he attracted students to an abstruse specialty. In that sense he might be called "the father of American chemistry," though surely even Rush would blush to accept the honor.

5

A rump session of the Carlisle college board of trustees, only ten of the forty members, most of them from Philadelphia, met at Dickinson's home on 15 September 1783. All took the loyalty oath ("We will not directly or indirectly do any act or thing prejudicial or injurious to the [Pennsylvania] constitution or government thereof . . ."), and Dickinson was elected president of the board. The first full meeting of the board was scheduled for the following April at Carlisle. At a second meeting held four evenings later at Rush's home, discussion centered on ways to raise money for the new school. Rush expected no trouble on that score, and nothing said at the meeting about the feebleness of "our resources and funds" could check his optimism.[27]

Early signs suggested that his hopes for a speedy endowment were not misplaced as wealthy friends in the city pledged moderately generous sums. But within a few weeks dismal reports came in from the backcountry. "The prospect is very dark," Reverend Black reported; people talk only of high taxes and lack of cash. Lancaster shows little interest, said another supporter. Pledges, it turned out, were easier made than collected. Aid from

abroad, which had helped so many colonial colleges before the war, somewhat understandably failed to materialize. "Friendship is not yet sufficiently
restored between the two countries," Richard Price wrote from London.
John Erskine from Edinburgh expressed doubts that the college could succeed and sent nothing; undaunted, Rush only determined to "remove his
prejudices in my next letters." Not too many months had passed before
Rush was pleading to British friends that "the sweepings of their studies
will be very acceptable in our illiterate wooden country."[28]

Finding a suitable "principal"—the title used in Scottish colleges and
preferred to "president" by Rush—seemed a more manageable problem.
Even before the charter had been granted he had settled on Charles Nisbet,
a clergyman he had met in Scotland sixteen years earlier. "I love the man's
character and am charmed with his disinterestedness," he had said then.
Nisbet by chance had refreshed the early good impression with a letter out
of the blue a few weeks before the charter passed, and Rush determined
instantly to attract him to Carlisle. Montgomery suggested an American
would do as well. Rev. William Linn from the backcountry suggested Samuel Blair, but "Samey," said Rush, suffered "from his habits of inactivity."
Reverend King accepted Nisbet's charms and scholarly achievements on
faith, but pleaded that before holding out too many inducements "we
should be satisfied that we are capable of holding up such encouragement
as would invite a man from thence, where if he is really such he will have
the great inducement to stay." Despite the warning, Rush virtually promised the post to Nisbet long before the April meeting in Carlisle, when the
full board would vote for the principal.[29]

Rush found time before the April board meeting to produce an essay
entitled "Of the Mode of Education Proper in a Republic." "It has cost me
a great deal of severe study," he said when done, admitting he had worked
at it off and on for more than four months. He might also have said it had
cost a great deal of self-study, for within the essay was a lengthy statement
of the guidelines Rush used to direct his life and to a striking degree practiced. In the process of setting down his conception of the ideal citizen of a
republic, this self-revealing credo came forth:

> He must watch for the state as if its liberties depended upon his
> vigilance alone, but he must do this in such a manner as not to
> defraud his creditors or neglect his family. He must love private

life, but he must decline no station however public or responsible it may be, when called to it by the suffrages of his fellow citizens. He must love popularity, but he must despise it when set in competition with the dictates of his judgment, or the real interest of his country. . . . He must avoid neutrality in all questions that divide the state, but he must shun the rage and acrimony of party spirit. He must be taught to love his fellow creatures in every part of the world, but he must cherish with a more intense and peculiar affection, the citizens of Pennsylvania and of the United States. I do not wish to see our youth educated with a single prejudice against any nation or country; but we impose a task upon human nature, repugnant alike to reason, revelation, and the ordinary dimensions of the human heart, when we require him to embrace with equal affection the whole family of mankind. He must be taught to amass wealth, but it must be only to increase his power of contributing to the wants and demands of the state. He must be indulged occasionally in amusements, but he must be taught that study and business should be his principal pursuits of life. Above all he must love life, and endeavor to acquire as many of its conveniences as possible by industry and economy, but he must be taught that this life "is not his own" when the safety of his country requires it.[30]

Rush said nothing here that would have displeased the mentors of his youth, Finley and Davies. The view that a college should reinforce "the principle of patriotism" and that a student should "be taught that he does not belong to himself, but that he is public property" echoed Davies' final sermon to the Class of '60. The stricture that religion and education must be tied together, for without religion "there can be no virtue, and without virtue there can be no liberty" could have been lifted from a sermon of Finley's. Rush admitted his views harked back to the past and that he resisted the liberal trend of the times, which judged "it is improper to fill the minds of youths with religious prejudices of any kind, and that they should be left to choose their own principles, after they have arrived at an age in which they are capable of judging for themselves."[31]

These old-fashioned views gave way when he turned to the details of his educational program. Here he had a number of reforms to suggest. Students should be prohibited from tasting spirituous liquors; their diet should be moderate, "consisting chiefly of broths, milk, and vegetables"; they should be taught to work with their hands. "Moderate sleep, silence, occasional solitude, and cleanliness should be inoculated upon them." The importance of singing "in civilizing the mind and thereby preparing it for the influence of religion and government" should not be overlooked. A prejudice against dormitory life dating from his own college days evoked the assertion that boys learn vices from one another and should be subjected "to those restraints which the differences of age and sex naturally produce in private families." Housing boys together in a hall "has a tendency to make them scholars, but our business is to make them men, citizens, and chieftains."

The curriculum proposed flouted current views. Ignore Latin and Greek in the early years and "teach our youth to read and write our American language with propriety and elegance," he said. "The French and German languages should likewise be carefully taught in all our colleges. They abound with useful books upon all subjects. So important and necessary are those languages, that a degree should never be conferred upon a young man who cannot speak or translate them." The study of eloquence should also be encouraged, for "it is the first accomplishment in a republic, and often sets the whole machine of government in motion." Along with history he urged the study of commerce for its humanizing effect upon mankind, its ability to check the rise of landed aristocracies, and "as the means of uniting the different nations of the world together by the ties of mutual wants and obligations." After token respect to the virtues of chemistry and the study of government, Rush ended with a plea for the liberal education of women, "who must concur in all our plans of education for young men, or no laws will ever render [the plans] effectual."[32]

Before departing for Carlisle he read the finished essay aloud to several friends. They "approve of my ideas," he reported, "and conceive more highly of the utility of our college than ever."[33]

16

Focus on the Backcountry

1784–1785

1

ON 2 APRIL 1784 Rush left for Carlisle on a ten-day trip that marked his longest absence from Philadelphia, except during the British occupation, since his return from Europe. For his wife, he honored the event by keeping a diary of the oddities met in the countryside that stretched beyond the city's borders.[1] Mrs. Rush remained in Philadelphia, pregnant with their sixth child who, when born on May 16, would be given the name Mary.

In 1784 the Pennsylvania backcountry comprised something over 150,000 people. More than a third, perhaps close to half, of them were German-speaking settlers of various denominations—Amish, Mennonites, Dunkards, River Brethren, Lutherans, Moravians, Schwenkfelders. Their settlements cut diagonally across the region in a broad swath that began at Easton in the northeast, curved through Bethlehem and Lancaster, and ended west of the Susquehanna in the vicinity of York. The Scotch-Irish, the other large group of settlers in the backcountry, were scattered through this belt but tended to be concentrated beyond the Germans closer to the frontier. Here and there among these two groups were pockets of English and Welsh Baptists, a few Quakers and Anglicans, and some Catholics. Little intermingling occurred among this diversity of settlers. Little Britain was "an Irish settlement" and in nearby York "the inhabitants are Dutch," one traveler found. New Oxford was "another settlement of the Scotch-

Irish," and close by it was a village, dominated by a Lutheran church, where the people spoke German and "an old kind Dutch landlady gave our horses for breakfast a dish of 'speltz.' "²

Rush traveled at a leisurely pace, attended by a servant, and treating himself to all the comfort that circumstances would allow. He began at a gentlemanly ten in the morning, pausing eleven miles later to feed the horses and take "a cold snack myself." With an eye for the good things in life, he took note of the "neat handsome Quaker girl" who served him and observed she "had all that cleverness about her that insures her making a good wife." Ten miles later came dinner at a tavern run by "a lively talking little Quaker," who hated Presbyterians and the constitution. In the midst of a harangue the man suddenly caught himself.

"But I ask pardon, sir," he said. "I hope—no offense. Perhaps, sir, you are a Presbyterian. I don't mean to be rude."

"Say on, friend," remarked Rush noncommittally. "You can't offend me by anything you can say of any sect." While Rush sat by drinking a quart of beer, the Quaker went on to praise his German neighbors who refused to take the loyalty oaths.

He stayed the first night out at a tavern run by a "full fed, fat Quaker Tory" who detested ex-President Reed, and remembered him once saying that "he would *bend*—or *break* the Quakers." After supping on a dish of tea, the evening was whiled away with a walk and some reading. Now and then he felt "an inclination for a pinch of snuff," but recollection of Mrs. Rush's "many pathetic, animated, and affectionate remonstrances" restrained him. He bedded down in a room shared by three other travelers. The next morning he paid an excessive bill "without *disputing*," having perhaps been warned by his wife to check his temper while away from home, and moved off through a raw, rainy day that ended at the Sign of the Bear in Lancaster, where John Dickinson joined him. The town's leading citizens stopped by through the evening to pay their respects to the Executive Council president, talk politics, and praise the idea of a college at Carlisle. On the remaining two days of travel, Rush eyed the farms as he passed out of the Pennsylvania Dutch country and toward the frontier, that "meeting point between savagery and civilization," as Frederick Jackson Turner was later to define it. He noted that the farms owned by Germans "bear all the marks of the industry of those people," but that farms of the Scotch-Irish had "houses without windows, water wasting itself in public roads instead of being drawn over the fields of grain, low or broken fences, and lean cattle."

Rush reached Carlisle on April 5. The next day fifteen of the college's trustees—General Armstrong, having capitulated to Rush's entreaties, was among them—gathered at the Episcopal Church to hear Reverend Black preach on "the utility of seminaries of learning." Montgomery honored the board with a dinner Rush judged "plentiful, elegant, and as well attended as any dinner I ever was at in a gentleman's house in Philadelphia." Afterward, the trustees trooped down to the courthouse where those who had not yet done so took the loyalty oath; they then proceeded to business. Presumably Rush now read his essay on education. The board requested Dickinson and Rush to prepare a seal for the college, and with that adjourned early in the evening.

The meeting on April 7 opened early with a "sensible prayer" and lasted all day. The Committee of Subscriptions reported that cash on hand to open the college amounted to only £257 15s and that the expected income from loan-office certificates and land would be "about £130 per annum." No one seemed fazed by these figures. The board agreed all endowed land should be sold and invested in bank shares. Nor were the members disturbed when they heard a letter from William Bingham read aloud. Bingham, then in Europe on business, was using his spare time to solicit funds for the college. He reported that he had thus far had no luck and did not expect to have much in the future. Committees were selected to solicit additional contributions from all parts of the state, to prepare a petition to the assembly for aid, and to draw up an appeal to a gathering of German Lutheran clergymen asking them to join in backing the college. In the afternoon the trustees visited the eastern edge of town to view what remained of a military encampment, or "public works" as it was called. If the college prospered, the dingy little building in the village where the first classes were scheduled to meet would soon prove inadequate. The "public works" was "judged proper for the accommodation of the pupils and professors" and the board voted to negotiate with Congress for its purchase.[3]

The following morning at eight the board, compliant to Rush's wishes, "elected unanimously our Principal Dr. Nisbet." James Ross, who had been master of the grammar school which would now house the college, was chosen professor of languages. Rush and Dickinson presented their suggestion for a seal—an open Bible, telescope, and liberty cap (these were

Rush's contribution) encompassed by the motto *Pietate et Doctrina Tuta Libertas* (suggested by Dickinson)—which the board accepted. The meeting ended with an "excellent prayer," then the citizens of Carlisle tendered "an elegant dinner" for the visitors. Montgomery thought the short talk delivered by Dickinson "effectually removed some jealousies that hung on some of our neighbors," and he was especially pleased "how pretty he touched on the upright intentions of those who first embarked in that glorious cause" of establishing a college on the edge of the wilderness.[4]

On April 9 a group of citizens accompanied the departing visitors for ten miles through a cold rain over a road covered in places with a foot of snow. Outside York another honor guard met the party to escort it into the town where six years earlier Rush had humbly handed in his resignation to Congress. If he recalled the day, it went unmentioned in the diary, though he did record that on April 10 he passed some time wandering about the village, visiting among other places the courthouse where Congress had sat. He enjoyed an hour of talk with a German artisan who agreed to make a mold for the college seal, dined in a large company with his friend and fellow trustee Thomas Hartley, then later in the day drank tea with James Smith, a local lawyer with whom he had collaborated on the Provincial Conference's address to Congress in 1776.

On Sunday, April 11, Rush felt sufficiently homesick or pressed for time to break the Sabbath with travel. He and Dickinson stopped the night at Wright's Ferry, where Susanna Wright, a friend of Franklin "who has been celebrated above half a century for her wit, good sense and valuable improvements of mind," reminisced away the evening. Monday morning Rush and Dickinson moved on early, dined near Lancaster, lodged one more evening away from home, and then arrived back in Philadelphia Tuesday afternoon.

2

With most men a trip of this sort would serve only as a diverting interlude. Not so with Rush. Out of his ten-day adventure came three spirited essays, each in its way a distinguished piece of work and all the direct result of ideas generated while sauntering through the backcountry.

The first, a follow-up of earlier attacks on the evils of drinking, came soon after he had returned to Philadelphia. It had occurred to him during the last day of travel that the contrast between German and Scotch-Irish farms owed a good deal to the stillhouse observable on nearly every Scotch-Irish plot. "The quantity of rye destroyed and of whisky drunk in these places is immense," he noted in the diary, "and its effects upon their industry, health, and morals are terrible." He hoped Dickinson College would introduce order, harmony, and enlightenment among the backcountry Presbyterians, but the omnipresent stillhouse was a mighty obstacle to that goal. Rush favored drinking; to judge by his own consumption, he found a quart of beer with lunch, a pint and a half of madeira after dinner, to be wholesome and moderate nourishment. He condemned only those liquors "obtained by distillations from fermented substances of any kind." The trip to Carlisle convinced him that ardent spirits lay at the root of *all* the Scotch-Irishman's troubles—his quarrelsome nature, his stump-filled fields and slovenly farmhouses, even his slack attendance at church. Within a few weeks after the return to Philadelphia, he had published *An Enquiry into the Effects of Spirituous Liquors Upon the Human Body, and their Influence upon the Happiness of Society*. Out of a fury for what he had seen of the way in which liquor demeaned his beloved Presbyterians, he broadened and sharpened an attack begun a decade earlier into what would become his most famous essay. He refined, enlarged, and revised it the rest of his life, and it remained in print, serving as a principal weapon in the arsenal of temperance workers, nearly a century after his death. Its power as propaganda has obscured its merits as medical literature: historically the essay ranks as the first to detail the physiological effects of alcoholism.

It opened with a vivid account of drinking's immediate effects upon men. It made them talkative and bawdy, and it predisposed them to swear, quarrel, and fight. Women, sad to say, who were suitably modest when sober performed "certain immodest actions" when drunk. The description of a man in "the paroxysm of drunkenness" combined the accuracy of a physician's report and the vividness of a preacher's sermon:

> He opens his eyes and closes them again—he gapes and stretches his limbs—he then coughs and pukes—his voice is hoarse—he rises with difficulty, and staggers to a chair—his eyes resemble balls of fire—his hands tremble—he loathes the sight of food—he calls for a glass of spirits to compose his stomach—now and then

he emits a deep-fetched sigh or groan, from a transient twinge
of conscience; but he more frequently scolds, and curses everything around him.

Rush moves on to detail the chronic effects of liquor on the body, blending
the mild with the mortal. Drinking leads to an obstructed liver, jaundice,
dropsy, diabetes, "rum-buds" on the face, a fetid breath, frequent belchings,
epilepsy, gout, and finally madness. Aside from the physical effects, it in-
evitably carries the drinker, and his family, too, into poverty, misery, crimes,
and infamy.[5]

The second literary product of the trip came a year later in a letter to
an English friend which, after still another year of mulling over, Rush
published in an expanded version as "An Account of the Progress of Population, Agriculture, Manners and Government in Pennsylvania." The essay
would in time prove to be a landmark in historiography, for a century later
Rush's perception of the stages of development on the Pennsylvania frontier
would be elaborated by Frederick Jackson Turner into a full-scale interpretation of the American experience. "The *first* settler in the woods,"
according to Rush, "is generally a man who has outlived his credit or fortune in the cultivated parts of the state." He carves a crude existence from
the wilderness, living close to starvation the first year and enduring "a great
deal of distress from hunger, cold, and a variety of accidental causes." Rush
admits he "seldom complains or sinks under" adversity, but otherwise
passes out no other praise. The ways of the first settler resemble those of
the barbarous and indolent Indian; he plants little more than maize, lets his
livestock run wild, and lives a disorderly life. "He loves spirituous liquors,
and he eats, drinks, and sleeps in dirt and rags in his little cabin." The
civilization he has fled catches up with him in two or three years, and he
endures it no more easily now than before. "He cannot bear to surrender
up a single natural right for all the benefits of government, and therefore
he abandons his little settlement and seeks retreat in the woods."

The second species of settler usually arrives with enough money to
make a substantial down payment on the farm the first man has developed.
He improves the cabin into a house, clears a meadow, plants an orchard,
builds a log barn, enlarges the fields and adds wheat and rye (for his
whisky) to the crop of maize. But this man, like his predecessor, still "bears

many marks of a weak tone of mind." Stumps continue to spot the fields, his fences soon fall into disrepair, the broken windows of the house are stuffed with old hats or pillows. He delights in company, spirituous liquors, and political meetings and generally refuses to contribute to his church or to the support of civil government. His ill-run farm leads to debts that "compel him to sell his plantation, generally in the course of a few years, to the *third* and last species of settler." This man first builds a stone barn to keep the livestock warm in winter, mends the fences, diversifies his crops, begins a kitchen garden, erects a milkhouse and smokehouse, improves the orchard, and, if he survives these labors, constructs a solid stone house for the family. The horses and cattle are always sleek and fat, the clothing worn is homespun, the table overflows with food. There is no whisky here but plenty of good beer, cider, and homemade wine. This third settler pays his taxes on time, supports his churches and schools. "Of this class of settlers are two-thirds of the farmers of Pennsylvania."

Rush deplores without pretending to understand the "passion for migration" of the first two types of settlers, but he also sees advantages in their desire to roam. They help to populate the interior of the continent. Moreover, as the pruning of suckers from an apple tree "increases the size of the tree and the quantity of the fruit," so their migration improves the country they have left behind. All these migrants go south, where the land is easier to till and the winters are milder. "From this you will see that our state is the great outport of the United States for Europeans, and that, after performing the office of a sieve by detaining all those people who possess the stamina of industry and virtue, it allows a passage to the rest to those states which are accommodated to their habits of indolence and vice." No doubt Rush intended these sentiments to be taken seriously rather than as a good-humored dig at the southern states.[6]

The original essay identified the settlers of the first and second stages as Scotch-Irish and those of the third as Germans. Rush dropped these identifications in the published version, perhaps because he found it difficult to censure publicly those who composed the majority of his church. In case anyone missed the praise bestowed upon those whom most Pennsylvanians called "the dumb Dutch," he eventually published "An Account of the Manners of the German Inhabitants of Pennsylvania." Rush here fleshed out the picture sketched earlier, making it quite evident that for him the

German stood forth as the ideal American—industrious and honest, devoted to his family and church, a supporter of education and government. "LEGISLATORS of Pennsylvania—learn from the history of your German fellow citizens that you possess an inexhaustible treasure in the bosom of the state," he admonished. "Do not contend with their prejudices in favor of their language. It will be the channel through which the knowledge and discoveries of one of the wisest nations in Europe may be conveyed into our country." Little about the essay seems striking until the modern reader is reminded that "nothing remotely comparable to it in informativeness and sympathetic understanding was written about the Pennsylvania Germans during the eighteenth century."[7]

Along with a natural sympathy for these solid citizens, Rush had a practical, pecuniary motive for promoting their virtues. He hoped his writings would encourage similarly stalwart farmers to emigrate to Pennsylvania and settle on some of the land he owned, for recently some of Rush's newfound prosperity from the medical practice had been diverted into speculative investments in backcountry land. As early as 1780 he had tried to interest Ramsay in joining with him, but Ramsay held he could get as good land in South Carolina "for one fourth the price." Rush had believed, mistakenly it turned out, that when the war ended emigrants would pour out of Europe, and on that hunch he had stepped up his purchases after 1783. These were modest compared with speculators like Morris and Wilson, who eventually were bankrupted by their dealings, and always undertaken with friends like Tench Coxe, Dr. William Plunkett, William Maclay, or Isaac Franks. With Franks, a patient and also a friend, listed in Rush's ledger as "broker," he bought a string of tracts in the center of the state in 1784. Enough settlers trickled in to keep alive hope of a handsome profit, and in 1787 he increased his investments. Rush's sporadic but intense interest in speculation, the colorful publicity he gave to the merits of Pennsylvania in essays and in letters to friends in Europe, never availed a great fortune, however. Part of the trouble was that pioneers, particularly the outrageous Scotch-Irish, preferred such distant places as Kentucky or the back sections of southern states. More important, Rush lacked both the talent and dedication to make a fortune. He displayed no more interest in piling up money than he did in accumulating power.[8]

3

Rush returned from the backcountry bursting with plans for the Carlisle college. He found time to carry on his practice, to meddle in politics, to publish in July the pamphlet on spirituous liquors, but most of his energy went to promoting the college's fortunes. A press release, probably prepared by him, appeared in the papers summarizing the Carlisle meeting and expanding on Reverend Nisbet's renown as a preacher and scholar. He dragooned Wilson into helping secure from Congress the "public works." He warned Montgomery his presence would be required in the city within a month, for the assembly must be pressed to give the school aid, and only he could convince doubtful deputies. He urged Black and King to be on hand when the synod met in order to promote contributions. Reverend Linn's desire to teach in the college was vetoed with flattery. "I do not wish to see Columbus chained to an oar," Rush wrote. "I have (ever since I became acquainted with your talents) desired you to a much higher sphere of usefulness than to teach boys to read and speak our languages with propriety."[9]

That deprecation of teaching notwithstanding, Rush fussed constantly with problems of staffing the school. He persuaded Rev. Robert Davidson, who had formerly taught history and geography at the College of Philadelphia, to accept a post at Dickinson. He had heard of an Episcopal minister, "a Whig in politics and a Calvinist in religion," who might make an excellent professor in moral philosophy and metaphysics. If he could find a good Lutheran clergyman to teach natural philosophy, "our plan will be complete." Gone was the hope of a strictly Presbyterian school. Now it would be "enough for us that the principal and a majority of the trustees are Presbyterians."[10]

Rush took special care with the letter to Nisbet announcing his election as principal, for he had learned that Witherspoon, then en route to Scotland on a fund-raising trip, had said before leaving he would advise Nisbet against coming to America. The resulting letter, a masterpiece of persuasive rhetoric, opens with the assumption that Nisbet would of course accept the honor accorded him and mentions at once an enclosed bill of exchange for £50 "to assist in defraying the expenses of your voyage to this country." A description of the board of trustees, of the village of Carlisle, and of the expected duties of the principal follow, then Rush proceeds to pour forth the charm that fifteen years earlier had melted Mrs. Witherspoon's resistance to the hazards of an American voyage. "Our college is as yet a newborn infant," he told Nisbet.

> It has all the parts and faculties of a man, but they require growth and extension. To *you,* sir, it lifts up its feeble hands. To you, to *you* alone (under God), it looks for support and nourishment. Your name is now in everybody's mouth. The Germans attempt to pronounce it in broken English. The natives of Ireland and the descendants of Irishmen have carried it to the western counties. The Juniata and Ohio rivers have borne it on their streams through every township of the state that lies beyond Carlisle. Our saints pray for you as the future apostle of the church in this part of the world. Our patriots long to thank you for defending the cause of America at a time and in a place where she had few friends.

Possibly Nisbet had heard slurs cast upon the college. "Ignorance, prejudice, party spirit, *self-interest,* and *jealousy* have all in their turns opposed it," Rush warns, adding by implication that the italicized words apply particularly to Witherspoon, who, he was sorry to say, "did not carry the same character back with him to Scotland that he brought from it to America. 'Demas hath forsaken me, having *loved* the *present* world.' "[11]

Demas was not the only one. In Scotland the Countess of Leven, mother of Lady Jane, depicted the college as "at best but an *indigested* scheme," and told Nisbet that Rush's "warm and lively temper" made him unreliable in projects of this sort. And from Philadelphia came a surprising letter by Dickinson urging Nisbet to turn down the offer. Dickinson had panicked at the October state election results; they gave the Constitutionalists once again a firm majority in the assembly, and he feared they might use this power to revoke the college's charter.[12]

Rush reacted predictably to this "treachery" by lashing out at a friend who had suddenly "become the most formidable enemy to our college that ever we have yet known." He canvassed those he knew in the assembly and found none who thought the school would lose its charter. He got the trustees in Philadelphia to answer Dickinson's letter and prodded Montgomery to have those in the Carlisle region do the same. He also visited Dickinson and spoke "very plainly," but the president stood fast, holding that "it became us to act with prudence," to which Rush answered as he headed for the door, "Prudence when *honor* is concerned is a rascally virtue." Where Rush's blandishments failed others succeeded, and a few days later Dickinson wrote a second carefully phrased letter to Nisbet. "Many of the friends of the college at Carlisle," he said, "are fully convinced that no attempts will be made against that establishment; or that, if they should be, that they will be unsuccessful. I must confess that my hopes are much stronger than they were in favor of the institution."[13]

The crisis passed. A short while later Rush received assurances from Nisbet that he would embark for Philadelphia the following spring. Rush replied suitably. "We have allotted a room in our house for your reception, which goes by the name of 'Dr. Nisbet's room.' My little folks often mention your name, especially my *boys,* who have been taught to consider you as their future master."[14] (None of Rush's sons ever attended Dickinson College.)

The battle that invigorated Rush had left Montgomery despondent. *"Give over our college!* God forbid!" he wrote to Montgomery toward the end of 1784. "We *must* succeed—unless the trustees at Carlisle are determined to chase learning as the Gadarenes once did Jesus Christ from their borders. I consider your languor as the only enemy we have now to encounter. We have overcome Mr. Dickinson's treachery." As Rush had said earlier: "Colleges, like children, I find are not born without labor pains. But all will end well. Our Brat will repay us hereafter for all the trouble it has given us."[15]

4

"I sincerely congratulate you on your growing foreign fame," a friend wrote Rush on his fortieth birthday. "You are now in the most valuable decade of human life." Fame had brought, along with a prosperous practice, all the honors but one—membership in the Royal Society—that he had chased after as a fledgling physician. It had also brought attacks. "Dr. Froth," as some called him, is as "changeable as the wind, fickle as the water, unstable as the ocean," wrote one newspaper correspondent. "He is contemptible in every point of view but one. *He is a mischievous and implacable enemy.* Tho' he contradicts himself ten times in a minute, yet if anyone also contradicts him, he is sure to attempt some mean revenge. A LIE is generally his instrument. The press or private conversation are alike vehicles of his poison."[16]

This particular attack both hit and missed the mark. Rush never consciously made lies his instrument but often deluded himself into propagating falsehoods as truth. His hatred toward Shippen and Ewing could burn long and hard, yet the phrase "implacable enemy" hardly characterizes one who could embrace with enthusiasm, later reject, and later still reembrace John Dickinson, John Witherspoon, and John Adams. To acquaintances he did appear changeable, fickle, and unstable, but close friends knew that he had been one of the first to favor independence and had never wavered once committed to the decision; that he had never backed off from the fight for a balanced government and a firm union of the states until these had been achieved; that when opposition to the college at Carlisle blazed on all sides and even the steady Montgomery faltered, he kept faith until the dream became a reality; that though his ideas on education after the peace were elaborated in succeeding years, as were those on slavery, the evils of drink, and the need for penal reform, they were never basically changed. Only in the realm of religion does the charge have credence. Rush here does appear changeable, fickle, and unstable.

It is easier to describe than to explain his shifting views on religion between 1784 and 1787. As early as April 1784, the month he went to Carlisle, though still a loyal Presbyterian, he showed an interest in the transmutation of the Anglican into the Episcopal Church—that is, into an *American* church whose revised articles of worship he admitted to "esteem very highly." A month later he offered to maintain before the Presbyterian synod then meeting in Philadelphia "a charge against Ewing for *lying, drunkenness, and unchristian language."* The offer went unnoticed and Ewing's influence in church and state remained undiminished. Rush continued, as he had since returning from Europe, to worship in the Second Presbyterian Church, listening to Sproat's sermons every Sunday but no longer as a devout Presbyterian. "I grow daily more and more disgusted with the folly and wickedness of our—I retract the word—*your* society," he told Montgomery in the summer of 1786. "After all *your* pains to prevent it, the Presbyterians in Pennsylvania seem destined only to be scaling-ladders and tools of Bryan and Ewing. The former looks more *pale,* the latter more *ruddy* with guilt than ever."[17]

From 1785 on Rush kept a close eye on the Episcopal Church as it adapted its mode of worship and doctrines to the American environment. The changes in baptism, marriage, and burial services and other alterations in the forms of worship, all "consonant to common sense as well as true Christianity," convinced him it would eventually become "the most popular church in America." He finally broke formally with the Presbyterians in August of 1787—the Constitutional Convention was then meeting in the city, but the juxtaposition of the two events appears only coincidental— when he learned that Sproat had proposed to Ewing "to keep up a friendly intercourse between their two societies [that is the Second and First Presbyterian Churches] by occasionally exchanging their pulpits." The decision to part, he confessed, came only after long deliberation and gave "great pain," for "the prejudices and friendships of my youth are among the Presbyterians, and most of my religious principles were derived from them." Though he proceeded to worship with the Episcopalians, a half year passed before Rush and his wife joined the church.[18]

Rush's own explanation of the break with the Presbyterians—his hatred of Ewing—fails to satisfy, but the deeper reasons can only be surmised. He had been baptized an Anglican, and some long-dormant desire to rejoin the church of his father, the church from which his mother had carried him, may have prompted the action. The parting came as he moved into his forties, a time when men sometimes reappraise themselves and often make a sharp change in their lives. Other friends at this time, notably Wilson, had also left the Presbyterians to join the Episcopalians. Moreover, in Rush's view his church broke first with him. "There are not more than ten Presbyterian families that employ me," he told a friend, "and most of them pass me without speaking to me in the streets." Political differences and disparate ideas on salvation had helped to isolate him from the Presbyterians. But so, too, did his new social position. Rush now had as friends such men as the prosperous Bingham, an Episcopalian, and William White, soon to become the church's first American bishop, "the only man I ever knew," said Rush, "of real abilities and unaffected purity and simplicity of manners that had not a single enemy."[19]

A broader and deeper influence may also have been at work. Rush's splintering off was symptomatic of a division that permeated Presbyterian-

ism much as it had at the time of the Great Awakening. Aware of this, Rush
went to the extreme of reviving old terms. Montgomery would have none
of this. "So we are to be amused with the old story of Old Side and New
Side," he wrote. "No, my friend, these old things will not now do. These
old prejudices are, I thank God, in a great measure wore off, and it sickens
me the naming of them." The terms may have been sickening and also
inaccurate, for the old alignments had dissolved—Rush now called himself
an Old Side—and new ones had come forth for which the former terms
were meaningless. Still, they revealed a truth the church wished to obscure:
Presbyterianism was once again riven with faction. One wing wished to
strengthen local, another central, control of church affairs. A recommendation to create a general assembly of the whole church, as in Scotland, to
set down overall policy tore the 1785 synod apart. Divisions over doctrine
also came to a head in 1785 when Presbyterians throughout Philadelphia
broke from their respective meetings to form a new society under the leadership of Rush's friend Elhanan Winchester, "who has openly and avowedly
preached the doctrine of final restitution." The complete Americanization
of the former Church of England occurred, under White, at the time Rush
was separating from his own meeting, and, to him, it made the Episcopalians especially attractive, socially as well as religiously. Rush, consciously or otherwise, was asking of religion what he had demanded of
education since the war ended—that it be adapted to the American experience. Beneath the clash soon to occur with Charles Nisbet lay the contrasting views of an Old World pedagogue and a New World visionary.[20]

5

Virtue, Rush once declared, "exists naturally in the human mind, as
fire does in certain bodies, in a latent or quiescent state. As collision renders
the one sensible, so education renders the other visible." The metaphor of
two colliding bodies could not have been better chosen, for when Rush
made it he had already collided with and, so to speak, been set afire by
Nisbet, Dickinson College's new guiding father.[21]

Rush fussed for weeks before Nisbet's arrival to assure a welcome "in
such a manner as to give him the most favorable ideas of the disposition of
our trustees towards him." He sent a long list of instructions to Montgomery about the Carlisle reception. Choose the best speaker among the

students to deliver the welcoming address, but make sure you get "Dr. Davidson to compose it for him." The trustees should travel out from Carlisle to meet Nisbet. The courthouse bell should be rung as he arrives. "The news of these things," Rush concluded, like a good public-relations man, "will make a clever paragraph in our Philadelphia papers and help to allure scholars to our college."[22]

Nisbet reached Philadelphia on 9 June 1785. He, his wife, and four children spent the next three weeks as guests of the Rush family, moving day after day from one reception to another arranged by their hosts. "I cannot tell you how many friends he has made in our city," Rush told Montgomery. "Indeed, my friend, in the arrival of Dr. Nisbet I conceive a new sun is risen upon Pennsylvania." John Dickinson came to call and left charmed. "I will do more for the college than ever I promised," he said. Rush dropped a practical hint. "A philosophical apparatus!" said Dickinson. "I will endow a professorship." (He did none of these things.)[23]

Nisbet on first impression seemed a younger and greater Witherspoon—a sound, perhaps even sounder Calvinist, a distinguished classicist, and a man of wit. He was, in short, the sort of Scotchman Rush had idolized some fifteen years earlier. But Rush, whether he knew it or not, had changed much since then. A man of wit no longer pleased him, especially when he served as target for the barbs. "His *wit* is like—to use a coarse simile—a certain ill-scented noise," he later told Montgomery, "which gives *him* pain while it is confined, and *everybody* pain when it is discharged."[24] Any lingering admiration that Rush might have had for a classical education had long ago died, as his proposals for the college curriculum made evident. He might deny it, but he could no longer be called a sound Calvinist; he now believed that though the Devil still resided in the world, the odds were good he would eventually be forced to vacate the premises. Above all, while he professed to admire the European university, he wanted Dickinson to become an American college designed to educate young men for life in a republic.

The Nisbets set out for Carlisle in high spirits, braced by Rush's ebullience. Their reception there on July 4 went off beautifully, but from that day on Charles Nisbet found little to elate him in the frontier village. The days by Scottish standards proved insufferably hot. The house provided for him had a roof that leaked. The college building, which had not been altered since the grammar school occupied it, he rightly judged a "hovel"; later, when an addition had been built on, he elevated it to the rank of "hogpen." He found the faculty inadequate and the students even worse. The heat, a toothache, and rheumatism soon laid his wife low, and within two weeks she had made "plans to return to Scotland or to convey *me* thither." When Nisbet himself came down with a fever, it helped little to have Rush dismiss it as something to which "all newcomers are more or less subject."[25]

While Nisbet was experiencing "a constant progressive decay of strength and natural spirits" early in August, Rush and his wife visited Carlisle for a trustees' meeting. They stayed with the Montgomerys. For some reason Rush failed to call on the ailing Nisbet, and a blunt note headed "Tomb of Dickinson" from the "much injured" principal did not encourage him to repair the discourtesy. Back in Philadelphia he continued to ignore Nisbet and, as in the past, sent out a string of instructions about the college to Montgomery: "The meadows on the public works should be drained. . . ." "I wish the masters would attend to the clothing of the boys. . . ." "Keep up Dr. Nisbet's spirits."[26]

Nisbet meanwhile had made up his mind—or his wife, a born complainer Rush thought, had made it up for him—to return to Scotland. None of Rush's eloquence could dissuade him from resigning "because he found that his constitution and time of life render him too weak to bear the heats of this climate." While waiting for the ship that had brought him over—he would return on no other—the trustees gave thought to a replacement. Rush liked Jonathan Edwards, Jr., whom he had heard was "eminent for his piety, prudence, and benevolence," and, he added with emphasis, *"has lately buried his wife."* Samuel Stanhope Smith, on the other hand, did have a wife, both outspoken and direct. She asked Rush why the trustees did not consider her husband, a professor at the College of New Jersey, for the vacant post. "Certainly, madam," came the answer, "he would not exchange Princeton for Carlisle." "Try him," Mrs. Smith replied.[27]

As the summer heat mellowed into a crisp autumn, Nisbet reconsidered the decision to depart. Montgomery favored taking him on again; Rush objected so vehemently it looked for a while that their friendship might end, "which would indeed give more uneasiness than a difference with the whole nation," a mutual friend remarked. Eventually Rush retreated, and Nisbet was reinstated on 9 May 1786. Rush, nonetheless, continued to carp. "Is it peculiar to Scotchmen and heads of colleges to be sordid and arbitrary?" he asked. "How melancholy the consideration that

Smith and Ewing, Witherspoon and Nisbet should all be so much alike in those *two* qualities." When Montgomery wrote that it was Rush who had urged Nisbet on the trustees, demanded a high salary for him, and excused his manners by saying a fever had made him "greatly disordered in his head," Rush gave thanks for the "long, friendly, and judicious letter" and then renewed the attack.[28]

Nisbet did not help matters when he held that "to erect a college in the corner of a grammar school is a scheme that never was thought of in any other age or place in the world." It is a credit to his character that he counted among the few men of the century who nearly drove Rush to distraction, pushing him so far as once to say: "We are an *undone* institution unless it shall please God to change Dr. N. or to take him to Himself." Aside from the clash of personalities, conflict between the men devolved from two issues. One dealt with practical matters. Nisbet looked at the college's situation squarely where Rush deluded himself and the public. "The difficulties in the establishment of our college are now nearly at an end," he wrote in April 1786, after the assembly had agreed to a modest grant of £500 and 10,000 acres of forest. The decision to publish an account of the college produced a candid report from Nisbet. "No proper place has yet been provided for teaching," was one of its milder statements. His report, however, was discarded and a more glowing and somewhat dishonest one substituted.[29]

A deeper source of difference between the two men sprang from their dissimilar backgrounds. Nisbet had been reared in the educational environment of Europe, where the faculty dominated academic affairs. Rush was accustomed to the American tradition, where a college was controlled largely by its board of trustees. When he complained that the plan of education drawn up by the board—actually he for the board—"had not been adopted by the professors of the college," Nisbet replied that of course it had not, for the board meddled in matters none of its business. The trustees generally and Rush in particular believed that as the collective father of their "brat" they had the right to comment on the content of courses, the methods of instruction, and, indeed, every side of the school's academic life as much as they had the right to direct the lives of their own children. Nisbet had never experienced such interference, and he objected at every turn.[30]

The finances of the college continued steadily to worsen. None of Rush's hopes materialized: the gifts in land proved of slight value, the loan-office certificates continued to be almost worthless, the Scotch-Irish community and the Presbyterian church gave little or nothing, and the wealthy of Philadelphia ceased to be interested. Rush did not help matters when he purchased some expensive equipment for the school at a time when the teachers had not been paid. He justified the extravagance mainly in terms of "the éclat a philosophical apparatus will give our college abroad," suggesting he seemed more interested in building a public image than a school.[31]

The slow, almost dismal growth of the college failed to deter Rush from continually expounding on its success. A British friend heard that "a class of near twenty young gentlemen" would graduate in the spring of 1787 (nine graduated in the fall of that year). A few weeks later Dickinson learned his namesake was "in a very flourishing condition," with pupils "coming and expected in great numbers from Maryland, Virginia, and North Carolina." These "press releases," as they might be called, were counterbalanced by less artful appraisals to Montgomery. "If Dr. Nisbet will only be prudent and silent upon the subject of our present difficulties," he wrote early in 1787, "we shall soon fill our college with pupils from every part of the nation." And so it went through the years. "Let us not be discouraged by the present low state of our funds and the declining number of our pupils," he wrote Montgomery in mid-1788. "Is there any *thing,* or any *body* in America that is *now* in a prosperous situation?"[32]

6

Less than two months after Nisbet had settled in at Carlisle and begun signaling complaints from the "tomb," Rush found himself involved in the promotion of another college, this one for the Germans of Pennsylvania. As late as May of 1785 he still expected to hire a German professor for Dickinson, hoping his presence would attract students. Soon afterward, however, Lutheran leaders revealed their fear that such a professor at Carlisle "would be accepted merely pro forma, and that it would finally lead to the rejection of the German language and the injury of the German people." They justified their suspicions by what had happened at the University of Pennsylvania, where a separate department had been created for German-speaking students. As the young men eased into college life, they

found themselves forced to reject their heritage or to endure such nick-
names as "Dutchmen" or "Sour Crouts." By mid-1785, the German community's leaders had set their minds on a college of their own. They wanted
to locate it outside both the city and Scotch-Irish territory, and in the heart
of Pennsylvania Dutch country either at Mannheim or Lancaster. They
turned to Rush, among others, for help.[33]

Rush bowed gracefully to the request, although he had counted
heavily on Germans joining in the Carlisle enterprise. But what in the short
run would hurt Dickinson College, he thought, would in the long run
benefit the nation, and that, after all, was what he had sought to do when
first plunging into the field of education. Rush initiated his campaign with
a pseudonymous letter "To the Citizens of Pennsylvania of German Birth
and Extraction: Proposal of a German College." Style and content gave the
author away. The essay began with praise for sectarian education, arguing
that it is easier to introduce religious instruction "into schools where all the
children are of one sect than where they are of different religious denominations." It praised the Germans as wise and temperate people whose lack of
educated leaders had put them "at the mercy of the lawyers of other societies, and of the quacks of their nation!"

He did not dodge the expected objections against a German college.
Would not such a school entrench the hold of the German language on
these people? Not at all, said Rush. Using their own language will make it
easier to educate them. Once a thirst for learning has been created, they
will turn naturally to English to further their education, especially when
they realize that language leads to distinction in medicine, law, and politics.
Would not such a college make a separate people more separate? "It is
ignorance and *prejudice* only that keeps men of different countries and
religions apart," came the answer. "A German college, by removing *these,*
will prepare the way for the Germans to unite more intimately with their
British and Irish fellow citizens and thus form with them one homogeneous
mass of people." To the objection that it would hurt the state to convert
its best farmers into scholars, Rush replied that government and the pro-
fessions had always taken its leaders "from the cultivators of the earth."[34]

As disillusionment with Nisbet increased, Rush immersed himself in
the founding of the German school. Though it would be located in the
backcountry, its promoters centered in Philadelphia, where both the money
and the German community's chief leaders resided. The ten who in De-

cember 1786 signed a petition to the assembly requesting a charter for the school and a grant of lands for an endowment were all Philadelphians and, except for Rush, Bingham, and McKean, all of German extraction. Perhaps on the suggestion of his friend Rush, the college would be named after Franklin, an ironical honor for one who had once called the Germans "boors." Lancaster would be its home, because of "its central and healthy situation, the character of its inhabitants, the conveniences with which students of every description may be accommodated with board and lodgings, and the probability that the necessary buildings may be immediately procured and at a moderate expense." There would be forty trustees, twenty-eight from Lutheran and Reformed churches, the rest from other denominations.[35]

Association with the new project delighted Rush, and the industry of the Germans impressed him. "With them I have no prejudices to combat, no lies to contradict, no Ewing to contend with," he told Montgomery, adding in a later letter, "We have no *hum's* and *ha's* among us nor no doubts or fears of our final success in the glorious undertaking." Once again energy and enthusiasm had been engaged, and at a time when Nisbet's complaints had made him wonder about Dickinson's chance of survival. "Dr. Franklin has given us £200 in specie. The 10,000 acres of land to be granted to us [by the state] will be situated next to the lands of our college at Carlisle." Mention of Dickinson led to another thought: "No, my friend, I can never forget the first fruits of our labors. My affections have been too much tied to Dickinson College to be weaned by a second child, as you are pleased to call Franklin College." He could find only one cause for regret: "Alas! our poor Presbyterians do nothing with zeal or spirit but quarrel, persecute, and oppress. I hope we are not destined with the Indians of our country to be annihilated for our vices."[36]

Naturally, Rush appeared among the new school's trustees, and shortly after the charter was granted in March 1787 he received an invitation to the first convocation. Events celebrated with "pomp and solemnity" delighted him, and he accepted at once. He and Bingham arrived in Lancaster on June 5 barely in time for the first trustees' meeting. After the session had been opened with a prayer, an awkward silence settled over the mixed group. William Rawle, a young Philadelphia lawyer, suggested Rush break the ice with a few remarks, knowing him never to be at a loss for words. He performed as expected, appropriately, and, at one point, when speaking of what the new school could accomplish, eloquently. "Our children will be bound together by ties of marriage, as we shall be by ties of friendship, and in the course of a few years by means of this college the names of German, Irishman, and Englishman will be lost in the general name of Pennsylvania."[37]

The emphasis in the brief talk on the Germans' role as citizens of Pennsylvania owed something to the presence in Philadelphia at that moment of the Constitutional Convention. Whatever the convention delegates wrought would in time have to be ratified by the people of Pennsylvania, and Rush, together with the other leading Philadelphians who had traveled out to Lancaster, was well aware of the importance of the German vote in securing statewide approval. Age as well as attendance at the convention had deterred Franklin from appearing at the ceremonies inaugurating the college named after him.

The convocation next day was attended by "several thousand people," according to the glowing report Rush sent to the newspapers. The odes, sermons, prayers, and music blended to provide "one of the highest entertainments I ever enjoyed in my life." In the afternoon came an elaborate banquet, designed "to make us better acquainted with each other." While William Hamilton, a wealthy gentleman who lived on an estate outside Philadelphia, "charmed everybody with his easy behavior," and Rawle "forced his way into their hearts" by conversing in German, Rush moved about chatting "alternately with a Lutheran, a Calvinist, a Roman Catholic, and a Moravian minister—all of whom I found to be sensible, agreeable men."[38]

Concern for Franklin College did not end with the ceremonies. Weeks later he sent out from Philadelphia a young Scotch-Irish immigrant as a candidate for instructor in English and Latin. He worked steadily to raise money for the school, but despite the efforts of the Germans and the energy of Rush, Franklin College at the end of 1787 found itself financially in the same position as Dickinson College—broke. "I lament the languor that has infected our trustees in this city," Rush wrote the college's principal, Rev. G. H. E. Muhlenberg, at the start of the new year. "I have tried in vain to bring about a meeting in order to collect our certificates and draw an interest on them. The present turbulent era is unfavorable to all peaceable enterprises. Nothing now fills the mind but subjects that agitate the passions. Let us not despair. As soon as our new government is established, the public spirit of our country will be forced to feed upon undertakings that have science or humanity for their objects."[39]

17

Reforms in Physic

1786–1787

1

O N 15 MARCH 1786, roughly two months after Rush's fortieth birthday, his third son, James, was born. Days later "a severe attack of
pleurisy" laid Rush low and left him limp with fatigue for months afterward. In June he pretended that "the warm weather and an excursion to
New Jersey" had restored his health, but even in mid-August he confessed
to Lettsom that "I find myself unequal in point of exertion to many objects
I wish to have seen executed before I leave the world." The supposed im-
mediacy of death may have spurred him onward, for in spite of uncertain
health the year was one of his busiest. He continued to practice—though the
main burden must have fallen on Hall—to teach, and to meddle in politics
and the affairs of Dickinson College. He left the Presbyterian Church. He
published an essay on public schools, one on the Pennsylvania frontier,
another on the "moral faculty." He wrote an article on the Confederation,
and saw three others printed in the volume of *Transactions* put out that
year by the American Philosophical Society.[1]

He also found the energy to help create in Philadelphia an institution
originated by Lettsom in London some fifteen years earlier—a free medical
dispensary for the poor. A copy of Lettsom's *Medical Memoirs of the General Dispensary in London,* published in 1774, undoubtedly found its way
to Rush, but politics then preoccupied him. Twelve years had to pass before
the chance came to follow the guidelines specified by his friend.

The poor of Philadelphia had never wanted for medical aid. All physicians had among their patients those whom they treated for nothing. The workhouse had an attending physician for the indigent, and those with serious illnesses were boarded without charge at the Pennsylvania Hospital. But "from the reduction of its funds by the late war," Rush lamented, the hospital's "usefulness is of late much circumscribed." He had always disliked the haphazard, patronizing system of treating the poor. It created a double standard: physicians visited the well-to-do in their homes while the poor had to go to the workhouse or the hospital. And it insulted their dignity to accept medical charity publicly.[2]

The Philadelphia Dispensary as set up in 1786 deviated hardly at all from Lettsom's pattern. It would be staffed by six attending and four consulting physicians and surgeons, a treasurer, and an apothecary. The attending physicians would give their time for nothing; whatever expenses arose in the course of treatment would be paid by voluntary contributions. The apothecary would double as administrator. He would receive all applications for admission, recording the necessary data about the patient along with the name of the contributor who recommended him, and then see to it he received the medicines prescribed by the physician. One physician would attend the dispensary while another made house calls. As with the hospital, twelve managers elected by the contributors would direct the dispensary.[3]

Rush only shared in the founding of the institution. Shippen, Jr., had a larger role, to judge by his attendance at organizational meetings—which may account for the limited appearances Rush put in—and Samuel Powel Griffitts still larger. Griffitts was a Quaker physician whose moral character Rush found "truly amiable."[4] Rush contributed his talents as a press agent. His prospectus printed in all Philadelphia newspapers was shrewdly designed to conjure contributions from the pockets of the suspicious. The dispensary was humane, for "the sick may be attended and relieved in their own houses." It was practical, for "the sick may be relieved at much less expense to the public than in a hospital, where provisions, bedding, firewood, and nurses are required for their accommodation." And, finally, it not only allowed those who lived in "virtuous poverty" to be treated with dignity but also in a manner "strictly agreeable to those refined precepts of Christianity, which inculcate secrecy in acts of charity and benevolence."[5]

The publicity succeeded so well that within a few months after the dispensary opened its door the number and amount of contributions had presaged a long life. During the first seven months, it treated 797 patients. Its success induced others the following year to found a lying-in hospital for the poor, but that project failed. Americans were not yet "ripe enough in vice or poverty for a lying-in hospital," Rush said. "Our dispensary supplies the necessity of such an institution at a tenth part of the expense that would attend it, and in a manner more consistent with female delicacy and the secrecy that is enjoined by the Gospel in acts of charity."[6]

The dispensary, meanwhile, flourished. In 1787 it served more than 1,500 patients at a cost Rush estimated at £500. Soon other cities were creating their own dispensaries, which led Rush to remark: "Thus have we applied the principles of mechanics to morals, for in what other way would so great a weight of evil have been removed by so small a force."[7]

The weight of another great evil was also in the process of being removed by a small force in 1786—Dock Creek. The legislature, at the urging of Rush, had authorized two years earlier that the polluted creek, with its muddy bed, its refuse, and its stench be covered over. It was a medical reform that Rush never bothered to include among his achievements. The "immense mass of animal and vegetable offal matters" dumped into it each day "poisoned the air by the exhalations arising from them," and Rush for years had prodded the assembly to cover over the creek.

"The people of the present day," a former student of Rush's wrote in 1811, "who now enjoy the great advantage of an airy street, and see the large stores built in place of the receptacles of poverty, vice, and filth, will learn with astonishment, that a violent opposition was made to the measure by many citizens, and that the benevolent and patriotic guardian of the public health 'stood alone' among his brethren in the recommendation of the measure." Not long after the creek had been covered typhus and cholera, "which destroyed so great a proportion of the children under the age of eighteen months, who were within the influence of the pestilential air of this creek," had "diminished so evidently as to strike even common observers."[8]

2

The first of Rush's three essays in the second volume of the American Philosophical Society's *Transactions* published in 1786 advanced a favorite theory of his—that the clearing of a land of trees promotes sickness by allowing the spread of miasmatic vapors from rivers, millponds, and marshlands.

If, however, after clearing the land men cultivated it, sickness would diminish. By cultivation he meant particularly draining off stagnant water where the "febrile miasmata" might concentrate. The millponds that dotted the farm country should be cleaned occasionally and around them trees should be planted. These trees acted mechanically by obstructing the passage of the vapors and *chemically* by absorbing "unhealthy air" and discharging "it in a highly purified state in the form of what is now called 'dephlogisticated air.'"

To these long-range recommendations in a program of preventive medicine were added several others that could be undertaken at once to reduce the mounting incidence of sickness. Cities were healthier than country places—an astonishing statement from Rush—mostly because fire, smoke, and heat destroyed "the effects of marsh miasmata upon the human body." Farmers were therefore advised to build large fires of brush every night, "between the spots from whence the exhalations are derived and the dwelling house," and to continue the practice until the first frosts descended. Rush melded into the advice his own prejudices—wear woolen and cotton rather than linen through the summer and fall, watch your diet, bathe frequently—and a generous helping of accepted medical lore. Vegetable offal, for instance, should be carted away from the dwelling house but animal dung offered no danger, for nature had endowed it with "a power of destroying the effects of marsh exhalations and of preventing fevers." The evening air should be avoided at all costs, and morning air should not be breathed before the sun rises or "until the body has been fortified with a little solid aliment or a *draught* of bitters."[9]

The second essay developed out of a successful treatment of tetanus or lockjaw during the war by substituting large doses of bark and wine for the standard remedy of opium. Rush had tried the cure several times since, generally with good luck. The cases described had resulted from gunshot wounds, from stepping on nails, and one from "sleeping in the evening on a damp brick pavement, after a day in which the mercury in Fahrenheit's thermometer had stood at near ninety degrees." Most of them had occurred during the summer, which caused Rush to believe tetanus a disease of warm climates and seasons and that relaxation "predisposed" a person to it. The cure, then, called not for a sedative like opium but for stimulants to promote a satisfactory "tone in the system." Rush considered this essay the most important of his three in *Transactions* and the suggested cure a major contribution to medicine. Earlier he had told Cullen and Lettsom about it and hoped they would propagate it in Great Britain. He spread the word among colleagues in Philadelphia but "my mode of treating the locked jaw," he admitted years later, "has not to this day been adopted by many of the practitioners in this city."[10]

The paper that attracted widest attention—the only one of the three to be reprinted in the press—dealt with a popular, much touted powder for curing cancer.

> A few years ago [Rush began] a certain Dr. Hugh Martin, a surgeon of one of the Pennsylvania regiments stationed at Fort Pitt, during the latter part of the late war, came to this city, and advertised to cure cancers with a medicine which he had discovered in the woods, in the neighborhood of the garrison. As Dr. Martin had once been a pupil of mine, I took the liberty of waiting upon him, and asked him some questions respecting his discovery. His answers were calculated to make me believe that his medicine was of a vegetable nature, and that it was originally an Indian remedy.[11]

Rush knew of the cancer powder before his ex-pupil had arrived back in Philadelphia. In July 1780 Martin had written from Fort Pitt that he had obtained a nostrum called "Dr. Bond's Cancer Powder" before leaving the city and that "as soon as I showed it here, the Indians knew immediately." Martin added that the Indians did not know the powder's "real virtues," but made "use of it to smell when their head aches and to smoke with their tobacco," offering what sounds like an early description of marijuana. "This last they are very fond of. It grows down the Ohio in great abundance, especially in the Cherokee nation."[12]

Rush for some reason preferred to overlook this letter and tell the story his own way. He confesses to experimenting with several roots— Rev. John King had sent some of the wild indigo plant which in powdered form had purportedly cured a local woman of cancer—but none proved effective.[13] Eventually he obtained from a friend at Fort Pitt "a powder which I had no doubt, from a variety of circumstances, was of the same kind as that used by Dr. Martin." That, too, failed to work. "After this, I should have suspected that the [Martin] powder was not a *simple* root, had not the doctor continued upon all occasions to assure me that it was wholly a vegetable preparation." After Martin's death, Rush inveigled a sample of the powder from the administrator of the estate, and after carrying out several chemical experiments he learned it contained a sprinkling of arsenic, a standard ingredient in cancer powders since ancient times. He assumed that "the principal and perhaps only design of the vegetable addition was to blunt the activity of the arsenic," and that probably any additive, common wheat flour for example, would have been equally satisfactory.[14]

The laboratory technique that revealed the powder's secret has been cited as "a single striking example" of Rush's "impeccably scientific methods."[15] The same could be said for his analysis of local mineral waters a decade earlier. His technique then excelled—as far it went; it failed, however, to identify the substance that produced the "fetid smell" from the water of the Philadelphia well. With Martin's powder he spotted the ingredient common to all such powders, but the "vegetable addition," which may have accounted for its success over other products on the market, was dismissed as unimportant and went unanalyzed. Yet to judge by Martin's letter to Rush in 1780, this additive may have been the ingredient that distinguished the powder.

The supposed revelation of the secret did not prompt Rush to condemn the powder. He encouraged its discriminate use. In cancerous tumors, the knife should be preferred; in cancerous ulcers, especially those seated "in the neck, in the breasts of females, and in the axillary glands, it can only protract the patient's misery." But on superficial cancerous sores, the powder, he believed, often promoted cures. The disease of cancer clearly puzzled him. He suspected treatment should center on diet "or in the long use of some internal medicine," but confessed "it remains yet to discover a cure for cancers that taint the fluids, or infest the whole lymphatic system." He ended justifying "this detail of a *quack* medicine" by reminding the audience who originally heard the paper at the American Philosophical Society "that it was from the inventions and temerity of quacks that physicians have derived some of their most active and useful medicines."[16]

3

Rush sometimes appeared to write with the speed of light. It led some to think he wrote, even on professional subjects, much as he sometimes acted —impetuously. In fact, however, Rush moved into print slowly. His essay on the "moral faculty" gestated for a dozen years. His first essay in which he generalized on the war from the military physician's point of view did not come forth until 1785, when he responded to his election to the Manchester Literary and Philosophical Society with some "Observations as Physician General in the Revolution," a brief piece based on experience rather than hearsay.[17]

The hospital, not the battlefield, caused the majority of deaths in the Revolution, Rush held, and blame for most of these centered on the putrid fever, "produced by the want of sufficient room and cleanliness." Soldiers billeted with families usually escaped the fever; convalescents and sots proved most susceptible. Those who slept in tents were more likely to come down with it than those who spread their bedrolls in the open air. (Despite this observation, Rush continued to believe night air harmful and slept till the day he died in a bedroom with the windows shut and a nightcap pulled over his head.) A man at home on furlough often caught the disease, but he could avoid it by "lying, for a few nights after his return to his family, on a blanket before the fire." The best remedy was a puke, followed by a laxative, bark, volatile salts, and wine—"two or three bottles a day in many cases."

Rush ended these observations saying that "after the *purveying* and *directing* departments were separated . . . very few of the American army died in our hospitals." That disingenuous, if not dishonest, conclusion was omitted from a revised version of the essay published in 1789. Military hospitals, those "sinks of human life," should be obliterated and an effort made to give sick soldiers "the conveniences and wholesome air of private houses," Rush now said. He denied that dysentery had been a serious disease during the war, except briefly in the summer of 1777; he mentioned that a gunshot wound at a joint was handled in the standard way, by amputation; and he slipped in a line about one soldier who lost his hearing from shell shock while another regained it. One of Rush's most durable statements in the piece came near the end: "Soldiers are but little more than adult children. That officer, therefore, will best perform his duty to his men, who obliges them to take the most care of their HEALTH."[18]

Rush never attempted an encompassing study of what he had seen or learned from his military experience, but in another essay, "An Account of the Influence of the Military and Political Events of the American Revolution Upon the Human Body," he made several perceptive observations:

> In the beginning of a battle I have observed *thirst* to be a
> very common sensation among both officers and soldiers. It oc-

curred where no exercise, or action of the body, could have excited it.

Soldiers bore operations of every kind immediately *after*
a battle with much more fortitude than they did at any time afterwards.

Militia officers and soldiers, who enjoyed good health during a campaign, were often affected by fevers and other disorders,
as soon as they returned to their respective homes.[19]

Rush gave the talk on Martin's cancer powder on 3 February 1786.
Three weeks later, on February 27, he delivered to another audience at the
American Philosophical Society what was to become the major medical
paper of his career, *An Enquiry into the Influence of Physical Causes upon
the Moral Faculty.* He had reflected on the ideas in the paper not for three
weeks but for twelve years or more, his interest in the subject dating back
to at least 1774 when he and Granville Sharp argued over man's knowledge
of good and evil, and Rush directed discussion to a topic that, said Sharp,
"you very properly call the '*moral faculty.'* "[20]

The concept of a moral faculty did not originate with Rush. A number of eighteenth-century philosophers accepted it under a variety of names
—moral sense (Francis Hutcheson), sympathy (Adam Smith), moral instinct (Rousseau). Rush preferred the term "moral faculty," which had
been coined by the Scottish poet-philosopher James Beattie, "because I conceive it conveys, with the most perspicuity, the idea of a capacity in the
mind of choosing good and evil." More accurately, he wanted to use a term
invented by a man whose work he admired rather than one accepted by
philosophers tainted with deism. Beattie had published in 1770 an *Essay
on the Nature and Immutability of Truth, in Opposition to Sophistry and
Scepticism,* which attacked David Hume and left a deep impression on
Rush. "I cannot think of him without fancying that I see Mr. Hume prostrate at his feet," Rush said later. "He was the David who slew that giant
of infidelity."[21]

At the start Rush added little to Beattie's discussion of the subject.
He distinguished between the moral faculty ("a lawgiver") and the conscience ("the witness that accuses or excuses us, of a breach of the law
written in our hearts"). He noted that "the state of moral faculty is
visible in actions, which affect the well-being of society." He argued that

the moral faculty is as important in men's makeup as the faculty of memory or of judgment. It is unrelated to reason and can flourish in the dullest person. All this had been said before. From this point Rush began to expound some fresh ideas.

He pointed out that mental derangement occurs when one or more of a person's faculties are impaired. The loss of memory is called amnesia; the loss of judgment upon one subject is called melancholia and upon all subjects mania. Those who suffer from these impairments "are considered, very properly, as subjects of medicine; and there are many cases upon record that prove that their diseases have yielded to the healing art." Impairment of the moral faculty can also be healed, said Rush, once it becomes apparent that it, like the mind of the mentally deranged, is influenced by the physical environment.

Rush, after confessing that he stepped "upon untrodden ground" here, pushed ahead. He gave, with accompanying illustrations, seventeen examples of physical causes that can weaken or strengthen the moral faculty, among them climate, diet, certain drinks, extreme hunger, diseases, idleness, and excessive sleep (more than six hours a night did more harm than good). The climate of the middle latitudes—Pennsylvania's, for example—"has been generally remarked for producing gentleness and benevolence." A vegetable diet calms tempers, and water "is the universal sedative of turbulent passions." The moral faculty can be strengthened in certain ways: by cleanliness, solitude (at least for those "who are irreclaimable by rational or moral remedies"), silence, music, eloquence from the pulpit, light ("how often do the peevish complaints of the night in sickness give way to the composing rays of the light of the morning!"), and particular medicines.

These outside forces are "the principal causes which act mechanically upon morals." There are others, such as the people one associates with and those matters that affect one's sensibility, that are of a compound nature, or, in modern language, psychological. Rush did not have much to say about these. He ended the essay, as might be expected, on a note of optimism, elaborating his favorite phrase "all will end well" into a paragraph:

> Should the same industry and ingenuity, which have produced
> these triumphs of medicine over disease and death, be applied to
> the moral science, it is highly probable that most of those bane-
> ful vices, which deform the human breast, and convulse the na-
> tions of the earth, might be banished from the world. . . . I am

fully persuaded that from the combined action of causes, which operate at once upon the reason, the moral faculty, the passions, the senses, the brain, the nerves, the blood and the heart, it is possible to produce such a change in his moral character, as shall raise him to a resemblance of angels—nay more, to the likeness of GOD himself.

Rush believed his essay the first to consider "the moral education of youth upon new and mechanical principles." It did much more. In one swoop he had virtually equated vice with disease, and in the process cracked open the door to psychiatry. All those failings of humans that lead to vice he now found traceable to physical causes. "It is vain to attack these vices with lectures upon morality," he said. They are curable if the physical or psychological environment is adjusted.[22]

The reception accorded to the address by the philosophical society's audience persuaded Rush almost immediately to have it printed. It was published as delivered, except for toning down what Benjamin Franklin called "that most extravagant encomium on your friend Franklin, which hurt me exceedingly in the unexpected hearing, and will mortify me beyond conception if it should appear from the press." The first printing sold out quickly and a second was ordered before the year ended. Rush, who still looked to England for accolades, persuaded Dilly to bring out a reprint in London, then turned to friends there to watch over his child. "As it contains some new opinions in religion and morals, as well as in physic, it will stand in need of the protection of my friends in London to preserve it from the rage of criticism," he wrote Richard Price. "If political prejudice blends itself with literature, I shall find no mercy from British reviewers. I have avoided everything that could awaken an idea of the folly of Great Britain in the late war. In science of every kind, men should consider themselves as citizens of the whole world."[23]

He worried needlessly about the British reception. A year later Dilly reported that "the demand has been very small—not fifty of the impressions have been sold."[24]

4

Rush wrote as he talked—constantly—and the spate of essays published in 1786 and 1787 only gave the illusion he was busier than usual with his pen. He was a compulsive writer, traveling through life as if all he saw and experienced must be put down on paper. He carried a pad and pencil wherever he went, for "many new ideas occurred to me when riding, walking, or between the times of my waking and leaving my bed in the morning." Eagerness to air his thoughts never slackened, not even during the sweltering summers that most Philadelphians used as an excuse to relax. "I obviated the usual effect of hot weather, in producing an inability to read, and thereby a waste of time, by spending the hot months in writing for the press," he said. "The greater the exertion necessary to compose, [than] to read, always obviated sleepiness. It had the same effect upon me after dinner and late at night."[25]

Rush wrote "from the impulse of the moment," often surrounded by a sleeping family—he took no more than four or five hours' rest a night—but more often in the midst of the household's daily confusion. "His mind was under such complete discipline," a friend said, "that he could read or write with perfect composure in the midst of the noise of his children, the conversation of his family, and the common interrogatories of his visiting patients."[26]

His medical lectures received the care given any essay he expected to publish. All were written out. Taking to heart his dictum that "too much pains cannot be taken to teach our youth to read and write our American language with propriety and elegance," he worked hard to make them "simple and always intelligible." They were drafted in a notebook in which the alternate pages were left blank. "On the blank side he entered, from time to time, every new fact, idea, anecdote, or illustration, that he became possessed of, from any source whatever," a former student recalled. "In the course of about four years, the blank was generally so far filled up, that he found it expedient to make a new set of lectures. In this way he not only lightened the various subjects on which it was his province to instruct his class, but the light which he cast on them, for forty-four successive years, was continually brightening."[27]

With notebook in hand, Rush seated himself in a chair on a raised platform before the class and proceeded to read what he had written, but read so well that one of his less enamored students admitted that though Rush was "a very ordinary speaker, he was one of the best public readers I have ever heard." The performance was less stiff than it might seem, for Rush found "teaching was the principal means of increasing new combinations in my mind." Often his text stirred up new ideas as he read it aloud. He would then pause, put down the notebook, take off his spectacles and deliver what had occurred to him "extempore to my pupils."[28]

Rush had written and thought enough about the process of education to know there was more to teaching than a deftly delivered lecture. "He possessed in a high degree those talents which engage the heart," an admirer said. "He took so lively an interest in everything that concerned his pupils, that each of them believed himself to be a favorite, while his kind offices to all proved that he was the common friend and father of them all."[29]

5

Rush's involvement in higher education spurred him to widen still further his field of action, and in 1786 he addressed to the assembly "A Plan for Establishing Public Schools in Pennsylvania." The essay is the first in American history to advance a program for government support from top to bottom of a statewide educational system.[30]

At the top, the plan called for a university located at Philadelphia. Below this, spread out as feeder schools, would be four colleges—located at Philadelphia, Mannheim (Lancaster in later editions after Franklin College had been founded), Carlisle, and Pittsburgh. The few Americans then concerned with establishing new schools centered their attention on the college, as had Rush previously. Now he broadened his perspective and called for the creation of free public schools in every township in the state. They should be supported by taxes from all, even bachelors, for "every member of the community is interested in the propagation of virtue and knowledge in the state." A system of free schools was not the farfetched dream it seemed, for it had already "long been used with success in Scotland" and in the state of Connecticut some six hundred such schools had been established.

The scheme had the neatness of Newton's picture of the solar system. "By this plan the whole state will be tied together by one system of education," Rush said. "The university will in time furnish masters for the colleges, and the colleges will furnish masters for the free schools, while the free schools, in their turns, will supply the colleges and the university with scholars, students, and pupils. The same systems of grammar, oratory, and philosophy will be taught in every part of the state. . . ."

Copies of this essay were sent as usual to friends around the state. Reactions this time were not especially favorable. People in Carlisle, one correspondent wrote, found themselves "so much involved in the care of one [college], and saw the state so much involved in burdens of another kind, that we thought this was not the time to make such a motion." Another friend questioned "whether it be for the benefit of this country to make learning too cheap."[31]

Generally, readers held he asked too much too soon of a state already steeped in debt. Rather than abandon the program, Rush thereupon adjusted it, putting aside for the time being the dream of state-supported colleges and restricting his advocacy to a system of public schools. An elaboration of earlier thoughts on this subject appeared in an open letter to the people of Philadelphia and its suburbs in March 1787. "The blessings of knowledge can be extended to the poor and laboring part of the community only by means of free schools," he said. Such schools are a remote possibility in the back and unsettled parts of the state, but the experiment can be begun here and now in Philadelphia. Remember, he warned, "where the common people are ignorant and vicious, a nation, and, above all, a republican nation, can never long be free and happy."[32]

Rush had worked out the plan and the arguments to promote it in detail. The schools should be tax-supported. "The price of a bottle of wine or of a single fashionable feather will pay the tax of an ordinary freeholder for a whole year to those schools," and for this slight cost the citizen helps sow the seeds of good morals and the habits of industry in the city's youth. Both girls and boys should attend the schools. All would be taught to read and write and be instructed in the principles and obligations of Christianity. The girls, in addition, would learn needlework, knitting, and spinning. The schools would be organized along sectarian lines, for "thereby religion and learning [will] be more intimately connected."

The scheme sought to relieve the poor but at the same time avoid the insult of charity by making all in the city share the burden of expense. "The present is an era of public spirit," Rush concluded, and if we are to "check the vice which taints the atmosphere of our city," if we are to banish "the profane and indecent language which assaults our ears in every street," then we must extend the right to education to all.

This proposal of Rush's met with a better reception, and he had great hopes something would soon materialize from it. "We met last night about our free schools," he told his wife in mid-1787. "The company was well chosen and truly respectable. A plan was adopted that cannot fail (heaven continuing to smile upon the undertaking) of succeeding and doing the most extensive good. O! Virtue, Virtue, who would not follow thee blindfolded!—Methinks I hear you cry out after reading this postscript, 'Alas! my poor husband! he is as crazy as ever.' "[33]

A month later Rush directed his thoughts on education to students of the Young Ladies Academy in Philadelphia, this time in a speech entitled "Thoughts upon Female Education, Accommodated to the Present State of Society, Manners, and Government in the United States of America."[34] Many of the ideas in the talk he lifted from François Fénelon's century-old *Treatise on the Education of Daughters,* but the language and style were his as well as the perceptions about the American woman's uniqueness.

Women in the United States, Rush began, "require a peculiar mode of education." Their early marriages limit the leisure they have to be educated, and thus in the short time available they should be taught mainly "the more useful branches of literature." The busy professional life of the American gentleman forces the women here to bear a larger share of the responsibility for the children's education than the European mother. The uncertain quality of servants in America forces women "to attend more to the private affairs of their families than ladies generally do of the same rank in Great Britain."

For these reasons, among others, American ladies must "know the English language well" and also be able to write "in a fair and legible hand," by which Rush meant one that conforms "to the simplicity of the citizens of a republic." Upon these twin foundations he erected a lofty curriculum. He would have the American female learn bookkeeping, for "there are certain occupations in which she may assist her husband with this knowledge," and if she should survive him "she cannot fail of deriving immense advantages from it." She must know the principles of Christianity. She should know something of geography, astronomy, natural philosophy, and chemistry, of history, travels, poetry, and moral essays. She should not neglect music, which soothes "the cares of domestic life" and also helps strengthen her lungs. Those who learn to play a musical instrument, however, generally waste their time, for given "the present state of society and manners in America," they lack the time to become pro-

ficient, and "their harpsichords serve only as sideboards for their parlors."
Dancing will also promote her health and in an age nearly destitute of good
conversation it works as "an agreeable substitute for the ignoble pleasures
of drinking and gaming."

Rush hoped his program of reading would, if nothing else, help
"subdue that passion for reading novels, which so generally prevails among
the fair sex." Mention of novels leads to a digression. They "hold up *life,*
it is true, but it is not as yet *life* in America," for "the intrigues of a
British novel are as foreign to our manners as the refinements of Asiatic
vice." British novels are not the only foolish fashion imported. "We behold
our ladies panting in a heat of ninety degrees under a hat and cushion
which were calculated for the temperature of a British summer." This
leads to a jibe at another British custom which figures in many of the
reform projects that currently engage Rush. "We behold our citizens condemned and punished by a criminal law which was copied from a country
where maturity in corruption renders public executions a part of the amusements of the nation. It is high time to awake from servility—to study our
own character—to examine the age of our country—and to adopt manners
in everything that shall be accommodated to our state of society, and to the
forms of our government."

Toward the end of the talk Rush suggests that the salvation of
America depends on an educated womanhood, and those who oppose their
enlightenment hold "the prejudice of little minds," unaware that it is the
ignorant woman who is the hardest for men to govern. "It will be in your
power, LADIES, to correct the mistakes and practice of our sex upon these
subjects, by demonstrating that the female temper can only be governed
by reason, and that the cultivation of reason in women, is alike friendly to
the order of nature and to private as well as public happiness."

6

"The state of our country for some years past has been unfavorable
to improvements of every kind in science," Rush wrote Lettsom in 1783.
"I approve of your plan for instituting a medical society in Philadelphia,
and am not without hopes of seeing it carried into execution as soon as
the minds of our literati are more perfectly detached from the political sub-

jects that have swallowed up all the ingenuity and industry of our country."
The time had come in 1787.[35]

Technically Rush was only one among twelve senior fellows of the
College of Physicians, as the society was called. At the first meeting on
January 2, John Redman, perhaps the only physician of stature in the city
who had avoided involvement in the Rush-Shippen-Morgan feud, was
elected president, a position he held until 1804 when he stepped down at
his own request. But the founding fathers recognized Rush's essential role
by asking him to deliver a talk February 6 on the objects of their college.
As usual he rose to the occasion and gave his colleagues an able, imaginative, some might even have said "inspiring," address.[36]

He opened with the felicitous reflection "that the late Revolution,
which has given such a spring to the mind in objects of philosophical and
moral inquiry, has at last extended itself to medicine, . . . before the human
faculties had contracted to their former dimensions. . . ." He got quickly
over the obvious advantages the college would offer in fellowship, such as
the chance to exchange professional opinions, so that he could emphasize
one his colleagues might not have considered: the opportunity to act as a
pressure group, for as "a college we shall be better able to attract the attention of the government of our country in matters that relate to the
health and happiness of our fellow citizens." He mentioned, as an example
of what could be done, that the College of Physicians of London had
petitioned Parliament against the pernicious effects of spirituous liquors.
(Rush's colleagues took the hint and a year and a half later copied the
British example by petitioning first the Pennsylvania Assembly, then Congress, "to increase the duty and excise upon spirits.")[37]

The core of Rush's talk was built around a program for the future.
Excerpts only hint at the range and variety of investigations Rush contemplated for American physicians:

> It remains yet to be discovered and recorded, whether
> the extent of human life has been increased or diminished in
> America.
> The comparative effects of the different articles of agricul-
> ture upon health, such as wheat, Indian corn, rice, tobacco, and
> indigo, remain yet to be explored in this country.
> It remains yet to be determined whether the increase of

fevers from [the cutting down of forests] is produced by the
increase of exhalation, or by the progress of easterly winds westward, as has been supposed by Mr. Jefferson in his *Notes on
Virginia.*

The comparative influence of the moon on diseases in this
country is a subject worthy of close investigation.

The effects of the mixture of the human species of different nations and countries upon health and life [has yet to be
determined].

Ten additional suggested avenues of research follow and Rush had still
not exhausted the possibilities. He turned next to diseases peculiar to
America. Physicians ought to investigate the cause of tooth decay, so frequent in this country. "The high price of firewood, makes it necessary to
examine the effects of fossil coal, and stove rooms, upon health and life."
Statistics should be collected in order to get a clearer picture of the epidemics that visit the city and state.

Be not disheartened by all that needs to be done, for "there does
not exist a disease in nature that has not an antidote to it," Rush concluded. "And when I consider the influence of liberty and republican forms
of government upon science, and the vigor which the American mind has
acquired by the events of the late Revolution, I am led to hope that a great
portion of the honor and happiness of discovering and applying these
antidotes may be reserved for the physicians of America."

The summer of 1787 proved eventful for the country—the Constitutional Convention met then—and for Rush. He traveled to Lancaster to
share in the opening ceremonies of Franklin College. He and his wife
joined the Episcopal Church. And the three-year partnership with James
Hall, which had given Rush enough freedom from his practice to engage
more fully than at any time except in 1776 and 1777 in public activities,
was terminated. The end of the partnership had been in sight for some
time. Rush's practice had declined steadily in recent years, partly because
his Presbyterian patients had deserted him, partly because some of his
colleagues had spread the word that in acquiring a partner he was preparing to abandon medicine for "public pursuits." He had hinted so often at
this in the past that now the denial went unheard. Dissolution of the

partnership was hastened by Hall's marriage during the summer of 1787 and his decision to open up his own practice in York.

Hall departed with his eyes filled with tears, unable to turn feelings into words. Rush found himself equally shaken. "He has left a blank in every part of the house," he said. "I feel without him as if I had lost my right arm." Soon afterward Mrs. Rush left for her annual vacation at Morven, leaving him alone with his apprentice, Benjamin Young. "To a mind like mine, which so soon (perhaps from its slender size) becomes plethoric with ideas and which delights so much in communicating them, it is a new and peculiar hardship to lose at once a domestic friend, a wife, and five children, to most of whom I had been in the habits of imparting every thought as soon as it rose in my mind," he wrote his wife in August. "Benny not only eats and drinks with me but sets constantly in the parlor, but this will not do," he told his wife. "He wants—I know not what. He has no relish for the lives of the poets—he has never visited with you the Hebrides. Even more, he dares not dispute nor contradict me, and this is not only the life of conversation but steel to the flint of genius. It awakens and excites the fire of the mind."[38]

18

"Through a Sea of Blunders"

1786–1788

1

THROUGH THE 1780s Rush kept a suspicious eye on the state assembly's direction of Pennsylvania's affairs. He followed the handling of the Wyoming Valley problem, a region in the northeast part of the state where citizens of Pennsylvania and Connecticut had fought more than a decade over land claimed by both states; his own holdings there, acquired with Franks, seemed safer when the assembly chose Timothy Pickering, a friend, to organize the disputed territory into a Pennsylvania county. He complained when the assembly repealed the Bank of North America's charter in 1785, exulted when the Republicans used their power to recharter it in 1786. The revision that year of the loyalty oath gave him further reason to hope for the future.

Rush made it seem nothing useful had emerged from the assembly until 1786, when the Republicans came to power. He somehow brushed aside an early enthusiasm for the funding bill passed by the Constitutionalists. Late in 1784 a committee of citizens, including Rush, recommended to the legislature that Pennsylvania should assume *all* debts owing to its residents from either the continental or the state government, fund them into one lump, and begin at once to pay the interest due on them. This recommendation pleased those eager to undermine the central government's power; it also attracted those like Rush who, though favoring a stronger central government, wanted a return on the currently worthless loan certificates. There were two principal objections to the proposal. Opponents pointed out that Pennsylvania, with one-eighth of the nation's population, would by this plan be assuming one-third of the United States's accumulated debt. They noted, too, that speculators would reap huge profits from certificates they had bought up for a pittance from original holders. President Dickinson's sharply worded remonstrance to the proposal dealt with this second point. He called for a plan that would distinguish between original and current holders of the certificates. "His reasonings are weak but very popular," said Rush, who saw Dickinson College's pitifully small endowment, the bulk of it in certificates, worth nothing if Dickinson had his way. Rush argued for the college and also for his own interests. Later, when speaking of the public creditors, he said "I belong to this class of citizens," and by implication counted himself among those who "deposited our ALL in the funds in the doubtful and gloomy year of 1777."[1]

The bill was amended to distinguish original and current holders of the certificates by putting interest rates on a sliding scale that varied from 20 per cent to 6; specific exceptions for institutions like Dickinson College classed them as original holders. Interest would be paid by a carefully controlled emission of paper money. The revised bill satisfied Rush and passed with his blessing in 1785, but recollection of this quickly faded when it became apparent, almost immediately, that it was one thing for the state to assume debts, another for it to pay even the interest on them. Rush was soon condemning the funding law as a tax that "like Aaron's rod swallows up all the strength and resources of the state." Pennsylvania's economy slumped seriously in 1785, and the tariff that had been passed to provide income for paying off the accumulated interest on the debt produced far less than expected. The paper money began to depreciate.[2]

Financial matters attracted Rush's concern as the state's depressed economy impinged on his private life. When an apprentice paid his fee in sterling, he confessed it would help "to wipe off a good deal of debt." A mounting anger provoked an essay in July 1786 on the evils of paper money, published under the somewhat pretentious pseudonym of "Nestor." His attack on this creature "so pregnant with mischief" hit first at "paper money when it circulates of an inferior value to gold and silver." It prevents private loans, promotes usury, leads to the withdrawal of specie from circulation. Worse, it undermines morals by promoting chicanery, lawsuits, and extravagance. Worse still, it encourages disunion by making men suspicious of their sister states' currency. Rush injected a passion, a lofty moral tone, into the discussion all his own; the thoughts were not his. Pennsylvania in 1785 had been the first state to inaugurate paper money, but by the time "Nestor" spoke forth six others had followed suit, and in all of them the arguments Rush advanced were circulating as freely as the currency itself.

However, the Pennsylvania currency presented a unique problem to those attacking it. It had depreciated much less than expected, something like 7.5 per cent after more than a year in circulation. The state was slowing down even that decline in value by retiring the money as it came back to the treasury. Even so, Rush had no good at all to say for the paper currency. The argument that it allows the loan office to finance those who wish to settle in the backcountry was rejected on the ground that private capital— some £2 million of it in 1774, Rush said—had always performed that task more than adequately. Substituting a state currency for gold and silver discouraged commerce, which prefers to deal in internationally accepted specie. Paper money, like breast milk and pap for infants, satisfied feeble colonies but was thin food for an independent state seeking its place in the world of nations. True, the currency was soundly based, "but in the present state of language, and with our imperfect measure of diffusing knowledge in Pennsylvania, how are farmers to know anything about funds, or the quantity of money that is in circulation? Besides, in the fluctuation of power and principles which have lately characterized Pennsylvania, who will trust a law beyond the duration of our annual assembly?"[3]

Rush liked the essay well enough to forward it to Ramsay for reprinting in a Charleston paper. Ramsay found the sentiments expressed "in general excellent—such as I wish to prevail universally." By the time Rush received the compliment, concern for Pennsylvania's financial affairs had become overshadowed by a greater issue.[4]

2

Rush's largely dormant interest in national affairs was aroused in the spring of 1786 by a proposal for the thirteen states to send delegates in September to a convention at Annapolis, Maryland. The delegates would assemble "for the purpose of agreeing upon certain commercial regulations and of suggesting such alterations in the Confederation as will give more extensive and coercive powers to Congress," Rush wrote Richard Price. "We entertain the most flattering hopes from this convention, especially as an opinion seems to have persuaded all classes of people that an increase of power in Congress is absolutely necessary for our safety and independence."[5]

Rush contributed his journalistic talents to publicizing the convention with an article on the defects of the Confederation.[6] Though not published until after the convention disbanded, he probably wrote the essay in May while recovering from "a return of my fever."[7] It opened with an observation made that month in a letter to Price and which he would make repeatedly until it became his most famous statement on the Revolution.

> There is nothing more common than to confound the terms of American revolution with those of the late American war. The American war is over; but this is far from being the case with the American revolution. On the contrary, nothing but the first act of the great drama is closed. It remains yet to establish and perfect our new forms of government, and to prepare the principles, morals, and manners of our citizens for these forms of government after they are established and brought to perfection.[8]

The job of reshaping and reeducating the people for republican society, he went on, is a long-term project that must wait until a more immediate problem is remedied: the defects of the Articles of Confederation.

The Annapolis Convention had been called to remedy only one of those defects—Congress's lack of authority over trade. Rush wished it would do more. It ought to recommend that each state surrender to Congress its power to emit money, for "a uniform currency will facilitate trade and help to bind the states together." He also wanted to see the end of the American custom of annual elections, a practice he had praised in 1776 and 1777 but now said was as absurd as it would be "to dismiss a general, a physician, or even a domestic as soon as they have acquired knowledge sufficient to be useful to us." Finally, he would substitute a bicameral for the single national legislature that currently existed. Several specific recommendations followed. He would call one house the Council of States, in which each state would have one representative, and the other the Assembly of States, to be composed of several delegates from each state. The President would be chosen annually by both houses, and he would "possess certain powers, in conjunction with a Privy Council, especially the power of appointing most of the officers of the United States." Comment on the division of power within the central government is avoided, but the question of state sovereignty is faced squarely. Sovereignty carries with it the power to make war and peace and to draw up treaties, powers that the states had long ago delegated to the Confederation. No state dares to call herself independent, said Rush, for "she is independent only in a union with her sister states in Congress."

From these recommended remedies for the Articles, Rush turned to a deeper concern: how to form the character of the American people along republican lines. It is important, he had told Price earlier, "to effect a revolution in our principles, opinions, and manners so as to accommodate them to the forms of government we have adopted," and to that end the essay proceeded to urge the creation of a federal university. This institution would serve doubly to unite the nation and to propagate republican ideas. It would complement the effectiveness of another institution—the post office, that "true nonelectric wire of government," Rush commented in an extraordinary metaphor, "the only means of conveying heat and light to every individual in the federal commonwealth."

The university would teach everything connected with government—the law of nature and nations, civil law, municipal law, the principles of commerce—everything connected with war, and, above all, everything that touched on the nation's economy—that is, "the principles and practices of agriculture and manufactures." The professor of economy should be given a "traveling correspondent" to report from Europe on the discoveries and improvements being made there. Eventually, no one would be allowed to serve in the United States government until he "had imbibed federal and republican ideas in this university."

The essay ended reprimanding those who held that Americans "are not proper materials for republican governments." "The United States are traveling peaceably into order and good government," he wrote, not knowing that Shays's Rebellion would occur in the next few months. "They know no strife but arises from the collision of opinion; and in three years they have advanced farther in the road to stability and happiness than most of the nations of Europe have done in as many centuries." To those who since the war have abandoned politics he pleaded for them once more to come forward: "Your country demands your services! . . . Hear her proclaiming, in sighs and groans, in her governments, in her finances, in her trade, in her manufactures, in her morals, and in her manners, 'The Revolution is not Over!' "

Rush said little when the Annapolis Convention failed to produce even a quorum of states; delegates from only five attended. The convention did nothing more than turn out another invitation to another convention, this one to meet in Philadelphia in May 1787. Nor did Rush say much when, after the convention adjourned, he learned of the uprising in the Massachusetts backcountry. Farmers there had been aroused by the state legislature's insistence that taxes, which had recently been increased, should be paid in hard money and by its refusal to issue paper money. In August they gathered in a mob and marched on the courts to block execution of the hundreds of foreclosures on the dockets; Daniel Shays, a likable former army captain but no born leader, more by accident than by design found himself at the head of it.

Rush published the essay on the Articles without bothering to bring it up to date with some comment on the Massachusetts insurrection, which was not smothered for another six months. Friends more enlightened politically told him Shays's Rebellion had made the chance of a strong union appear dimmer than ever. He heard proposals to break up the Confederation into three confederacies, with New York joining the Eastern Confederacy and Pennsylvania becoming the keystone of the Middle Confederacy. "These confederacies, they say, will be united by nature, by interest, and by manners, and consequently they will be safe, agreeable and durable," he reported. Whatever his true reaction to Shays's Rebellion, he disguised it in letters to friends abroad. "The commotions in New England have happily subsided without the loss of a life or the effusion of one drop of kindred blood," he wrongly informed Price. He followed this misrepresentation with what was to become perhaps his most famous utterance: "The kingdoms of Europe have traveled into their present state of boasted tranquillity through seas of blood. The republics of America are traveling into order and wise government only through a sea of blunders."[9]

3

Through the first half of 1787, Rush was far from being totally absorbed in continental politics. The dispensary, Dock Creek, a public-school system, the new medical society, Pennsylvania politics—all these were providing the main outlets for energy. In March he joined the Pennsylvania Abolition Society. He became a founding member of the Society for Promoting Political Inquiries, but the paper he read at the second meeting, held in March at Franklin's home, was devoted to penal reform rather than politics. His only activity on the national scene concerned his friend Franklin.

When the assembly first chose delegates for the Constitutional Convention, as it would be called, Franklin's name did not appear on the slate. Rush complained to his friends George Clymer and Thomas Fitzsimons about the omission. Fitzsimons said the assembly had understood Franklin's "health rendered him unable to attend, and as the suggestion was supposed to come from his friends I was unwilling to bring him again into view for the appointment." Rush persisted, reprobated the action as "ungrateful and impolitic," and said his name would do much to recommend the Constitution to the people when it came time for ratification. After further prodding, Fitzsimons checked with a "particular friend of the doctor" and learned Franklin would be delighted to accept the honor. The assembly promptly added him to the delegation.[10]

Rush had reason to be pleased, for the most part, with Pennsylvania's eight-man delegation. In addition to Franklin, it contained two good friends—Clymer and Fitzsimons; two politicians he respected above all others—James Wilson and Robert Morris; and two moderate Constitutionalists—Thomas Mifflin and Jared Ingersoll—whom he could tolerate. He knew only slightly the eighth member, Gouverneur Morris, a New Yorker temporarily living in Philadelphia—cynical, witty, and, as a bachelor who never appeared to be without female companionship, suspected of loose morals; he was not Rush's kind of man. Seven of the eight resided in Philadelphia, and Mifflin lived just five miles out of town. Six were determined nationalists who could be counted on to work for a strong central government in the convention.

As the delegations from other states straggled into the city in the early weeks of May, Rush could here and there spot a friend from the days of '76. John Dickinson arrived as a delegate from Delaware, where he now made his home. Elbridge Gerry was again representing Massachusetts and Roger Sherman was again in Connecticut's delegation. More striking, and perhaps something of a shock to Rush, were the number of old allies missing. John Adams was serving as the American minister to England, Thomas

Jefferson in a similar capacity to France. Samuel Adams and John Hancock had stayed home, as had Richard Henry Lee and Patrick Henry; Henry refused to come because he "smelt a rat." Rush knew some of the younger men, like James Madison and Alexander Hamilton, but he had never been close to them.

In the days it took the delegates to collect a convention quorum—they had to wait until May 25—Rush became involved with a petition he and friends planned to submit to them, asking that they "make the suppression of the African slave trade in the United States an essential article of the new confederation." Rush, in addition of course, was also concerned with the problems of government. Here he once again deferred to John Adams. The first of Adams' three volumes on the *Defence of the Constitutions of Government of the United States of America*—an elaborate, prolix promotion of the virtues of bicameralism and a strong executive—had reached Philadelphia in the spring, and at Rush's instigation it was reprinted in time for the gathering delegates to pick up from the local bookstalls if they were curious about what Adams had to say. "Mr. Adams' book has diffused such excellent principles among us that there is little doubt of our adopting a vigorous and compounded legislature," he said soon after the delegates had assembled. "Our illustrious minister in this gift to his country has done us more service than if he had obtained alliances for us with all the nations in Europe." And to Adams he wrote: "You have laid the world and posterity under great obligations by your remarks. I am not more satisfied of the truth of any one proposition in Euclid than I am of the truth of your leading propositions in government."[11]

Rush committed himself to the results of the convention even before it got down to business. The delegates had hardly assembled when he had an essay in the press praising them for what they were about to do. In another article he became the first, so he later boasted, to promote George Washington for President and John Adams for Vice President. The convention figured in his social life throughout the summer; several of the delegates he invited to his house for dinner, and late in July Washington came to tea and carried away several of Rush's pamphlets on education.[12]

Rush left the city for the convocation at Franklin College encouraged by what he had heard was secretly transpiring in the State House. Franklin had told him that the convention was "the most august and respectable assembly he ever was in in his life," and "that he thinks they will soon finish their business, as there are no prejudices to oppose nor errors to refute in any of the body." John Dickinson reported "they are all *united* in their objects, and he expects they will be equally united in the means of attaining them." Both gentlemen spoke to Rush at a time when the convention, though little more than a week old, was rife with dissension and seemed to some on the verge of breaking up. They obviously used Rush's loquacity to disseminate a false impression of what was occurring behind the closed doors.[13]

Rush remained busy, happy, and innocent. "The same enthusiasm now *pervades* all classes in favor of *government* that actuated us in favor of *liberty* in the years 1774 and 1775, with this difference, that we are more *united* in the former than we were in the latter pursuit," he wrote Price in June. "When our enemies triumph in our mistakes and follies, tell them that we are *men,* that we walk upon two legs, that we possess reason, passions, and senses, and that under these circumstances it is as absurd to expect the ordinary times of the rising and setting of the sun will be altered as to suppose we shall not *finally* compose and *adopt* a suitable form of government and be happy in the blessings which are usually connected with it."[14]

The word "adopt" deserved the emphasis given, for already signs abounded that some in Pennsylvania would resist whatever the convention produced. Its work, true, "will excite factions among us, but they will be of a temporary duration," Rush predicted. "Time, necessity, and the gradual operation of reason will carry it down," he went on, adding ominously, "and if these fail *force* will not be wanting to carry it into execution, for not only all the wealth but all the military men of our country (associated in the Society of the Cincinnati) are in favor of a wise and efficient government. The order of nature is the same in the political as it is in the natural world—good is derived chiefly from evil. We are traveling fast into order and national happiness."[15]

August was an arduous month, personally and politically. He left the Presbyterian Church. The family went to Morven, and as with every summer Rush still found it difficult to lose a family "to most of whom I had been in the habit of imparting every thought as soon as it rose in my mind." He tried to forget the silent, empty house by reading, but books lost their relish, he confessed, without his wife there to hear read aloud some passage that pleased him. The day's only pleasure came when he returned fatigued "from my morning's business" at the hospital to find a letter from Mrs. Rush on the table.[16]

As the convention continued to meet through the humid August days, rumors expanded, then congealed into an opposition composed mainly of fervent supporters of Pennsylvania's constitution who were determined to undermine whatever the delegates did. Sometime during the month, John Dickinson dropped a note to Rush asking him to take the lead in promoting a favorable public opinion of the convention's work. Rush accepted the invitation, pleased to be back at the center of political affairs. Essays by him began appearing in the press—all under pseudonyms and none of which have been definitely identified—and letters flowed out to friends who might help influence the public.[17]

Though in these letters he wrote about the new national government, he could not resist one more blast at the Constitution of Pennsylvania and Reverend Ewing. "The new federal government like a new continental wagon will overset our state dung cart with all its dirty contents (reverend and irreverent) and thereby restore order and happiness to Pennsylvania," he wrote in late August. The "new federal government" came from the State House on September 17. A week later Rush's exuberance reached a peak. It "is very acceptable to a great majority of our citizens and will certainly be adopted immediately by *nine* and in the course of a year or eighteen months by *all* the states," he told Lettsom. "When this shall happen, *then* to be a citizen of the United States *with all its consequences* will be to be a citizen of the freest, purest, and happiest government upon the face of the earth."[18]

4

The Pennsylvania legislature on September 28, with its scheduled adjournment only a day away, tried to set a date and place for the state's ratifying convention, though it had not yet received official word from the Continental Congress that the Constitution was being submitted to the states for ratification. Nineteen assemblymen, all proponents of the Pennsylvania Constitution of 1776 who would later rally around the banner of Anti-Federalists, blocked a vote on a ratifying convention by refusing to attend the legislative session, thus preventing a quorum. The next day, when word

347

arrived that Congress had agreed to submit the Constitution to the states, the recalcitrant nineteen, banking on an overturn in the assembly's membership at the election only two weeks away, continued to absent themselves. The Republicans (or Federalists, as they were beginning to call themselves) aroused public sympathy for their dilemma. On the afternoon of the twenty-ninth a mob carried two of the truants by force into the assembly chamber, and while they sputtered from their seats a quorum was declared and the session opened. The decision to hold the ratifying convention on November 21 in Philadelphia was quickly voted, and the assembly soon afterward adjourned.[19]

The resolution to hold a ratifying convention provoked Pennsylvania's bitterest barrage of opinion in the press since the exchanges over adoption of the state's constitution of 1776. Both sides saw the local struggle as decisive in molding the nation's attitude toward the Constitution. The Federalist leaders in this new war of words were Wilson, one of the principal architects of the new Constitution, and Rush, both of whom spoke as well as wrote for the cause, and Tench Coxe, who only wrote for it.

The first week in October, according to the *Pennsylvania Packet,* "a very large concourse of people attended at the State House on Saturday evening, to fix on a ticket of representatives for the ensuing General Assembly." That done, Wilson, followed by Rush, spoke at length for the Constitution. Wilson discussed the objections that had been raised against it. He justified the omission of a bill of rights on the ground that "it would have been superfluous and absurd to have stipulated . . . we should enjoy those privileges of which we are not divested." He spoke up for the clause that would permit a standing army as necessary to preserve tranquillity. The Senate, he promised, could never become the seat of a "baneful aristocracy" since it was fettered on one side by the House of Representatives and on the other by the President. He ridiculed those opposed to giving the new government the power of direct taxation as men "alarmed with visionary evils." "The state of Pennsylvania particularly, which has encumbered itself with the assumption of a large proportion of the public debt, will derive considerable relief and advantage," he said prophetically of what would come to be known as Alexander Hamilton's assumption program. "For, as it was the imbecility of the present confederation which gave rise to the funding law, that law must naturally expire when a competent and energetic federal system shall be substituted. The state will then be discharged from an extraordinary burden, and the national creditor will find it to be his interest to return to his original security."

Wilson warned the audience that those who opposed the Constitution would do so from self-interest. The new government will "necessarily turn the stream of influence and emolument into a new channel," he said, and that man who gains power and profit from the current state governments "will object to the proposed innovation; not, in truth, because it is injurious to the liberties of his country, but because it affects his schemes of wealth and consequence." Wilson ended admitting he was not "a blind admirer of the Constitution, that there were parts of it that "if my wish had prevailed, would certainly have been altered." But given the variety of differences that flourished among Americans, "I am satisfied that anything nearer to perfection could not have been accomplished."[20]

Rush followed Wilson's thoughtful, analytical speech with a burst of emotional rhetoric. He spoke "in an elegant and pathetic style," according to one in the audience, "describing our present calamitous situation, and enumerating the advantages which would flow from the adoption of the new system of federal government." He saw the Constitution clearing the way to a millennium. It would advance commerce, agriculture, and manufacturing, the arts and science. It would encourage immigration, lead to the abolition of paper money, annihilate party divisions, and prevent war. "Were this the last moment of my existence," he concluded, "my dying request and injunction to my fellow citizens would be to accept and support the offered Constitution."[21]

Rush's name, along with those of Wilson, McKean, Hilary Baker, and George Latimer, made up the slate of Federalists in the city for the November 3 election of delegates to the ratifying convention. The Anti-Federalists, as a stratagem and apparently without his permission, put Franklin's name at the head of their list, hoping he would draw votes to their other candidates. The Federalists took the field, but the light vote gave them no reason to think the outcome reflected popular feeling. Latimer, a merchant, led the ticket and Rush, with 1,200 votes, ranked second. Franklin drew only 235 votes and none of his companions got more than 150. Interest elsewhere in the state rose no higher than in the city. The Anti-Federalists later complained that less than 19 per cent of the eligible voters cast ballots for convention delegates and that two-thirds of the members had been chosen by a total of only 6,800 ballots or about 10 per cent of the state's voters.[22]

Rush's delight in returning to public life, however briefly, was capped five days after the election with the birth of his fourth son, William. The sixty-nine delegates convened in Philadelphia on November 21. The average age of those who had come to oppose ratification was forty-six, and of those who favored it forty-two. Among the pros, Rush, slightly more than a month away from turning forty-two, for once could be considered average.[23]

Rush sparked discussion immediately on the convention floor over a matter many delegates regarded as trivial. After Frederick A. C. Muhlenberg, brother of Franklin College's president, had been chosen to chair the meetings, Rush moved "that a committee be appointed to request the attendance of some minister of gospel tomorrow morning, in order to open the business of the convention with prayer." Some objected it would be "impossible to fix upon a clergyman to suit every man's tenets." Besides, no precedent existed for such action; the convention that framed the Pennsylvania Constitution had got along without an opening prayer. That, replied Rush, "is probably the reason that the state has ever since been distracted by their proceedings." The convention voted to postpone further discussion, then the next day made Rush a member of the committee on rules, where apparently the issue was resolved.[24]

The first business day of the convention, November 24, was devoted to a long speech by James Wilson on "the general principles that have produced the national Constitution." Wilson dominated every convention discussion from first to last; Rush spoke often but played a secondary role to Wilson's. He tangled first with William Findley, a backcountry foe of the Constitution, over the aptness of a metaphor. Findley considered it the duty of the convention to examine the new "house" that had been erected for the United States; the delegates should determine if its parts were "fitting and combining . . . with each other" and reject "everything that is useless and rotten."

"That is not our situation," Rush answered. "We are not, at this time, called upon to raise the structure. The house is already built for us, and we are only asked, whether we choose to occupy it. If we find its apartments commodious, and upon the whole that it is well calculated to shelter us from the inclemencies of the storm that threatens, we shall act prudently in entering it; if otherwise, all that is required of us is to return the key to those who have built and offered it for our use." The purpose here was to block any effort to amend the Constitution, a maneuver that its opponents had made clear from the outset they would employ in their fight against the document.[25]

Rush continued the block-amendments strategy when he rose on November 30 to answer his friend Thomas Hartley of York on the absence of a bill of rights. He argued first that a balanced government rather than a list of rights best preserved men's liberties. "While the honorable convention who framed this system were employed in their work, there are many gentlemen who can bear testimony that my only anxiety was upon the subject of representation," he said. "And when I beheld a legislature constituted of three branches, and in so excellent a manner, either directly or indirectly, elected by the people and amenable to them, I confess, sir, that here I cheerfully posed all my hopes and confidence of safety." He went on to argue that "our rights are not yet all known," and therefore "why should we attempt to enumerate them." At one point he got carried away by his own rhetoric, saying: "I am happy, sir, to find that the convention hath not disgraced this Constitution with a bill of rights," a statement he would not be allowed to forget. Finally, he reminded Hartley that the new government was not going to be administered by "strangers to our habits and opinions and unconnected with our interests and prosperity," but by men as eager as he to protect the rights and privileges of Americans.[26]

Discussion the next day, Saturday, December 1, turned on the abridgment of state sovereignty under the Constitution. Findley, according to a press report, "delivered an eloquent and powerful speech, to prove that the proposed plan of government amounted to a consolidation, and not a confederation, of the states." Over the weekend Rush worked up an answer which was delivered when the convention continued on December 3. Rush told the delegates he rejoiced to see the annihilation of state sovereignty. "This passion for state sovereignty despoiled the union of Greece. A plurality of sovereigns is political idolatry." He delighted that with the new Constitution the sovereignty of Pennsylvania was ceded to the United States. "I have now a vote for members of Congress. I am a citizen of every state." A strong central government gives "more security for my property," and it will do much more. The new government, he promised, would abolish paper money, tender laws, and religious tests. "Commerce will hold up her declining head under the influence of general, vigorous, uniform regulations. The communication of the Mississippi with the Atlantic will be opened under the new Constitution." The public debt will be thrown back on Congress. Thanks to the end of state sovereignty, there will be "an increase of freedom, knowledge, and religion" throughout the land.[27]

The rest of the day was spent dealing with Rush's free-swinging speech. The remark of one opponent—"I never heard anything so ridiculous"—apparently summed up the feelings of many left uneasy by Rush's extravagant claims for the government the Constitution would bring into being. Findley commented in passing that he found it odd to hear Rush condemn Pennsylvania's funding of the state and national debt owing its citizens since he had been a member of the committee that had urged the assembly to do just this. Rush, according to a newspaper report, "observed that he did not think the [funding] system would have extended so far," an answer the convention must have regarded as lame.[28]

On Wednesday, December 12, the two leading opponents of the Constitution—Findley and John Smilie—presented their closing arguments, then a vote on ratification was called for. At that moment occurred an event that must have stunned the entire convention and left Wilson white with rage. Rush rose and asked the indulgence of the delegates for a few moments.

> He then entered into a metaphysical argument, to prove that the morals of the people had been corrupted by the imperfections of the government; and while he ascribed all our vices and distresses to the existing system, he predicted a millennium of virtue and happiness as the necessary consequence of the proposed Constitution. To illustrate the depraved state of society, he remarked, among other things, the disregard which was notorious in matters of religion, so that between the congregation and the minister scarcely any communication or respect remained. Nay, the doctor evinced that they were not bound by the ties of common honesty, on the evidence of two facts, from which it appears that several clergymen had been lately cheated by their respective flocks of the wages due for their pastoral care and instruction. Doctor Rush then proceeded to consider the origin of the proposed system, and fairly deduced it from heaven, as-

serting that he as much believed the hand of God was employed in this work, as that God had divided the Red Sea to give a passage to the children of Israel, or had fulminated the Ten Commandments from Mount Sinai! Dilating sometime upon this new species of *divine right,* thus transmitted to the future governors of the Union, he made a pathetic appeal to the opposition, in which he deprecated the consequences of any further contention, and pictured the honorable and endearing effects of an unanimous vote, after the full and fair investigation which the great question had undergone.

The reporter of the speech up to this point had paraphrased Rush's remarks, but the concluding part came forth as a direct quotation of what he said:

It is not, sir, a majority however numerous and respectable, that can gratify my wishes. Nothing short of an unanimous vote can indeed complete my satisfaction. And, permit me to add, were that event to take place, I could not preserve the strict bounds of decorum, but, flying to the other side of this room, cordially embrace every member who has hitherto been in opposition as a brother and a patriot. Let us then, sir, this night bury the hatchet and smoke the calumet of peace![29]

Rush was not to have his way. He had opened up again the business of debate, and it wound on through the evening. Robert Whitehill of Cumberland County said he "regretted that so imperfect a work should have been ascribed to God," and then presented a number of petitions calling for, among other changes in the document, a bill of rights. The petitions were tabled and a vote on the Constitution once again called for. By a vote of forty-six to twenty-three the convention ratified the Constitution.[30]

5

The haste for ratification had been calculated. As Pennsylvania went, so went the nation—it was hoped. If the richest state, and one of the largest and most populated, ratified the document, then others surely would follow, as they had in 1776 when Pennsylvania, after reversing its stand, favored independence. The national implications in Pennsylvania's decision caused Rush and Wilson to continue their work for the Constitution after its ratification. They formed the nucleus of a select committee which, according to the Anti-Federalists, was "assiduously employed in the manufacturing of deception in all its ensnaring colors, and having an adequate fund at their command, they are deluging the country with their productions." "James the Caledonian" (Wilson) headed the group, but "Dr. Puff's" (Rush's) work was not to be slighted. "Dr. Puff, the paragraphist, has scarcely slept since his appointment, having received orders to work double tides," "Centinel," an Anti-Federalist, snidely observed. "Beneath his creative pen thousands of correspondents rise into view, who all harmonize in their sentiments and information about the new Constitution."[31]

Among others, Rush wrote to Gen. William Irvine, with the Continental Congress now meeting in New York, asking to have that city's papers publish extracts of one of his convention speeches. Similar letters went out to Ramsay in South Carolina and Belknap in Massachusetts. The defection of Presbyterian friends in the backcountry, like Hartley, induced him "to look up my German brethren (indulge the term)," he explained to Frederick Muhlenberg. "On them I rely chiefly to *outvote,* to *outwork,* and to *outpray* the Anti-Federalists in our state. I hope you do not neglect to fill your gazette with federal essays, anecdotes, and intelligence."[32]

Rush nearly worked himself to death during these early months of 1788, but for reasons that may not have borne directly on the nation's welfare. On January 15 his two-month-old son William died, leaving Mrs. Rush "much afflicted," and probably her husband, too, though his reactions went unrecorded. In March, a day or two after going out one night "too thinly clad, I was attacked upon my return from church by a severe pleurisy." He lay for nine days near death. His slave William Grubber sat through the night at his bedside when the crisis came. "If massaw die, put me in de grave with him," he said. "He be de only friend I got in dis world." Shortly after he had been declared out of danger, Rush told John Montgomery what had gone through his mind those terrible days:

> For my own part, I had taken leave of life. I not only settled all my worldly affairs but gave the most minute directions with respect to everything that related to my funeral. It pleased God to enable me to do this with an uncommon degree of composure, for the promise of the Gospel bore up my soul above the

fear of death and the horrors of the grave. O! my friend, the religion of Jesus Christ is indeed a reality. It is comfortable in life, but in a near view of the last enemy its value cannot be measured or estimated by the pen or tongue of a mortal.

What Montgomery could read between the lines of that confession Rush later made explicit to his children. "My faith, it is true, was weak," he said, "but my hopes in the mercy of God as a Redeemer were strong."[33]

The aftereffects of the illness lingered on, and months later he confessed to finding himself "unequal in point of exertion to many objects I wish to have seen executed before I leave the world." But neither his weakened constitution nor the continuing opposition of the Anti-Federalists in the state caused despair. "The new government *will be* established, nor will its establishment be followed with a civil war anywhere," he predicted. "Then will its enemies become like the enemies and opposers of independence—infamous and contemptible." For Bryan and Ewing, both Anti-Federalists, he reserved a vivid metaphor: "I view them as oxen decorated with ribbons parading the streets of a great city previous to their being led to the place of their destruction."[34]

Early in 1788 Rush distributed an open letter on exactly where he stood as an answer to an attack on opinions of his aired at the ratifying convention. He largely repeated arguments used in the convention—that a government of checks and balances and one in which the people were fully represented offered much more security for liberty than a bill of rights; that those who called for such a bill "have not recovered from the habits they acquired under the monarchical government of Great Britain." He flayed those who favored "a simple democracy," that is, an unbalanced government. He also dared to question the moral character of the American people. Time has shown "too plainly," he said, "that the people are as much disposed to vice as their rulers, and that nothing but a vigorous and efficient government can prevent their degenerating into savages or devouring each other like beasts of prey."[35]

Rush had lived through the critical years after the Revolution without being driven either to distraction or despair. Now, however, with the Constitution ratified—approval in May by the ninth state, New Hampshire, made it the law of the land—he saw the past as a decade of misery. The Constitution "makes us a nation," he exulted to John Adams on July 2, exactly twelve years after Congress had declared independence. "It rescues us from anarchy and slavery. It revives agriculture and commerce. It checks moral and political iniquity. In a word, it makes a man both willing to *live* and to *die*. To *live,* because it opens to him fair prospects of great public and private happiness. To *die,* because it insures peace, order, safety, and prosperity to his children."[36]

Two days later, on the Fourth of July, he witnessed the grandest parade America had ever seen, gotten up to honor both Independence Day and official acceptance of the Constitution. It began at eight in the morning, wound through three miles of the city's streets, and ended at one in the afternoon on the sprawling grounds of William Hamilton's estate at the edge of town, where some seventeen thousand citizens spent the afternoon picnicking, and where, out of that great mob, Rush did not spy a single intoxicated person. Francis Hopkinson, who had stage-managed the parade, wrote a long account for the newspapers, which Rush, after reading it, felt the need to supplement with a version of his own. He did not describe the parade so much as his reactions to it. He suppressed family pride—no mention was made that on a float that personified the Constitution in the form of an eagle rode his brother Judge Jacob Rush and that aboard the Ship of Union rode son John as one of the crew—to emphasize that this was an *American* parade, where farmers and tradesmen made up the majority of marchers, where a rabbi walked with arms linked between a Catholic priest and a Protestant clergyman to underscore the point that the Constitution opened "all its power and offices alike not only to every sect of Christians but to worthy men of *every* religion." Every float, every body of marchers, expressed once again to Rush the glories the Constitution would spread throughout the land. " 'Tis done! We have become a nation," he ended. "America has ceased to be the only power in the world that has derived no benefit from her declaration of independence."[37]

Rush did not lay down his pen once the Constitution had been accepted. Elections for Congress would be held in November and he joined with others to secure the best men to represent the state. He urged John Dickinson to stand for the Senate. Dickinson, from his Delaware farm, pleaded ill health forbade further public service. " 'To do good' is the business of *life,*" Rush admonished. " 'To enjoy *rest*' is the happiness of heaven." Dickinson still refused to run, and the Federalists eventually nominated Robert Morris and Rush's good friend William Maclay. The

Republican-Federalist-controlled assembly decided that to contain the power of the Anti-Federalists, who were strongest in the backcountry, congressional districts would not now be created and the election for the House of Representatives would be held on a statewide basis.[38]

Rush continued during the campaign to write for the Federalists, mainly blaming everything that had gone wrong with Pennsylvania since 1776 on the Constitutionalists, who now masqueraded as Anti-Federalists. The opposition soon chose him as their main target. "Galen," as one of the attackers dubbed him, "has done more to destroy the harmony of Pennsylvania and forward the vassalage of her citizens to the *rich and aspiring* than all the other firebrands of party and instruments of ambition." If the jibe cut, the election results soothed any pain. Morris and Maclay won the Senate race, and the Federalists collected all eight seats in the House, with his friends Fitzsimons and Clymer among the victors. Rush, with Wilson, Coxe, and Maclay, worked to create a slate of electors—the men who would cast the state's vote for President and Vice President—favorable to John Adams for the second post. Washington's election to the Presidency was assumed by all. By October he confided to a friend in New England that Adams would "have all the votes of our state."

Rush had but a single reservation about all that happened. "Many pious people wish the name of the Supreme Being had been introduced somewhere in the new Constitution," he told John Adams a year later. "Perhaps an acknowledgement may be made of His goodness or of His providence in the proposed amendments. In all enterprises and parties, I believe the *praying* are better allies than the *fighting* part of communities."[39] Otherwise the Constitution seemed to him perfect. "Citizen of the United States! you have a well-balanced Constitution established by general consent, which is an improvement on all republican forms of government heretofore established," he exulted. "It possesses the good qualities of monarchy, but without its vices. The wisdom and stability of an aristocracy, but without the insolence of hereditary masters. The freedom and independence of a popular assembly, acquainted with the wants and wishes of the people, but without the capacity of doing those mischiefs which result from uncontrolled power in one assembly. The end and object of it is public good. If you are not happy it will be your own fault."[40]

19

Reforms in the Cause of Virtue

1787–1789

1

IN NEW ENGLAND Rush had a clergyman friend who did not think much of those who condescended to call him "Dr. Puff" or "Dr. Froth." "Dear Doctor," Jeremy Belknap wrote, "I can compare you to nothing better than *Mr. Great Heart* in Bunyan who attacks without mercy all the giants, hydras, hobgoblins, etc., which stand in the way of his Pilgrims and conducts them thro' all opposition to the Celestial City." The compliment from Belknap, then in the midst of writing and publishing a history of New Hampshire, had been prompted by Rush's latest drive to form a better nation. An urgency infused this campaign that had been absent in earlier ones. On three occasions since 1780 he had come close to death. Each time his strength returned more slowly, and the tedious recovery in 1788 left him thinking more than ever about death. " 'Behold he cometh!'—and 'The time is short,' " he wrote Belknap. "This, my dear friend, is my apology for troubling the world with so many of my opinions on paper. A weak breast daily tells me that I hold my life by a precious tenure."[1]

The supposed nearness of death once again brought Rush "trem-blingly alive." After learning that the requisite nine states had ratified the Constitution, he dropped politics for the moment and in June of 1788 dashed off an open letter to clergymen of all denominations on a favorite subject: American morality. He wrote to hasten that "revolution in our principles, opinions, and manners," spoken of so often before. It is a curious letter, revealing little in America worth praise. In it he deplores popular elections of magistrates and militia officers as a vice so shocking "the twelve apostles could all be raised from their graves"; the country fair as a Pandora's box that tempts people "to extravagance, gaming, drunkenness, and uncleanness"; lawsuits, which expose men who attend court "to idleness, drinking, and gaming"; a licentious press that undermines the cause of liberty by personal calumnies—doubtless labeling his own attacks against Shippen in the public interest rather than libelous. Amusements engaged in without female company—horse racing, cockfighting, dining at men's clubs—are "unfriendly to morals and of course to the liberties of our country." Another evil, enjoying oneself on the Sabbath, can possibly be remedied by Sunday schools for the poor, an innovation recently inaugurated in England. "Who can witness the practices of swimming, sliding, and skating, which prevail so universally on Sundays in most cities of the United States, and not wish for similar institutions to rescue our poor children from destruction." Rush never perceived the number of institutions, varying from Sunday schools to a medical dispensary, he urged America to import from the hopelessly corrupted land of Britain.

This buckshot approach to vice ended with a call for "a new species of federal government for the advancement of morals in the United States." Rush envisioned "a general convention of Christians, whose business shall be to unite in promoting the general objects of Christianity." The convention would shun discussion of doctrine, which each sect determined for itself, as the federal government avoided interference in matters over which the states had jurisdiction. The convention would deal only with issues of common interest to all Christians, specifically questions of morality. A federalism of religious sects would teach Christians "to love each other and to unite in the advancement of their common interests."[2]

The imaginative suggestion of applying a political concept to religion was lost for many in a tract that verged close to pious ranting. For those who knew his medical writings, the essay must have seemed odd—the morally conservative religionist juxtaposed with the socially liberal physician. While the physician sought to narrow the definition of immorality by arguing that moral failings were rooted in physical or psychological ills, the layman worked to broaden it by including under the label of vice whatever vexed his soul about Americans and the way they led their lives.

2

One night in a dream Rush came upon a beautiful country inhabited by a band of cheerful Negroes. "We perceive you are a *white man*," someone said as he approached. "That color which is the emblem of innocence in every creature of God, is to us a sign of guilt in man." Suspicion melted and the people embraced Rush when they learned his name. But any self-satisfaction he felt died as the dream took a curious turn:

> All at once, the eyes of the whole assembly were turned from me, and directed towards a little white man who advanced towards them, on the opposite side of the grove, in which we were seated. His face was grave, placid and full of benignity. . . . While I was employed in contemplating this venerable figure— suddenly I beheld the whole assembly running to meet him—the air resounded with the clapping of hands—and I awoke from my dream, by the noise of a general acclamation of ANTHONY BENEZET.[3]

The dream can be taken as a literary device used to praise Benezet or as Rush's oblique way of confessing his own belated commitment to the antislavery movement. Benezet had prodded him about the evils of slavery since the early 1770's. He got from Rush one essay, and, except for a rebuttal to a critic, nothing more. Rush continued to retain a slave. He did not join the abolition society formed in 1774, and he had nothing to do with the abolition law passed by the assembly in 1780; while Rush had sat by silently or worrying in print about inflation or the evils of Shippen, Benezet had quietly interviewed every deputy and kept pressure on all of them until his pet bill passed. When the old abolition group was reorganized in 1784 under the name of the Pennsylvania Society for Promoting the Abolition of Slavery and the Relief of Free Negroes Unlawfully Held in Bondage, Rush did not appear among the members. He did not commit himself to the society until March of 1787. A month later Franklin joined it and, with his election as president, Rush was chosen one of the secretaries, though most of the work was done by his fellow secretary Tench Coxe. He had a hand in the petition condemning slavery which was sent to the Constitutional Convention, and he was pleased by the clause in the Constitution calling for an end to the slave trade after twenty years. "The prospect of this glorious event more than repays me for all the persecution and slander to which my principles and publications exposed me about sixteen or seventeen years ago," he said at the time.[4]

The assembly gave further reason to brag in March 1788, when it passed a law plugging loopholes in the earlier legislation against slavery. "I am encouraged by the success that has finally attended the exertions of the friends of universal freedom and justice," he said soon afterward, "to go on in my romantic schemes (as they have often been called) of serving my countrymen."[5]

Two months later Rush took time off from his "romantic schemes" to make a statement which was witnessed by two colleagues, Samuel Powel Griffitts and Benjamin Young, his former apprentice.

> I, Benjamin Rush of the city of Philadelphia, doctor of physic, having purchased a Negro slave named William of Captain David McCullough, and being fully satisfied that it is contrary to reason and religion to detain the said slave in bondage beyond such a time as will be a just compensation for my having paid for him the full price of a slave for life, I do hereby declare that the said William shall be free from me and from all persons claiming under me, on the twenty-fifth day of February on the year of our Lord one thousand seven hundred and ninety four. In witness whereof I have hereunto set my hand and seal on this twenty-fourth day of May one thousand seven hundred and eighty eight.
>
> Benj. Rush[6]

The statement makes it difficult to believe that Rush approached the antislavery movement with the moral indignation evoked in his letters. William is to gain freedom only after Rush has received "just compensation for my having paid for him the full price of a slave for life," which means six more years of bondage. But for that phrase "just compensation" it could be said Rush delayed manumission until he considered William adequately educated and trained to cope for himself in the world. Even without it no sign of fury, no real compassion, appears to underlie his commitment against slavery.

Worse still, the affidavit raises a question about Rush's veracity and subjects to doubt his apparently consistent distaste for slavery. He once said William was "liberated after he had served me ten years." Yet legally he could not have purchased him after 1780, which means he served a minimum of fourteen years as a slave. And morally he could not have bought him after 1773, the year of his original antislavery pamphlet, unless he wished publicly to be classed as a hypocrite. Regardless of when William was purchased, Rush positively owned him in 1776 and mentioned him in a letter to his wife. Rush rarely if ever consciously lied, yet it would seem that a strong feeling of guilt over his ownership of a slave persuaded him to obscure the truth of the matter from his children and posterity.[7]

It can be said for Rush that he did agree to free William, for the law did not manumit those in Pennsylvania already enslaved. He made this agreement at an inconvenient time, when his practice had slumped, he was in debt, and his large family had become expensive to maintain. He could only hope that by 1794 he could afford a paid servant to carry out tasks William had performed without wages. When the time came to give William his freedom, the bargain was kept. For a while he stayed on as a paid servant. A notebook of household expenses lists payments to him in 1794 for such chores as weeding the garden and gathering in the potatoes. Soon afterward he went to sea, but the warm relationship between former master and slave continued. "He was when I first bought his time a drunkard and swore frequently," Rush recalled upon William's death in 1799. "In a year or two he was reformed from both these vices, and became afterwards a sober, moral man and faithful and affectionate servant. His integrity extended to trifles, and was of the most delicate nature. . . . He obtained some of my hair secretly, and had it put into a ring in London, which ring he gave to one of the maids to keep for him, with an injunction 'not to tell me of it.' "[8]

Rush's antagonism toward slavery as a moral evil—an evil he had not bothered to include in the letter to clergymen detailing what was wrong with American society—deepened in the years after 1790, and he came to deserve the reputation as a leader in the antislavery movement. But in 1788 he appeared to attack the institution as a physician rather than as a moralist. He worried about the diseases Negroes suffered as a direct result of enslavement and about the effect of slavery upon their well-being: the difficulty in childbearing because of a pelvis distorted by a master's kicks; lockjaw, which he thought arose "from the heat and smoke of their cabins in which the children are born and from their being exposed afterwards to the cool air"; hypochondriasis or *mal d'estomac,* which "is occasioned wholly by grief and therefore stands justly chargeable upon slavery"; the usual chronic diseases due to an inadequate diet. The sense of degradation slavery imposed on its victims sapped their moral and intellectual energy, which in turn made them psychologically susceptible to disease. In 1788 he told Jacques Pierre Brissot de Warville, a visiting Frenchman, it was "much more difficult to treat and to cure Negro slaves than white people and that the Negroes have much less resistance to serious and prolonged illnesses. This is so because they do not have the will to live; they are virtually without vitality and life force."[9]

3

Many who sympathized with Rush's "romantic schemes" were put off by his godlike view of the world's ills. "Ever since I was one-and-twenty years of age I have unfortunately been engaged in combating vulgar errors or popular prejudices," he wrote in 1788. This self-satisfied certainty about the right and wrong of every issue no doubt irritated many who might otherwise have sided with him in his lonely battles to make the world a better place. Consequently when it came to parceling out credit for a reform achieved, Rush's work often passed unnoticed. He deserved praise for the penal reforms initiated in Pennsylvania late in the 1780's, yet most of the honor fell on Judge William Bradford, who originally viewed them "with good-humored ridicule," then promoted them in a "learned and eloquent pamphlet"; and on Benjamin Franklin, although Franklin "never wrote a line nor uttered a sentiment in favor of it to my knowledge, neither before nor after it had taken place in Pennsylvania."

In 1786, Rush's schemes for reform had not yet extended to criminals when Constitutionalists and Republicans, urged on by Quakers, had united to carry through the assembly a revision of Pennsylvania's penal laws that sharply reduced the number of offenses calling for the death penalty. The revision did not alter, however, the long-accepted proposition that criminals' punishment should be public and humiliating. To that end the new code required prisoners to work on public projects—dig ditches, clean streets, repair roads. A distinctive prison garb and shaved heads made them conspicuous wherever their work took them, and the wheelbarrows they pushed elicited the epithet "wheelbarrow men."

Rush did not comment on the legislation when it passed. "It is your duty," he had said in a stern tone a few years earlier, "to rejoice in seeing punishment inflicted upon a criminal who has disturbed the peace of the society to which you belong." It took an accidental meeting with a group of "wheelbarrow men" to arouse his interest in penal reform. He came upon them sweeping the street before his house. He offered the men molasses beer, and while chatting as they refreshed themselves he found that he had sympathy, perhaps even respect, for the way they bore their humiliation, overcoming the distaste he would have felt.[10]

As a result of that incident, Rush became among the first to attack Pennsylvania's much praised penal law. He did so in a speech given in March 1787 before the recently created Society for Promoting Political Inquiries, which held its meetings in Benjamin Franklin's living room. "There was no formality of discussion," one member later recalled. "Dr. Rush, who had great powers of conversation, commonly took the lead"; another member, however, held that Rush's "incessant talking disturbed us very much." Rush advanced two radical propositions: first, he called for a reversal of the centuries-old Anglo-colonial tradition that criminals should be publicly punished and demanded "that crimes should be punished in private, or not punished at all"; secondly, he took an extraordinary stand on penology—that "the only design of punishment is the reformation of the criminal." These views reveal once again the influence of the British humanitarian movement on Rush. He could have drawn some of his thoughts from William Paley's *Principles of Moral and Political Philosophy* or Cesare Beccaria's *Essay on Crimes and Punishments,* both of which expressed similar notions and were written by favorite authors of his, but the greatest influence came from the English reformer John Howard's *State of the Prisons in England and Wales, with Preliminary Observations, and an Account of Some Foreign Prisons,* first published in 1777. Rush knew the book well enough a decade later to call himself "a pupil and admirer of the celebrated Mr. Howard," and to confess still later "that all the improvements in the treatment and punishment of criminals in our country are derived from it."[11]

The reforms to *reform* the criminal that Rush advanced in the talk at

Franklin's home came directly from Howard. He advocated a large house whose name shall "convey an idea of its benevolent and salutary design." There will be cells for the solitary confinement of the refractory, a room for carrying on handicrafts, another for worship, and a garden adjoining the house. Prison terms will be adjusted to the crime and fixed by law, but the prisoner will not know the length of his sentence, for uncertainty agitated the imagination and hastened the reformation. The prisoner's "labor should be so regulated and directed as to be profitable to the state." They would derive their food from gardens "cultivated by their own hands." Punishments should consist in general "of bodily pain, labor, watchfulness, solitude and silence," but when it came to attaching a specific punishment to a specific crime he confessed "my subject begins to oppress me." He knew every crime had "its cure in moral and physical influence"—just as every disease had its antidote—but the trick was "to find the proper remedy or remedies for particular vices."[12]

Those who heard the speech praised it enough to encourage publication. It came forth as an anonymous pamphlet which in some quarters was attributed to Franklin, a mistake Rush only half succeeded in correcting. Public reception contrasted with the private one. "The principles contained in this pamphlet were opposed with acrimony and ridicule in the newspapers," a friend reported. "They were considered as the schemes of a humane heart but a wild and visionary imagination which it was impossible from the nature of man and constitution of his mind ever to realize, and as being much more adapted to the government of an Utopia than to those living under that of Pennsylvania." Rush ignored the outcry, and as usual spread his work everywhere. When a Boston newspaper ascribed it to Franklin he told a friend there he had "no objection to that mistake being corrected."[13]

The pamphlet helped to encourage the creation of the Philadelphia Society for Alleviating the Miseries of Public Prisons, most of whose members were Quakers. Rush became one of the four consulting physicians who advised on health measures for local prisons. Soon after assuming the assignment he told Lettsom about the reformation that "has lately taken place in the jails of this city in favor not only of humanity but of virtue in general." He did not know how much permanent good would be achieved by the program, but "men grow *good* by attempting it." Of that he was certain. "A prison sometimes supplies the place of a church and outpreaches the preacher in conveying useful instruction to the heart."[14]

A toe dipped into the pool of prison reform quickly led to complete immersion. In 1788 Rush elaborated into a pamphlet a remark on capital punishment in his original essay. He argued that it contradicted both reason and divine revelation and noted in passing that even the Indians opposed capital punishment except for prisoners of war. "There are many crimes," he said, "which unfit a man much more for human society than a single murder." He suggested several substitutes for "punishing murder by death": for murder of the first degree—solitude, darkness, "and a total *want* of employment"; of the second degree—"solitude and labor, with the benefit of light"; and of the third degree—confinement and hard labor. Rush had a high opinion of the reforming qualities of solitude. "A wheelbarrow, a whipping post, nay even a gibbet are all light punishments compared with letting a man's conscience loose upon him in solitude," he said. "Company, conversation, and even business are the opiates of the Spirit of God in the human heart. For this reason, a bad man should be left for some time without anything to employ his hands in his confinement. Every *thought* should recoil wholly upon *himself*."[15]

This second essay was judged the "boldest attack I have ever made upon a public opinion or a general practice." Out it went to friends at home and abroad. He urged reprinting it in local papers and let it be known he did not mind public acknowledgment of his authorship. A few months later the assembly repealed the law that had brought Rush into penal reform. With the abandonment of public punishment, it inaugurated a reform of the prison system. Hard labor behind prison walls, solitary confinement, and a system of fines were substituted for the old punishments. General regulations for the new program were drawn up and provisions made for inspectors to initiate revisions as needed. The legislature saw the reform as an experiment and, said a contemporary, "as if apprehending that the new system would not ultimately answer, limited the law to five years." Rush judged the innovations highly satisfactory: "Truth has at last prevailed upon the subject of our *penal* laws."[16]

4

Friends often accused him "of polygamy in studies," but Rush disagreed. "Unlike a plurality of wives," he said, "my studies all agree and are handmaids to each other." Anything "unfriendly to the progress of morals, knowledge, and religion" in the United States—be it Negro slavery, capital punishment, spirituous liquors, or the study of Latin and Greek— sooner or later engaged his attention. The intensity of interest varied with the particular reform and from year to year, except on the subject of education.

Rush lacked what has been called "the energy of true vigor," that is, the "energy which goes into maintaining things in good repair day in and day out." When Dickinson College went through a grim spell in 1788 and appeared doomed to extinction, he transferred the dreams once cherished for that school to another vision, expanding old ideas on a federal university in an essay published in October 1788. Only university graduates could qualify for public office after it had been in operation thirty years. "We are restrained from injuring ourselves by employing quacks in law; why should we not be restrained in like manner, by law, from employing quacks in government?"[17]

Rush's lifelong antipathy to Latin and Greek manifested itself in their absence from the proposed curriculum and, in June 1789, in "An Enquiry" into their supposed usefulness.[18] The title misled, for Rush did not inquire; he attacked. (In later editions the title was altered to "Observations . . . .") The classical languages undermined morals and religion by exposing youngsters to the "indelicate amours and shocking vices both of gods and men." They also, Rush held, obstructed the growth of an American literary style. "The present is the age of simplicity in writing in America," he had said in the essay on the federal university. "The turgid style of Johnson, the purple glare of Gibbon, and even the studied and thickset metaphors of Junius are all equally unnatural and should not be admitted into our country." He wanted to democratize the language, to cleanse it of words like *festivity, celebrity, hilarity, amenity,* and other favorites of Johnson which "have corrupted and weakened our language, and which are unintelligible to three-fourths of common English readers." Out, too, would go such "equally disgusting" additions as *exit, fecit, excudit, pinit, acme, finis, bona fide, ipso facto, ad valorem,* as well as such accretions from the French and Italian as *éclat, amateur, douceur, en passant, corps, dilettanti, con cuore, piano*—"all of which impair the uniformity and dignity of the English language."[19]

A pure English (or American) would give the nation a language intelligible to the common people. There were other equally honorable reasons to reject the classics as un-American. We must not forget the country in which we live. What serves as a practical language in Europe for treaties, laws, and official letters is no more useful in America than a heavy overcoat in Cuba. A fixed and frozen Latin cannot keep pace with a changing society. Where, for instance, he asked, "shall we find Latin words to convey just ideas of the many terms which electricity, chemistry, navigation, and many other sciences have introduced into our modern languages?"

The American language, came the prediction, "will probably be spoken by more people in the course of two or three centuries than . . . any one language at one time since the creation of the world." A misguided affection for Latin and Greek can only delay that great day. "We occupy a new country," Rush said, ending with an admonishment. "Our principal business should be to explore and apply its resources, all of which press us to enterprise and haste. Under these circumstances, to spend four or five years in learning two dead languages, is to turn our backs upon a gold mine, in order to amuse ourselves in catching butterflies."[20]

Rush sent the essay to John Adams, knowing it would provoke a rejoinder. "I should as soon think of closing all my window shutters, to enable me to see," Adams replied, "as of banishing the classics to improve republican ideas." Not a hint of humor tinged this colloquy. "I shall only ask two questions," Rush said in his prompt reply:

> Who are guilty of the greatest absurdity—the Chinese who press the feet into deformity by small shoes, or the Europeans and Americans who press the brain into obliquity by Greek and Latin?
>
> Do not men use Latin and Greek as the scuttlefish emit their ink, on purpose to conceal themselves from an intercourse with the common people?

Adams said the merits of his own literary style, whatever they were, developed from his classical training. Rush held that the overblown, affected style of his youth came from exposure to Latin and Greek, and not until he had read Hume and Swift did he learn to write a simple declarative sentence.[21]

Toward the end of his essay Rush had said that the decline of the classical languages in America would diminish "the present immense disparity which subsists between the sexes in the degrees of their education and knowledge." He believed a source of misery in many marriages might "be sought for in the *mediocrity* of knowledge of the women." This passing remark, he now told Adams, would be elaborated in another essay addressed to American women. The essay was never written, but Rush outlined to Adams what he planned to say. "They are not perverted by any prejudice upon this subject," he said. "They will hear from me the language of reason and nature, and their influence will render my opinions sooner or later universal." He ended with a final jab at his friend: "From the character you once gave me of Mrs. Adams and which I have had confirmed by all who have conversed with her, I anticipate support from her in my undertaking."[22]

5

Rush escaped the usual bout with spring sickness in 1789 but continued "still feeble" through the rest of the year. He enjoyed "good spirits" yet complained that "public and private pursuits since the year 1774 have nearly worn me out." Steadily through the year his concern for reforming America diminished. He stared ahead toward death with a "hope which looks with composure and sometimes with joy beyond the grave." He attacked a vice hitherto neglected, but otherwise only the campaign against spirituous liquor continued to engage his attention.[23]

Tobacco came forth as the new vice, and Rush made war against it with what to modern eyes rates as one of his most trenchant essays.[24] He brushed aside tobacco's virtues as largely illusory, like those of strong drink. True, it relieves uneasiness after a full meal, "but why should we cure one evil by producing another?" Those who chew it to ward off contagious diseases only delude themselves, for it has no immunization effect. Tobacco aids "intellectual operations" no more than distilled spirits do. In fact, it is "often used rather to supply the *want* of ideas than to *collect* or excite them."

The ill effects of tobacco on men's health that Rush ticked off must have startled contemporaries, for no one before had attacked the weed from this point of view. It impairs the appetite, he said, prevents easy digestion, and produces "many of those diseases which are supposed to be seated in the nerves." He spoke of one Philadelphian who lost his "teeth by drawing the hot smoke of tobacco into his mouth by means of a short pipe," and of another who acquired "a cancer on the lip which terminated fatally from the same cause." That anecdote perhaps distinguishes Rush as the first physician in history publicly to connect smoking with cancer. Others since the day King James referred to tobacco as a vile weed had condemned it as a moral evil, but Rush's analysis contributed something new. Not only was tobacco unhealthy, it led to idleness, "the root of all evil," to a "neglect of cleanliness," and, since its addicts were offensive to nonusers, to rudeness—and "whoever knew a rude man completely or uniformly moral?" At the heart of the indictment lay Rush's distress over the growing use of tobacco among children. "Who can see groups of boys of six or eight years old in our streets smoking segars, without anticipating such a depreciation of our posterity in health and character, as can scarcely be contemplated at this distance of time without pain and horror!"

Rush waited nine years to publish the essay. It served as his lone outcry in the antitobacco campaign. Perhaps as a frustrated snuff taker he lacked the heart for battle. Perhaps he sensed the ridiculous in comparing the smoker to the alcoholic. Whatever the reason, little of the spirit and none of the dedication given to the war against liquor were transmitted to the antitobacco campaign.

The two campaigns differed fundamentally, for Rush wanted to end the use of tobacco but only "the *abuse*" of spirituous liquors. This more reasonable goal seemed attainable, and after four years of preaching temperance, success did not seem too distant. The Philadelphia Society for promoting Agriculture and Rural Affairs let him carry on the war under its banner, and he prodded the College of Physicians to petition the assembly to raise the duty on spirits as a way of inhibiting consumption. Annually before every harvest the *Pennsylvania Packet* reprinted his *Enquiry into the Effects of Spirituous Liquors,* and now associations, he reported in the spring of 1789, began "forming in many places to give no spirits at the ensuing harvest." The battle extended to other states, with Belknap serving as a lieutenant in Massachusetts and Ramsay in South Carolina. *"Much* less rum will be used this year than last in this and the adjoining states of New Jersey, Delaware, and Maryland," he predicted in July. Though visible, the triumph would not, however, come quickly. "The good effects of our labors will appear in the next generation," he said. "In the year 1915 a drunkard I hope will be as infamous in society as a liar or a thief, and the use of spirits as uncommon in families as a drink made of a solution of arsenic or a decoction of hemlock."[25]

Rush in 1789 also added a new weapon to the arsenal of those armed against vice: A Moral and Physical Thermometer. The top half of the thermometer, which ranged from 0 to 70, indicated the degree of temperance. Those who favored anything from strong beer (10) to cider (40) could expect "cheerfulness, strength, and nourishment, when taken only at meals and in moderate amounts." A small beer (50), molasses and water (60), or plain water (70) generate "health, wealth, serenity of mind, reputation, long life and happiness." Degrees of intemperance were calibrated on the bottom half: punch (−10), toddy (−20), grog (−30), slings (−40), bitters (−50), and "rum, gin, brandy, and Jamaica spirits in the *morning*" (−60) and *"during the day and night"* (−70). Adjacent to this calibration were not only vices ranging from idleness (−10) through obscenity (−40) and hatred of just government (−60) to murder and suicide (−70) but also both the diseases and punishments relevant to the degree of intemperance: tremors and black eyes (−10), pains in the limbs and the poor house (−40), dropsy and the whipping post (−55), and DEATH and the GALLOWS (−70).

The moral thermometer issued forth as Rush altered the focus of his crusade. Up to now he had believed that an appeal to reason would win men from liquor. Gradually he came to recognize that "habitual drunkards are beyond the influence of *reason*." The Quakers' and Methodists' success in checking alcoholism showed that "the business must be effected finally by religion alone." He began to work through the churches rather than only the press, speaking to a conference of Methodist clergymen, writing to Bishop John Carroll of the Catholic Church, and urging his own Bishop White that the Episcopal Church must not stand "neuter in this interesting business." He remained full of hope. "Spirituous liquors give way in every part of the United States to beer and cider," he said. "But we must not relax in our publications against them. The *perseverance* as well as the *arm* of Hercules will be necessary completely to expel those monsters from our country."[26]

In the struggle to make America virtuous, Rush at the same time strove toward another goal—isolation from Europe. Fear of European corruption threads itself through every attack on vice. A depraved Europe had sent whisky and slavery to America. Idle amusements like cockfighting and horse racing, extravagant tastes, and affected manners were among the baneful imports. What viruses ships failed to bring in to impregnate America with evil were slipped into the country through the classical languages, those carriers of a bankrupt civilization. "Avoid filling your paper with anecdotes of British vices and follies," Rush advised a friend who planned to start a newspaper. "What have the citizens of the United States to do with the duels, the elopements, the crim. cons., the kept mistresses, the murders, the suicides, the thefts, the forgeries, the boxing matches, the wagers for eating, drinking, and walking, etc., etc., of the people of Great Britain? Such stuff when circulated through our country by means of a newspaper, is calculated to destroy that delicacy in the mind which is one of the safeguards of the virtue of a young country."[27] For all the vices he found to expostulate about, America was still, in comparison with the decadence of Europe, a virtuous young nation.

6

The years that Rush busied himself with a multitude of reforms were also the years that marked a turning point in his career as a physician, when he at last committed himself for good to medicine. While with one hand he worked to renovate society morally, physically, and politically, with the other, incredibly, he carried on a full-time medical practice as well as professorial duties at the college of Philadelphia, developed a new system of medicine he hoped would overthrow Cullen's medical theories, and laid the basis for his reputation as the founding father of American psychiatry.

By 1787 Rush was already, at the age of forty-one, America's best-known physician and the only one with an international reputation. Colleagues acknowledged his eminence by inviting him to join their medical societies as, year by year, they came to be organized through the country. The Massachusetts society extended its invitation in 1787 immediately after its founding, and New Haven followed suit in 1788. The London Medical Society, founded by Lettsom, honored Rush with its silver medal for the "valuable memoirs" he had sent across the water since becoming a corresponding member.[28]

Fame did not excuse Rush from earning a living. His practice continued moderately large—nowhere near what Redman's had been but considerably more sizable than Morgan's, which had diminished steadily since Shippen's acquittal. The usual intermitting, remitting, and inflammatory fevers appeared and disappeared at the expected times, and little out of the ordinary in diseases manifested itself. In July 1787 swellings of lips and eyelids affected a number of people; the swellings came suddenly and left in two or three days. The disease, which Rush suspected was a variant form of scarlatina anginosa, reappeared the following year "with different degrees of violence in many parts of the city." In 1789 "the epidemic cold" or influenza struck the city, the state, and the entire nation with such force that Rush thought it worth a paper.[29]

By 1787 Rush had acquired a second medical practice, a by-product of fame and seventeen years of teaching. As former students and apprentices left Philadelphia to start their own practices, they often turned to him for advice on puzzling cases. This mail-order practice brought in little cash —Rush charged strangers but rarely former students—but it took a good deal of his time, increasingly so as his fame spread. He prescribed cautiously in these letters, aware of the danger involved in trying to judge a case by another's description of it. When asked to suggest treatment for a cancer of the breast that afflicted George Washington's mother he offered little hope. He suggested Martin's cancer powder to retard the tumor's growth and a decoction of red clover to cleanse it. "Give anodynes when necessary, and support the system with bark and wine," he added. "Under this treatment, she may live comfortably many years and finally die of old age." Her death a month later pointed up the risks involved in mail-order consultation, for obviously Rush's correspondent had failed to report accurately the progress of the disease through Mrs. Washington's body.[30]

The report Rush had made in 1773 on mineral waters in and around Philadelphia had been an unimaginative, naïve appraisal by an innocent young physician-chemist. He had come a long way since then. In the fall of 1789 he listened to an acquaintance tell about taking the waters at Sweet Springs, Virginia, where annually two hundred to five hundred invalids visited and in the past seventeen years only sixteen had died. Rush gave the waters little credit for the low death and high recovery rates. The good effects of the waters came first, he said, from the leisurely journey to the isolated spa; second, from the pure air of the high Blue Ridge country; third, from "temperate living and freedom from care and hopes excited by histories of cures"; and finally, from the waters.[31]

In the years since his return from Europe, Rush had come to place greater importance on the role of the mind and environment in effecting a cure. But the brand of medicine he practiced remained pretty much Cullen's. Exactly how much appears in an essay he wrote for his friend Timothy Pickering on July 3 and 4, 1787. Pickering, who had moved from Massachusetts to Pennsylvania, had been selected by the assembly to organize the disputed Wyoming Valley into Luzerne County. Before going off into the wilderness, he asked Rush to prepare a brief manual describing the diseases most common in Pennsylvania and suggesting cures for them. A draft of Rush's essay survives in one of his commonplace books. It is a remarkably succinct and complete report of the diseases that afflicted eighteenth-century Pennsylvanians and also of Rush's medical views only a year or so before he rebelled against Cullenian medicine (see Appendix).

Cullen's influence on Rush's treatments is evident in the repeated injunction of "bleeding, if the pulse be full and tense," be it for a headache or lockjaw. A tense patient must be relaxed before any cure can be effected. Moreover, the body's system must be cleansed at both ends by heavy doses of purges and pukes. After these requirements have been carried out, Rush then appears to follow the dictum of his old mentor Redman: let nature take its course in the healing process. The absence of mercury and opium (except in one instance) indicate another break with Philadelphia colleagues, but otherwise Rush's materia medica—castor oil and rhubarb for laxatives, tartar emetic to promote vomiting, jalap and salts for purges—differed little from other physicians of the day. Rush's heroic dosages of laudanum—from ten drops for putrid fever to forty for dysentery—were considered normal for the day. Like his colleagues he continued to use blisters for such localized infections as toothaches, inflammatory fevers, and inflamed eyes. Nor, to judge by his cure for piles, was he above drawing on tried-and-tested folklore. The poultice of milk and bread, the hog's lard for the itch were prescriptions at least as old as America. Two specific treatments—those for lockjaw and for worms—Rush regarded as his own contributions to the advancement of medicine. These, however, were minor refinements rather than breaks with his master's teaching. In 1787 Rush was still a practicing disciple of Dr. Cullen.

7

The Pennsylvania Hospital had always rated high among the numerous sights to see in Philadelphia. After Rush became a consulting physician there it rated especially high with those visiting dignitaries who were allowed to accompany him on the day it was his turn to make the rounds.[32] Rush, a stickler for punctuality, arrived at the hospital promptly and rounds began as soon as he had reached the third floor, where between twenty and thirty medical students awaited him outside the women's ward. The ward was a large, clean room, well aired and lighted by tall windows that stretched down two sides. "Blacks are here mingled with the whites and lodged in the same apartments," one visitor noted. Rush made the rounds, another visitor said, "with a great deal of formality," and the moment he entered the ward a "most profound silence and order were preserved." He moved from bed to bed flanked by the attending physician, who reviewed the patient's progress, and the apothecary, who noted down prescriptions as Rush called them out. "In every case worthy of notice, he addresses the young physicians, points out its nature, the probable tendency, and the reason for the mode of treatment which he pursues." Rush's courtly manners among the female patients slackened when he and the entourage moved down to the men's ward on the second floor, where, according to a lay visitor, "most of the cases were chronic, many of them swellings and ulcerations, and some of them very singular." Rush imputed their troubles "to their drinking spirituous liquors and did not fail to remind them of it"; he went on to tell his visitor that "the greater proportion of his patients in the city were similar cases and originated from the same cause."

From the men's ward Rush walked down to the basement, where the lunatics were housed in cells. "These cells are about ten feet square, made as strong as a prison," Manasseh Cutler wrote after Rush had shown them to him in 1787. He added:

> On the back part is a long entry, from which a door opens into each of them; in each door is a hole, large enough to give them food, etc., which is closed with a little door secured with strong bolts. On the opposite side is a window, and large iron grates

within to prevent their breaking the glass. They can be darkened at pleasure. Here were both men and women, between twenty and thirty in number. Some of them have beds; most of them clean straw. Some of them were extremely fierce and raving, nearly or quite naked; some singing and dancing; some in despair; some were dumb and would not open their mouths; others incessantly talking. It was curious indeed to see in what different strains their distraction raged. This would have been a melancholy scene indeed, had it not been that there was every possible relief afforded them in the power of man. Everything about them, notwithstanding the labor and trouble it must have required, was neat and clean.

At the time Cutler toured the cells of the insane, Rush had obtained exclusive charge of these patients. "You see from this desperate undertaking I am still fond of voyages to Otaheite [Tahiti] in medicine," he told Lettsom.

Rush began his new assignment in 1787 with no clear plan of treatment that differed radically from what had been tried before. "The remedies on which I place my chief dependence are the warm and cold baths," he told Lettsom soon after taking charge of the insane. "In some cases I have used them after the Indian method—that is, I direct the cold to succeed the use of the warm bath while the patient is in the lowest state of debility and the highest state of irritability from the action of the warm water." He was beginning, in other words, with a treatment based on Cullen's system of medicine. Other than that he had no preconceived plan of treatment, except to deal kindly with his patients. "I shall carefully record the effects of these and other remedies upon my patients," he concluded to Lettsom, "and if any new facts should occur I shall not fail of communicating them to you."[33]

Rush knew he undertook a nearly hopeless task. Not only the patients but the public resisted his efforts to cure the insane. Many people still believed that insanity was God's way of punishing evildoers. Even among physicians who regarded it as a natural disease there were few who thought it curable. In his essay on penal reform he had wondered "why should receptacles be provided and supported at an immense expense, in every country, for the relief of persons afflicted with bodily disorders, and an objection be made to providing a place for the cure of the diseases of the mind?" He found resistance to improving the insane's living conditions even among the managers of the hospital. Two years after undertaking direction of the lunatics, he told the managers that any hope for improvement was being "rendered abortive by the cells of the hospital. These apartments are damp in winter and too warm in summer. They are, moreover, so constituted as not to admit readily of a change of air; hence the smell of them is both offensive and unwholesome." But the patients continued to live in their subterranean cells, continued to suffer from cold and occasionally to die from pneumonia. And Rush continued to fight for them against a public opinion he had so many times before found incredibly obtuse.[34]

8

Sometime in 1786 Rush determined—or as he would have it, "my countrymen have applied to me"—to publish a collection of his literary and medical essays written since he had returned from Europe in 1770. He told Lettsom of the project in June, sending along a table of contents and asking his friend to handle all the negotiations involved in getting it published in London. On 26 August 1787 he told Mrs. Rush the volume would go to the printer the next day, and that it would be dedicated to Cullen. For reasons never explained, more than a year and a half passed before the volume, which ended up being dedicated to Redman, was printed.[35]

Medical Inquiries and Observations, as Rush entitled the volume, came forth early in 1789 as the first larger-than-pamphlet-size collection of medical essays by an American physician published in the United States. It incorporated nearly everything Rush had previously published on medical matters and several pieces he had been unable to have printed. Like all authors, he believed his work to be a bold and radical venture. The essays, he told his wife, "contain more new opinions in medicine than ever I have published in morals or metaphysics." Every one of them, he thought, challenged some accepted medical cliché. Only in his account of the Revolution's effect on the human body did he think he wrote something acceptable to all his colleagues, "as it opposes no popular prejudice." He expected great opposition to the essay on worms, which he had never before been able to get published, and to the one that called for exercise and fresh air for consumptives. "In all of these," he said with a touch of sanctimony, "truth and utility, not novelty or fame, have been the sole objects of my inquiries." He wrote, he might have added, for laymen as well as colleagues, for he had always held that medicine was not an occult art in which only the practitioners could talk with one another.[36]

Medical Inquiries and Observations was published in January. In February Rush concluded his chemistry course for the year—and forever it turned out, though he would not know this for several months—with a lecture on the duties of a physician and his means for improving medicine.[37] He directed the talk particularly to those in the class who would eventually have a country practice, doubtless the large majority. They were advised to settle on a farm. A farm, he said, will promote a sense of equality among your patients and "prevent envy"; it "will serve your country," for you can use your knowledge of chemistry to advance agriculture; it will provide you with plenty of exercise and thus distract you from drinking grog.

Rush passed out the usual advice physicians had been handing students for centuries. "Take care of the poor. . . . Go regularly to some place of worship. . . . Avoid intimacies with your patients if possible, and visit them only in sickness. . . . Never dispute about a bill. . . . Never make light (to a patient) of *any* case." He gave out a few tricks of the trade. "Don't insert trifling advice or services in a bill," he warned. "You can incorporate them with important matters such as pleurisy or the reduction of a bone." Charge what the traffic will bear—"let the number and *time* of your visits, the nature of your patient's disease, and his rank in his family or society, determine the figures in your accounts"—and "the sooner you send in your accounts after your patients recover, the better." He pointed out traps to avoid. Refuse, "especially in the *forenoon*," he said, the drink of strong liquor invariably offered on visits or you may be "innocently led by it into habits of drunkenness."

Once a path had been cleared through the homilies Rush had some original things to say. Listen to old wives' tales, for their homemade remedies often cure where physicians fail. Quacks—medical quacks, at least, as opposed to quacks in law—can also teach, for out of their temerity have come "many of our most useful remedies." Admittedly Franz Mesmer was a quack, but "the facts which he has established clearly prove the influence of the imagination, and will, upon disease," Rush said. "Let us avail ourselves of the handle which those faculties of the mind present to us, in the strife between life and death." At another point he held it the duty of physicians to rescue metaphysics, or "the anatomy of the human mind" as he preferred to call it, from academics and theologians. "It can only be perfected by the aid and discoveries of medicine," he said.

He ended with a plea to put medicine like government on an American footing. Field and forest should be searched for indigenous medicines. "Who knows but that, at the foot of the Allegheny Mountains there blooms a flower that is an infallible cure for the epilepsy? Perhaps on the Monongahela or the Potomac there may grow a root that shall supply by its tonic powers the invigorating effects of the savage or military life in the cure of consumptions." That hopeful note was sustained to the rousing peroration: "All the doors and windows of the temple of nature have been thrown open by the convulsions of the late American Revolution. This is the time, therefore, to press upon her altars."

9

In March 1789, a decade after the College of Philadelphia had been transmuted into the University of Pennsylvania, the state assembly returned the property to its original holders. Ewing vacated the provost's house, allowing William Smith to return to his old home. Rush assumed that the revived college spelled death for the university, whose endowed funds would then be split between Dickinson and Franklin colleges. Ewing, the university trustees, and the assembly thought differently; the university stayed alive, kept its funds, and, after one false move, came to share the new hall of the American Philosophical Society. Its continued existence posed a problem for some of the medical professors. Not for Rush, of course, who had vehemently opposed the assembly's conversion of the college into a state-affiliated university. He resigned from the university at once. Kuhn followed his lead. Morgan's apathy about professional matters prevented him from deciding one way or the other. Shippen, torn in his allegiance, accepted appointments at both institutions.

When the college's medical department began classes again in November, Shippen appears to have taken the lead in the campaign for abandoning the bachelor of medicine degree. Morgan had introduced the degree at the department's birth, arguing that it suited a young country needing physicians and one where many students lacked the money to stay the distance for the doctor of medicine degree. As the years passed, fewer and fewer undergraduates bothered going on for the higher degree, for, as a foreign visitor pointed out, it gave "no advantage, in honor or remuneration, over other practitioners and bunglers." In 1789, then, the college determined to honor with the title "doctor" only those who had fulfilled the stiffer graduate requirements, the most important of which was submission of a thesis (it could be written in either Latin or English—a modification of European standards Rush may have pushed through).

What looked like a reform in medical education to Shippen, and no doubt Rush, eventually proved a setback. The faculty realized America was not yet ready for a strict graduate course in medicine; when it voted to give the M.D. it demanded more than it had asked for the M.B., but a good deal less than formerly required for the doctorate. "Thus a dangerous precedent was set," one scholar has said, "to be followed for a century and more by other schools that sprang up over all the country. Most of these had no university connections and the M.D. finally became meaningless until the twentieth century."[38]

On October 15, only two weeks before the reborn college would inaugurate its fall series of medical lectures, a messenger arrived at Rush's home with news that Morgan was dying. When Rush reached his old colleague he

> found him dead in a small hovel, surrounded with books and papers, and on a light dirty bed. He was attended only by a washerwoman, one of his tenants. His niece, Polly Gordon, came in time enough to see him draw his last breath. His disorder was the influenza, but he had been previously debilitated by many other disorders. What a change from his former rank and prospects in life! The man who once filled half the world with his name, had now scarcely friends enough left to bury him.[39]

Two days later Rush attended the funeral at Saint Peter's Church, where Morgan was buried beneath the floor next to his wife. The following week the college trustees elected Rush to the professorship of theory and practice of medicine, now vacant with Morgan's death. On November 2 Rush opened his course with a eulogy on Morgan—a man whose career and Rush's had been so closely linked in the quarter century past.

20

"Only a Spectator of
Public Measures"

1789–1790

1

IN 1789 Rush began to lead what by his standards was "a most unrepub-
lican life." He ceased to be concerned with public affairs. Few if any
essays aimed at reforming society issued forth from his study. He no longer
believed men could be swayed by reason to improve either themselves or
the world around them. "What did reason do in the council or the field in
the last American war?" he asked John Adams. "Man is indeed fallen! He
discovers it every day in domestic, in social, and in political life." But for
one who through so many black times had always held that "all will end
well," that bitter sentiment had to be adulterated. "Let us not despair," he
went on, for it seems "probable that man is becoming a more rational
creature in America than in other parts of the world."[1]

Years later Adams chastised his friend for refusing to be drawn back
into the public arena. Rush defended his stand by recounting a "singular
dream" that had occurred sometime around 1790. He found himself in the
dream traveling up a Philadelphia street, headed toward Christ Church.
Near the church he came upon a crowd gazing upward at a man "seated
on the ball just below the vane of the steeple." When Rush asked what
was going on, an acquaintance explained: "The man whom you see yon-

der has discovered a method of regulating the weather, and that he could produce rain and sunshine and cause the wind to blow from any quarter he pleased."

> I now joined the crowd in gazing at him. He had a trident in his hand which he waved in the air, and called at the same time to the wind, which then blew from the northeast, to blow from the northwest. I observed the vane of the steeple while he was speaking, but perceived no motion in it. He then called for rain, but the clouds passed over the city without dropping a particle of water. He now became agitated and dejected, and complained of the refractory elements in the most affecting terms. Struck with the issue of his conduct, I said to my friend who stood near to me, "The man is certainly mad." Instantly, a figure dressed like a flying Mercury descended rapidly from him, with a streamer in his hand, and holding it before my eyes bid me read the inscription on it. It was: *De te fabula narratur.* [The story is told of you yourself.]

The dream stunned Rush. Like the man on the church steeple, he, too, had played God in the drive to reform America and had "complained of the refractory elements" when people failed to listen. Now his subconscious had come forth to declare him, like the man in the dream, mad. "The impression of these words was so forcible upon my mind," he told Adams, "that I instantly awoke, and from that time I determined never again to attempt to influence the opinions and passions of my fellow citizens upon political subjects."[2]

The dream only determined a decision that had been brewing for some time. "I am gradually withdrawing myself from public duties and public life," he said early in 1788, adding "—not because I am hurt by the slander of my enemies or the ingratitude of my friends, but because my health will not bear as formerly more labors than the duties of my profession." There was also his family to consider. "My boys, too, begin now to require some of those evenings which I formerly gave to my country." Finally, it had to be admitted that Rush did not so much abandon politics as the politicians abandoned him.[3]

2

After Pennsylvania's ratification of the Constitution, Rush had puffed John Adams in the press for Vice President. He did not boast to Adams of his efforts, but instead went out of the way to praise the work of friends like Coxe (he "has had great merit in holding up your name to the public"), Wilson ("could his advice have prevailed *fully,* you would have had *ten* instead of eight votes from Pennsylvania"), Morris ("likewise"), and Maclay ("a scholar, a philosopher, and a statesman"), all electoral college members.[4]

Mixed motives prompted the efforts of this group. They believed that Adams as Vice President would bring distinction to the new government. Moreover, his election would give the Pennsylvania Federalists who helped bring it about a pipeline to the center of power, for it was then assumed the Vice Presidency would be an office of importance, which it might have been if Washington had not disliked Adams so thoroughly. Finally, according to Maclay, "we knew his vanity and hoped by laying hold of it to render him useful among the New England men in our scheme of bringing Congress to Pennsylvania."[5]

Rush opened the drive to make Philadelphia the capital of the United States before Congress convened. "There is an expectation here, which I have humored, that your influence will be exerted immediately in favor of a motion to bring Congress to Philadelphia," he wrote Adams in February 1789. In mid-March he sent another long letter—really an essay—in which he questioned whether the virtue of Congress could be safe in New York where a third of the citizens were Anti-Federalists and another third were Americans "with *British hearts.*" This praise for Philadelphia—"she is wholly and *highly* federal"—came from one who conveniently forgot he had once called it "a seat of corruption."

> Here the human mind is in a state of fermentation. Here pleasure yields to business, and eating and drinking to useful conversation. Here Quakers and Germans tincture everything with simplicity, industry, and republicanism. Here the people and their rulers will be alive. Here the people are *natives* of America and

visibly interested in its prosperity. Here learning, manufactures,
and human improvements of every kind thrive and flourish.

In the midst of this high-sounding rhetoric came a discerning comment,
which, if heeded, would have prevented the capital of the United States
from becoming a southern city, in effect a captive of the South for the
next seventy years. "By *delaying* the removal of Congress to Philadelphia,"
he warned Adams, "you will probably be dragged in a few years to the
banks of the Potomac, where Negro slaves will be your servants by day,
mosquitoes your sentinels by night, and bilious fevers your companions
every summer and fall, and pleurisies every spring."[6]

On 30 April 1789 Washington took the oath of office and the new
government began to function in New York City, picking up where the
Continental Congress had sat out its last days waiting for the Constitution
to be ratified. Rush did not attend the inauguration, nor did he have anything to say about it in letters, though a testy one in June to John Adams
implied, without saying why, he did not like the way the first month under
Washington had gone. "I would not be jolted two hours in the stage that
plies between New York and Philadelphia to be the prime minister of the
United States," he said, noting belligerently: "Under all circumstances, I
hope I shall be excused in *thinking* for myself at all times and upon all
subjects."

Rush believed New York to be "the *sink* of British manners and politics," and by June he could see signs of the city's influence on the new
government. "The citizens of Pennsylvania are truly republican," he told
Adams, "and will not readily concur in a government which has begun so
soon to ape the corruption of the British court, conveyed to it through the
impure channel of the city of New York." It would appear that these fears
of a corrupted government were pricked alive by Maclay, who, while
visiting for tea, would fill Rush's ears with news of doings in New York.
Maclay disliked Adams and managed to instill distrust in Rush, whose letters to his old friend now become filled with discussions about republicanism, the evils of titles, and the dangers of monarchy. Maclay derided both
the Senate and Adams when he came for tea one afternoon in mid-August:

He observed that half the Senate were lawyers; that he never
knew one of them [to] retract or alter an opinion after the fullest

discussion of it, which he ascribed to their habits of contending for victory instead of truth at the bar. He added further that he had heard John Adams say in a private company, "The more ignorant people are, the more easily they will be governed."[7]

Nonetheless, the friendship between Rush and Adams remained solid. The acid tone that crept into Rush's side of the correspondence late in 1789 owed little or nothing to Adams' supposed defection from republicanism. The persecutions that public life had exposed Rush to had left him friendless, he told Adams, in a city where he had "devoted . . . sixteen years to my country." An unnamed but trusted person has "employed his talents for evil and ridicule against me in the public papers." Worse still, "I see many high in power or affluent in office who in the year 1776 considered me as one of the firebrands of independence," not making it clear whether he thought the men in power were ignoring him or that he should be one of the men in power. "That man will be egregiously disappointed who expects the rewards of his patriotism or successful enterprises on this side of the grave," he warned young Noah Webster, who was giving thought to a political career. *"Expect* to be persecuted for doing good, and *learn* to rejoice in persecution." These injections of self-pity reveal the pain Rush felt in being forced out of politics.[8]

Though he had "applied for no office and shall apply for none," Rush had hoped the new government would reward him with a post overseas. "My knowledge of several European languages and of many eminent literary characters would have added frequent opportunities to my disposition to serve my country," he told Adams. Seldom before had he set his heart on a less attainable, less realistic goal. The debt-ridden federal government could afford to send few ministers abroad; the few posts available went to men who knew something about diplomacy. Probably even Adams believed his friend unqualified by temperament and training for a foreign post, but if he had not vetoed such an assignment, Washington certainly would have. Still, Rush had reason to feel misused. Others had done as much but no one more to hasten ratification of the Constitution. All the friends he had worked with held offices in the federal government—Wilson on the Supreme Court, Coxe in the Treasury Department, Morris and Maclay in the Senate—yet nothing had been offered to him.[9]

The insult of being ignored helped to weaken Rush's commitment to Washington's government. For this and other reasons, he began to shed the Federalist cloak. His commitment to republicanism, his fear of corruption, his opposition to aristocracy all joined to convince him that under Washington, whom he had never greatly admired, the principles of the Revolution were being plowed under, that out of the battle for a strong central government had come a behemoth controlled by an aggrandizing elite determined to manage the great beast for their own interests. "I already see a system of influence bordering upon corruption established in our country which seems to proclaim to innocence and patriotism to keep their distance," he told Adams before the new government had passed its first birthday. Every bit of news out of New York sent him deeper into gloom, until by mid-April 1790 he had, so he said, become so indifferent as well as disgusted with national politics that it was doubtful whether he would "give a vote at our next election."[10]

3

Rush might more easily have accepted the slight handed out by the federal government if friends at home had not at the same time heaped upon him a greater insult by denying him the chance to share in the creation of a new constitution for Pennsylvania. None in the state had fought harder for this goal. Even the opposition admitted he "bore away the palm and shone conspicuous beyond all the imps of the *well-born*" during the thirteen years he had attacked the constitution of 1776. His disgust for the evils wrought by that document stayed intact to the end. "It is below a democracy," he told Adams in 1789. "It is a *mobocracy,* if you will allow me to coin a word." The chance to slay a dragon long pursued carried Rush back to the center of the political arena. Battle plans were concocted around the fireside in his parlor early in March. Present were his friends Gerardus Wynkoop, Maclay, Fitzsimons, and Wilson. "My parlor will therefore be the *Bingham's porch* of the new constitution," Rush told his old partner in the Dickinson College venture.[11]

According to plan, a rump meeting of the assembly was held a few nights later at the City Tavern, then on 24 March 1789 the legislature voted that the sense of the people should be polled on whether or not to call a constitutional convention. The triumph "of reason and virtue in Pennsylvania" seemed about to occur, but to make sure the assembly's resolution did not end as an empty gesture, Rush joined in a campaign to start moving petitions favoring a convention toward the legislature. "The sooner you set about this business the better," he told Montgomery. "Otherwise the Antis will be beforehand with you. We shall have the best government in the Union."[12]

By early September the assembly had received petitions with more than ten thousand signatures calling for a convention, and the request was quickly acceded to by the deputies. Several weeks later a statewide election for delegates was held. A caucus at the home of Samuel Powel, mayor of Philadelphia, produced a ballot of five candidates to represent the city in the convention. James Wilson headed the list; Rush's name did not appear on it. Other caucuses elsewhere in the city altered the list slightly but one constant always remained: the absence of Rush's name. At a town meeting held in the State House yard, citizens were given twenty-seven suggested candidates; again Rush was not proposed. Why suddenly he had become political poison puzzled him, or if he knew why he refused to divulge the reason. Had the times passed him by? He thought so. When the convention convened in late November, he found the seats "all filled with men who were either unknown in 1776 or known only for timidity or disaffection."

Rush's apathy toward public affairs dipped so low "that I often pass whole weeks without reading our newspapers," he told Adams. Not even reports from Paris that everything was "in a ferment" could arouse him from his lethargic attitude toward current events. Throughout these months the press overflowed with news on the progress of the French Revolution, but neither news of France, New York, nor of his own state could dispel Rush's abrupt disinterest in political affairs.[13]

The state constitutional convention sat for ten months and Rush ostentatiously ignored it. "I have never once been within the doors of our convention, nor have I broken bread with a single member of the body who compose it," he said. But he must have known something of what was going on behind the closed doors, for seven months before completion of the new constitution, which would give Pennsylvania the two-house legislature and strong executive he had long contended for, he wrote: "The reformation of our state government has completed my last political wish." Compared with the run of men, Rush was a relatively modest person, but at this juncture in his life he felt the need to boast. "Hitherto I have never known a defeat or final disappointment in any one of [my political wishes]. I ascribe my successes wholly to my *perseverance.* I claim this virtue boldly, since all my enemies admit my possessing it at the time they deny me every other virtue or quality of a politician." He had seen first the ship of the United States and now the ship of Pennsylvania safely moored. Let their officers repair the rigging and stop the leaks, he said. "I am only a passenger."[14]

4

The Philadelphia Rush had known since youth had changed considerably in recent years. The population had doubled—from twenty-five thousand to about fifty thousand. New faces had appeared in positions of power and old ones had begun to fade. Morgan died in 1789, and early in 1790 came word from Edinburgh that Cullen had died. This news had hardly been absorbed when Rush learned of the end of the last of his youthful heroes. "Last evening at 11 o'clock died the venerable Dr. Franklin," he wrote on April 18. As a physician, he noted that Franklin "had been reduced by the stone in his bladder, but died finally of a pleurisy which terminated in an abscess in his lungs from which he discharged matter a few days before his death." As a lifelong spokesman on the dangers of night air, Rush could not forbear to add, somewhat smugly, that "this pleurisy was caught with his windows open."[15]

Franklin retained his reason to the end but lost the use of his voice a day or two before death. This distressed Rush, for it prevented Franklin from speaking "of his future existence or expectation beyond the grave." Mrs. Rush wished he had left "a short testimony in favor of Christianity." Her husband felt "that if he had, he would have overset much stronger evidences of its truth, for we are told 'that not many *wise* are called,' and that 'the world by *wisdom* knew not God.'" He brooded for days on Franklin's tenacious attachment to deism. It cheered him to learn (incorrectly) that Franklin's will called for an epitaph that compared his body to the discarded cover of an old book that he hoped would be reissued in a new, more elegant edition, "revised and corrected by the Author." "By this request he has declared his belief in the Christian doctrine of a resurrection," Rush said.

The day after Franklin died, Rush visited the house to view the body. "It was much reduced but not changed," he reported. "Had his beard been shaved after his death, he would have looked himself, but this was forbidden by Mr. Bache [his son-in-law]." He begged for a lock of Franklin's hair, which Bache later gave him. A few strands went to Richard Price in England and a few more to Lafayette in France. Rush had little to say about the funeral except that "the concourse of spectators and followers were supposed to amount to twenty thousand people."[16]

5

These were among the most difficult years in Rush's life. Ostracized from politics, unsettled by the death of old friends, dubious about the new government in New York, startled by the rapidity of change that had descended upon Philadelphia, and uneasy about the apparent imminence of his own death, he retreated into his work as a physician and into his family, which by now had reached considerable proportions. On 3 July 1789 his wife gave birth to another son, Benjamin, who lived only a short time. Benjamin became the fourth of the children—along with Susanna, Elizabeth, and William—to be buried. Five remained among the living—John (aged twelve), Anne Emily (ten), Richard (eight), Mary (five), and James (three). Rush, as usual, missed them terribly during the summer excursions to Morven. All were "affectionate and dutiful and promising," but John continued the pet, a favoritism his father justified on principle. "Where the eldest son or daughter is honored and preferred by parents," he said, "a family is never without government in the absence of parents from home, and when these parents are removed by death there is a foundation laid in the habits of the younger children for a continuance of subordination in a family."[17]

Twenty years later this eldest son, preferred by his parents, would be brought home incurably insane. "Neither the embraces nor tears of your mother, father, sister, nor brother could obtain a word nor even a look from him," Rush wrote to James, then in Edinburgh studying medicine. "This evening we conveyed him to the hospital. . . . I do not despair, with the medical resources of the hospital, of his recovery," he added, but John was a patient there until he died in 1837.[18] Richard, perhaps the least favored of the sons, went on to become American ambassador to Great

Britain and then Secretary of the Treasury under John Quincy Adams, the
son of his father's old friend, ending his career as minister to France.
James, alone of the boys, followed his father's profession though only
desultorily after marrying one of Philadelphia's richest women. Anne
Emily, the elder daughter, married a Canadian and died in Quebec in 1850.
Mary wed a British army officer and moved to England, where she died
in 1849.

Mrs. Rush would give her husband four more children: Benjamin,
who was born in 1791; Julia, in 1792; Samuel, in 1795; and William, in
1801. She was forty-two when her thirteenth and last child was born. She
continued to be everything her husband demanded of a wife—the steel to
his flint, the fire to his mind. "Had I married a fool," he told her one day,
"I never should have disturbed a single sleeping prejudice upon any subject." The strictures preached on female education he practiced with her.
"I long to put Paley's *Moral Philosophy* into your hands," he once wrote
during the annual absence to Morven. "I enjoy it only by halves from not
reading it with you." Reading it would also better qualify her to educate
their children, which his duties prohibited him from overseeing. "By directing *your* studies, therefore, I shall instruct them—and this, too, after
I am removed from them, for I have no idea of surviving you."[19]

His firm ideas about rearing children did not fit with the times. He
believed in rewarding them when they did good. After the age of three or
four, he held, they should never be whipped; solitude seemed a more effective punishment, knowing his own dread for it. He once confined both
John and Richard to their rooms for two full days for some unmentioned
offense. The punishment impressed John so strongly that he begged to be
flogged rather than ever again to be sent to his room.[20]

After 1789, Rush spent nineteen out of twenty evenings at home. He
once described the family scene to John Adams:

> At the same table where I now set, I have had the pleasure of
> seeing my dear Mrs. Rush engaged in reading Millot's "Account
> of the Manners and Laws of the Ancient Egyptians," my eldest
> son plodding over Rollin's "History of Cyrus," and my second
> boy just beginning Goldsmith's *History of England*. In the course
> of the evening, frequent applications were made to me to explain
> hard words to my boys. One of them, who has just finished Ovid

at school, asked me if there was such a river as the Nile or such
a country as Egypt.

That led to some strong remarks he knew Adams would enjoy on the
stupidity of teaching youngsters Latin before they had learned the rudiments of geography. Having aired that sentiment, Rush went on to complete the scene. His eldest daughter sat by "employed in her sewing but
partook in all the conversation of the evening." His mother, now seventy-
five, spent the evening in her room. "She is often indisposed in body, but
all the powers of her mind are in their full vigor," he said. "Such is my
veneration for this excellent parent that I never look forward to that hour
which must perhaps soon part us without feeling an anguish which I cannot describe."[21]

The outward peace radiated by this scene obscured the feelings of a
temporarily embittered man, one who considered himself isolated from
the times, betrayed by friends, and doubly desperate because he now rode
the tides of life without a religious anchor. In 1789 he left the Episcopal
Church "in consequence of an alteration made in the forms of baptism and
the communion service." Thereafter he shuttled between the Episcopal and
Presbyterian churches, without belonging to either. He still attended
services regularly, "but alas! with coldness and formality," he recalled later.
"I was under the influence of an unholy temper, and often wounded the
peace of my mind by yielding to it."[22]

Rush doubtless thought in 1789 that the three recent brushes with
death gave him little time to live. But ahead lay twenty-four years as full
and busy and productive as the quarter of a century behind him. The work
for which posterity would remember him best had only begun. Publication
in 1789 of his *Medical Inquiries and Observations* signaled the new direction his life would take. Medicine would cease to be simply a way to
earn a living. It would supplant politics and humanitarian projects and
become the core of his new life. Out of his college lectures on the theory
and practice of medicine came a new theory of disease that he hoped would
replace Cullen's doctrines and win the fame for him in medicine that
Newton had achieved in physics. That honor never came, but from his
work at the Pennsylvania Hospital, where he supervised the treatment of
the mentally ill, he gathered material for his most famous medical work, a
book on the diseases of the mind. Each year the size of his classes at the col-

lege and the number of those who read his books increased. For good or ill, the most influential physician in the history of American medicine down to the Civil War became Benjamin Rush.

Though his energies poured into new channels after 1790, Rush continued to be the man he was—Dr. Froth to some, Mr. Good Heart to others. His wife still thought he resembled Martin Luther while Rush still preferred to liken himself to that fulminating prophet, Jeremiah, a man of *strife*. His complex personality defied a single assessment, but the judgment of an Irish lady upon an equally contentious contemporary came perhaps as close as possible. "All you call him is true," she said of her friend. "And there are more names still he deserves. But do you remember how alive he was? Ah, so alive he was."

Appendix

Directions for the Treatment of Such Disorders as are Most Common in Pennsylvania, and for Such Complaints as are Common in All Families

DRAWN UP AT THE REQUEST OF
TIMOTHY PICKERING, ESQ.
BY HIS FRIEND
BENJAMIN RUSH

Philadelphia
July 3, 1787

Directions for the Cure of Sundry Common Diseases Suited to Country Gentlemen in the United States

COMMON INTERMITTING FEVER

Begin by giving two or three grains of tartar emetic, dissolved in six tablespoonfuls of water and one spoonful to be taken every twenty minutes, till it pukes two or three times. Work it off with warm water or any kind of weak herb tea.

In habits where *pregnancy,* a disposition to puke or spit *blood,* or *ruptures* forbid the use of vomits, the stomach and bowels may be cleansed by half an ounce of salts or by twenty grains of jalap with five grains of calomel made into a pill with a little soft bread. In case the vomits should operate too harshly at any time, it may easily be checked by giving thirty or forty drops of *laudanum.*

After the above evacuations, give a teaspoonful of *bark* every hour in milk, or anything agreeable in the absence or interval of the fever. If it purges, add two drops of laudanum to each dose; if it binds the bowels, add to each dose two grains of *rhubarb.* In obstinate intermittents, bleed in *winter* and *spring* and use blisters in the *summer* and *autumn.*

INFLAMMATORY FEVER

Bleeding and opening the bowels should begin the cure; afterwards give ten or twelve grains of niter every two hours.

Blisters where the fever is attended with local pain may be applied to the part affected.

COMMON BILIOUS OR REMITTING FEVERS

Bleeding, if the pulse be full and tense, and gentle puke as before directed, and the gentle laxatives before mentioned should begin the cure. If these fail of curing the fever, blisters should be applied to the wrists on the third or fifth day. Afterwards give the bark as before directed.

395

PLEURISY, INFLAMMATORY SORE THROAT, AND RHEUMATISM

The same as inflammatory fever.

PUTRID SORE THROAT

Bleed if the pulse be full and tense. Give gentle pukes of ten grains of ipecacuanha and five grains of calomel every day for two or three days, according to the violence of the disorder. Restrain a lax[ative] by giving ten drops of *laudanum*. Let the throat be kept clean by frequently gargling it with *sage tea* and *vinegar*.

DISCHARGE OF BLOOD

1. *From the lungs:* Bleed if the pulse be full or tense and give a tablespoonful of dry salt and repeat it daily till the discharge ceases.

2. *From the stomach by vomiting:* Give thirty drops of laudanum every hour till it ceases and afterwards open the bowels with a half ounce of salts or fifteen grains of rhubarb.

3. *From the womb:* Give laudanum as in the last case and apply cloths wet with cold *vinegar* or water to the parts adjacent. Enjoin *rest* till the discharge is completely checked.

4. *From the nose:* Thrust a large plug made of rag up the nostril from whence the blood *flows,* or apply a cloth wet with cold water to the neck or armpits.

DYSENTERY

Bleed if the pulse be full or tense and give a half an ounce or six drams of salt or two or three tablespoonfuls of *castor oil* every morning or every other morning or forty drops of *laudanum* every night. Let your patient drink plentifully of weak fresh broth or bran or flaxseed tea.

COLIC

Bleed if the pulse be full or tense and give thirty or forty drops of *laudanum* every half hour till the pain abates. Afterwards open the bowels with salts and cream of tartar or clysters.

CHOLERA MORBUS OR VOMITING AND PURGING

Give thirty or forty drops of laudanum every half hour till the symptoms abate, and let the mint tea be drunk plentifully. This disease frequent among children, to whom laudanum may be given but in much smaller quantity, according to their ages.

WORMS

Give a dose of jalap with five or six grains of calomel in it, according to the age of the patient. The dose of jalap for an adult is half a dram. For all children above two years old from fifteen to twenty-five grains; below two years old it may be a good rule to give nearly the same number of grains of rhubarb and jalap as the children have lived months.

CATARRH OR COLD

Bleed occasionally, if the pulse is hard or full. Abstain from eating meat and butter. Drink freely of bran or flaxseed hysop teas. Take ten grains of niter three or four times a day. When cough attends and is troublesome, take thirty or forty drops of *laudanum* every night at bedtime.

Keep bowels open with the pills made of aloes and soap.

INFLAMED EYES

Bleed as formerly directed and take a purge of jalap or salts. Bathe the eyes frequently with half a pint of water in which half a dram of sugar of lead has been dissolved. If these fail of curing them, small blisters should be applied behind the ear.

TOOTHACHE

If emulsion cannot be practiced, take laudanum in doses of thirty drops till the pain is relieved, and apply a blister behind the ear nearest the part affected.

HEADACHE

Bleed if the pulse be full and tense. Take a purge, apply cold water to the head and go to bed.

BURNS

When much inflamed, wash them frequently with cold water, apply to them a poultice of bread and milk and wash them frequently with lead water prepared as for inflamed eyes.

LOCAL INFLAMMATIONS TENDING TO ABSCESS

Ripen them with a poultice made of bread boiled in beer or stale cider, and a few spoonfuls of strong lye with a little *lard* or *oil* and when ripe open it with a lancet, or a plaster made of flour, *honey* and the yolk of an egg.

PILES

Keep the bowels gently open with *castor oil,* sulphur, or salts, and by no means with aloes. Bathe the part affected with cold water. When the inflammation is reduced apply an ointment made of equal parts of tar and hog's lard and after the bowels are open if the pain continues give a dose of *laudanum.* . . .

WHOOPING COUGH

Bleed when the pulse is hard and full, give occasionally gentle pukes or a few grains of ipecac; open the bowels when costive with small doses of rhubarb and calomel; give gentle anodynes of laudanum at bedtime.

The *radical cure* for this disorder is change of air and exercise, purges occasionally, and abstain from animal food and butter. . . .

ITCH

Anoint the part affected with sulphur and hog's lard or anoint the inside of the wrists, elbows, and knees for three successive nights with mercurial ointment.

APHTHA OR SORE MOUTH

Purge the bowels gently with rhubarb. Touch the sores in the mouth frequently with molasses or with molasses and water in which a little salt-peter (niter) has been dissolved.

LOCKED JAW

Bleed if the pulse be full or tense. Give bark and wine in large doses and excite inflammation in the part which has been wounded (if it arises from a wound) by applying spirits of *turpentine* to it. Use likewise the *cold bath.* Opium and laudanum which has been used so much in this disorder seldom does much service, but it may be given to ease pain.

Philadelphia

Benjamin Rush

July 4th, 1787

Bibliography

and

Notes

B ENJAMIN RUSH left behind one of the largest collections of private
papers to come down from eighteenth-century America. The material held by the Library Company of Philadelphia, now on deposit at the
Historical Society of Pennsylvania, centers around forty-five thick volumes of
correspondence, comprised mainly of letters to Rush, and some twenty boxes
of papers that range from land leases, calling cards, and invitations—Rush
saved everything—to unpublished medical lectures. There are in addition
series of ledgers and account books that list Rush's medical patients, their
illnesses, his diagnoses, and his prescriptions as well as a number of notebooks that contain such material as drafts of essays and letters, snatches of
autobiography, intermittently kept diaries, and household accounts.

This only taps the lode. Rush's letters, literally hundreds of them, can
be found in libraries scattered through virtually all the thirteen original
states. His collected published essays add up to seven volumes, and seven
more could probably be produced if fugitive writings in contemporary
newspapers and magazines were also gathered between hard covers.

Nathan G. Goodman deserves honor for charting a course through
this sea of paper. His biography, published in 1934, was the first full study
of Rush. Anyone who has followed the route Goodman pioneered knows
the high quality of his work. Others who have since written on Rush—
notably James Thomas Flexner, whose essay in *Doctors on Horseback*
(1937) remains the best brief sketch, and Dr. Carl Binger, who contributed
the insights of a psychiatrist to his sympathetic study published in 1966—
have followed Goodman's lead and drawn on his research.

Groundwork for a more extensive biography has since been laid by
two other scholars. George W. Corner made an indispensable contribution
with his edition of *The Autobiography of Benjamin Rush. His "Travels
Through Life" together with his* Commonplace Book *for 1789–1813*
(1948). This was soon followed by the equally splendid two-volume edition of selected *Letters of Benjamin Rush* (1951), edited with skill and

grace by Lyman H. Butterfield. Today anyone who studies Rush must give deep thanks to Goodman, Corner, and Butterfield. Scholars who have written specialized essays on various aspects of Rush's multifaceted career also deserve thanks. The work done during the past thirty-five years has made it possible at last to present a full-length study of one of the least known of the Founding Fathers.

Several abbreviations have been introduced into the notes that follow. Benjamin Rush, for instance, becomes BR; the Historical Society of Pennsylvania becomes HSP; the *Pennsylvania Magazine of History and Biography* becomes *PMHB*. Quotations from correspondence in the Butterfield volumes are noted as from the *Letters* and those from Corner's edition of *The Autobiography* as from *Auto*. Citations from the manuscripts at the HSP have required a more complicated shorthand. A footnote that reads, for example, 41 BR-MSS 13 indicates that the material comes from volume 41 of Rush's correspondence, page 13.

STARTING OUT

1. Youth: 1746–1760

A genealogy of the Rush family is found in *A Memorial containing Travels through Life, or Sundry Incidents in the Life of Dr. Benjamin Rush . . . Written by Himself . . .* (1905), edited by Louis Alexander Biddle. The little else that can be turned up about Rush's ancestors comes principally from his *Autobiography* and *Letters.* Information about the Rush family in Byberry Township is presented in Joseph C. Martindale's *History of Byberry and Moreland* (1867). The maternal side of Rush's family tree is covered in J. Hall Pleasants, "Hall Family of Tacony, Philadelphia County, Pennsylvania," *William and Mary Quarterly,* 1st ser. 22 (1913), pp. 265–268.

An important and also provocative work is Alan Heimert's *Religion and the American Mind from the Great Awakening to the Revolution* (1966); it is especially helpful in its perspective on Finley and Davies. Another excellent, useful volume is Leonard J. Trinterud's *The Forming of an American Tradition—A Re-examination of Colonial Presbyterianism* (1949). No full-length study of Finley has been made, but sketches of the man can be found in William B. Sprague's *Annals of the American Pulpit* (9 vols., 1857–1869), vol. 3, pp. 96–101, and in Archibald Alexander's *Biographical Sketches of the Founder and Principal Alumni of the Log College* (1845). Rush's *Autobiography* gives the fullest account of Nottingham Academy.

Rush said surprisingly little about his days at the College of New Jersey. The best general study of the school in its early years is by Thomas J. Wertenbaker, *Princeton 1746–1896* (1946), but the most complete on the years Rush attended is in John MacLean's *History of the College of New Jersey, from its Origin in 1746 to the Commencement of 1854* (2 vols., 1877). William H. Foote's references to Davies in *Sketches of Virginia, Historical and Biographical* (1850) can be supplemented by those in MacLean, Trinterud, and Sprague. The only detailed study of Davies is G. H. Bost's "Samuel Davies, Colonial Revivalist and Champion of Religious Toleration," a 1942 Ph.D. dissertation at the University of Chicago Library. Rush's remarks on Davies' innovations are analyzed by Francis L. Broderick's "Pulpit, Physics, and Politics: The Curriculum of the College of New Jersey, 1746–1794," *William and Mary Quarterly*, 3rd. ser. 6 (1949), pp. 42–68. Sketches of Rush and his classmates are given in Samuel Davies Alexander's *Princeton College during the Eighteenth Century* (1872).

1. BR to John Adams, 26 December 1811, *Letters.*

2. BR to Noah Webster, 13 February 1788; to Enoch Green, 1761; to John Montgomery, 27 June 1783; to Thomas Jefferson, 6 October 1800—all in *Letters.* "Croaking frogs": Albert Cook Myers, ed., *Sally Wister's Journal . . . 1777–1778* (1902), p. 35.

3. BR to Adams, 8 August and 13 July 1812, *Letters.*

4. *Auto.,* p. 24; BR to Jefferson, 6 October 1800, *Letters;* Mary Manning to BR, 27 January 1802, 11 BR-MSS 25; BR to wife, 1 June 1776, *Letters;* BR to Jefferson, 6 October 1800, ibid.

5. BR to Adams, 8 August 1812, ibid.

6. BR to Adams, 13 July 1812, ibid.; *Auto.,* pp. 25, 26, 27n, 167, 293.

7. David Ramsay to James Rush, 10 July 1813, Robert L. Brunhouse, ed., *David Ramsay, 1749–1815. A Selection from his Writings,* in American Philosophical Society *Transactions* n.s. 55 (1965), p. 176.

8. BR to Adams, 13 July 1812, *Letters;* J. F. Watson, *Annals of Philadelphia and Pennsylvania in the Olden Time* (2 vols., 1857), vol. 2, p. 376; J. Thomas Scharf and Thompson Westcott, *History of Philadelphia, 1609–1884* (3 vols., 1884), vol. 1, p. 213.

9. BR to Adams, 13 July 1812, *Letters.*

10. Carl Bridenbaugh, *Cities in Revolt* (1955), pt. 1, *passim;* [Jacob Duché], *Caspipina's Letters Containing Observations on a Variety of Subjects* (1777), p. 3.

11. *Pennsylvania Gazette,* 15 May 1776.

12. Carl Bridenbaugh, ed., *Gentleman's Progress. The Itinerarium of Dr. Alexander Hamilton, 1774* (1948), p. 21.

13. Ibid., pp. 22, 23–24.

14. Ibid., p. 20.

15. *Auto.,* pp. 24, 27, 168; *Letters,* p. 1153n.

16. *Auto.,* pp. 26, 27, 168; *Pennsylvania Gazette,* 24 October 1751.

17. *Auto.,* pp. 27–28, 166.

18. Ibid., p. 88.

19. Davies, *Religion and Public Spirit,* quoted in Heimert, *Religion and the American Mind,* p. 329.

20. Tennent, Davies, and Finley as quoted in Heimert, *Religion and the American Mind,* pp. 51, 32, 305.

21. Gilbert Tennent, *Danger of an Unconverted Ministry* (1740).

22. *Auto.,* pp. 32, 34, 190. For a biographical sketch of Finley see Sprague, *Annals of the American Pulpit,* vol. 3, pp. 96–101.

23. *Auto.,* pp. 29–30; BR to wife, 31 July 1791, *Letters.*

24. *Auto.,* pp. 30, 31, 32.

25. Ibid., p. 31. For BR's later thoughts on Finley see "A Dream Containing a Dialogue between Dr. Sam. Finley, Rev. Sam. Davies, Dr. Wm. Cullen and Dr. B. Rush," in "Letters and Thoughts," BR-MSS 70.

26. BR to Adams, 21 July 1789, *Letters; Auto.,* p. 33; BR to B. R. Floyd, 21 April 1812, *Letters.* For Finley's recommendation to president of the College of New Jersey, see Finley to Jacob Green, 26 April 1759, *PMHB* 70 (1946), p. 85.

27. Quoted in Wertenbaker, *Princeton,* p. 39.

28. *Auto.,* p. 36.

29. Jackson Turner Main, *Social Structure of Revolutionary America* (1965), pp. 246–247, 117, 118.

30. BR, "Oration . . . on the Moral Faculty," *Medical Inquiries and Observations* (1789 ed.), p. 46; BR to Walter Minto, 24 March and 24 September 1792, *Letters.*

31. BR to Enoch Green, 1761, ibid.

32. *Auto.,* p. 35.

33. Davies' diary in Foote, *Sketches of Virginia,* p. 285; Davies on Negroes quoted in Winthrop D. Jordan, *White Over Black* (1968), p. 188.

34. Davies' sermon *Curse of Cowardice* (1755), from Trinterud, *Forming of an American Tradition,* p. 134. Quotation on Washington is in James Thomas Flexner, *George Washington: The Forge of Experience (1732–1775)* (1965), p. 134.

35. Ashbel Green, *Discourses* (1822), quoted in Wertenbaker, *Princeton,* p. 45.

36. *Auto.,* p. 36. For Davies' affection for poetry of Young and Thomson see Heimert, *Religion and the American Mind,* p. 173.

37. BR, "A Lecture" (ca. 1795), quoted in Harry G. Good, *Benjamin Rush and His Services to American Education* (1918), p. 241; the "Synoptical," dated 3 July 1760, is found in Box 9 (1760–1794), BR-MSS.

38. *Auto.,* p. 36; Davies' views on government, as recalled by BR, are in "A Dream Containing a Dialogue . . .," in "Letters and Thoughts," BR-MSS 70.

39. BR to Enoch Green, 1761, *Letters.*

40. Quotations from Davies' *Religion and Public Spirit. A Valedictory Address . . .* come from a copy printed in Portsmouth, New Hampshire, 1762, now in the Rare Book Room of Dartmouth College Library.

41. The anonymous report appeared in the *Pennsylvania Gazette,* 9 October 1760.

2. Apprenticeship: 1760–1766

William S. Middleton's "John Redman," *Annals of Medical History* 10 (1926), pp. 213–223, contains several excellent excerpts from contemporary reports on the doctor, but the fullest, most recent account of him is in Whitfield J. Bell, Jr., "John Redman, Medical Preceptor, 1722–1808," *PMHB* 81 (1957), pp. 157–169. Bell's annotation refers to almost all the material in print and manuscript relevant to Redman.

Cecil K. Drinker writes of the quality of Philadelphia health and medicine during the eighteenth century in *Not So Long Ago* (1937), drawing much from the contemporary diary of an ancestor. Carl and Jessica Bridenbaugh's *Rebels and Gentlemen. Philadelphia in the Age of Franklin* (1942), gives in chapter 8, "The Medical Profession: A Coalition of Able Men," the best secondary account, which, though unannotated, has a full bibliographical essay. John Duffy's *Epidemics in Colonial America* (1953) is especially helpful in equating colonial with modern nomenclature of diseases. Richard Shryock's "Eighteenth Century Medicine in America," *Proceedings of the American Antiquarian Society* 59 (1949), pp. 275–292, can be supplemented by his *Medicine and Society in America 1660–1860* (1954); both are of great use. Rush reveals most of the little that is known about medical apprentices' work in the early pages of his *Autobiography;* he also gives one of the fullest accounts of medicine in Philadelphia from 1760 to 1766 in the final volume of his *Medical Inquiries and Observations* (4 vols., 2nd ed., 1805). Redman wrote *An Account of the Yellow Fever as it Prevailed in Philadelphia in the Autumn of 1762* (1865) some thirty years after the event. Rush summarizes the same epidemic in *An Account of the Bilious Remitting Yellow Fever . . . in . . . 1793, Medical Inquiries and Observations* (1805 ed.), vol. 3, pp. 13–14, drawn from an apparently lost notebook kept during his apprenticeship.

David Riesman offers a brief, admiring introduction to *Thomas Sydenham* (1926). Kenneth Dewhurst's excellent "Thomas Sydenham (1624–1689), Reformer of Clinical Medicine," *Medical History* 6 (1962), pp. 101–118, carries a lengthy bibliography. Essays on Sydenham are also found in Knud Faber, *Nosography in Modern Internal Medicine* (1923); Henry E. Sigerist, *The Great Doctors. A Biographical History of Medicine*

(1933); and Charles-Edward Amory Winslow, *The Conquest of Epidemic Disease. A Chapter in the History of Ideas* (1943). Of the three, Winslow's excels. Sydenham's writings are most easily consulted in the edition edited by Rush in 1809. The latest evaluation of Hermann Boerhaave appears in Lester S. King, *The Medical World of the Eighteenth Century* (1958), wherein the physician is discussed both as a systematist and as a scientist.

Rush's eulogy to Gilbert Tennent appears at the end of Finley's sermon, *The Successful Minister of Christ Distinguished in Glory . . .* (1764), under the title *Funeral Eulogy, Sacred to the Memory of the Late Reverend Gilbert Tennent*. Though signed only "by a gentleman of Philadelphia," David Ramsay revealed the author in his *Eulogium* of Rush (1813), p. 136.

The most comprehensive account of Shippen appears in the introduction and annotation of Betsey Copping Corner's *William Shippen, Jr., Pioneer in American Medical Education. With Notes and the Original Text of Shippen's Student Diary, London, 1759–1760; together with a translation of his Edinburgh Dissertation, 1761* (1951). Bell has also explored Morgan's career with thoroughness in *John Morgan, Continental Doctor* (1965). The Johns Hopkins Press reprint (1937) of Morgan's *A Discourse upon the Institution of Medical Schools in America* (1765) contains not only his commencement address outlining the plan for a medical school but also the lengthy Preface wherein he defends his plan for specialization in medicine. George W. Corner's *Two Centuries of Medicine. A History of the School of Medicine, University of Pennsylvania* (1965) offers the latest and best treatment of the College of Philadelphia's medical department.

1. John Sanderson, *Biography of the Signers of the Declaration of Independence* (5 vols., 2nd ed., 1828), vol. 3, p. 29; *Autobiography of Charles Biddle* (1883), p. 223; T. L. Wharton, *A Memoir of William Rawle* (1840), p. 25.

2. BR to Enoch Green, 1761, *Letters; Auto.,* p. 36.

3. *Ibid.,* pp. 36–37; Finley to BR, 30 January 1761, 33 BR-MSS 79; BR to Enoch Green, 1761, *Letters.*

4. Finley to BR, 30 January 1761, 33 BR-MSS 79; *Auto.,* p. 37.

5. Middleton, "John Redman," pp. 218, 222; BR to Hazard, 21 May 1765, *Letters.*

6. Bell, "John Redman," pp. 157–160.

7. Redman to BR, 4 April 1767, 22 BR-MSS 10; Redman to Morgan, 13 March 1764, quoted in Bell, "John Redman," p. 166.

8. *Auto.*, p. 38.

9. J. F. Watson, *Annals of Philadelphia* (2 vols., 1857), vol. 2, p. 374; Drinker, *Not So Long Ago*, p. 43; Isaac Cathrall's medical handbook (1799) quoted in King, *Medical World*, pp. 318–319; Henry Burnell Shafer, *American Medical Profession, 1783 to 1850* (1936), pp. 97, 101.

10. BR, *Medical Inquiries and Observations* (1815 ed.), vol. 4, pp. 229–231; vol. 3, p. 125.

11. Redman, *Account of Yellow Fever*, pp. 11, 29, 30. Mention of closed schools appears in Alexander Graydon, *Memoirs of His Own Times* (1846 ed.), p. 43.

12. BR to Hazard, 27 September 1762, *Letters.*

13. *Auto.*, p. 38.

14. Dr. Thomas Young, "To the Public," *Pennsylvania Journal*, 5 July 1775.

15. William Douglass, *A Summary, Historical and Political, . . . of the British Settlements of North-America* (2 vols., 1749–1752), vol. 2, pp. 352, 394; Bridenbaugh, ed., *Gentleman's Progress*, p. 116.

16. Advertisement quoted in Corner, *William Shippen, Jr.*, p. 100; *Auto.*, p. 322; *Pennsylvania Gazette,* 2 December 1762, as quoted in Harold Donaldson Eberlein and Cortlandt V. D. Hubbard, *Diary of Independence Hall* (1948), p. 107.

17. BR to Hazard, 7 November and 2 August 1764, *Letters.*

18. Edward B. Krumbhaar, "The State of Pathology in the British Colonies of North America," *Science, Medicine and History*, vol. 2, p. 131; Jacques Pierre Brissot de Warville, *New Travels in the United States of America, 1788* (1964), p. 279; BR to Vine Utley, 25 June 1812, *Letters.*

19. BR to Hazard, 19 March 1765, ibid.

20. BR to Hazard, 21 May 1765, ibid.

21. Ibid.; Watson, *Annals of Philadelphia,* vol. 2, p. 376.

22. Bell, *Morgan*, pp. 77, 74, 107.

23. Quotations are from Morgan's *Discourse* and the long Preface he added to the published version to justify his vision.

24. Redman to Morgan, 13 March 1764, quoted in Bell, *Morgan*, p. 113; Bell, "An Eighteenth Century American Medical Manuscript. The Clinical Notebook of John Archer, M.B., 1768," *The Library Chronicle of the Friends of the University of Pennsylvania Library* 22 (1956), p. 2; BR to Hazard, 21 May 1765, *Letters.*

25. *Pennsylvania Gazette,* 9 May 1765, quoted in Bell, *Morgan,* p. 117.

26. Morgan, *A Discourse.*

27. Bonds and mortgages in 34 BR-MSS 82 (for £500, dated 1774); p. 83 (bond of Richard Morris, 1770); p. 84 (bond of Richard Morris, 1759); p. 88 (Mrs. Morris sells a town lot, 1767); p. 95 (bond for £200, dated 1773); p. 96 (bond for

£200, dated 1774); p. 104 (bond for £700, dated 1773); and p. 105 (mortgage, 1777). These suggest that BR's mother Susanna Morris and possibly his step-father floated loans to help pay for his education at Princeton, as an apprentice with Redman, and abroad.

28. BR to Hazard, 21 May 1765; BR to Thomas Bradford, 15 April 1768, both in *Letters*.

29. BR to Hazard, 21 May and 27 June 1765, ibid.

30. BR to Hazard, 27 June and 8 November 1765, ibid.

31. Trinterud, *Forming of an American Tradition*, p. 237.

32. BR to Hazard, 8 and 18 November 1765, *Letters*.

33. BR mentions the society to Hazard, 10 April 1765, ibid.; it is also discussed in Corner, *Two Centuries of Medicine*, p. 30.

34. BR to Hazard, 23 January, 22 February, 30 March 1766, 39 BR-MSS 17, 18, and 19; *Auto.*, p. 164.

35. BR to Hazard, 29 March 1766, *Letters*.

36. BR to Hazard, 2 July 1766; BR to Montgomery, 5 August 1801; BR to wife, 15 August 1791, ibid.

37. BR to Hazard, 2 July 1766, ibid.; *Auto.*, p. 33; BR, "Contrast between the Death of a Deist and a Christian, David Hume and Samuel Finley," *United States Magazine* (February 1779), pp. 65–72.

3. Edinburgh: 1766–1768

Rush's reports on the Edinburgh years in the *Letters* and *Autobiography* can be supplemented by his Scottish Journal, located at Indiana University Library. The best brief secondary account is Josiah C. Trent, "Benjamin Rush in Edinburgh, 1766–1768," in *Science, Medicine and History: Essays on the Evolution of Scientific Thought and Medical Practice in Honour of Charles Singer* (2 vols., 1953), edited by E. Ashworth Underwood, vol. 2, pp. 179–185. Whitfield J. Bell, Jr., has written two useful articles and edited a third: "Some American Students of 'That Shining Oracle of Physic,' Dr. William Cullen of Edinburgh, 1755–1766," *Proceedings of the American Philosophical Society* 94 (1950), pp. 275–281; "Philadelphia Medical Students in Europe, 1750–1800," *PMHB* 67 (1943), pp. 1–29; and especially "Thomas Parke's Student Life in England and Scotland, 1771–1773," *PMHB* 75 (1951), pp. 237–259. Samuel Bard's letters to his father in John McVickar's *A Domestic Narrative of the Life of Sam-*

uel Bard (1822) describe university life from the viewpoint of a New York. An excellent and helpful secondary work is Henry Gray Graham, *The Social Life of Scotland in the Eighteenth Century* (2 vols., 1900).

John Thomson's *An Account of the Life, Lectures and Writings of William Cullen, M.D.* (2 vols., 1832–1859) presents the fullest treatment of Rush's hero. The early judgments in the Scottish Journal are amplified by Rush's eulogy to Cullen delivered in 1790, and found in his *Essays, Literary, Moral and Philosophical* (1798), pp. 321–343. R. W. Johnstone's "William Cullen," *Medical History* 3 (1959), pp. 33–46, offers a recent, brief, and competent estimate. Cullen's nosology is discussed by Walther Riese, "History and Principles of Classification of Nervous Diseases," *Bulletin of the History of Medicine* 18 (1945), pp. 465–512; in Edgar Goldschmid's "Nosologia Naturalis" in Underwood, ed., *Science, Medicine and History*, vol. 2, pp. 103–122; and in the volumes of Shryock and King mentioned in chapter 2.

Joseph Black is authoritatively summarized in J. R. Partington, *A History of Chemistry* (4 vols., 1961–1964), vol. 3, pp. 109–159, and by Henry, Lord Brougham in *Great Chemists* (1961), edited by Eduard Farber, pp. 211–226.

Lyman H. Butterfield's *John Witherspoon Comes to America. A Documentary Account Based Largely on New Materials* (1953) details Witherspoon's relations with Rush and, in passing, describes the religious scene of Scotland as it relates to America. Butterfield's "Love and Valor; or Benjamin Rush and the Leslies of Edinburgh," appeared in the *Princeton University Library Chronicle* 9 (1947–1948), pp. 1–12.

The subject of digestion and the eighteenth century's views on it are discussed briefly by King and at some length in Michael Foster's *Lectures on the History of Physiology* (1901), pp. 200–223. Donald G. Bates, "The Background to John Young's Thesis on Digestion," *Bulletin of the History of Medicine* 36 (1962), pp. 341–361, has considerably more material relevant to Rush than the title indicates. David F. Musto's "Benjamin Rush's Medical Thesis, 'On the Digestion of Food in the Stomach,' Edinburgh, 1768," College of Physicians of Philadelphia, *Transactions and Studies* 33 (1965), pp. 121–138, accompanies his translation of BR's dissertation with a superb historical introduction, which makes the point that the essay "carried little influence."

1. The material in this section is drawn from *Auto.,* pp. 39–42; BR to Bradford, 25 October 1766, in Lyman H. Butterfield, "Further Letters of Benjamin Rush," *PMHB* 78 (1954), pp. 7–10; BR's Scottish Journal; BR to Bradford, 2 September 1766, and BR to Franklin, 22 October 1766, *Letters.*

2. BR to [?], 29 December 1766, ibid.

3. Sanderson, *Biography of the Signers,* vol. 3, p. 88; *Auto.,* pp. 51–52; BR, *Sermons to Gentlemen upon Temperance and Exercise* (1772).

4. BR to [?], 29 December 1766, *Letters.*

5. BR to trustees of Dickinson College, 21 October 1786, ibid.; BR, "An Eulogium upon . . . Cullen," *Essays, Literary, Moral and Philosophical,* p. 335; BR to Morgan, 16 November 1766, *Letters.*

6. Ibid.

7. BR to Jonathan Bayard Smith, 30 April 1767, ibid.

8. Bell, ed., "Thomas Parke," p. 249; Scottish Journal, p. 70.

9. Ibid., pp. 73, 72–73.

10. Thomas S. Kuhn, *The Structure of Scientific Revolutions* (1962), pp. 69, 70; Bell, ed., "Thomas Parke," p. 249; Scottish Journal, p. 71.

11. BR to Smith, 30 April 1767, *Letters;* manuscript notes of BR's chemistry lectures, 1771, quoted in Trent, "BR in Edinburgh," p. 182.

12. Scottish Journal, pp. 57, 64, 55.

13. Samuel Miller, *Brief Retrospect of the Eighteenth Century* (2 vols., 1803), vol. 2, pp. 281–282.

14. Riese, "Nervous Diseases," pp. 468–469.

15. Samuel Bard to his parents, 5 December 1762, McVickar, *Bard,* pp. 36–37; BR to Smith, 30 April 1767, *Letters.*

16. *Auto.,* pp. 42–43.

17. Ibid., pp. 47–48; Scottish Journal, pp. 75–145; BR to Smith, 30 April 1767, and BR to Lady Jane Belsches, 21 April 1784, *Letters.*

18. *Auto.,* pp. 47–50; Scottish Journal, pp. 75–145; Michael Kraus, *The Atlantic Civilization: Eighteenth Century Origins* (1949), p. 223.

19. *Auto.,* pp. 47, 164; Scottish Journal, pp. 66–67.

20. BR to Samuel Fisher, 28 July 1768, *Letters;* Scottish Journal, pp. 28–29; Walter Jones to Thomas Jones, 15 August 1766, as quoted in Main, *Social Structure,* p. 146; BR to Morgan, 20 January 1768, *Letters.*

21. *Auto.,* p. 46.

22. BR's certificate of membership is found in Box 9 (1760–1794) of BR-MSS.

23. BR to Smith, 30 April 1767, *Letters;* Butterfield, *Witherspoon,* xii, quoting from Green in Sprague, *Annals of the American Pulpit,* vol. 3, p. 297.

24. BR to Witherspoon, 25 March 1767, *Letters.*

25. BR to Witherspoon, 23 April 1767, ibid.

26. Scottish Journal, pp. 31–32; *Auto.,* pp. 50–51; Witherspoon to Charles Nisbet, 25 May 1767, quoted in Butterfield, "The Reputation of BR," *Pennsylvania History* 17 (1950), p. 3.

27. Scottish Journal, p. 30; BR to Morgan, 20 January 1768, *Letters.*

28. Samuel Bard to John Bard, 4 February 1764, McVickar, *Bard,* pp. 55–56.

29. *Pennsylvania Journal,* 11 June 1772.

30. BR to Morgan, 20 January 1768, *Letters;* Redman to BR, 21 December 1767 and 12 May 1768, 22 BR-MSS 10 and 11.

31. BR to Witherspoon, 30 April 1768, *Letters;* BR to Hazard, 21 April 1768, ibid.; Witherspoon to BR, 18 May 1768, Butterfield, *Witherspoon,* p. 75.

32. Samuel Bard to John Bard, 15 May 1765, McVickar, *Bard,* pp. 68–69.

33. Scottish Journal, pp. 33–34; *Auto.,* p. 43.

34. BR to Morgan, 20 January 1768, *Letters.*

35. BR to Colina Campbell Hogg, 5 July 1768, Butterfield, ed., "Further Letters," p. 11.

36. BR to Bradford, 15 April and 3 June 1768, *Letters.*

37. BR to Bradford, 15 April and 3 June 1768; BR to Morgan, 16 November 1766 and 20 January 1768, all ibid.

38. BR to Morgan, 27 July 1768, ibid.; Morgan to BR, 10 May 1769, 25 BR-MSS 1.

39. BR to Hazard, 14 June 1768, 39 BR-MSS 22.

40. BR to Morgan, 27 July 1768, *Letters; Auto.,* p. 43; BR to James Rush, 19 March 1810, *Letters.*

4. London and Paris: 1768–1769

William L. Sachse's *The Colonial American in Britain* (1956) is a meticulous account of its subject and of some relevance here. Arnold Chaplin, *Medicine in London during the Reign of George III* (1919), places Rush's experience in the context of the times. An even clearer picture emerges in "Thomas Parke's Student Life in England and Scotland, 1771–1773," edited by Whitfield J. Bell, Jr., *PMHB* 75 (1951), pp. 237–259.

The Hunter brothers are discussed in George C. Peachey's *A Memoir of John and William Hunter* (1924) and more recently in a popular biography by John Kobler, *The Reluctant Surgeon. A Biography of John Hunter* (1960), which deals as much with William Hunter and the medical world of the eighteenth century, with Edinburgh as well as London, as it does with the subject of its title. The best contemporary discussion of the Hunter-Hewson research on lymphatic glands appears in Samuel Miller, *Brief Retrospect of the Eighteenth Century* (2 vols., 1803), vol. 1, pp. 208–211. Two short but useful accounts of London surgeons and hospitals are by Leo M. Zimmerman, "Surgeons and the Rise of Clinical Teaching in England," *Bulletin of the History of Medicine* 37 (1963), pp. 167–177, and Genevieve Miller, "Medical Education and the Rise of Hospitals. The Eighteenth Century," *Journal of American Medical Association* 186 (7 December 1963), pp. 938–942.

R. Hingston Fox's *Dr. John Fothergill and his Friends. Chapters in Eighteenth Century Life* (1919) is still the most complete work to date on Fothergill. Thomas Joseph Pettigrew's *Memoirs of the Life and Writings of the Late John Coakley Lettsom, M.D. . . . With a Selection from His Correspondence* (3 vols., 1817) contains some twenty letters from Rush, though all were written at a later date than the period covered in this chapter. Lettsom's own memories of his friend are found in the slim volume, *Recollections of Dr. Rush* (1815). The most recent biography is by James Johnston Abraham, *Lettsom: His Life, Times, Friends, and Descendants* (1933), but an excellent brief introduction is Josiah C. Trent's "John Coakley Lettsom," *Bulletin of the History of Medicine* 22 (1948), pp. 528–542.

On Mrs. Macaulay, see Lucy M. Donnelly, "The Celebrated Mrs. Macaulay," *William and Mary Quarterly* 6 (1949), pp. 173–207. A solid account of Rush's day with Johnson is found in Lyman H. Butterfield's privately printed essay *Reminiscences of Boswell and Johnson* (1936). The Quaker druggists, Timothy Bevan and sons, are described in Ernest C. Cripps, *Plough Court: The Story of a Notable Pharmacy* (1927).

The Pierpont Morgan Library of New York City possesses the Rush journal of his trip to Paris, a copy of which is also on deposit at the Historical Society of Pennsylvania. A major part of the diary has been reprinted in Dagobert D. Runes, ed., *The Selected Writings of Benjamin Rush* (1947), pp. 373–395, under the title "On Manners."

1. Richard Peters to Timothy Pickering, 7 October 1797, quoted in *Letters*, p. 1210.
2. BR to Morgan, 27 July 1768, ibid.; *Auto.*, p. 52.
3. Isaac Chanler to BR, 27 April 1770, 3 BR-MSS 45; Kobler, *Reluctant Surgeon*, p. 166; Corner, *William Shippen, Jr.*, pp. 66–67; *Auto.*, p. 53.

4. BR to Morgan, 21 October 1768, *Letters.*

5. *Auto.,* pp. 52–53; see especially Corner's footnote on p. 53.

6. *Auto.,* p. 53. Bell, ed., "Thomas Parke," and Corner, *William Shippen, Jr.,* both give a full account of the life of the medical student in mid-century London.

7. *Auto.,* pp. 53, 54; BR to Morgan, 21 October 1768, *Letters.*

8. BR to Morgan, 21 October 1768, *Letters.*

9. Ibid.; BR, "Containing the New Method of Inoculating for the Smallpox . . . 1781," in appendix of *Medical Inquiries and Observations* (1789), p. 7; Carl Binger, *Revolutionary Doctor, Benjamin Rush* (1966), p. 77.

10. Benjamin Waterhouse to Joseph Willard, 20 August 1822, quoted in Butterfield, "The Reputation of BR," p. 3; *Auto.,* p. 55.

11. Betty Fothergill, quoted in Abraham, *Lettsom,* p. 87; Lettsom, *Recollections,* pp. 5–6.

12. BR to Samuel Fisher, 28 July 1768, *Letters; Auto.,* p. 55.

13. *Auto.,* p. 63; Lyman H. Butterfield, "The American Interests of the Firm of E. and C. Dilly, . . ." Bibliographical Society of America, *Papers* 45 (1951), pp. 285, 286, 288, 290.

14. *Auto.,* pp. 58–59.

15. BR to James Abercrombie, 22 April 1793, *Letters; Auto.,* pp. 58–60.

16. *Auto.,* p. 60.

17. BR to Hazard, 22 October 1768, *Letters.*

18. Ibid.

19. Heimert, *Religion and the American Mind,* p. 357; *Auto.,* p. 62; *Pennsylvania Gazette,* 3 July 1779.

20. *Auto.,* p. 61; Donnelly, "Mrs. Macaulay," p. 181.

21. BR to Mrs. Macaulay, 18 January 1769, *Letters.*

22. *Auto.,* pp. 61–62; BR to [Jacob Rush], 19 January 1769, *Letters.*

23. BR to [Jacob Rush], 19 and 26 January 1769, *Letters.* They appeared in the *Pennsylvania Journal,* 30 March and 6 April 1769.

24. Ibid.

25. *Auto.,* p. 66.

26. The material that follows on the Paris trip comes from BR's account in the *Auto.,* pp. 66–73, and the copy of his journal at the HSP.

27. BR to John Adams, 21 July 1789, *Letters.*

28. *Auto.,* pp. 73, 74.

29. *Auto.,* p. 69; Fothergill to James Pemberton, 16 May 1769, quoted in Butterfield, "The Reputation of BR," p. 4.

30. *Auto.,* pp. 74–77.

31. Ibid., pp. 77–78; James Thacher, *American Medical Biography, or Memoirs of*

Eminent Physicians who have Flourished in America (2 vols., 1828; reprint ed., 1967), vol. 2, pp. 56–57.

32. Quoted in Thacher, *American Medical Biography,* vol. 2, p. 57.

5. Fledgling Physician: 1769–1773

Records of Rush's professional practice are found in the account and daybooks on deposit at the Historical Society of Pennsylvania. Journal A, used for this chapter and the next, covers his daily visits from August 1769 to June 1774. His habit was to keep a rough daily account of visits—listing the patient, the illness, and the prescribed treatment—which was later written up in the ledger by an apprentice. Rush's extant ledgers extend to nineteen volumes.

Historians of chemistry in America have paid full attention to Rush. Herbert S. Klickstein discusses him along with other early chemists in "A Short History of the Professorship of Chemistry of the University of Pennsylvania School of Medicine, 1765–1847," *Bulletin of the History of Medicine* 27 (1953), pp. 43–68. Wyndham Miles expands his brief remarks in "Joseph Black, Benjamin Rush and the Teaching of Chemistry at the University of Pennsylvania," *The Library Chronical of the Friends of the University of Pennsylvania Library* 22 (1956), pp. 9–18, in the more detailed "Benjamin Rush, Chemist," *Chymia* 4 (1953), pp. 37–77. All three articles are elaborately annotated. Donald J. D'Elia's "Dr. Benjamin Rush's Key to a Thousand Sources of Knowledge," *Journal of General Education* 19 (1967), pp. 112–118, one of several excellent articles on Rush, discusses the relationship of chemistry to his general thought. A facsimile reprint of the 1770 edition of Rush's *Syllabus of a Course of Lectures on Chemistry* has been published (1954) with an introduction by Lyman H. Butterfield and a bibliographical note by Robert F. Sutton.

For general accounts of American physicians Rush knew and corresponded with, see the essays written by contemporaries in James Thacher, *American Medical Biography, or Memoirs of Eminent Physicians who have Flourished in America* (2 vols., 1828; reprinted in 1 vol., 1967). These sketches can be supplemented by Maurice Bear Gordon, *Aesculapius Comes to the Colonies* (1949). The correspondence of Lionel Chalmers, Rush's wise friend from South Carolina, should be read in conjunction with Joseph

Ioor Waring's "Lionel Chalmers, Medical Author," *Bulletin of the History of Medicine* 32 (1958), pp. 349–355.

Rush's apprentices are listed, along with his occasional brief characterizations of them, in James E. Gibson, "Benjamin Rush's Apprenticed Students," *Transactions and Studies of the College of Physicians of Philadelphia* 14 (1946), pp. 127–132.

The quotations from the Dillys' letters were taken from the manuscripts before it was known that Butterfield had published virtually all their side of the correspondence in "The American Interests of the Firm of E. and C. Dilly, with Their Letters to Benjamin Rush, 1770–1795," Bibliographical Society of America, *Papers* 45 (1951), pp. 283–332.

Most of what is known about Sarah Eve appears in "Extracts from the Journal of Miss Sarah Eve. Written While Living near the City of Philadelphia in 1772–73," *PMHB* 5 (1881), pp. 19–40, 191–205.

1. *Auto.,* pp. 78–79.

2. Journal A, BR-MSS. BR visited McPherson August 18.

3. Rush on deaths 1771–1809, quoted from 1810 charge to medical graduates in James Mease, *The Picture of Philadelphia . . .* (1811), p. 45.

4. Duffy, *Epidemics in Colonial America,* pp. 134, 100, 176–177, 199–200.

5. Robbing of BR's house in *Pennsylvania Journal,* 22 March 1770; *Pennsylvania Chronicle,* 19 March 1770, gives list of stolen goods. Rebecca Stamper, in *Auto.,* p. 78; years later, after she had married a gentleman named Wallace, she expressed her affection for BR in a letter dated 13 November 1787, 33 BR-MSS 1.

6. Comments on apprentices are found in Gibson, "BR's Apprenticed Students." Mention that "prentices no longer board with you," made by Jacob Rush to BR, 24 January 1771, 34 BR-MSS 44. Advice to apprentice in BR to Elisha Hall, 13 July 1773, letter in private hands. Letters in 2B BR-MSS 128–137 to Timothy Bevan indicate orders for medicine. Franklin debt repaid in *Auto.,* p. 74.

7. Fothergill quotation in McVickar, *Bard,* pp. 80–81. Practice among poor, *Auto.,* pp. 79–80, 84.

8. Ibid., pp. 80–81.

9. McPherson's wife, Journal A, 3 October 1769, BR-MSS; *Auto.,* pp. 84–85.

10. Journal A, 1 August 1769, BR-MSS; *Auto.,* p. 81.

11. *Pennsylvania Journal,* 5 September 1771.

12. BR, "Notes on Various Subjects" (1770–1809), BR-MSS.

13. The definition of chemistry, quoted in Miles, "BR, Chemist," p. 50, with Black's definition, p. 50n.

14. "I shall not risk . . ." from a 1771 student notebook of BR's lectures, quoted in Trent, "BR in Edinburgh," p. 183. On experiments, see Miles, "BR, Chemist,"

pp. 52–53. On *"absolute levity,"* see BR to Jonathan Bayard Smith, 30 April 1767, *Letters*. On antidotes: Miles, "BR, Chemist," p. 61.

15. BR to Franklin, 1 May 1773, *Letters*.

16. BR on examinations: given to John Warren, 12 October 1782, ibid. On commencements, *Pennsylvania Journal,* 11 July 1771, 28 July 1773. On Nicholas Way, BR to Gates, 3 Setember 1797. On toast to Boerhaave: *Auto.,* p. 82.

17. Lionel Chalmers to BR, 12 September 1772, 3 BR-MSS 36, 37.

18. William Barker to BR, 2 July 1770, 2B BR-MSS 6.

19. Peter Dott Fayssoux to BR, 4 August 1770, 5 BR-MSS 7; Isaac Chanler to BR, 27 April 1770, 3 BR-MSS 45; Thomas Coombe to BR, 12 March 1770, 33 BR-MSS 36.

20. Jacob Rush to BR, 24 January 1771, 34 BR-MSS 41; Huck to BR, 3 February 1772, 7 BR-MSS 163; Journal A, BR-MSS.

21. Huck to BR, ca. 1773, 7 BR-MSS 166.

22. Huck to BR, 9 March 1771, 7 BR-MSS 162.

23. "Philopaidos" appeared in *Pennsylvania Journal,* 12 April 1770.

24. Coombe to BR, 12 March 1770, 33 BR-MSS 36; Dilly to BR, 20 July 1770, 31 BR-MSS 2; John Millar to BR, 16 July 1770, 10 BR-MSS 40.

25. *Pennsylvania Journal,* 9 August 1770; Thomas Pratt to BR, 12 July 1771, 13 BR-MSS 150.

26. American Philosophical Society, *Transactions* 1 (1771), pp. 318–322. BR spelled "stramonium" with a double m.

27. Dilly to BR, 31 July 1771, 31 BR-MSS 6; Dilly to BR, 13 July 1774, 31 BR-MSS 9.

28. *Pennsylvania Gazette,* 26 December 1771 and 9 January 1772; *Pennsylvania Packet,* 17 February 1772; BR, Preface, *Sermons to Gentlemen.*

29. *Auto.,* pp. 82–83; Dilly to BR, 2 May 1772, 31 BR-MSS 5. The lady's critique appeared in the *Pennsylvania Journal,* 4 June 1772, with BR's reply following on 11 June 1772 in the same newspaper.

30. Coombe to BR, 29 November 1769, 33 BR-MSS 45; Huck to BR, 9 March 1771, 7 BR-MSS 162.

31. Lionel Chalmers to BR, 30 July 1772, 3 BR-MSS 35; Huck to BR, 3 February 1772, 7 BR-MSS 163.

32. Notations on Jacob Rush appear on flyleaf of "Notes on Various Subjects" (1770–1809), BR-MSS.

33. Huck to BR, 9 March 1771, 7 BR-MSS 162; Hazard to BR, 10 November 1770, 14 January 1771, 39 BR-MSS 25, 26; Coombe to BR, 23 April 1771, 33 BR-MSS 40.

34. Coombe to BR, 6 October 1770, 33 BR-MSS 37; BR to Franklin, ca. 1771, Butterfield, ed., "Further Letters," p. 13. Paper on colds mentioned in *Pennsylvania Journal,* 16 September 1772, and first published in *Columbian Magazine* 1 (1787), pp. 427–431.

35. Mrs. Coxe to BR, September 1770, 27 BR-MSS 20.

36. On Miss Graeme, see Sachse, *Colonial American in Britain,* p. 163.

37. Mrs. Coxe to BR, 11 July and 19 September 1770, 27 BR-MSS 19, 20; Hannah (Jeffries) Hayling to BR, 16 February 1773, 26 BR-MSS 82; Richard Baker to BR, 14 July 1773, 24 BR-MSS 8.

38. BR to Dubourg, 29 April 1773, *Letters;* Lionel Chalmers to BR, 2 November 1772, 23 BR-MSS 28; Richard Baker cites the figure fifteen hundred guineas in a letter to BR, 24 November 1772, 24 BR-MSS 7.

39. Huck to BR, 18 February 1773, 7 BR-MSS 164; Baker to BR, 24 November 1772, 24 BR-MSS 7; BR to Dubourg, 29 April 1773, *Letters;* BR to Elisha Hall, 10 November 1774, letter in private hands; Journal A, BR-MSS.

6. Politics Intrude: 1773–1774

The daybook for Rush's first three years in practice is missing, but the one for November 1772 to May 1775 is with his papers at the Historical Society of Pennsylvania. This daybook gives a rough day-by-day listing of patients visited. The name of each patient in the daybook is lined through after the entry has been placed in the ledger. There, under the individual's name, charges for medicines and care for each visit are given and a notation made whether or not the bill was paid.

The full story of mineral waters in and around Philadelphia has been told by F. H. Shelton, "Springs and Spas of Old-Time Philadelphia," *PMHB* 47 (1923), pp. 196–237.

Rush's early role in the antislavery crusade is told briefly in Leonard J. Trinterud, *The Forming of an American Tradition* (1949), where his pamphlet of 1773 is called "the first outspoken and clear denunciation of slavery as an institution by a Presbyterian. . . ." Bernard Bailyn places the pamphlet in the context of the times in *The Ideological Origins of the American Revolution* (1967). The most detailed early account is in M. S. Locke, *Anti-Slavery Sentiment in America, 1619–1808* (1901); this work has been superseded by Winthrop D. Jordan's superb *White Over Black* (1968).

John Adams' comments on Rush are most accessible in the new edition of the *Diary and Autobiography of John Adams* (4 vols., 1961), edited by Lyman H. Butterfield. Until recently only one side of the Rush-

Sharp correspondence was known to exist, that of Sharp, whose letters are on deposit at the Historical Society of Pennsylvania. A few of Sharp's and all of Rush's letters have now been edited by John A. Woods, "The Correspondence of Benjamin Rush and Granville Sharp, 1773–1809," *Journal of American Studies* 1 (1967), pp. 1–38. Rush's side of the Rush-Ramsay correspondence is lost, but all of Ramsay's letters have been edited by Robert L. Brunhouse from the manuscripts at the Historical Society of Pennsylvania and published under the title *David Ramsay, 1749–1815: Selections from His Writings* as a separate volume in the American Philosophical Society *Transactions* (new series, vol. 55, pt. 4, 1965).

1. Hazard to Jeremy Belknap, 3 February 1788, quoted in *Letters,* p. 6n.
2. Sarah Eve Diary, 27 May 1773, *PMHB,* p. 191; Francis Alison's notation on the Philadelphia well quoted in Drinker, *Not So Long Ago,* p. 25. BR's essay read before the American Philosophical Society 18 June 1773 and published soon afterward as *Experiments and Observations on the Mineral Waters.*
3. Ibid., p. 30.
4. John Stuart to BR, 14 March 1771, 16 BR-MSS 79; BR to William Smith, 10 August 1802, *Letters.*
5. *Pennsylvania Journal,* 2 February 1774, gives an account of A Society for Inoculating the Poor. Mention of BR as a member of the Hand-in-Hand Fire Company in *PMHB* 46 (1922), p. 252. His membership in The Society of Sons of Saint Tammany of Philadelphia is noted in an essay on the society by Francis Von A. Cabeen, *PMHB* 25 (1901), pp. 433–451.
6. BR to Dubourg, 29 April 1773, *Letters.* In *Auto.,* p. 246, under date 17 June 1799, BR notes that William Grubber remained his slave for ten years. The accuracy of this statement is questioned in chapter 19. Let it be said here that there is no proof he owned Grubber prior to 1773. It is assumed, however, that he did; it is hard to believe BR would have risked the charge of hypocrisy if he had purchased him *after* publication of his antislavery essays, a charge he especially would have preferred to avoid once it was known he had written *An Address* and *Vindication.* The admission of few new arguments in the essays is in BR to Sharp, 1 May 1773, *Letters.*
7. Benezet quoted in Jordan, *White Over Black,* p. 275. BR, *An Address,* pp. 2, 15, 20, 22, 23–25, 27, 30.
8. The *Pennsylvania Packet* has an advertisement for the pamphlet 18 January 1773. BR to Dubourg, 29 April 1773, *Letters;* [Nesbit], *Slavery Not Forbidden by Scriptures* (1773), p. 22.
9. BR, *A Vindication of the Address,* pp. 4, 6, 25, 30.
10. Ibid., p. 26.

11. BR to Sharp, 1 May 1773, *Letters;* [Walter] Jones to BR, 2 November 1773, 8 BR-MSS 123; Ramsay to BR, Brunhouse, ed., *David Ramsay,* pp. 51–52.

12. Journal A, BR-MSS; *Auto.,* p. 83. BR's own record of income for 1773 and 1774 is found on the flyleaf of Journal A.

13. Sharp to BR, 21 February 1774, 28 BR-MSS 74; idem, 27 July 1774, 28 BR-MSS 77. BR's letters to Sharp, 1 May and 29 October 1773, appear in Woods, "Correspondence of Rush and Sharp," pp. 2–3.

14. *Auto.,* pp. 109, 190; BR to William Gordon, 10 October 1773; BR, "To His Fellow Countrymen: On Patriotism," 20 October 1773, both in *Letters.* Additional essays signed "Hampden" appear in *Pennsylvania Packet,* 18 and 25 October 1773.

15. BR, "On Patriotism," *Letters.*

16. *Pennsylvania Journal,* 22 December 1773.

17. Ibid., 15 February 1775.

18. *Auto.,* pp. 109, 110, 149, 155.

19. BR, "Notes on Various Subjects," BR-MSS, contains the early draft of essay on Indians.

20. The friendly critic was Huck in letter to BR, 31 August 1774, 7 BR-MSS 165. The original edition of *An Oration . . . Containing an Enquiry into the Natural History of Medicines Among Indians in North-America, and a Comparative View of their Diseases and Remedies, with those of Civilized Nations . . .* (1774), was compared with BR, *Medical Inquiries and Observations* (1794–1798).

21. BR to Elisha Hall, 10 November 1774, letter in private hands. BR, *An Oration* (1774 ed.), p. 85.

22. Ibid., pp. 88, 84, 66, 61, 102.

23. The unchanged peroration appears on pages 74–75 of the 1794–1798 edition.

24. Ramsay to BR, 29 July 1774, Brunhouse, ed., *David Ramsay,* p. 51; Dilly to BR, 13 July 1774, 31 BR-MSS 9; Franklin to BR, 22 July 1774, Albert H. Smyth, ed., *Writings of Benjamin Franklin* (10 vols., 1901–1907), vol. 6, p. 235.

25. Huck to BR, 31 August 1774, 7 BR-MSS 165.

26. Abraham, *Lettsom,* p. 132.

27. BR to Arthur Lee, 4 May 1774, *Letters.*

28. Butterfield, ed., *Adams Diary,* 29 August 1774, vol. 2, p. 115.

29. *Auto.,* p. 110.

30. Butterfield, ed., *Adams Diary,* 14 September 1774, vol. 2, p. 134. Soon after Congress adjourned, Charles Lee asked BR to "inquire of Mrs. Yard if she has any letters for me—if she has send 'em." *Lee Papers,* New-York Historical Society, *Collections* (4 vols., 1871–1874), vol. 1, p. 144.

31. On city librarian: William Bradford, Jr., to James Madison, 17 October 1774, Bradford Letterbook, Historical Society of Pennsylvania.

32. Journal A, BR-MSS; quotation on smallpox, *Auto.,* p. 110n.
33. *Auto.,* p. 111.
34. BR to Sharp, 1 November 1774, Woods, "Correspondence of Rush and Sharp," p. 13.
35. *Auto.,* pp. 111–112.
36. Ibid., p. 111.
37. BR to Lewis Johnson, 15 November 1774, *Letters;* Edward Dilly to BR, 22 September 1774, 31 BR-MSS 10.
38. *Pennsylvania Packet,* 12 December 1774; last page of BR to Lady Jane Leslie, 28 September 1774, 39 BR-MSS 27. Evidence that Rush escorted other girls in 1774 is found in a letter from Baker to BR, July 1774, 39 BR-MSS 27, in which he speaks of one of BR's lady friends as "hard-hearted and irascible," adding that he was "sure the fair Quaker surpasses her much in every instance." Captain Eve's payment for services rendered is found in BR's Journal AA under June 1775.
39. *Pennsylvania Journal* also ran the announcement, 28 December 1774.

IN THE MIDST OF A REVOLUTION

7. The Revolution Begins: 1775–1776

The still untold story of the United Company has been sketched largely from contemporary newspaper sources by William R. Bagnall, *The Textile Industries of the United States* (1893). Lyman H. Butterfield gives details of the interception of Rush's letter to Thomas Ruston in "The Milliner's Mission in 1775; Or the British Seize a Treasonable Letter by Dr. Benjamin Rush," *William and Mary Quarterly* 3d ser. 8 (1951), pp. 192–203. Much of the political story covered here and in more detail in the following chapter can be mined from *Extracts from the Diary of Christopher Marshall, Kept in Philadelphia and Lancaster, during the American Revolution, 1774–1781,* edited by William Duane (1877). The manuscript of Adam Stephen's "The Ohio Expedition of 1754" remains in the Rush Papers at the Historical Society of Pennsylvania with an endorsement in Rush's hand—"Col. Steven's life written by himself for B. Rush in 1775." It has been published in the *PMHB* 18 (1894), pp. 43–50.

1. BR, "An Account of the Influence of the Military and Political Events of the American Revolution Upon the Human Body," *Medical Inquiries and Observations* (1794–1798 ed.), vol. 1, pp. 271–272.

2. Butterfield, ed., *Adams Diary,* 30 January 1768, vol. 1, p. 337.

3. *Auto.,* p. 112.

4. Journal AA, BR-MSS. His cash income from the practice alone came to £675, with £880 credit still on the books at the end of the year. He did not bother to list the sums brought in from the apothecary shop, the classes at the college, or the fees from apprentices.

5. Lionel Chalmers to BR, 30 September 1775, 3 BR-MSS 38.

6. Number of students in medical class listed on next to last page of daybook for 1772–1773, BR-MSS. On Priestley: Thomas Henry to BR, 1 April 1775, 7 BR-MSS 94.

7. *Pennsylvania Packet,* 24 November 1774; *Pennsylvania Journal,* 25 January

1775. The two brief essays were combined in the *Pennsylvania Magazine* for June 1775, probably on the initiative of Thomas Paine, also interested in the subject, who had published his own findings earlier.

8. *Pennsylvania Gazette,* 22 February 1775.

9. A manuscript version of BR's speech exists in the Wetherill Papers, University of Pennsylvania. A more accessible copy can be found in the *Pennsylvania Evening Post* for 11 and 13 April 1775.

10. Duane, ed., *Extracts from the Marshall Diary,* 24 April 1775; *Auto.,* p. 112.

11. On inoculation of Patrick Henry see Journal AA for July, BR-MSS and *Auto.,* pp. 110–111. On London Coffee House: Scharf and Westcott, *History of Philadelphia,* vol. 1, pp. 279n–281n. On Washington: BR to John Adams, 12 February 1812, *Letters,* and *Auto.,* pp. 112–113. On use of Davies' sermon, see footnote 4, p. 1125, *Letters.* On Jefferson: BR to Jefferson, 6 October 1800, ibid.

12. Butterfield, ed., *Adams Diary,* 24 September 1775, vol. 2, p. 182; John Adams to James Warren, 24 July 1775, *Warren-Adams Letters* (2 vols., 1917–1925), vol. 1, p. 88; *Auto.,* p. 142.

13. Charles Lee to BR, 19 September, 10 October, 12 December 1775, *Lee Papers,* vol. 1, pp. 206, 207, 211, 212, 226.

14. Butterfield, ed., *Adams Diary,* 24 September 1775, vol. 2, p. 182; Lyman H. Butterfield, ed., *Adams Family Correspondence* (2 vols., 1963), 20 July 1776, vol. 2, p. 54.

15. BR to wife, 16 August 1787, *Letters.*

16. John R. Howe, Jr., *The Changing Political Thought of John Adams* (1966), and Gordon S. Wood, *The Creation of the American Republic 1776–1787* (1969), interpret John Adams' thought in the 1770's in a way that leaves hardly any distinction between his outlook and Rush's. It is difficult to believe that the forty-year-old Adams, who had endured the riotous pre-Revolutionary period depicted in Hiller B. Zobel, *The Boston Massacre* (1970), came to Philadelphia filled with the great faith in the peculiar virtues of the American people that enthralled the younger Rush.

17. Bailyn, *Ideological Origins,* p. 19.

18. Butterfield, ed., *Adams Diary,* 2 July 1771, 30 June 1772, 1 January 1773, vol. 2, pp. 43, 62, 76.

19. BR to Thomas Ruston, 29 October 1775, *Letters.*

20. BR to John Adams, 12 February 1812, ibid.; *Auto.,* pp. 179–180.

21. Letter to John Benezet for Committee of Safety, 3 July 1775, in *PMHB* 36 (1912), p. 256. BR to Adams, 13 April 1790, 29 June 1805, *Letters.* The row galleys are fully described in Scharf and Westcott, *History of Philadelphia,* vol. 1, pp. 299–300.

22. James McHenry to BR, 9 October 1775, 43 BR-MSS 30.

23. *Auto.,* pp. 113–115; BR to James Cheetham, 17 July 1809, *Letters; Auto.,* p. 323.

24. Ibid., p. 114; William Duane to Thomas Jefferson, 27 November 1802, *Proceedings of the Massachusetts Historical Society,* 2nd ser., 20 (1907), p. 279.

25. *Auto.,* p. 114; BR to Cheetham, 17 July 1809, *Letters.*

26. *Auto.,* p. 323.

27. Ibid.; BR to Nathanael Greene, 4 September 1781, Butterfield, ed., "Further Letters," p. 19.

28. BR to Lady Jane Belsches, 21 April 1784, *Letters; Auto.,* pp. 115–116.

29. BR to Lady Jane Belsches, 21 April 1784 and 4 July 1785, *Letters.*

30. Journal AA, October–December 1775, BR-MSS.

31. Charles G. Sellers, *Charles Willson Peale* (2 vols., 1939, 1947), vol. 1, p. 128.

32. Thacher, *American Medical Biography,* vol. 2, p. 57n.

33. Daybook, 11–18 January 1776, BR-MSS.

34. BR to wife, 27 and 29 May 1776, *Letters.*

35. BR to Hogg, 16 September 1783, Butterfield, ed., "Further Letters," p. 21.

8. Pennsylvania Politics: 1776

For the most part this chapter repeats in brief what is covered more extensively in David Hawke, *In the Midst of a Revolution* (1961).

1. [Walter] Jones to BR, 20 February 1776, 8 BR-MSS 149.

2. Duane, ed., *Extracts from the Marshall Diary,* 20 January, 7 and 12 February 1776; list of Pennsylvania Hospital staff as appointed in May in *Pennsylvania Gazette,* 15 May 1776. The judgment of Matlack made by Joseph Shippen to Edward Shippen, 29 February 1776, Shippen Papers, vol. 12, HSP.

3. Edward Shippen to Jasper Yeates, 11 March 1776, Shippen Papers, vol. 2, HSP.

4. Edward Burd to James Burd, 15 March 1776, Shippen Papers, vol. 7, HSP.

5. Joseph Shippen to Edward Shippen, 12 March 1776, ibid.; *Auto.,* p. 116.

6. *Auto.,* pp. 263, 265; P. Wroth to H. W. Smith, 8 February 1872, in H. W. Smith, *Life and Correspondence of Reverend William Smith* (2 vols., 1880), vol. 2, pp. 504–505.

7. "Cato," *Pennsylvania Gazette,* 13 March 1776.

8. *Pennsylvania Evening Post,* 27 April 1776.

9. Paine, "A Serious Address to the People of Pennsylvania on the Present Situation of Their Affairs," *Pennsylvania Packet,* 5 December 1778, in Philip S. Foner, ed., *The Complete Writings of Thomas Paine* (2 vols., 1945), vol. 2, pp. 287–288; "Elector," *Pennsylvania Packet,* 29 April 1776.

10. Richard Bache to Benjamin Franklin, 7 May 1776, Franklin Papers, American Philosophical Society; BR to John Adams, 11 July 1806, *Letters.*

11. Quoted in Charles H. Lincoln, *The Revolutionary Movement in Pennsylvania 1760–1776* (1901), p. 249.

12. House for sale advertised in *Pennsylvania Gazette,* 29 May 1776; "Extracts from the Diary of Dr. James Clitherall," *PMHB* 22 (1898), p. 468.

13. The May 10 resolution appears in Edmund C. Burnett, *The Continental Congress* (1941), p. 157.

14. Ibid., p. 158.

15. Charles Francis Adams, *Life and Works of John Adams* (10 vols., 1850–1856), vol. 2, p. 491.

16. Caesar Rodney to Thomas Rodney, 17 May 1776, Burnett, *Continental Congress,* pp. 159–160.

17. BR to wife, 29 May 1776, *Letters.*

18. George Read to Caesar Rodney, 10 May 1776, G. H. Ryden, ed., *Letters to and from Caesar Rodney 1756–1784* (1933), p. 76.

19. BR to wife, 29 May 1776, *Letters.*

20. Journal AA, May 18 and 19.

21. *Pennsylvania Gazette,* 22 May 1776.

22. Caesar Rodney to Thomas Rodney, 22 May 1776, Ryden, ed., *Rodney Letters,* p. 83; *Pennsylvania Gazette,* 22 May 1776.

23. BR to Richard Henry Lee, 22 May 1776, Butterfield, ed., "Further Letters," pp. 14–15.

24. Duane, ed., *Extracts from the Marshall Diary,* 23–25 May 1776; *Pennsylvania Gazette,* 29 May 1776.

25. Duane, ed., *Extracts from the Marshall Diary,* 24 May 1776.

26. BR to wife, 1 June 1776, *Letters.*

27. All quotations from BR to wife can be found in *Letters* under the dates 27 and 29 May and 1 June 1776.

28. Thomas Rodney, "Diary," 10 March 1781, in Edmund C. Burnett, ed., *Letters of the Members of the Continental Congress* (8 vols., 1921–1936), vol. 6, p. 20.

29. Christopher Marshall to J. B. at New Jersey, 30 June 1776, Marshall Letterbook, HSP.

30. Graydon, *Memoirs,* pp. 122–123; Marshall to J. B., 30 June 1776, Marshall Letterbook, HSP.

31. Proceedings of Provincial Conference, in *Pennsylvania Archives,* 2nd ser. (19 vols., 1874–1890), vol. 3, pp. 652–653.

32. Broadside, dated 26 June 1776, in Broadside Collection, HSP; BR to "Citizens of Pennsylvania of German Birth . . ." 31 August 1785, *Letters.*

9. In and Out of Congress: 1776–1777

The two great collections of material on Congress are Worthington Chauncey Ford's edition of the *Journals of the Continental Congress, 1774–1789* (34 vols., 1904–1937), of which volumes five and six are applicable here, and the *Letters of the Members of the Continental Congress* edited by Edmund C. Burnett (8 vols., 1921–1936), of which volume two pertains to the time of Rush's tenure.

Background on the period covered by Rush's first tour of military duty can be found in W. S. Stryker's detailed *Battles of Princeton and Trenton* (1898), Alfred Hoyt Bill's succinct *Campaign of Princeton, 1776–1777* (1948), and James Thomas Flexner's *George Washington in the American Revolution 1775–1783* (1968), which tells the story most effectively from its subject's point of view.

The essential parts of Rush's small notebook on the Continental Congress have been extracted by S. Weir Mitchell, "Historical Notes of Dr. Benjamin Rush, 1777," and published in the *PMHB* 27 (1903), pp. 129–150.

1. BR to Charles Lee, 23 July 1776, *Letters.*

2. Ibid. Rush had not won in a walk. Duane, ed., *Extracts from the Marshall Diary,* under 20 July 1776, gives the balloting as follows: Franklin, 78; James Wilson, 74; John Morton, 71; George Clymer, 75; George Ross, 77; Col. James Smith, 56; Benjamin Rush, 61; George Taylor, 34.

3. BR to John Adams, 13 April 1790, *Letters.*

4. *Auto.,* p. 119. BR says here he took a seat July 20, but for correct date see *Letters,* p. 105n. BR to John Adams, 20 July 1811, *Letters.*

5. BR to Charles Lee, 23 July 1776, *Letters.*

6. *Auto.,* pp. 140–141.

7. Ibid., pp. 119, 150, 139, 147, 140, 141, 148; BR to Adams, 13 April 1790, *Letters.*

8. BR to wife, 23 July 1776, *Letters.*

9. *Auto.,* p. 121. Quotations of BR's speech come from two versions, one in Butterfield, ed., *Adams Diary,* vol. 2, pp. 247–248; the other in Julian Boyd, ed., *Papers of Thomas Jefferson* (18 vols. to date, 1950–   ), vol. 1, p. 326.

10. See Ford, ed., *Journals of Continental Congress,* vol. 5, under appropriate dates.

11. Flexner, *Washington in the Revolution,* pp. 116, 117, 121; BR to Adams, 13 April 1790, *Letters; Auto.,* pp. 140, 120.

12. BR to Adams, 29 June 1805; BR to wife, 14 September 1776, *Letters.*

13. BR to Dubourg, 16 September 1776; BR to wife, 18? September 1776; BR to Wayne, 24 September 1776, all *Letters.*

14. John C. Fitzpatrick, ed., *Writings of George Washington* (39 vols., 1931–1944), vol. 32, p. 76; BR to Wayne, 24 and 29 September 1776, *Letters.*

15. Ford, ed., *Journals of Continental Congress,* 20 August 1776.

16. BR to Shippen, September 1776, published by Shippen in *Pennsylvania Packet,* 18 November 1780.

17. Shippen to BR, 10 November 1776, *Pennsylvania Packet,* 13 July 1779; Ford, ed., *Journals of Continental Congress,* 12 November 1776.

18. Ford, ed., *Journals of Continental Congress* shows BR appointed to committee to expedite production of powder August 6; to medical committee August 7; to committee to expedite supplies to northern army September 24; to committee on prisoners October 8; and to committee on intelligence October 17. William Hooper to Joseph Hewes on Pennsylvania Committee of Safety, 16 November 1776, Burnett, ed., *Letters of Continental Congress,* vol. 2, p. 156.

19. BR to wife, 23 July 1776, *Letters.*

20. BR to wife, 14 and 18? September 1776, ibid.

21. Daybook and Journal AA, BR-MSS. BR to wife, 23 July 1776, *Letters.*

22. Daybook and Journal AA, BR-MSS.

23. BR to Wayne, 29 September 1776, *Letters.*

24. Ford, ed., *Journal of Continental Congress,* 22 November 1776; John Morgan quoting from BR testimony at Shippen court-martial, *Pennsylvania Packet,* 7 October 1780. Mention of gravedigger and smallpox in Nicholas B. Wainwright, ed., " 'A Diary of Trifling Occurrences' Philadelphia, 1776–1778," *PMHB* 82 (1958), pp. 420, 421, 425. BR to Shippen, 28 November 1776, published by Shippen in *Pennsylvania Packet,* 18 November 1780.

25. Duane, ed., *Extracts from the Marshall Diary,* 2 and 10 December 1776; Wainwright, ed., " 'Diary of Trifling Occurrences,' " under date December 13, p. 416.

26. *Auto.,* p. 123.

27. Ibid.

28. Maj. James Wilkinson on Philadelphia, quoted in Bill, *Campaign of Princeton,* p. 18. On Reed: BR to General Cadwalader, 3 March 1783, in John G. Johnson, *A Criticism of Mr. Wm. B. Reed's aspersions on the character of Dr. Benjamin Rush . . . By a member of the Philadelphia Bar* (1867), pp. 11–12.

29. BR to Lee, 21 December 1776, *Letters.*

30. The quotations come from this small flood of letters from BR to Lee: 21 December, 25 December, 30 December 1776, 6 January (two letters), 7 January, 14 January (two letters), and 15 January 1777. All appear in *Letters* except those for December 25 and the second for January 6, which are found in Butterfield, ed., "Further Letters."

31. BR to Lee, 30 December 1776, *Letters.*

32. *Auto.,* p. 124.

33. Ibid., p. 125; BR to Lee, 30 December 1776, *Letters.*

34. *Auto.,* p. 126.

35. Ibid., p. 127.

36. Ibid., pp. 127–128.

37. BR to Lee, 14 January 1777, second letter, *Letters; Auto.,* p. 128.

38. *Auto.,* p. 128; BR to John Adams, 19 August 1811, *Letters.*

39. Sellers, *Peale,* vol. 1, p. 153; BR to Lee, 6 January 1777, *Letters;* second letter same day, Butterfield, ed., "Further Letters," p. 17.

40. *Auto.,* p. 128; BR to Lee, 7 January 1777, *Letters.*

41. *Auto.,* pp. 130, 129; BR to Lady Jane Belsches, 21 April 1784, *Letters.*

42. BR to Lee, 7 January 1777, *Letters.*

43. Foner, ed., *Writings of Thomas Paine,* vol. 1, p. 50; BR to Lee, 14 January 1777, first letter, *Letters.*

44. BR to Lee, 14 January 1777, first letter, *Letters.*

45. BR to wife, 24 and 31 January 1777; BR to Robert Morris, 8 February 1777, *Letters.*

46. Sanderson, *Biography of the Signers,* vol. 5, p. 60; Thornton's letter is dated 23 January 1777.

47. BR to Wayne, 24 September 1776; BR to Adams, 12 February 1790, *Letters; Auto.,* p. 142; BR to Adams, 12 October 1779, *Letters.*

48. BR to Adams, 13 April and 24 February 1790, *Letters;* BR to General Cadwalader, 3 March 1783, in Johnson, *A Criticism of Reed's Aspersions,* p. 12; *Auto.,* p. 142.

49. Mitchell, ed., "Historical Notes of BR," pp. 132, 133.

50. Ibid., pp. 135, 136.

51. Ibid., pp. 136, 139.

52. Ibid., pp. 139–140.

53. Ibid., p. 140; also BR on Adams in *Auto.,* p. 141.

54. Mitchell, ed., "Historical Notes of BR," pp. 141–142.

55. *Pennsylvania Journal,* 17 July 1782.

56. BR to Robert Morris, 22 February 1777, *Letters.* Also E. James Ferguson, *The Power of the Purse* (1961), p. 35.

57. George Washington to Congress, 14 February 1777, in Louis C. Duncan, "Medical Men in the American Revolution," in *Army Medical Bulletin* no. 25 (1931).

58. BR to wife, 24 January 1777, *Letters.*

10. "Here Ends the Chapter": 1777

The Pennsylvania Constitution is discussed briefly in David Hawke, *In the Midst of a Revolution* (1961), and fully in J. Paul Selsam, *The Pennsylvania Constitution of 1776* (1936) and Elisha P. Douglass, *Rebels and Democrats* (1955). The most recent and perhaps most perceptive account is found in Gordon S. Wood, *The Creation of the American Republic 1776–1787* (1969). Quotations from Rush's *Observations Upon the Present Government of Pennsylvania. In Four Letters to the People of Pennsylvania* (1777) were drawn from the copy in the Library Company of Philadelphia.

1. John Adams to Abigail Adams, 2 June 1777, Butterfield, ed., *Adams Family Correspondence,* vol. 2, p. 252.
2. Burnett, ed., *Letters of Continental Congress,* vol. 2, p. lxv.
3. Paine, *Crisis No. 2,* in Foner, ed., *Writings of Thomas Paine,* vol. 1, p. 64. Mitchell, ed., "Historical Notes of BR," pp. 143–145, has reprinted BR's rough draft of this essay. This version, unlike that published in the *Pennsylvania Packet,* 18 March 1777, makes clear how Braxton sparked the piece.
4. A record of BR's peregrinations from March 24 to July 23 is found in his hand on the front flyleaf of Notebook 2 of "Mss. Notes on Continental Congress, 1777–1778" (3 notebooks), BR-MSS. BR's daybook and Journal AA give the story of his medical practice. BR, 8 April 1777, in Mitchell, "Historical Notes of BR," p. 146; BR to Wayne, 2 April 1777, *Letters.*
5. Gates quoting Henry: BR to Adams, 12 February 1812, *Letters.* Mifflin on Washington, ibid. Ford, ed., *Journals of Continental Congress,* vol. 6, pp. 161–164, gives the medical reorganization plan that BR's committee submitted to Congress on 27 February 1777. The figures for the sick in Washington's army are found in James E. Gibson, *Dr. Bodo Otto and the Medical Background of the American Revolution* (1937), p. 141.
6. See Ford, ed., *Journals of Continental Congress,* under dates noted. See also Gibson, *Otto,* pp. 138–141, and Duncan, "Medical Men," pp. 192–198.
7. Daybook, BR-MSS.
8. BR to wife, 14 April 1777, *Letters.* Mrs. Rush's arrival is noted on flyleaf of Notebook 2, "Notes on Congress," BR-MSS.
9. This essay is reprinted in *Letters,* pp. 140–145.
10. *Auto.,* p. 131; on Young, see *Letters,* p. 149n.
11. *Pennsylvania Packet,* 7 October 1780; BR to Adams, 12 February 1812, *Letters; Auto.,* pp. 131–132.

12. *Auto.,* p. 132.

13. BR to wife, 23 July 1776, *Letters;* BR, *Observations,* p. 12.

14. Cannon broadside, 26 June 1776, HSP.

15. Theodore Thayer reproduces the constitution in an appendix in *Pennsylvania Politics and the Growth of Democracy 1740–1776* (1953), pp. 211–227.

16. BR to Wayne, 24 September 1776; BR to Dickinson, 1 December 1776, both *Letters.*

17. BR to Wayne, 2 April and 19 May 1777, *Letters.*

18. BR to Patrick Henry, 16 July 1776, in Lyman H. Butterfield, "Dr. Rush to Governor Henry on the Declaration of Independence and the Virginia Constitution," *Proceedings of the American Philosophical Society* 95 (1951), p. 252.

19. The letters, republished as the pamphlet *Observations,* appeared in the *Pennsylvania Journal,* May 21, 28, June 4 and 11.

20. *Observations,* p. 4.

21. Ibid., pp. 5–7; John Adams to Abigail Adams, 4 June 1777, Butterfield, ed., *Adams Family Correspondence,* vol. 2, p. 255.

22. *Observations,* pp. 9, 8–9.

23. Adams, *Thoughts on Government,* in George A. Peek, Jr., ed., *The Political Writings of John Adams* (1954), p. 88; Wood, *Creation of the American Republic,* p. 230.

24. *Observations,* pp. 13–14, 15–16, 18–19.

25. Ibid., p. 21.

26. BR to Wayne, 18 June 1777, *Letters.*

27. Rush, "Defects of the Confederation," as quoted in Wood, *Creation of the American Republic,* p. 374.

28. Ibid., p. 255.

29. Date of departure noted on flyleaf of Notebook 2, "Notes on Congress," BR-MSS.

11. In and Out of the Army: 1777–1778

As the annotation of this chapter reveals, the best of the mass of material dealing with Rush's brief tour of duty has been culled by Butterfield for his edition of the *Letters.* Volume 29 of the Rush correspondence contains much more, beginning with the document on page 110 entitled "Substance of information and evidence given against Dr. Shippen Junior." More can be found in James E. Gibson's *Dr. Bodo Otto and the Medical*

Background of the American Revolution (1937), and still more in the running battle of letters and vindications carried on by Shippen, Rush, and Morgan in the *Pennsylvania Packet* through the summer of 1779 and resumed in the fall of 1780.

The abbreviated diary Rush kept of his travels during 1777–1778 appears as part of S. Weir Mitchell's "Historical Notes of Dr. Benjamin Rush, 1777," *PMHB* 27 (1903), pp. 129–150.

A full and admirable account of Rush's relations with Washington, centering around his fateful letter of 12 January 1778, is found in Appendix I of the *Letters,* pp. 1197–1208.

1. BR to Adams, 8 August 1777, *Letters.*
2. Wainwright, ed., " 'A Diary of Trifling Occurrences,' " *PMHB* 82 (1958), pp. 437–438, 439.
3. BR, *Medical Inquiries and Observations* (1794 ed.), vol. 1, p. 260; James Tilton, *Economical Observations on Military Hospitals* (1813), quoted in Nathan G. Goodman, *Benjamin Rush, Physician and Citizen, 1746–1813* (1934), pp. 86–87.
4. Wainwright, ed., " 'A Diary of Trifling Occurrences,' " pp. 443, 444; *Auto.,* p. 132; BR to Adams, 1 October 1777, *Letters.*
5. BR to Adams, 1 October 1777, ibid.; Wainwright, ed., " 'A Diary of Trifling Occurrences,' " p. 450.
6. Mitchell, ed., "Historical Notes of BR," p. 147.
7. BR to Adams, 31 October 1777, *Letters.*
8. BR to Adams, 13 October 1777, ibid.
9. BR to Gates, 27 July 1803; BR to Adams, 21 October 1777, both ibid.
10. Gibson, *Otto,* pp. 142, 143, 144, 244.
11. BR to Adams, 1 October 1777, *Letters.*
12. BR to Adams, 31 October 1777, ibid.
13. Thomas Bond, Jr., "Eulogy on Dr. Shippen," *Port Folio* 1 (1813), p. 108; BR to Adams, 1 August and 21 October 1777, *Letters.*
14. *Pennsylvania Packet,* 7 October 1780.
15. Quoted in Gibson, *Otto,* p. 225; BR to Adams, 31 October 1777, *Letters.*
16. BR to wife, 10 November 1777; BR to James Searle, 19 November 1777; BR to Elizabeth Graeme Ferguson, 24 December 1777, all ibid.
17. BR to Washington, 26 December 1777, ibid.
18. BR to Greene, 2 December 1777, ibid.
19. BR to Shippen, 2 December 1777; BR to Duer, 8 December 1777, both ibid.
20. Ibid.

21. BR to Duer, 13 December 1777, ibid.

22. BR to Washington, 26 December 1777, ibid.

23. BR to Morgan, June 1779, ibid.; Washington to BR, 12 January 1778, quoted in ibid., p. 182n.

24. BR to Adams, 12 February 1812, ibid.; Mitchell, ed., "Historical Notes of BR," p. 148; Duane, ed., *Extracts from the Marshall Diary,* 7 January 1778.

25. BR to wife, 15 January 1778; BR to James Searle, 21 January 1778, both *Letters.*

26. BR to wife, 15 January 1778, ibid.

27. Ibid.

28. BR to Henry, 12 January 1778, ibid.

29. This friendship is revealed in an earlier letter written by BR to Henry on 16 July 1776; it is reprinted by Butterfield in "Dr. Rush to Governor Henry," pp. 250–255.

30. Charles Lee to BR, 13 August 1778, *Lee Papers,* vol. 2, pp. 228–229.

31. Fitzpatrick, ed., *Writings of Washington,* vol. 6, p. 453.

32. BR to Adams, 22 January 1778, *Letters.*

33. Quoted in Gibson, *Otto,* p. 213.

34. BR to Adams, 22 January 1778; BR to James Searle, 21 January 1778, both *Letters.*

35. BR to Henry Laurens, 25 January 1778, ibid.

36. BR to Morgan [June ? 1779], ibid.

37. Ibid.

38. Ibid.

39. Ibid.

40. Graydon, *Memoirs,* pp. 306–307; BR to Adams (draft), 12 February 1812, *Letters,* p. 1125n; BR to Morgan [June ? 1779], ibid.

41. BR to Henry Laurens, 30 January 1778, *Letters.* A note from Witherspoon to BR, 2 February 1778, 43 BR-MSS 46 makes it clear BR wrote out two forms of his resignation, gave them to Witherspoon, and left town immediately.

42. BR to wife, 15 January 1778, *Letters.* Even close friends like Richard Peters found it hard to speak out wholeheartedly in favor of BR. "There is so much said on both sides that I fancy both were wrong at least in some degree," Peters wrote Robert Morris, 3 February 1778, Dreer Collection, New Series, HSP.

43. Adams to BR, 8 February 1778, quoted in Goodman, *Rush,* pp. 96–97.

44. Witherspoon to BR, 2 February 1778, 43 BR-MSS 46; BR to Greene ?, 1 February 1778, *Letters.*

45. BR uses "last legacy" phrase in letters to Gates, 4 February 1778, and to Greene, 1 February 1778, ibid. The fully annotated "To the Officers in the Army of the United American States: Directions for Preserving the Health of Soldiers," appears in ibid., pp. 140–147.

46. BR to Shippen, 1 February 1778; BR to Greene ?, 1 February 1778, both ibid.

47. BR to Roberdeau, 9 March 1778, ibid.

48. Ibid.; travels recorded in Mitchell, ed., "Historical Notes of BR," pp. 149–150; Finley affidavit in BR to Washington, 25 February 1778, *Letters.*

49. BR to Washington, 25 February 1778, ibid.; Washington to Henry, quoted in Goodman, *Rush,* p. 115.

50. BR to Roberdeau, 9 March 1778, *Letters.*

51. Mitchell, ed., "Historical Notes of BR," p. 149; BR to William Henry Drayton, Samuel Huntington, and John Banister, 20 April 1778, *Letters.*

52. *Auto.,* p. 137; BR to Dickinson, 20 March 1778, Dickinson Papers, formerly with Library Company, now with HSP.

53. *Auto.,* pp. 137–138; Mitchell, ed., "Historical Notes of BR," p. 150.

12. Back in Philadelphia: 1778–1780

Robert L. Brunhouse's *The Counter-Revolution in Pennsylvania 1776–1790* (1942) is indispensable for anyone attempting to unravel the political events of this period. His account of the conversion of the College of Philadelphia into a university can be supplemented by Edward Potts Cheyney's *History of the University of Pennsylvania 1740–1940* (1940), which is notably fair to Rush's enemies and their effort to "broaden the bottom" of education.

The most authoritative account of Shippen's trial, amply annotated, is in Whitfield J. Bell Jr.'s *John Morgan* (1965), chapter 13.

Rush's "Account of the Bilious Remitting Fever, As it Appeared in Philadelphia in the Summer and Autumn of the Year, 1780," is part of his *Medical Inquiries and Observations* (1789), pp. 89–100. References to the essay in the notes below are based on a reprint of it that appeared in the *American Journal of Medicine* 11 (1951), pp. 546–550, which happened to be more accessible.

On the Humane Society of Philadelphia, see Elizabeth H. Thomson, "The Role of Physicians in the Humane Societies of the Eighteenth Century," *Bulletin of the History of Medicine* 37 (1963), pp. 43–51; a briefer description is in Horace Mather Lippincott's *Early Philadelphia, Its People, Life and Progress* (1917).

1. *Auto.,* p. 138; BR to Abigail Adams Smith, 3 September 1778, *Letters.*

2. Daybook No. 2; Journal AA; C. W. Peale to David Ramsay, ca. late 1778, Brunhouse, ed., *David Ramsay,* p. 57; BR to wife, 24 August 1778, *Letters.*

3. BR to wife, 24 August 1778, 30 July 1779, *Letters;* Howard Peckham, ed., "Dr. Berkenhout's Journal, 1778," *PMHB* 65 (1941), p. 87.

4. Ramsay to BR, 3 February 1779, Brunhouse, ed., *David Ramsay,* p. 58; BR to Ramsay, 5 November 1778, *Letters.* BR mentions his gray hair to Lady Jane Belsches, 21 April 1784, ibid. The letters being held for BR at the post office are mentioned in *Pennsylvania Packet,* 24 October 1778. Reference to "long confinement," *Auto.,* p. 138.

5. BR to wife, 24 August 1778, *Letters;* Lee to BR, 26 September 1779, 19 December 1781, *Lee Papers,* vol. 2, pp. 370, 467–468.

6. BR to Ramsay, 5 November 1778; BR to William Gordon, 10 December 1778; BR to Gates, 1 March 1779, all *Letters.*

7. Washington quoted in Flexner, *Washington in the Revolution,* p. 336; Adams quoted in Wood, *Creation of the American Republic,* p. 420.

8. *Pennsylvania Packet,* 25 July 1787; BR to Wayne, 24 September 1776; *Auto.,* p. 117; Roberts as "infamous Tory" in *Pennsylvania Packet,* 27 August 1778. Roberts' guilt noted in ibid., 7 November 1778.

9. Number of students in chemistry class listed on sixth page from end of Daybook No. 2. Material on Stockton drawn from Alfred Hoyt Bill, *A House Called Morven* (1954), pp. 48–50.

10. BR, "Contrast," pp. 65–72.

11. Bill, *Morven,* pp. 49–50.

12. "Journal of Rev. James Sproat," *PMHB* 27 (1903), p. 505.

13. "Manly decision": BR to Wayne, 18 June 1777. Oath of allegiance: BR to John Montgomery, 5 November 1782, both *Letters.* On Bryan: Graydon, *Memoirs,* pp. 287–288. Reed's visit to BR's bedside: BR to Adams, 24 February 1790, *Letters.*

14. Reference to acts of assembly on prohibition of whisky, suppression of vice, abolition of slavery are found in the *Pennsylvania Packet,* 4 March, 8 and 11 May 1779. BR to Ramsay, 5 November 1778, *Letters; Auto.,* p. 158. BR's name attached to an address by the Republican Society appears in *Pennsylvania Packet,* 25 March 1779. Journal AA.

15. BR to James McHenry, 2 June 1779, *Letters.*

16. *Pennsylvania Packet,* 3 July 1779, reprinted in *Letters,* pp. 230–237.

17. Quoted in *Letters,* p. 236n. Dissatisfaction with the essay was not confined to Congress. "I applaud your zeal, but cannot approve your delicacy in concealing from public view the names of those who are misapplying public money," "Socrates" observed in the *Pennsylvania Packet,* 13 July 1779. "Leonidas'" limp retort appeared in the newspaper on July 20.

18. *Pennsylvania Packet,* 22 and 29 July 1779. *Pennsylvania Gazette,* 28 July 1779.

19. Paine, *Pennsylvania Packet,* 14 August 1779; "Leonidas," ibid., 27 August 1779. BR's essay apparently followed an earlier one in the *Packet,* 1 August 1778, by "Gallo-Americanus," who has been identified as BR by William C. Stinchcombe, *The American Revolution and the French Alliance* (1969), p. 130n.

20. Daybook No. 2; Journal AA; BR to Adams, 12 October 1779; BR to wife, 30 July 1779, *Letters.*

21. The material on Fort Wilson comes from Charles Page Smith, "The Attack on Fort Wilson," *PMHB* 78 (1954), pp. 177–188. BR commented on the episode to Adams, 12 October 1779, *Letters.*

22. BR to Charles Lee, 24 October 1779, *Letters.* In a lost letter to Ramsay, BR apparently spoke of retirement, for Ramsay, 23 January 1780, replied: "You may talk of retirement from business. I cannot." Brunhouse, ed., *David Ramsay,* p. 65.

23. "Broad bottom," Ewing's phrase, from *Pennsylvania Packet,* 26 February 1785.

24. Cheyney, *University of Pennsylvania,* pp. 120–137; Brunhouse, *Counter-Revolution,* pp. 77–79.

25. BR in *Pennsylvania Packet,* 2 March 1785.

26. Cheyney, *University of Pennsylvania,* p. 135; James Hall to BR, 27 April 1780, 33 BR-MSS 96.

27. BR to James McHenry, 19 January 1780, *Letters.* Morgan's *Vindication* begins in the *Pennsylvania Packet,* 17 June 1779. BR to Morgan [June? 1779], *Letters.*

28. BR to Morgan, 17 July 1779, in Duncan, "Medical Men," p. 294. Charges quoted in Gibson, *Otto,* p. 267.

29. BR to Adams, 19 October 1779, *Letters.*

30. BR to wife, 17 March 1780, ibid.

31. BR to John Marshall, 5 September 1804, ibid.; Flexner, *Washington in the Revolution,* p. 374n.

32. BR, "Notes on Congress," Notebook No. 2, BR-MSS; BR, "Substance of information and evidence against Dr. Shippen, Junr.," 29 BR-MSS 110; Morgan, quoting BR at trial, *Pennsylvania Packet,* 7 October 1780.

33. BR to Adams, 28 April and 13 July 1780, *Letters.*

34. BR to Adams, 13 July 1780, ibid.

35. On pledges: Robert C. Alberts, *Golden Voyage: The Life and Times of William Bingham 1752–1804* (1969), p. 89; Brunhouse, *Counter-Revolution,* p. 86; Bray Hammond, *Banks and Politics in America from the Revolution to the Civil War* (1957), pp. 40–44. BR's contribution is listed in Scharf and Westcott, *History of Philadelphia,* vol. 1, p. 409n, and *Pennsylvania Packet,* 27 June 1780.

36. Journal B, BR-MSS.

37. BR, "An Account of the Bilious Remitting Fever, As it Appeared in Philadelphia in the Summer and Autumn of the Year 1780," reprinted in *American Journal of Medicine* 11 (1951), p. 546. The forty-three inoculations are listed in Journal B (1779–1781), under April.

38. "An Account of the Bilious Remitting Fever," p. 546. Journal B gives Wilson as a patient first in May. BR mentioned the deaths from cold water to John Adams, 23 August 1780, *Letters.* The Humane Society's aims are given in Lippincott, *Early Philadelphia,* p. 20, but the fullest record appears on Reel No. 42 of the filmed records of the Pennsylvania Hospital on deposit at the American Philosophical Society. These records show that BR was chosen vice president of the society on 5 September 1780, and that he served on the reorganization committee in 1787. James Hall to BR, 27 April 1780, 33 BR-MSS 96, quotes his former mentor on preventive medicine.

39. Journal B and Daybook No. 2; BR to John Dickinson, 3 September 1780, Dickinson Papers, formerly with Library Company, now at HSP; BR, "An Account of the Bilious Remitting Fever," p. 546.

40. BR, "An Account of the Bilious Remitting Fever," pp. 547, 548, 549.

41. Ibid., p. 550.

42. *Auto.,* pp. 85–86.

43. Binger, *Revolutionary Doctor,* pp. 154–155.

44. *Pennsylvania Packet,* 25 November 1780; Bell, *Morgan,* p. 236.

45. *Pennsylvania Packet,* 18 November 1780.

46. Whitfield Bell, Jr., "The Court-Martial of Dr. William Shippen, Jr.," *Journal of the History of Medicine* 19 (1964), p. 231. Bell, in reprinting the article as a chapter in his biography of Morgan, changed "morally indefensible" to "hardly defensible," p. 234.

47. Morgan's new attack began in the *Pennsylvania Packet,* 2 September 1780, and lasted until 23 December 1780. On patients see Journal B. BR to Shippen, 18 November 1780, *Letters.*

48. *Pennsylvania Packet,* 2 and 9 December 1780.

49. Ibid., 23 December 1780.

50. BR to Boudinot, 30 January 1781, *Letters; Pennsylvania Packet,* 14 July 1781.

13. "All Will End Well": 1781–1782

1. BR to Adams, 21 January 1781, *Letters.*

2. On Morris: BR to Gates, 5 September 1781, ibid. BR's share in Bank of North America noted in Forrest McDonald, *We the People. The Economic Origins of the Constitution* (1958), p. 174.

3. BR to Gates, 5 September 1781, *Letters.*

4. *Pennsylvania Packet,* 23 October and 2 November 1781.

5. BR to Greene, 30 October 1781, *Letters.*

6. Journal B; after mid-August 1781, see Journal C. BR's Preface is dated 13 April

1781. On the American edition of Cullen's work, see BR to Cullen, 16 September 1783, *Letters.* The lecture on inoculation appeared in 1781 (see advertisement in *Pennsylvania Packet,* August 18) and in an appendix of *Medical Inquiries and Observations* (1789), pp. 3–20. BR's humble remarks, p. 3.

7. *Pennsylvania Packet,* 14 November and 16 December 1780; *Freeman's Journal,* 26 September 1781.

8. Bell, *Morgan,* pp. 244–245.

9. *Freeman's Journal,* 26 September 1781.

10. Ibid., 3 and 10 October 1781.

11. Ibid., 17 October 1781; also 7, 14, and 21 November 1781, ibid.

12. Reel No. 29 of Pennsylvania Hospital Records at American Philosophical Society: "Notes Taken from Dr. Rush's Lectures in the Winter of 1781 & 1782" by Reading Beatty, dated 20 February 1783.

13. Ramsay to BR, 9 February 1782: "I shall very cheerfully accept a room in your house if you can spare one, on my arrival, which I suppose will be about the 20th of March," in Brunhouse, ed., *David Ramsay,* p. 68. BR on "Sukey" to Elias Boudinot, 30 January 1781; BR on Ramsay to Jacob Read, 23 April 1782, both in *Letters.*

14. BR to Elizabeth Graeme Ferguson, 16 July 1782, *Letters.*

15. E. James Ferguson, "The Nationalists of 1781–1782 and the Economic Interpretation of the Constitution," *Journal of American History* 56 (1969), p. 246; idem, *Power of the Purse,* pp. 112–115, 152–153.

16. Journal C. The nine essays appeared in the *Pennsylvania Journal,* 15, 22, 29 May, 19 June, 4, 10, 17, 31 July, and 14 August 1782. The first, second, and fourth were signed "Retaliation," the others were signed "Leonidas." The final four essays also appeared in the *Pennsylvania Gazette,* 3, 10 and 17 July, and 14 August 1782.

17. "Retaliation," *Pennsylvania Journal,* 19 June 1782.

18. Lee to BR, 26 September 1779, *Lee Papers,* vol. 2, p. 371.

19. "Leonidas," "On the United States Navy," *Pennsylvania Journal,* 4 July 1782; also *Letters,* pp. 273–277.

20. "Leonidas," "On Public Credit as the Means of Obtaining a Navy," *Pennsylvania Gazette,* 10 July 1782.

21. Peale to BR, 13 December 1782, in Sellers, *Peale,* vol. 1, pp. 222–223. BR's debt to Bingham is mentioned in Alberts, *Golden Voyage: Bingham,* p. 503.

22. *Pennsylvania Gazette,* 10 July 1782; McDonald, *We the People,* p. 174.

23. "Leonidas," "The Subject of an American Navy *continued,*" *Pennsylvania Gazette,* 31 July 1782.

24. "Leonidas," "For the Pennsylvania Gazette," *Pennsylvania Gazette,* 17 July 1782.

25. Ibid.

26. BR to Wayne, 16 September 1782; BR to Greene, 16 September 1782, both *Letters.*

27. Rev. John Coleman to BR, 6 May 1782, 3 BR-MSS 89; *Auto.,* pp. 163–164.

28. On Fletcher, see Leslie Stephen, *History of English Thought in the Eighteenth Century* (2 vols., 1962 paperback ed.), vol. 2, pp. 362–363. *Auto.,* p. 164; advertisement in *Freeman's Journal,* 31 July 1782.

29. On Wilson, see Trinterud, *Forming of an American Tradition,* p. 256. On Blair, see BR to Price, 29 July 1787, *Letters.*

30. BR to Price, 2 June 1787, ibid.

31. BR, "Against Spirituous Liquors," *Pennsylvania Journal,* 26 June 1782, reprinted in *Letters,* pp. 270–273.

32. BR to Greene, 16 September 1782, *Letters.*

33. BR to Montgomery, 5 November 1782, ibid.

34. BR to Montgomery, 15 October 1782, ibid.

35. Petition, dated 31 October 1782, in *Pennsylvania Journal,* 13 November 1782.

14. The Spirit of Peace: 1783–1784

1. Brunhouse, *Counter-Revolution,* pp. 137–140.

2. BR to Montgomery, 27 June 1783, *Letters;* BR to Montgomery, 16 July 1783, 43 BR-MSS 93. BR's efforts to pacify the mutinous soldiers is discussed in James E. Gibson, "Benjamin Rush Terminates a Post-War Mutiny among Troops Demanding Their Discharge," College of Physicians of Philadelphia *Transactions and Studies,* 4th ser., 13 (1945), pp. 134–138.

3. BR to Montgomery, 4 July 1783, *Letters.*

4. Paine to BR, 13 June 1783, Foner, ed., *Writings of Thomas Paine,* vol. 2, pp. 263–265, 1209–1210. The letter appears to be misdated; it must have been written in July.

5. BR to Boudinot, 2 August 1783, *Letters.*

6. Thomson to Peters, 10 August 1783, Burnett, ed., *Letters of Continental Congress,* vol. 7, p. 256.

7. Journal C for BR's practice. He attended more than 100 patients every month from April through October, reaching a high of 127 in September. BR to Montgomery, 30 September 1783, 41 BR-MSS 43.

8. "Clarendon," in *Freeman's Journal,* Postscript, 10 October 1783.

9. BR to Montgomery, 20 October 1783, 41 BR-MSS 45.

10. BR to Montgomery, 15 November 1783, *Letters;* BR to Montgomery, 24 October 1783, 41 BR-MSS 46.

11. Journal C. His cash income averaged about £50 a month, occasionally as in January, April, and September, soaring to well over £100.

12. Morgan to Pennsylvania Hospital Managers, 24 May 1783, Thomas G. Morton assisted by Frank Woodbury, *History of the Pennsylvania Hospital, 1751–1895* (1897), pp. 448–449. See also Reel No. 2 of the hospital records at American Philosophical Society, especially pp. 298, 312, 315, and 318.

13. Quoted in Bell, *Morgan,* p. 242.

14. Ibid., p. 249. Official notice of BR's appointment found in Box 9, BR-MSS.

15. *Pennsylvania Packet,* 7 October 1783.

16. Miles, "BR, Chemist," p. 47.

17. BR, "An Account of the Scarlatina Anginosa as it appeared in Philadelphia in the Years 1783 and 1784," *Medical Inquiries and Observations* (1789), pp. 101–108. BR to Montgomery, 1 September 1783, *Letters.*

18. "An Account," pp. 102, 103.

19. Ibid., pp. 107, 108; "Added Observations upon Scarlatina Anginosa," *Medical Inquiries and Observations* (1794–1798 ed.), vol. 1, pp. 111.

20. BR to Lady Jane Belsches, 21 April 1784, *Letters.* The number of BR's patients slipped to between sixty and seventy-five a month during the first half of 1784, but cash income rose appreciably. In the first six months of the year, he collected more than £800 in cash and during the latter half of the year nearly £500. Journal C.

21. BR to Lady Jane Belsches, 21 April 1784, *Letters.* BR referred to her as "our sister Sukey" in letter to Elizabeth Graeme Ferguson, 16 July 1782, ibid. She is not to be confused with Susan Boudinot, whom he also called "Sukey" in letter to Elias Boudinot, 30 January 1781, ibid.

22. The statement that Mrs. Morris and Mrs. Stamper were running the dry-goods and china shops is based on bills for 1783 and 1784 in 34 BR-MSS 98, 99, 102. The hint of financial tension comes from BR to Boudinot, 25 December 1783, a letter owned by Lloyd W. Smith, a photostat of which is at the American Philosophical Society. BR refers to his "truly amiable" in-laws in letter to Lady Jane Belsches, 21 April 1784, *Letters.* BR to wife, 12 July 1783, ibid.

23. BR to Lady Jane Belsches, 21 April 1784; BR to wife, 12 July 1783, both *Letters.*

24. BR to John Bayard, 2 July [actually 2 August] 1783, ibid.

25. Armstrong to BR, 6 January 1784, 41 BR-MSS 51 and 52; BR to Montgomery, 17 February 1784, 41 BR-MSS 57; Armstrong to BR, 28 February 1784, 41 BR-MSS 58.

26. BR to Montgomery, 12 July 1784, 41 BR-MSS 76.

27. BR to [Edward Hand?], 10 November 1784, *Letters.*

28. Ibid.

29. Two parts of BR's pamphlet published in 1784 were printed in the *Pennsylvania Gazette,* 18 May and 15 June 1785. The quotations are taken from here.

30. BR to Montgomery, 4 January 1785, *Letters;* Hartley to BR, 8 January 1785, 41 BR-MSS 105.

31. BR to Price, 22 April 1786; BR to Adams, 21 February 1789, both *Letters.*

32. Roberts' guilt noted in *Pennsylvania Packet,* 7 November 1778. "Journal of Samuel Rowland Fisher," *PMHB* 41 (1917), p. 177; BR to Mrs. Ferguson, 25 December 1787, *Letters.* BR to Executive Council, 14 June 1780, re. Mrs. Coxe, Gratz Collection, case 1, box 20, folio 4, HSP; on Kuhn: *Letters,* p. 1113n; BR to Mrs. Ferguson, ca. January 1781, Amherst College Library, photostat at American Philosophical Society.

33. BR to Adams, 24 February 1790; BR to John Bayard, 2 July 1783, both *Letters.*

34. Huck (-Saunders) to BR, 11 March 1784, 43 BR-MSS 98; Mrs. Coxe to BR, 4 August 1783, 16 February 1786, 27 BR-MSS 23, 24.

35. Cullen to BR, 20 June 1783, 24 BR-MSS 55; Lettsom to BR, 8 September 1783, 28 BR-MSS 3; Andrew Duncan to BR, 29 May 1783, 21 BR-MSS 73.

36. BR to Cullen, 22 December 1784; BR to Lettsom, 15 November 1783, both *Letters;* Lettsom to BR, 28 February 1784, 28 BR-MSS 4.

37. BR to Hogg, 16 September 1783, Butterfield, ed., "Further Letters," p. 20; Charles Elliott to BR, 3 July, 16 October, 25 October 1784, 4 BR-MSS 140, 141; 21 BR-MSS 85.

38. Timothy Bevan to BR, 1783, 39 BR-MSS 30; 2 February 1785, 39 BR-MSS 31; Joseph Bevan to BR, 6 April 1784, 29 September 1787, 15 February 1793, 39 BR-MSS 32, 33, 34.

39. Charles Dilly to BR, 26 June 1783, 15 March 1784, 26 February 1785, 5 July 1786, 31 BR-MSS 12, 14, 19, 22.

40. Dilly to BR, 8 August 1785, 5 July 1786, 31 BR-MSS 20, 22.

41. BR to Lettsom, 15 November 1783; 8 April 1785; BR to King, 2 April 1783, all *Letters.*

42. Ramsay to BR, 16 August 1784, Brunhouse, ed., *David Ramsay,* p. 81; Dilly to BR, 5 July 1786, 31 BR-MSS 22.

43. BR, "An Account of the Influence of the Military and Political Events of the American Revolution Upon the Human Body," *Medical Inquiries and Observations* (1794–1798 ed.), vol. 1, pp. 263–278. Quotations are from pp. 273–274.

44. Ibid., p. 277.

45. BR to Nisbet, 5 December 1783; BR to Sharp, 27 April 1784, both *Letters.*

46. BR to Cullen, 22 December 1784, ibid.; BR to William Peterkin, 27 November 1784, Butterfield, ed., "Further Letters," p. 26; BR to Nisbet, 5 December 1783; BR to Price, 22 April 1786; BR to Nisbet, 28 November 1784, all *Letters.*

47. BR to Lettsom, 8 April 1785, ibid.; BR to Peterkin, 27 November 1784, Butterfield, ed., "Further Letters," pp. 26–27; BR to John Howard, 14 October 1789, *Letters.*

A MULTITUDE OF CAUSES

15. The Birth of "Our Brat": 1783–1784

The general remarks on the Founding Fathers' ideas on education owe much to David Tyack's excellent article, "Forming the National Character. Paradox in the Educational Thought of the Revolutionary Generation," which appeared in the *Harvard Educational Review* 36 (1966), pp. 29–41. Thanks go to Joseph F. Sinzer for calling attention to it.

Few colleges in America enjoy a more complete record of their early years than Dickinson. The primary sources are abundant and secondary works are numerous and in several instances excellent. The most recent study, told through Rush's eyes, is James A. Bonar's detailed and thoroughly researched 1965 Ph.D. dissertation, "Benjamin Rush and the Theory and Practice of Republican Education in Pennsylvania," on deposit at the Milton S. Eisenhower Library, Johns Hopkins University in Baltimore. This work, despite the title, deals mainly with Rush's relations with Dickinson College. The full bibliographical essay notes with pertinent comment all earlier work done on the subject.

The material in this chapter comes principally from volumes forty-one and forty-two in the Rush MSS, which contain some three hundred letters to and from Rush covering the first years of the college. The standard history of the college is James Henry Morgan's *Dickinson College. The History of One Hundred and Fifty Years, 1783–1933* (1933). A succinct and satisfactory account of the school's beginnings appears in Saul Sack, *History of Higher Education in Pennsylvania* (2 vols., 1963). Details of the story are filled in with three first-rate essays drawn from the Boyd Lee Spahr Lectures in Americana: Lyman H. Butterfield, "Benjamin Rush and the Beginnings of 'John and Mary's' College over the Susquehanna," *Bulwark of Liberty. Early Years at Dickinson College* (1950); Whitfield J. Bell, Jr., "The Other Man on Bingham's Porch," in *John and Mary's College* (1956); and A. O. Aldridge, "Dickinson College and the 'Broad Bottom'

of Early Education in Pennsylvania," in *Early Dickinsoniana* (1961).
Ernest J. Moyne writes on the candidacy for principal of Dickinson of "The
Reverend William Hazlitt and Dickinson College," in *PMHB* 85 (1961),
pp. 289–302.

1. BR to John Armstrong, 19 March 1783, *Letters.*

2. Washington and Jefferson quoted in Tyack, "Forming the National Character,"
p. 32, Rush quoted p. 33.

3. Ibid., p. 31.

4. Ewing to BR, 17 December 1773, 4 BR-MSS 122.

5. BR in *Pennsylvania Packet,* 17 February 1785; "School of Prophets" mentioned
in Good, *BR and American Education,* p. 110n; a college for ministers put by
BR to Armstrong, 30 July 1783, 41 BR-MSS 34 and 35; BR to Armstrong, 19
March 1783, *Letters.*

6. BR to Armstrong, 19 March 1783; BR to Nisbet, 27 August 1784, ibid.

7. BR, "Hints for Establishing a College at Carlisle," 3 September 1782, 41
BR-MSS 1.

8. Ibid.; Patrick Alison to BR, 12 February 1783, 41 BR-MSS 14, 15, 16; John
Floyd to BR, 17 February 1783, 41 BR-MSS 17.

9. Ewing to BR, 17 December 1773, 4 BR-MSS 122.

10. BR to Montgomery, 7 July 1783, 41 BR-MSS 33.

11. BR to Armstrong, 19 March 1783, *Letters.* Armstrong's dissolving resistance first
becomes apparent in letter to BR, 15 April 1783, and Montgomery's to BR, 16
April 1783, 41 BR-MSS 26 and 27.

12. BR to King, 2 April 1783, *Letters;* Montgomery to BR, 15 April 1783, 41 BR-MSS
27; BR to King, 2 April 1783, *Letters.*

13. King to BR, 24 March 1783, 41 BR-MSS 22; BR to King, 2 April 1783, *Letters.*

14. Black to BR, 21 June 1783, 41 BR-MSS 31; BR to Montgomery, 27 June 1783,
Letters.

15. Petition, in BR's hand, 41 BR-MSS 3 and 4; BR to King, 2 April 1783; BR to
Montgomery, 1 September and 15 November 1783, all *Letters.*

16. BR to Montgomery, 1 September 1783, *Letters.*

17. BR to Cullen, 16 September 1783, *Letters;* Journal C, and Daybook (June 1783–
June 1785).

18. Watson, *Annals of Philadelphia,* vol. 2, pp. 382–383.

19. *Auto.,* p. 86; list of lunatics in Pennsylvania Hospital, 31 BR-MSS 31.

20. Journal C, Daybook; Hall to BR, 18 October 1783, 7 BR-MSS 11.

21. *Auto.,* p. 86; BR to wife, 23 August and 27 August 1787, *Letters.*

22. *Auto.,* pp. 175–176; BR to Mary or Susan Stockton, 30 July 1784, Butterfield, ed.,
"Further Letters," pp. 22–25.

23. BR to wife, 27 June 1787, *Letters*.

24. Michaelis to BR, 22 July 1783, 10 BR-MSS 24; Ramsay to BR, 8 April 1784, Brunhouse, ed., *David Ramsay*, p. 78; Robert Dougan to BR, 5 April 1784, 4 BR-MSS 81; BR to Thomas Hogg, 16 September 1783, Butterfield, ed., "Further Letters," p. 20; BR to Cullen, 17 June 1786, *Letters*, provides a typical letter of introduction.

25. Miles, "BR, Chemist," pp. 47, 48, 54.

26. Ibid., pp. 76, 77.

27. BR to Armstrong, 19 March 1783, *Letters;* Armstrong to BR, 6 January 1784, 41 BR-MSS 51 and 52.

28. Black to BR, 8 January 1784, 41 BR-MSS 53; James Jacks to BR, 3 February 1784, 41 BR-MSS 56; Price to BR, 1 April 1783, 41 BR-MSS 11; on Erskine: BR to Montgomery, 15 November 1783; BR to Lettsom, 8 April 1785, both *Letters*.

29. BR to Witherspoon, 1 August 1767, ibid.; Nisbet to BR, 5 August 1783, 41 BR-MSS 37; Linn to BR, 25 September 1783, 41 BR-MSS 41; BR to Montgomery, 9 October 1783, 41 BR-MSS 44; King to BR, 12 January 1784, 41 BR-MSS 54.

30. BR, "Of the Mode of Education Proper in a Republic," *Essays, Literary, Moral and Philosophical*, pp. 11–12.

31. Ibid., pp. 7, 10, 8.

32. Ibid., pp. 13–19.

33. BR to Montgomery, 9 March 1784, 41 BR-MSS 60.

16. Focus on the Backcountry: 1784–1785

1. Lyman H. Butterfield, ed., "BR Journal of a Trip to Carlisle in 1784," *PMHB* 74 (1950), pp. 443–456.

2. Robert C. Albion and Leonidas Dodson, eds., *Philip Vickers Fithian: Journal, 1775–1776* (1932), pp. 6, 7, 8–9.

3. On meeting, see Morgan, *Dickinson College*, pp. 26–27, and Sack, *Higher Education in Pennsylvania*, vol. 1, p. 48. On Bingham, see Alberts, *Golden Voyage: Bingham*, p. 130. Bingham's letter is dated 10 August 1783.

4. Montgomery to BR, 7 May 1784, 41 BR-MSS 67; BR to Nisbet, 15 May 1784, *Letters*.

5. The quotations here are taken from the sixth edition (1811).

6. "To Thomas Percival: An Account of the Progress of Population, Agriculture, Manners, and Government in Pennsylvania" [26 October 1786], *Letters*, pp. 400–407.

7. BR, "An Account of the Manners of the German Inhabitants of Pennsylvania," *Essays, Literary, Moral and Philosophical*, pp. 226–248.

8. BR's real estate dealings at this time are difficult to assess, for the Tench Coxe Papers at the HSP, which contain the bulk of his letters on the subject, are currently closed to scholars. Letters to William Plunkett covering the BR-Franks negotiations are found in 32 BR-MSS 62-92. These date from late 1784 through September 1789. The fullest account of BR and Franks as partners is in Morris Jastrow's "Documents Relating to the Career of Colonel Isaac Franks," *Publications of the American Jewish Historical Society,* vol. 5, pp. 7-34. Ramsay's remarks to BR on land were made 23 January 1780 and 18 August 1787, Brunhouse, ed., *David Ramsay,* pp. 64, 113.

9. BR to Montgomery, 15 April 1784, *Letters;* BR to Linn, 4 May 1784, ibid.

10. BR to Linn, 4 May 1784; BR to Montgomery, 15 April 1784, both ibid.

11. BR to Nisbet, [19 April 1784], ibid.

12. Samuel Miller, *Memoir of Rev. Charles Nisbet . . .* (1840), pp. 104, 109, quoted in *Letters,* p. 375n; Dickinson to Nisbet (copy), 25 October 1784, 41 BR-MSS 97.

13. Trustees to Nisbet, 15 November 1784, 41 BR-MSS 99; BR to Montgomery, 13 November 1784, *Letters;* Dickinson to Nisbet, 15 November 1784, 41 BR-MSS 98.

14. BR to Nisbet, 28 November 1784, *Letters.*

15. BR to Montgomery, 4 January 1785, 13 November 1784, ibid.

16. Ramsay to BR, 14 December 1784, Brunhouse, ed., *David Ramsay,* p. 94. Quotation on "Dr. Froth" is found in *Early Dickinsoniana* (1961), p. 104.

17. BR to Sharp, 27 April 1784; BR to Ashbel Green, 11 August 1787, *Letters;* BR to Montgomery, 8 August 1786, 42 BR-MSS 21.

18. BR to Price, 15 October 1785; BR to Green, 11 August 1787, *Letters.*

19. BR to Montgomery, 20 February 1786; BR to Price, 27 October 1786, ibid.

20. Montgomery to BR, 6 October 1785, 41 BR-MSS 156; BR to Price, 15 October 1785, *Letters.* On Presbyterianism at this time, see Trinterud, *Forming of an American Tradition,* pp. 280–284.

21. BR, "Influence of Physical Causes upon the Moral Faculty," *Medical Inquiries and Observations* (1794–1798 ed.), vol. 2, p. 16.

22. BR to Trustees of Dickinson College, 23 May 1785; BR to Montgomery, 27 June 1785, both *Letters.*

23. BR to Montgomery, 14 June 1785, ibid.; BR to Montgomery, 27 June 1785, 41 BR-MSS 131 and 132.

24. BR to Montgomery, 21 July 1786, 42 BR-MSS 18.

25. Montgomery to BR, 6 July 1785, 41 BR-MSS 134; BR to John Erskine, 25 October 1785, *Letters;* BR to Montgomery, 25 September 1786, 42 BR-MSS 27; Nisbet to BR, 18 July 1785, 41 BR-MSS 136.

26. Nisbet to BR, 24 August 1785, 41 BR-MSS 142; Nisbet to BR, 10 August 1785, 41 BR-MSS 139; BR to Montgomery, 20 August 1785, *Letters.*

27. Nisbet's resignation is dated 18 October 1785, 41 BR-MSS 157; BR to Montgomery, 11 September 1785, 28 December 1785, *Letters.*

28. King to BR, 8 April 1786, 41 BR-MSS 11; BR to Montgomery, 18 June 1786, 42 BR-MSS 16; Montgomery to BR, 12 September 1786, 42 BR-MSS 25; BR to Montgomery, 13 September 1786, 42 BR-MSS 26.

29. Nisbet to BR, 9 January 1786, 41 BR-MSS 174; BR to Montgomery, 25 September 1786, 42 BR-MSS 28; BR to Trustees, [April] 1786, *Letters;* Nisbet to Trustees on Present State of Dickinson College, 15 November 1786, 42 BR-MSS 36. The complimentary report appeared in the *Pennsylvania Packet,* 7 February 1787, and is reprinted in Goodman, *Rush,* p. 335.

30. Sack, *Higher Education in Pennsylvania,* vol. 1, pp. 65–66.

31. BR to Trustees, 21 October 1786, *Letters.*

32. BR to Price, 14 February 1787; BR to Dickinson, 5 April 1787; BR to Montgomery, 17 February 1787, all ibid.; BR to Montgomery, 10 May 1788, 42 BR-MSS 48.

33. "Pro forma" remark quoted in Joseph Henry Dubbs, *History of Franklin and Marshall College* (1903), p. 7.

34. BR to Trustees of Dickinson College, 23 May 1785, *Letters;* BR, "To the Citizens of Pennsylvania . . . ," ibid., pp. 364–368.

35. Dubbs, *History of Franklin and Marshall,* pp. 17–26.

36. BR to Montgomery, 21 January and 17 February 1787, *Letters.*

37. BR's report on the convocation appears in BR to Annis Boudinot Stockton, 19 June 1787, *Letters.* An earlier edition by Butterfield, *A Letter by Dr. Benjamin Rush Describing the Consecration of the German College at Lancaster in June, 1787* (1945), contains a helpful introduction.

38. BR to Annis Boudinot Stockton, 19 June 1787, *Letters.*

39. BR to Muhlenberg, 15 February 1788, ibid. Further letters revealing BR's ties with the college are found in 24 BR-MSS 124–126, 159–160.

17. Reforms in Physic: 1786–1787

Once again Wyndham Miles's essay "Benjamin Rush, Chemist," *Chymia* 4 (1953), pp. 37–77, has guided the way through this side of Rush's life. An oblique approach to his medical reforms is contained in James Mease, *The Picture of Philadelphia . . .* (1811), which has essays on most of the organizations he was connected with, such as the dispensary and the College of Physicians.

Daniel J. Boorstin, *The Lost World of Thomas Jefferson* (1948), places Rush's concept of the moral faculty in the social-intellectual setting of eighteenth-century America.

On the College of Physicians, see William S. W. Ruschenberger, *An Account of the Institution and Progress of the College of Physicians at Philadelphia . . .* (1887), and Horace Mather Lippincott, *Early Philadelphia, Its People, Life and Progress* (1917). Rush's "A Discourse Delivered Before the College of Physicians of Philadelphia, Feb. 6, 1787. On the Objects of Their Institution," has been reprinted in College of Physicians *Transactions,* 4th ser., 4, Supplement, "Commemoration of the 150th Anniversary of the Founding" (1937), pp. 5–10.

1. The "warm weather": BR to Montgomery, 18 June 1786, *Letters.* The illness must have been unusually severe, for mention of it turns up often in letters to and from BR. See, for example, BR to Dickinson, 14 April 1786, *Letters;* Solomon Birckhead to BR, 28 June 1786, 2B2 BR-MSS 13; BR to James Wilson, 14 April, *PMHB* 24 (1900), p. 233. BR's remark to Lettsom was written 16 August 1786, *Letters.*

2. Abraham, *Lettsom,* pp. 109, 198; BR to Belknap, 8 January 1788, *Letters.*

3. The fullest account of the dispensary appears in Mease, *Picture of Philadelphia,* pp. 236–240.

4. Attendance at the early meetings is found in the dispensary records, incorporated with the Pennsylvania Hospital records, which have been microfilmed by the American Philosophical Society. See particularly film roll No. 41. BR on Griffitts to John Dickinson, 4 October 1791, *Letters.*

5. Good, *BR and American Education,* p. 94; Mease, *Picture of Philadelphia,* p. 236.

6. BR to Belknap, 8 January 1788, *Letters.*

7. Ibid.

8. Mease, *Picture of Philadelphia,* pp. 38–39.

9. BR, "An Enquiry into the Cause of the Increase of Bilious and Intermitting Fevers in Pennsylvania, with Hints for preventing them," American Philosophical Society *Transactions* 2 (1786), pp. 206–212.

10. BR, "Observations on the Cause and Cure of Tetanus," ibid., pp. 225–231. BR to Lettsom, 15 November 1783, *Letters;* BR to Cullen, 22 December 1787, ibid.; *Auto.,* p. 85; BR to wife, 10 September 1793, *Letters.*

11. BR, "An Account of the late Dr. Hugh Martin's Cancer Powder, with brief Observations on Cancers," *Transactions* 2 (1786), pp. 212–217. The quotation is from pp. 212–213.

12. Martin to BR, January 1780 and 1 July 1780, Box 9, BR-MSS. BR's essay was also published in the *Pennsylvania Gazette,* 30 August 1786.

13. John King to BR, 3 March 1783, 41 BR-MSS 18. An indication of widespread

interest in the nostrum appears in John Tyler to BR, 15 November 1786, 17 BR-MSS 75 and Josiah Bartlett to BR, 43 BR-MSS 78. See also BR to Bartlett, 23 February 1783, Dartmouth College Library.

14. BR, "Dr. Martin's Cancer Powder," *Transactions,* pp. 215–216.

15. Lyman H. Butterfield, "BR as Promoter of Useful Knowledge," *Proceedings of the American Philosophical Society* 92 (1948), p. 33.

16. BR, "Dr. Martin's Cancer Powder," *Transactions,* pp. 216, 217.

17. BR, "To Thomas Henry: Observations as Physician General in the Revolution," 22 July 1785, *Letters,* pp. 358–361.

18. The revised essay was entitled "The Result of Observations made upon The Diseases which Occurred in the Military Hospitals of the United States during the Late War," and appeared in *Medical Inquiries and Observations* (1789), pp. 180–185. It appeared further revised in ibid. (1794–1798), vol. 1, pp. 255–262.

19. Ibid. (1789), pp. 263–278.

20. BR to Sharp, 9 July 1774, reprinted by Woods, "Correspondence of Rush and Sharp," pp. 6–8; Sharp to BR, 31 October 1774, 28 BR-MSS 78, and Woods, "Correspondence of Rush and Sharp," pp. 12–13.

21. BR to _____, 13 May 1794, *Letters.*

22. The full essay appears in *Medical Inquiries and Observations* (1794–1798 ed.), vol. 2, pp. 1–56.

23. Franklin to BR, quoted in William Pepper, *The Medical Side of Benjamin Franklin* (1911), p. 101; BR to Price, 22 April 1786, *Letters.*

24. Charles Dilly to BR, 26 February 1787, 31 BR-MSS 24.

25. *Auto.,* p. 91.

26. BR to Webster, 13 February 1783, *Letters;* Thacher, *American Medical Biography,* p. 48.

27. BR, "Of the Mode of Education Proper in a Republic," *Essays, Literary, Moral and Philosophical,* p. 15; Thacher, *American Medical Biography,* p. 55.

28. Hariott W. Warner, ed., *Autobiography of Charles Caldwell* (1855), p. 116; *Auto.,* p. 91.

29. Thacher, *American Medical Biography,* p. 55.

30. The "Plan" appeared bound with "A Mode of Education Proper in a Republic" as a pamphlet in the spring of 1786, was reprinted in the *Pennsylvania Gazette,* 10 May 1786, and led off BR's *Essays, Literary, Moral and Philosophical,* pp. 6–20.

31. King to BR, 25 May 1786, 42 BR-MSS 15; Alexander Addison to BR, 10 August 1786, 1 BR-MSS 3.

32. BR, "To the Citizens of Philadelphia: A Plan for Free Schools," 28 March 1787, *Letters.*

33. BR to wife, 27 June 1787, ibid.

34. BR, "Thoughts upon Female Education," *Essays, Literary, Moral and Philosophical,* pp. 75–92. Good, *BR and American Education,* p. 234, takes note of BR's debt to Fénelon. BR to a degree sought to practice what he preached by giving a series of twelve lectures on chemistry to the ladies who had heard his original talk. Marion B. Savin and Harold J. Abrahams, "Benjamin Rush's Course in Chemistry at the Young Ladies' Academy," *Journal of Franklin Institute* 262 (1956), pp. 425–435, draw extensively from the notebooks BR used to prepare for this course, which might be described as the first course in home economics given in America.

35. BR to Lettsom, 15 November 1783, *Letters.*

36. Lippincott, *Early Philadelphia,* p. 178.

37. BR, "A Discourse Delivered Before the College of Physicians," *Transactions,* p. 6; BR to Lettsom, 16 August 1788, *Letters.*

38. *Auto.,* p. 86; BR to wife, 27 June and 16 August 1787, *Letters.*

18. "Through a Sea of Blunders": 1786–1788

The Counter-Revolution in Pennsylvania 1776–1790 (1942) by Robert L. Brunhouse continues here as earlier to help chart Rush's path through the politics of his state. The single most important volume on ratification in Pennsylvania is John B. McMaster and Frederick D. Stone, *Pennsylvania and the Federal Constitution 1787–1788* (1888), mainly a collection of newspaper accounts on the ratification convention. Merrill Jensen's *The New Nation* (1950) is excellent for putting the Pennsylvania story into the national setting.

1. Brunhouse, *Counter-Revolution,* pp. 170–171, 185; BR under pseudonym of "Nestor," *Pennsylvania Packet,* 21 July 1786.

2. On "Aaron's rod," see "Nestor," ibid.; on tariff, see Brunhouse, *Counter-Revolution,* pp. 172–173.

3. BR to wife, 26 August 1787, *Letters.* Identification of BR as "Nestor" is in Ramsay to BR, 6 August 1786, Brunhouse, ed., *David Ramsay,* p. 105, and in BR to Price, 2 August 1786, in *Proceedings of the Massachusetts Historical Society* 2nd ser. 17 (1903), p. 349. Ramsay speaks of two essays, but a careful search of Philadelphia papers for this period has turned up only the one, "Thoughts on Paper Money," published in the *Pennsylvania Gazette,* 19 July 1786, and reprinted two days later in the *Pennsylvania Packet.* On Pennsylvania's paper currency see also Jensen, *New Nation,* pp. 313, 316, 317.

4. Ramsay to BR, 6 August 1786, Brunhouse, ed., *David Ramsay,* p. 105.

5. BR to Price, 25 May 1786, *Letters.*

6. BR, "An Address to the People of the United States . . . on the Defects of the Confederation," reprinted in Good, *BR and American Education,* pp. 198–206.

7. BR to Wilson, 14 April 1786, Wilson Papers, vol. 3, p. 28, HSP.

8. BR, "Defects of the Confederation," Good, *BR and American Education,* p. 198. A polished version of the statement appears in BR to Price, 25 May 1786, *Letters.*

9. BR to Price, 27 October 1786, ibid.

10. The paper was published in *Essays, Literary, Moral and Philosophical* under the title of "An Enquiry into the Effects of Public Punishments upon Criminals, and upon Society. Read in the Society for Promoting Political Enquiries, Convened at the House of Benjamin Franklin, esq., in Philadelphia, March 9th, 1787," pp. 136–163. Fitzsimons to BR, 29 July 1789, 25 BR-MSS 9. This letter appears written to reassure BR he deserved credit for getting Franklin chosen a delegate to the convention.

11. BR to Price, 14 February 1787, Butterfield, ed., "Further Letters," p. 29; BR to Lettsom, 18 May 1787; BR to Adams, 2 July 1788; BR to Price, 2 June 1787, all *Letters.*

12. BR to Adams, 12 February 1812, ibid.; Washington to Clement Biddle, 10 September 1787, Fitzpatrick, ed., *Writings of Washington,* vol. 29, p. 272. See also John Fitzpatrick, ed., *Diaries of George Washington 1748–1799* (4 vols., 1925), vol. 3, under date 24 July 1787.

13. BR to Price, 2 June 1787, *Letters.*

14. Ibid.

15. Ibid.

16. BR to wife, 16, 22, 26 August 1787, all ibid.

17. *Auto.,* p. 160.

18. BR to Pickering, 30 August 1787; BR to Lettsom, 28 September 1787, both *Letters.*

19. Brunhouse, *Counter-Revolution,* pp. 200–203.

20. *Pennsylvania Packet,* 10 October 1787.

21. Ibid.

22. Duane, ed., *Extracts from the Marshall Diary,* under 7 November 1787, gives votes for BR; official notification of his election is found in Box 9, BR-MSS. Anti-Federalist complaints are in *Pennsylvania Packet,* 18 December 1787, and *Independent Gazetteer,* 18 November 1787.

23. Average age of delegates given in Brunhouse, *Counter-Revolution,* p. 292, footnote 52.

24. McMaster and Stone, *Pennsylvania and the Federal Constitution,* p. 214.

25. Ibid., pp. 218–231 for Wilson speech, pp. 234–235 for BR's.

26. Ibid., pp. 294–295.

27. Ibid., pp. 300, 771.

28. Ibid., pp. 771, 310.

29. Ibid., pp. 419–425.

30. Ibid., pp. 424, 425.

31. Brunhouse, *Counter-Revolution,* pp. 211–213. The attack on "Dr. Puff" by "Centinel" on 30 January 1788 appears in McMaster and Stone, *Pennsylvania and the Federal Constitution,* pp. 642–643.

32. BR to Irvine, 21 December 1787, 9 Irvine MSS 107, HSP; BR to Muhlenberg, 15 February 1788; BR to Ramsay, March or April 1788, both *Letters.*

33. BR to Pickering, 29 January 1788, *Letters; Auto.,* p. 246, where BR misdates his illness as 1787. BR to Montgomery, 9 April 1788, *Letters; Auto.,* p. 165.

34. BR to Montgomery, 9 April 1788, *Letters.*

35. BR to Ramsay, March or April 1788, ibid.

36. BR to Adams, 2 July 1788, ibid.

37. BR to Boudinot ?, 9 July 1788, entitled, "Observations on the Federal Procession in Philadelphia," ibid. John Rush's invitation to ride the Ship of Union, 2 July 1788, 32 BR-MSS 1. Mention of Judge Rush appears in Rufus Wilmot Griswold, *The Republican Court or American Society in the Days of Washington* (1854), p. 106.

38. BR to Dickinson, 15 July 1788, *Letters;* Brunhouse, *Counter-Revolution,* p. 216; BR to Belknap, 7 October 1788, *Letters.*

39. Attack on "Galen" by "Centinel," 14 November 1788, in McMaster and Stone, *Pennsylvania and the Federal Constitution,* p. 683. "Centinel" identifies BR as "Lucullus" in this piece. BR to Belknap, 7 October 1788, *Letters.* Plea for recognition of God in Constitution made to John Adams, 15 June 1789, ibid.

40. David Ramsay, *History of the American Revolution* (2 vols., 1789), vol. 2, p. 354. Brunhouse, ed., *David Ramsay,* p. 41n, points out that a note in the Library Company of Philadelphia's copy of Ramsay's work identifies the peroration as by BR.

19. Reforms in the Cause of Virtue: 1787–1789

The best modern study of the American reformer and reforms of this period continues to be Michael Kraus's *The Atlantic Civilization: Eighteenth Century Origins* (1949). Robert L. Brunhouse, *The Counter-Revolution in Pennsylvania, 1776–1790* (1942), touches on most of the reforms in which Rush was involved. The best contemporary work on the various reform societies Rush worked with is James Mease's *Picture of Philadelphia . . .* (1811).

Asa Earl Martin's "The Temperance Movement in Pennsylvania Prior to the Civil War," *PMHB* 49 (1925), pp. 105–230, contains the most detailed study on the subject. The last few pages of Joseph Hirsch, "Enlightened Eighteenth-Century Views of the Alcohol Problem," *Journal of Medical History* 4 (1949), pp. 230–236, discusses Rush's approach to drinking. David Brion Davis, "The Movement to Abolish Capital Punishment in America, 1787–1861," *American Historical Review* 63 (1957), pp. 23–46, is an excellent essay, though it mentions Rush only in passing. More relevant is Albert Post, "Early Efforts to Abolish Capital Punishment in Pennsylvania," *PMHB* 68 (1944), pp. 38–53.

Albert Deutsch provides a general account of *The Mentally Ill in America. A History of Their Care and Treatment from Colonial Times* (1949, 2nd ed.), but a more extended discussion of BR's role appears in Norman Dain's excellent *Concepts of Insanity in the United States, 1789–1865* (1964).

1. Belknap to BR, 7 October 1790, quoted in *Letters,* p. lxix; BR to Belknap, 31 January 1789, ibid.
2. BR, "To the Ministers of the Gospel of All Denominations: An Address . . . ," 21 June 1788, ibid., pp. 461–467.
3. BR, "Paradise of Negro Slaves—A Dream," *Essays, Literary, Moral and Philosophical,* pp. 315, 320.
4. BR to Lettsom, 18 May 1787; BR to Mrs. Ferguson, 25 December 1787, both *Letters.* Evidence of Tench Coxe's work with the Abolition Society can be found in the society's papers, HSP. Also at the HSP is W. J. Buck's manuscript "History of the Pennsylvania Abolition Society," of which vol. 1 details Benezet's achievements as well as the early history of the society. BR explains to Lettsom, 28 September 1787, *Letters,* disingenuously and perhaps for foreign consumption, that "no mention was made of *Negroes* or *slaves* in the Constitution only because it was thought the very words would contaminate the glorious fabric of American liberty and government."
5. BR to Belknap, 6 May 1788, *Letters.*
6. Pennsylvania Abolition Society, Manumission Book A, 1780–1793, p. 46, HSP. The affidavit also appears in the society's Box of Manumissions, ROD-SAV, also at HSP.
7. *Auto.,* p. 246; BR to wife, [23 July 1776], *Letters.*
8. BR, "Original Manuscript Accounts, 1794–1799," of personal expenses, BR-MSS; *Auto.,* p. 246.
9. BR to Lettsom, 21 April 1788, *Letters;* Brissot de Warville, *New Travels,* p. 233n.

10. BR to Belknap, 19 August 1788; BR to Adams, 11 July 1806, both *Letters*. "Leonidas," *Pennsylvania Packet*, 24 August 1779. On "wheelbarrow men": BR to wife, 22 August 1787, *Letters*.

11. BR, "An Enquiry into the Effects of Public Punishments upon Criminals and upon Society," *Essays, Literary, Moral and Philosophical*, pp. 136–163. On the society's meetings: Wharton, *Memoir of William Rawle*, p. 25; *Autobiography of Charles Biddle* (1883), p. 223. On Howard: BR to Lettsom, 18 May and 8 June 1787, *Letters*.

12. BR, "An Enquiry into . . . Public Punishments," *Essays, Literary, Moral and Philosophical*, pp. 150–156.

13. Mease, *Picture of Philadelphia*, p. 161; BR to Belknap, 19 August 1788, *Letters*.

14. BR to Lettsom, 28 September 1787, ibid.

15. BR, "An Enquiry into the Justice and Policy of Punishing Murder by Death," *Essays, Literary, Moral and Philosophical*, pp. 164–182.

16. BR to Belknap, 19 August, 7 October, 5 November 1788, *Letters;* Mease, *Picture of Philadelphia*, p. 162.

17. BR on "my studies": quoted in Butterfield, ed., *A Letter by BR Describing Consecration of German College*, p. 6n. On "energy of true vigor": Eric Hoffer, *Temper of Our Time* (1967), p. 95. BR, "To Friends of a Federal Government: A Plan for a Federal University," *Letters*, pp. 491–495.

18. BR, "An Enquiry into the Utility of a Knowledge of the Latin and Greek Languages, as a Branch of Liberal Education, with Hints of a Plan of Liberal Instruction without Them . . . ," *American Museum* 5 (1789), pp. 525–535. In the *Essays, Literary, Moral and Philosophical*, pp. 21–56, the title becomes "Observations upon the Study of the Latin and Greek Languages. . . ."

19. *Essays, Literary, Moral and Philosophical*, pp. 42–43.

20. Ibid., pp. 38, 35, 39.

21. Adams to BR, 19 June 1789, quoted in *Letters*, p. 518n; BR to Adams, 21 July 1789, ibid.

22. BR, "Observations upon . . . Latin and Greek," *Essays, Literary, Moral and Philosophical*, p. 44; BR to Adams, 21 July 1789, *Letters*.

23. BR to Belknap, 13 July 1789, ibid.

24. BR, "Observations upon the Influence of the Habitual Use of Tobacco upon Health, Morals, and Property," *Essays, Literary, Moral and Philosophical*, pp. 263–274.

25. BR to Belknap, 6 May, 13 July, 19 August 1788; BR to Lettsom, 16 August 1788, all *Letters*. "An open letter to the Philadelphia Society for Promoting Agriculture and Rural Affairs" appears in the *Pennsylvania Gazette*, 7 June 1786, signed "B."

26. "The Moral and Physical Thermometer" appears in *Letters* opposite p. 512. BR to Belknap, 19 August, 7 October, 5 November 1788, ibid.

27. BR, "To Andrew Brown: Directions for Conducting a Newspaper in Such a Manner as to Make It Innocent, Useful, and Entertaining," 1 October 1788, ibid.

28. Invitations to join the medical societies found in Box 9, BR-MSS. The one from Massachusetts is dated 20 May 1787; from New Haven, 29 November 1788; from London, 5 January 1789.

29. BR, "Added Observations upon the Scarlatina Anginosa," vol. 1, pp. 109–110, 111–112. "The epidemic cold," mentioned in Drinker, *Not So Long Ago,* p. 69. BR wrote "An Account of the Influenza, as it appeared in Philadelphia, in the Autumn of 1789, in the Spring of 1790, and in the Winter of 1791," in *Medical Inquiries and Observations,* (1794–1798 ed.), vol. 2, pp. 245–262.

30. BR to Elisha Hall, 6 July 1789, *Letters.*

31. *Auto.,* under date 18 September 1789, pp. 178–179.

32. The descriptions that follow are based on accounts by Brissot de Warville and Manasseh Cutler, both of which are found in Morton, *History of the Pennsylvania Hospital,* pp. 162–163, 448–449.

Lettsom, 28 September 1787, ibid.

34. BR, "An Enquiry into . . . Public Punishments," *Essays, Literary, Moral and Philosophical,* p. 153; BR to the Managers of the Pennsylvania Hospital, 11 November 1789, *Letters.*

35. BR to Lettsom, 2 June 1786; BR to wife, 26 August 1787, both *Letters.*

36. BR to wife, 26 August 1787; BR to James Currie, 11 December 1787, both ibid. Publication of volume mentioned BR to Belknap, 31 January 1789, ibid. BR to Lettsom, 28 September 1787, ibid.

37. BR, "Observations on the Duties of a Physician, and the Methods of Improving Medicine Accommodated to the Present State of Society and Manners in the United States," *Medical Inquiries and Observations* (1794–1798 ed.), vol. 1, Appendix, pp. 315–338. The essay was reprinted in 1951 in the *American Journal of Medicine,* pp. 551–556.

38. Corner, *Two Centuries of Medicine,* p. 41.

39. *Auto.,* p. 180.

20. "Only a Spectator of Public Measures": 1789–1790

1. BR to Adams, 13 April 1790, *Letters.*

2. BR to Adams, 23 March 1805, ibid.

3. BR to Noah Webster, 13 February 1788; BR to Lettsom, 16 August 1788, both ibid.

4. BR to Adams, 22 January, 21 February, and 4 June 1789, ibid.

5. Charles A. Beard, ed., *The Journal of William Maclay, 1789–1791* (1927 ed.), p. 83.

6. BR to Adams, 21 February and 19 March 1789, *Letters.*

7. BR to Adams, 4 June 1789, ibid.; *Auto.,* 14 August 1789, p. 176.

8. BR to Adams, 12 and 24 February 1790; BR to Webster, 29 December 1789, all *Letters.*

9. BR to Adams, 24 February 1790, ibid.

10. Ibid.; BR to Adams, 13 April 1790, ibid.

11. "Centinel," 13 November 1788, quoted in McMaster and Stone, *Pennsylvania and the Federal Constitution,* p. 677; BR to Adams, 22 January 1789; BR to Montgomery, 27 March 1789, both *Letters.*

12. Brunhouse, *Counter-Revolution,* pp. 221–225; BR to Montgomery, 27 March 1789, *Letters.*

13. The various caucuses held are mentioned throughout the September 1789 issues of *Pennsylvania Packet.* On list submitted to town meeting, see *Independent Gazetteer,* 8 October 1789. On French Revolution: *Pennsylvania Packet,* 8 September 1789, refers to Paris in "a ferment"; BR's apathy mentioned to Adams, 12 February 1790, *Letters.*

14. BR to Adams, 12 and 24 February 1790, ibid.

15. *Auto.,* p. 182.

16. BR to Boudinot, 18 April 1790, *Letters; Auto.,* p. 183; BR to Price, 24 April 1790, *Letters.*

17. BR to Elihu Hall, 6 July 1789; BR to Adams, 12 February 1790; BR to Enos Hitchcock, 24 April 1789, all *Letters.*

18. BR to James Rush, 7 February 1810, *Letters.*

19. BR to wife, 16 and 22 August 1787, ibid.

20. BR to Enos Hitchcock, 24 April 1789, ibid.

21. BR to Adams, 24 February 1790, ibid.

22. *Auto.,* p. 165.

Index

phlogiston theory, 294

physicians: status in 18th-century America, 25; laymen as, 27; contents of medical bag, 27; apprentice training of, 27–28; and Sydenham's theories, 30; and Boerhaave's theories, 31–32; Morgan's plans for improving status of, 36; in Britain, 65–66, 67, 91–92; in France, 77; regarded as "apprentices let loose," 127; BR views on role in army, 209; research projects for, 335–336; BR on duties of, 378–379

physics: and Boerhaavian medicine, 31

Pickering, Timothy: and Wyoming Valley, 338, 374; BR writes essay for on diseases and treatment of, 374, 395–398

piles: effect of mineral waters on, 102; treatment of, 374, 398

Pittsburgh: as possible college site, 287, 290, 331

Pitt, William. *See* Chatham, Earl of

"Plain Truth": planned title for *Common Sense*, 138

pleurisies: and bloodletting, 27; BR downed by (1786), 320; (1788), 354; Franklin dies of, 388; mentioned, 28

Pluckemin (New Jersey): Leslie buried at, 180

Plunkett, William: investor in land, 306

poetry: Davies on, 20; women should know something of, 333

pokeberries: as cure for cancer, 27

Portsmouth (New Hampshire), 108

post office: "nonelectric wire of government," 342

potassium nitrate. *See* saltpeter

Potomac River: effect on government if national capital made on banks of, 384; mentioned, 379

Potts, John, Jr.: freed, 274

Potts, Jonathan: BR's companion abroad, 43, 44, 46, 47; catches itch en route to Edinburgh, 45; Franklin on, 51; departs for home, 53; names first son Benjamin, 53–54; gets M.D., 89; informs on Shippen, 222

Powel, Samuel, 387

Presbyterian Church: BR's mother takes family into, 11; in 1730s, 12–13; in Virginia,

Presbyterian Church—*cont.*
19; and Redman, 26; BR breaks with, 311, 320, 346; fails to support Dickinson College, 316; BR attends without belonging, 391

Presbyterians: and Stamp Act, 39; in Liverpool, 44; in Edinburgh, 53; and BR's medical practice, 82, 85, 274; and Pennsylvania Constitution, 197; and College of Philadelphia, 235; BR's practice among declines, 274; BR wants college for, 285; and postwar political power of, 286; divided by Dickinson College scheme, 289; backcountry Quaker on, 300; demeaned by liquor, 303; BR breaks with, 310–311; division among after Revolution, 311–312; censured, 318; desert BR as physician, 336. *See also* New Lights *and* Old Lights

Presbyterian synod: BR charges Ewing before, 310

prescriptions, 27, 85, 395–398

Price, Elisha: at Provincial Conference, 159

price regulation: and Committee of Inspection and Observation, 143; congressional debate on, 184–185; Philadelphia debates (1779), 231–232; and Republicans, 234

Price, Richard: BR meets, 70; BR corresponds with, 269, 329, 340–341, 342, 343, 345; ties with renewed, 277; and Dickinson College, 296; sent lock of Franklin's hair, 389

Priestley, Joseph: paper on air, 88; experiments of, 127; BR follows work of, 294

Princeton (New Jersey): college moved to, 17; home of Stocktons, 55; Witherspoons arrive at, 59; BR visits, 139; battle of and aftermath, 178–179, 180–181, 196; BR stationed at, 204; wounded troops in, 211; BR departs from for York, 213; BR asked to explain absence from, 217; BR plans to retire to, 217, 234; in retirement at, 223; Congress in, 264–265; influence of college's presence on land values in, 288; mentioned, 220

Princeton University. *See* College of New Jersey